T0366235

# Information and Communication Technologies in Support of the Tourism Industry

Wayne Pease, University of Southern Queensland, Australia

Michelle Rowe, Edith Cowan University, Australia

Malcolm Cooper, Ritsumeikan Asia Pacific University, Japan

**IDEA GROUP PUBLISHING**

Hershey • London • Melbourne • Singapore

| | |
|---|---|
| Acquisition Editor: | Kristin Klinger |
| Senior Managing Editor: | Jennifer Neidig |
| Managing Editor: | Sara Reed |
| Assistant Managing Editor: | Sharon Berger |
| Development Editor: | Kristin Roth |
| Copy Editor: | Jennifer Young |
| Typesetter: | Michael Brehm |
| Cover Design: | Lisa Tosheff |
| Printed at: | Yurchak Printing Inc. |

Published in the United States of America by
    Idea Group Publishing (an imprint of Idea Group Inc.)
    701 E. Chocolate Avenue
    Hershey PA 17033
    Tel: 717-533-8845
    Fax: 717-533-8661
    E-mail: cust@idea-group.com
    Web site: http://www.idea-group.com

and in the United Kingdom by
    Idea Group Publishing (an imprint of Idea Group Inc.)
    3 Henrietta Street
    Covent Garden
    London WC2E 8LU
    Tel: 44 20 7240 0856
    Fax: 44 20 7379 0609
    Web site: http://www.eurospanonline.com

Library of Congress Cataloging-in-Publication Data

Information and communication technologies in support of the tourism industry / Wayne R. Pease, Michelle Rowe and Malcolm Cooper, editors.
    p. cm.
  Summary: "This book examines the process of transformation as it relates to the tourism industry, and the changes to that industry from modern electronic communications. It covers not only geographically support-ive technologies in communication, but also in terms of culture, economics, marketing, social, and regional issues"--Provided by publisher.
  Includes bibliographical references and index.
  ISBN 978-1-59904-159-9 (hardcover) -- ISBN 978-1-59904-161-2 (ebook)
  1. Tourism--Information technology. I. Pease, Wayne R., 1953- II. Rowe, Michelle, 1961- III. Cooper, Malcolm, 1946-
  G155.A1I453 2007
  910.285--dc22
                    2006033771

British Cataloguing in Publication Data
A Cataloguing in Publication record for this book is available from the British Library.

All work contributed to this book is new, previously-unpublished material. The views expressed in this book are those of the authors, but not necessarily of the publisher.

# Information and Communication Technologies in Support of the Tourism Industry

## Table of Contents

### Section I:
### Use of Computers and the Internet in Tourism

# Foreword

Information communication technologies (ICTs) have been transforming tourism globally. The ICT driven re-engineering has gradually generated a new paradigm-shift, altering the industry structure and developing a whole range of opportunities and threats. ICTs empowers consumers to identify, customise, and purchase tourism products and supports the globalisation of the industry by providing tools for developing, managing and distributing offerings worldwide. Increasingly ICTs play a critical role for the competitiveness of tourism organisations and destinations. ICTs are becoming a key determinant of organisational competitiveness and a wide range of technological developments propel this evolution. Successful ICT deployment requires innovative management to constantly review developments and adopt the suitable technological solutions in order to maximise organisational competitiveness.

Increasingly, it is evident that ICTs evolve constantly, providing new tools for tourism marketing and management. They support the interactivity between tourism enterprises and consumers and as a result they reengineer the entire process of developing, managing and marketing tourism products and destinations. This book has identified a number of key changes in hardware, software and networking that will impact on the tourism industry in the future. Although the exact impacts are far from clear, the future of eTourism will be focused on *consumer centric* technologies that will enable organisations to focus on their profitability through a network of partnerships. Consumers will be more sophisticated and experienced and therefore more difficult to please. The availability of powerful ICTs empowers both suppliers and destinations to enhance their efficiency and re-engineer their communication strategies.

This book deals with a number of key aspects of ICTs for tourism. It explore generic technical issues such as online delivery of tourism services; the use of computers and the internet for making travel decisions by older adults as well as cutting edge technological innovations such as ontology-based tourism application generation and visual tourism recommender systems. It then investigates the transformation of the tourist industry with cases from the airline, tour operating, and hospitality industries and also through the emerging location-based services and virtual reality.

It is evident that increasingly ICTs will provide the "info-structure" for the entire industry and will take over all mechanistic aspects of tourism transactions. Innovative tourism enterprises will have the ability to divert resources and expertise to servicing consumers and provide higher value-added transactions. Agile strategies are required at both strategic and tactical management levels to ensure that the ICT raised opportunities and challenges are turned to the advantage of tourism organisations to enhance their innovation and competitiveness.

*Dr. Dimitrios Buhalis*
*University of Surrey, UK*

*Dimitrios Buhalis is a reader in business information management, a course leader MSc in tourism marketing and leader of e-tourism research at the School of Management University of Surrey (UK). Dr. Dimitrios is also adjunct professor of the MBA in Hospitality Management at the Institut de Management Hotelier International (Cornell University-Ecole Superieure des Sciences Economiques et Commerciales ESSEC) in Paris. He also teaches regularly on postgraduate courses around the world. Dimitrios has been an active researcher in the areas of ICTs and tourism and he was the UniS-based principle investigator for a number of projects including the European projects FP5 SMART-UP (e-commerce and e-learning for hospitality SMEs), Harmonise (harmonisation of standards in tourism), FP6 NoE EPOCH (ICTs for cultural heritage) as well as for the Knowledge Transfer Partnership (KTP) project eLearning for Hospitality Professionals and the World Travel Tourism Council project eTourism Stakeholders. He is a registered European Commission IST evaluator and reviewer and he was the cluster rapporter for the IST tourism projects for the period 2000-2004. He is also a specialist reviewer in Hospitality, Leisure, Recreation, Sport, and Tourism for the Quality Assurance Agency for Higher Education in the UK and external examiner at the Swansea Institute, University of Wales and at the University of Greenwich.*

*He serves as vice chairman on the International Federation of Information Technology and Tourism (IFITT) Board and he is the chair of events and meetings and a member of the executive council of the Tourism Society. Dimitrios was the immediate past chairman of the Association of Tourism Teachers and Trainers (ATTT). He has editorial roles in a number of academic journals and he has written, edited, or co-edited 8 books on e-tourism, tourism strategic issues, and distribution channels of tourism.*

# Preface

Tourism is fundamental to the world economy. The World Travel and Tourism Council Tourism reports travel and tourism in 2006 is expected to post US$6.477 trillion of economic activity (total demand) and this is forecast to grow to US$12.119 trillion by 2016. It is estimated that in 2006 the travel and tourism industry will contribute 3.6% to worldwide GDP. The broader classification of travel and tourism economy indicates that the industry will contribute 10.3% to world GDP in 2006, making it arguably the largest single industry worldwide. The importance of the industry also is evident in terms of employment; in 2004 the tourism sector provided approximately 214 million jobs or 8.1% of global employment. It is expected that the industry will provide 260 million jobs (or 8.6% of world employment) by 2014.

For many regions throughout the world, reliance on tourism is considerable. It is the lifeblood of many local economies. It also has a significant influence on culture. This is especially true for many less-developed nations as much as for rural and regional areas in developed nations. Growth of the magnitude mentioned above has brought and will bring many opportunities and many problems to both source and destination markets, just as earlier growth patterns in manufacturing and mining or agricultural sectors has done. One of those opportunity/problem areas is the exchange of information within and external to the tourism industry.

New information communication technologies (ICT) are dramatically transforming spatial relationships within all industries, at every scale from local to global. It provides improved linkage, command, and control systems. This book examines that process of technological transformation as it relates to the tourism industry. It is about the changes that modern electronic communications are supporting, or could support, in the world of tourism, not only geographically but in terms of culture, economics, marketing, social, and regional issues. Issues covered in the book range from the use of the Internet to supply information, to the emerging patterns of tourist decision making and investment based on such information. The book is about developing an informed appreciation of a wide range of issues arising from the growth of information technology and the Internet in particular and ICT in general for the tourism industry.

Tourism leads the way with respect to ICT uptake and development. The main aim of the book is thus to enhance the reader's knowledge as to the developments and application of ICT within the industry. It takes a multidisciplinary perspective of cybertourism and considers the role of ICT in the evolving world of tourism in the 21$^{st}$ century. The Internet is especially relevant to tourism since it enables knowledge about the consumer or tourist to be gathered, as well as providing information to them. Online technologies within the tourism industry have significantly impacted on communications, transactions, and relationships between the various industry operators and with the customer, as well as between regulators and operators (Clayton & Criscuolo, 2002; Dogac et al., 2004; Galloway, Mochrie, & Deakins, 2004; Sharma, Carson, & DeLacy, 2000; Sheldon, 1998; Werthner & Klien, 1999; World Tourism Organisation, 1999). The benefits of ICT, particularly those of the Internet for tourism are substantial. These benefits are no longer dependent on proprietary information systems as has been the past experience, since the Internet is a commonly available technology. The Internet can enhance the level of collaboration between tourist operators, important especially for tourism destinations, and brings about greater levels of interoperability with internal and external applications, previously available only to the larger players via proprietary systems such as Galileo for example.

Awareness of the functionality of the Internet, as well as resources and expertise necessary to take advantage of this functionality may be lacking, especially with respect to small and medium tourism enterprises (SMTEs). It is not yet clear that individual SMTEs are able to use this intelligence, or indeed even recognize its value. Information potentially available therefore is lost, but even if it is used, infrastructure issues such as access to reliable broadband may impede its effectiveness. These issues may especially be relevant for tourism operators in countries where infrastructure is less developed.

The book is divided into three sections: the first discusses the use of computers and the Internet in tourism; the second the transformation of the tourist industry under the influence of ICT; and the third provides a set of case studies.

# Section I: Use of Computers and the Internet in Tourism

Section I provides an overview of ICT, its development and application to tourism. This section, which comprises 3 chapters, is designed to introduce the reader to these developments and applications. This is especially the case with respect to Chapters I and III. Chapter II provides more detail regarding the use of the Semantic Web and ontologies that underpin the same.

In **Chapter I**, *Online Delivery of Tourism Services: Developments, Issues and Challenges*, John W. Houghton presents an overview of recent developments in online delivery of tourism services, highlighting major issues and challenges. The chapter notes that the tourism sector is among the leaders in online marketing and sales, but considerable potential remains, with the sector lagging in the adoption of supply chain related systems and the use of ICT for internal efficiency. The Internet brings new opportunities and challenges, with both disintermediation and the emergence of new intermediaries. Key policy issues include the need to carefully monitor the competition effects of online service delivery and take advantage of the potential for the development of destination management systems that provide an integrated front-end for SMTEs.

**Chapter II**, *A Framework for Ontology-Based Tourism Application Generator*, by Roopa Jakkilinki and Nalin Sharda, provides an overview of tourism ontology and how this can be used for developing e-tourism applications. The Semantic Web is the next generation Web; it uses background knowledge captured as ontology and stored in machine-processable and interpretable form. Ontologies form the core of the Semantic Web and can be used to develop intelligent applications. However, generating applications based on ontology still remains a challenging task. This chapter presents a framework that provides a systematic process for developing intelligent e-tourism applications by using tourism ontologies.

**Chapter III**, *ICT and the Travel Industry: Opportunities and Challenges for New Zealand Travel Agents*, by Vladimir Garkavenko and Simon Milne, provides an in-depth study of how ICT has influenced the New Zealand travel agent's market. The authors focus on the impact of ICT on the travel industry. Key findings from a longitudinal study of New Zealand travel agents (TA) conducted during 2000-2004 are presented. These findings are compared and contrasted with information gathered from in-depth interviews with tourism consumers. The study explores major pressure factors on TA businesses: direct airline-consumer sales, introduction of the Internet, and the increasing sophistication of the tourist consumer. There is great variation in the extent to which New Zealand TAs use the advantages associated with new technology and their perception of ICT.

# Section II: Transformation of the Tourist Industry

This section, being the core of the book, contains 8 chapters that address a broad range of more specific applications of ICT to tourism. The intention of this section is to focus on specific aspects of ICT, many of which are emerging and cutting-edge.

**Chapter IV**, *The Transformation of the Distribution Process in the Airline Industry Empowered by Information and Communication Technology*, by Patrick S. Merten, reviews the historical evolution of the airline market and its first-generation airline reservation and distribution systems. The development and diffusion of computer reservation systems (CRS) and global distribution systems (GDS) is discussed extensively in order to provide a comprehensive overview of the state of business in the 1990s. Based on this evaluation, the influence of modern ICT on the airline distribution system environment is discussed.

**Chapter V**, *Design and Implementation Approaches for Location-Based, Tourism-Related Services*, by George Kakaletris, Dimitris Varoutas, Dimitris Katsianis, and Thomas Sphicopoulos discusses design and implementation approaches for location-based, tourism-related services. The recent globally observed slump in the mobile services market has led mobile network operators to seek opportunities to provide other value added services. This chapter presents the key concepts, capabilities, and considerations of infrastructures and applications targeted to the mobile tourist. It covers data and content delivery, positioning, systems' interactions, platforms, protocols, security, and privacy as well as business modelling aspects.

**Chapter VI**, *Developing Visual Tourism Recommender Systems*, by Mohan Ponnada, Roopa Jakkilinki, and Nalin Sharda, develops this theme further. The authors note that tourism recommender systems (TRS) have become popular in recent years; however, most lack visual means of presenting the recommendations. This chapter presents ways of developing visual travel recommender systems (V-TRS). The two popular travel recommender systems used today are the TripMatcher and Me-Print. Tour recommendation using image-based planning using SCORM (TRIPS) is a system that aims to make the presentation more visual. A case study demonstrating the operation of current TRS also is presented. Further research in this area should aim to improve user interaction and provide more control functions within a V-TRS to make tour-planning simple, fun, and more visually interactive.

The next two chapters look at the development of virtual reality approaches to the task of informing the potential tourist of markets and attractions. **Chapter VII**, *Virtual Reality Applications in Tourism*, by Călin Gurău, starts with a description of the present development of virtual reality technology and applications. The physical tools and the software programmes required to interact with virtual reality applications are presented, and on the basis of their description, various hardware/software systems of virtual reality are identified and discussed. **Chapter VIII**, *Virtual Reality Mapping Revisited: IT Tools for the Divide Between Knowledge and Action in Tourism*, by Malcolm Cooper and Neil MacNeil, deepens this discussion by providing a brief overview of the available technologies and opportunities for the use of virtual reality in tourism marketing. It acknowledges that in almost all formulations of the tourism marketing model to date, much has been made of the notion that tourism is unique because production and consumption occur not only at the same time but in the same place. Location or proximity is therefore often a critical determinant of the take-up of tourism opportunities. The chapter then goes on to posit the question: what if the place variable could be removed from this equation through the further development of virtual reality techniques?

**Chapter IX**, *Towards Improved Business Planning Decision Support for Small-to-Medium Tourism Enterprise Operators* by G. Michael McGrath, reports on the use of system dynamics (SD) in the modelling and analysis of the problem domains for tourism businesses such as rapid change, complexity, and uncertainty. The chapter discusses the development and implementation of a "tourism enterprise planning simulator" (TEPS) based largely upon SD constructs and technologies. Scenarios in which TEPS might be used to good effect in small business are outlined and the potential benefits of this deployment are detailed. Michelle Rowe and Alfred Ogle take this discussion further in **Chapter X**, *Collaborative Commerce and the Hotel Industry*, by proposing a framework to consider the application of collaborative commerce (c-commerce) in the hotel industry. C-commerce and some general characteristics of the hotel industry are examined followed by a discussion of the likelihood of c-commerce adoption by hotels. Corporate structure, IT and its importance to organization strategy, the role and attitudes of the General Manager of each hotel to IT, as well as the social identity of the hotel, emerge as issues critical to c-commerce. This area of study is in its infancy and further research is required to more fully consider the issues.

The final chapter in this section, *Sex Tourism and the Internet: Information, Amplification, and Moral Panics*, by Jerry Eades, looks at sex tourism and the Internet. Probably no sector of the tourist market has been more affected by the rise of the Internet than that of sex tourism. In fact, as shown in **Chapter XI**, until the advent of the Internet sex tourism as a concept, sex tourism was rarely discussed in the media, even though sex as a motivation for travel has a very long history. But the relationship between sex tourism and the Internet also is extremely complex and contested, as befits such a controversial subject. The author argues that in relation to tourism the Internet has proved a double-edged sword. Even though it has provided greatly enhanced opportunities for members of a wide variety of sexual interests, orientations and subcultures to contact and interact with each other, it also has provided an environment in which certain types of sex tourism have been increasingly demonized by the media, civil society and the politicians, resulting in the imposition of increasingly severe regulation and sanctions in a number of countries.

# Section III: Case Studies

The final section is a compilation of three case studies that consider the application of IT with respect to demographic features such as culture and age and innovative behaviour of the tourist.

In **Chapter XII**, *Digital Imaging Trek: A Practical Model for Managing the Demand of the Digitally Enabled Traveller*, Stephen C. Andrade and Hilary Mason note that in recent years digital communication platforms and technologies have evolved and become accessible to a wide mainstream audience of tourists and travellers. Organizations engaging in travel and tourism commerce need to understand this wave of innovative behaviour among their customers. What does a traveller need to know to keep current with changing technologies? It is critical that service providers and travellers alike stay informed, because one thing is certain, technological innovation and change will be a constant companion for the travel and tourism industry. This chapter provides insight into evolving technologies that will be helpful to the practitioner, student, educator and the tourist-travellers themselves. Being prepared to meet the new demands of customers will provide rewarding experiences for parties on all sides of the tourism equation.

**Chapter XIII**, *Feeling Welcome: Internet Tourism Marketing Across Cultures*, by Wolfgang Arlt, discusses the way in which cross-cultural marketing via the Internet can be used to make visitors feel welcome—or not. In this chapter the author notes that if used in a proper way, the Internet can be a powerful cross-cultural incoming tourism communication tool. This chapter examines to what extent the opportunities are utilized which are offered in the virtual sphere to extend across physical and cultural distances a welcoming hand to potential visitors from far-away source markets. The discussion is based on the results of a study about the non-german language Web sites of Central European destination marketing organizations (DMOs), conducted in 2002 and updated in 2006, and the results of a study of German-language Web sites of non-European national tourism organizations (NTOs) and DMOs, conducted in 2005. It was found that an increase in multilingual Web sites within the period under review can be recognized, but that an increase in cross-cultural awareness of the providers of such Web sites is still lacking.

**Chapter XIV**, *Changing Technological Trends in the Travel Behaviour of Older Tourists*, by Ian Patterson, looks at changing technological trends in the travel behaviour of older tourists. The chapter examines the growth in usage of information technology and the Internet by older adults. As many countries are now experiencing, we are becoming an ageing society with seniors and baby boomers now responsible for a larger share of all holiday spending. But, while the Internet provides a perfect vehicle for the travel industry, many seniors are still fearful about using it, and perceived problems still exist with credit card security, quality control and privacy issues. In the future, Internet travel bookings are likely to increase with the growth in baby boomers who generally prefer to use the Internet. This will further encourage the use of discount fares but also will place increased pressure on the future role of the travel agent.

Throughout the book we have concentrated on what Dimitrios Buhalis considers is the defining characteristic of the changing ICT environment with respect to tourism—it is evident that ICTs evolve constantly, providing new tools for tourism marketing and management. This evolution promotes and requires the interactivity between tourism enterprises and consumers and potentially enables the reengineering of the development, management and marketing of tourism products and destinations. The book has identified a number of key changes in hardware, software, and networking that will impact on the tourism industry in the future. It has explored generic technical issues such as online delivery of tourism services but also has looked at cutting edge technological innovations. The past two decades have brought profound change to the way in which the tourism industry functions as a business and the place tourism has in the economy, at a regional, national, and international level. The tourism industry can be seen as one of the first business sectors whose business functions are almost exclusively using ICT in their operation. This book makes a significant contribution to knowledge in terms of the use of ICT within the industry and will become both a repository of information and a source for demonstrating and generating awareness of innovative approaches.

# References

Clayton, T., & Criscuolo, C. (2002). *Electronic commerce and business change.* Retrieved April 16, 2005, from http://www.statistics.gov.uk/cci/article.asp?ID=139

Dogac, A., Kabak, Y., Laleci, G., Sinir, S., Yildiz, A., Kirbas, S., et al. (2004). Semantically enriched Web services for the travel industry. *SIGMOD Rec., 33*(3), 21-27.

Galloway, L., Mochrie, R., & Deakins, D. (2004). ICT-enabled collectivity as a positive rural business strategy. *International Journal of Entrepreneurial Behaviour and Research, 10*(4), 247-259.

Sharma, P., Carson, D., & DeLacy, T. (2000). National online tourism policy initiatives for Australia. *Journal of Travel Research, 39*(2), 157-162.

Sheldon, P. J. (1998). *Tourism information technology.* New York: CABI Publishing.

Werthner, H., & Klien, S. (1999). *Information, technology, and tourism: A challenging relationship.* Vienna, Austria: Springer.

World Tourism Organisation. (1999). *Marketing tourism destinations online: Strategies for the information age.* Madrid.

# Acknowledgments

The editors wish to acknowledge the help of the many people who have contributed to this project, without whose support this book could not have been satisfactorily completed.

All of the authors of the chapters included in this book also served as referees for articles written by the other authors. Without their hard work and cooperation in this process this book would not have been written. We also would like to acknowledge the assistance of two external reviewers, Jacqui Blake and Graham Young, who provided invaluable assistance in this process by providing constructive and comprehensive reviews that were well received by all involved.

We also would like to thank the staff at Idea Group Inc. for recognising the value of this project, for their very helpful and well written guidelines, and for their invaluable assistance throughout the process. Our special thanks go to Kristin Roth for her effort in keeping us on track, including those occasional reminders about outstanding tasks. Without you, Kristin, we would not have finished the project.

Of course, all of this would not have been possible without the love and support of our families throughout the process. Despite late nights, tantrums, and other distractions (burning computers) they stood by us even at our lowest points which says something for the role of family in this task.

Once again our many thanks for everyone involved in this project.

*Wayne Pease*
*Michelle Rowe*
*Malcolm Cooper*

# Section I

# Use of Computers and the Internet in Tourism

## Chapter I

# Online Delivery of Tourism Services:
## Developments, Issues, and Challenges

John W. Houghton, Victoria University, Australia

## Abstract

*This chapter presents an overview of recent developments in online delivery of tourism services, highlighting major issues and challenges. Many tourism services are highly amenable to online delivery and, in OECD countries, the adoption of e-commerce and online service delivery in tourism has been rapid. The tourism sector is among the leaders in online marketing and sales, but considerable potential remains, with the sector lagging in the adoption of supply chain related systems and the use of ICTs for internal efficiency. The Internet brings new opportunities and challenges, with both disintermediation and the emergence of new intermediaries. Key policy issues include the need to carefully monitor the competition effects of online service delivery and take advantage of the potential for the development of destination management systems that provide an integrated front-end for small to medium sized tourism enterprises.*

# Introduction

Many tourism services are highly amenable to online delivery, with booking and reservation based on the exchange of information and payments. In OECD countries, the adoption of e-commerce and online service delivery in tourism has been rapid, and the tourism sector is among the leaders in online marketing and sales. Nevertheless, considerable potential remains, with most tourism sectors lagging in the adoption of supply chain related systems and the use of ICTs for internal efficiency. Recent developments such as the Internet bring new opportunities and challenges, with both disintermediation and the emergence of new intermediaries. Key policy issues include the need to carefully monitor the competition effects of online service delivery and to take advantage of the potential for the development of destination management systems that provide an integrated front-end for small to medium tourism enterprises (SMTEs).

# Industry Structure

Tourism services include elements of transport services (e.g., passenger transport), auxiliary activities (e.g., travel agency and tour operator services), accommodation and food services (e.g., hotel accommodation and restaurants), entertainment and recreational services (e.g., historical sites, museums, theme parks, etc.) and a range of related products and services (e.g., retailing, manufacturing, financial, and property related services). Thus the tourism sector exhibits a range of industry structures, competitive environments, business models, value chains, and critical success factors.

According to E-Business Watch (2002), key characteristics of the tourism sector include:

- The complex nature of the product, with the overall product being the sum of different activities (e.g., transport, accommodation, meals, recreational activities, etc.)
- The diverse industry structure, with a large number of small businesses (e.g., family hotels, guesthouses, campsites, guided tour operators, etc.) and some very large ones (e.g., airlines)
- The prevalence among small to medium tourism enterprises (SMTEs) of family run businesses, some with very different drivers to those operating in listed firms (e.g., "lifestyle" businesses)

- The mix of public and private sector enterprises catering to similar markets (e.g., public museums and galleries, and private galleries and entertainment venues including theme and amusement parks)
- The dominance of large integrated firms in certain parts of the value chain, such as travel distribution (e.g., tour operators and tour agencies) and transport (e.g., airlines)
- Deregulation and privatisation in some segments, leading to greatly increased competition (e.g., airlines, including airline routes and airports) (E-Business Watch, 2002)

With such diversity, the various sub-sectors exhibit different characteristics and business dynamics, and different levels and foci of ICT adoption and use.

## Transport Services

There are many forms of transport involved in tourism services—including airlines, bus lines, car rental companies, railways, boat operators, and boat hire firms. Air transport is among the most important. Air travel has been expanding rapidly, driven by world economic growth, globalisation and increasing international trade and investment, deregulation and privatisation, increasing business travel, and increases in leisure time for both workers and retirees (E-Business Watch, 2002).

*Figure 1. Comparison of distribution costs for a USD 300 US domestic air ticket, 2000 (USD) (Source: Pappas, 2001)*

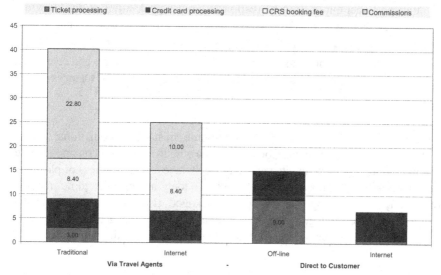

The airline industry is characterised by volatile demand and high fixed costs relating to the operation and maintenance of aircraft fleets. Many factors affect demand, with the events of September 11, 2001 and recent SARS fears demonstrating how profound an effect exogenous events can have on passenger demand (E-Business Watch, 2002). Privatisation of airlines and the deregulation of routes have had, and are having, a major effect. Many airlines have struggled to maintain profitability and some national flag carriers have failed, leading to mergers and consolidation within the industry. One consequence has been much greater competition. This has been exacerbated by the emergence of low-cost, "no-frills" airlines, which seek to extend air travel to a wider public through lower fares based on lower cost structures.

Airlines have long been advanced users of ICTs, leading in such areas as reservation systems for many years. Nevertheless, the Internet has had a profound effect, allowing airlines to sell direct to their customers (i.e., passengers) and, thereby, to greatly reduce commission and other costs, as well as enhance their relationship with customers (e.g., through membership and frequent flyer programs). The cruise shipping, passenger railway and car rental industries exhibit many similar characteristics.

## Intermediation Services: Tour Operators and Travel Agencies

There are two main business types in intermediation services:

- **Tour operators:** Who purchase services from other tourism services firms (e.g., transport, accommodation, recreation and amusement activities, and tours) and package them into standardised packages sold through travel agencies
- **Travel agencies:** Who purchase individual services (e.g., flight, car rental or accommodation bookings) or packages from the tour operators and resell them to consumers on a commission or fee-for-service basis (E-Business Watch, 2002)

There are relatively few tour operators, with some substantial international firms in the industry (e.g., TUI, Thomas Cook, etc.). The pursuit of different business strategies makes industry participants varied. Some pursue a core business of packaged travel services, which they seek to expand as widely as possible; some integrate horizontally, bringing together a range of packaged travel, transport, and ground services; and others integrate vertically, with airlines entering the travel agency and/or package tour businesses. One important dynamic in the sub-sector is the increase in consumer customised packages and in the individual booking of package elements in a personalised and flexible way. This is leading to a decline in demand for the standardised package tour—a phenomenon often described as the decline in package tourism and rise in do-it-yourself tourism (E-Business Watch, 2002). Such do-it-yourself tourism is enabled by the Internet, in part driven by adoption of ICTs and in part a driver. Another trend is that towards more specialised tours, following hobbies or special interest themes. These trends present challenges for integrated majors and niches for smaller operators.

There are far more travel agencies, many operate as small, single business shop-fronts, while others operate national and international agency chains. Both have come under pressure from other participants in the value chain, with others now following the lead of airlines towards low- or no-commission ticket sales through agencies. As a result, travel agencies have sought other sources of revenue, such as charging service fees to the customer instead of commissions to the tourism service provider (E-Business Watch, 2002). Travel agencies also are under pressure from the rise of the Internet and online delivery, being the point in the value chain most susceptible to disintermediation.

## Recreation and Amusement Services

Businesses in the recreation and amusement industry are highly diverse, as are the services they offer. They may be private sector (e.g., amusement parks) or public sector (e.g., museums and historical sites). Their shared characteristics include theme and/or location, and, like hotel and accommodation enterprises, a dependence upon the skills of their employees for service quality (E-Business Watch, 2002). Their ties to location make such businesses natural collaborators in destination market-ing/management activities.

The impacts of Internet e-commerce and e-business applications vary greatly, although the ability to provide information worldwide, 24/7 at relatively low cost is clearly important. The possibility of direct to customer online reservations and ticket sales also is important, both for reach and for process efficiency and the possibility of disintermediation. Nevertheless, it is unlikely that many recreation and amusement sector enterprises could afford to risk significant channel conflict, as they depend to a greater or lesser extent on major tour and package operators driving ticket sales. More immediate opportunities exist in communication relating to content (e.g., online access to museum and gallery collections) and more immediate visitor information, which enhances awareness and attractiveness, enabling individuals and groups to get to know more about the destination beforehand and to plan visits. There also are opportunities in enabling online shopping at the gallery, museum or park shop (e.g., The Louvre—www.louvre.fr).

## Accommodation and Food Services

E-Business Watch (2002) noted that the accommodation sub-sector incorporates a very large number of businesses, which vary greatly in the type and scale of both management and the product on offer (e.g., from luxury five-star hotels to basic one-star accommodation, from hotel chains to family-run inns, from campsites to residences and rental accommodation, from farm holidays to bed and breakfasts, etc.). All are characterized by close links with their local setting and a close relationship between the quality and capacities of employees and the quality of service offered. What they have in common is that they supply service "packages," ranging from overnight accommodation to a series of complementary services, the quality and variety of which are dependent upon the size and type of the business. Accommodation businesses also are natural collaborators in destination marketing/management activities.

Recent developments in accommodation include: increasing concentration, with relatively few major hotels chains (albeit, often branded with multiple brands); and increasing aggregation among businesses, through franchising—allowing branding of affiliated hotels and increased bargaining power, greater potential to develop and use customer relationship management and supporting back office systems, greater brand visibility and the ability to engage in more widespread marketing, and greater potential to set and manage quality standards (E-Business Watch, 2002).

Food services businesses are typically small and fragmented, with obvious exceptions among a relatively few well-known global brands and franchises. Online information relating to service offerings, time, menu, location, and related nearby attractions can help to promote the business to a wider travelling audience, while online ordering and payment systems can enhance local reservations and take-away food business. There also is potential to link into destination marketing/management activities, to promote the business and enable participation in possible special interest tourism related activities (e.g., food and wine lover groups, specific locations or architecture).

## ICT in the Tourism Value Chain

Tourism services involve both business-to-business (B2B) and business-to-consumer (B2C) transactions, with the distinction sometimes difficult to maintain (e.g., direct to customer vs. travel agent mediated hotel bookings). E-Business Watch (2002) noted that the tourism services sector had already been profoundly affected by ICTs. They also noted that there had been three main waves of ICT related innovation: the development of computer reservation systems (CRS) during the 1970s; the development of global distribution systems (GDS) during the 1980s; and the emergence of the Internet during the 1990s. Computer reservation systems (CRS) began the process of automating reservations (especially for airline bookings). Global distribution systems (GDS) provided the means by which to connect and integrate automated reservation systems, and are still the principal means by which reservations are made through travel agencies worldwide. There are four main systems operating—SABRE, Amadeus, Galileo and Worldspan. They are proprietary systems, operating through a network of agreements between partner firms. The Internet brought a fundamental change in that all categories of firms, large and small, form anywhere in the value chain, can now communicate directly with their end customers. Importantly, whereas CRS and GDS were highly complex, proprietary systems that required access agreements and significant investment in ICT infrastructure and skills to use them, the Internet is a "free," open network that can be used without bearing the full cost of implementation of the entire network. As a result it is transforming the tourism services value chain—a transformation that is more advanced in developed countries than elsewhere.

In the past, integration into the GDS was sometimes problematic and costly for hotel and car rental providers, and could only be effectively achieved by such means as the hotel industry switch companies (e.g., Pegasus, HotelBank, WizCom, Worldres, etc.) providing a shared interface into GDS. More recently, tourism service providers (e.g., hotels, car rental firms and airlines) have used the Internet to enhance their links with their customers by implementing systems that enable direct links to end users for reservations, and so forth and customer relationship management (CRM) features, such as frequent flyer/user and loyalty reward programs. For their part, the traditional travel intermediaries (e.g., travel agencies and tour operators) have used the Internet to broaden their activities and as an additional channel through which to sell to the end customer (e.g., in addition to shop front sales). The major participants in proprietary global distribution systems have either brought their databases onto the Internet directly (e.g., Amadeus and Galileo) or through new brands (e.g., SABRE established Travelocity.com). There also are new participants, such as travel portals (e.g., expedia.com and lastminute.com) and national, regional or local tourist and travel portals (e.g., www.franceguide.com, www.enit.it, and www.visitbritain.com) (E-Business Watch, 2002). Increasingly, these latter are linked to destination management systems (DMS), which provide a database of local tourism service suppliers and support for single destination specific front-end Web sites or portals. Hence, there is both disintermediation (e.g., airlines bypassing travel agents and selling direct to customers via their own Web sites) and new intermediaries (e.g., travel portals and ticketing sites such as Expedia.com and Ticketclic.com).

Figures 2 and 3 show the tourism services value chain before and with the Internet. Prior to the emergence of the Internet, tourism services providers (i.e., produc-

*Figure 2. The tourism services value chain before the Internet (Source: UNCTAD, 2001)*

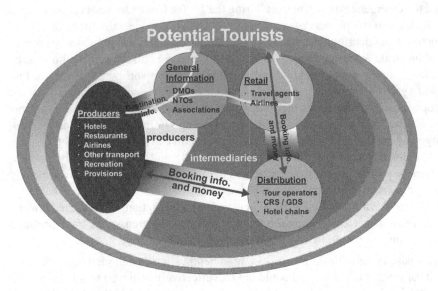

*Figure 3. The Internet enabled tourism services value chain (Source: UNCTAD, 2001)*

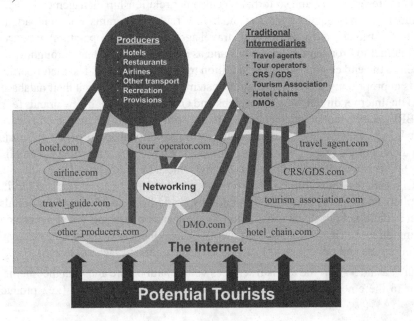

ers) fed information through general information intermediaries (e.g., destination management organisations, national and regional tourist offices) and through travel intermediaries (e.g., travel agencies and tour operators). Payments were taken by the intermediaries (i.e., travel agencies and tour operators), and a share remitted back to the service providers after the deduction of commissions (Figure 2).

With the emergence of the Internet, both service providers (i.e., producers) and the traditional intermediaries (i.e., travel agents and tour operators) link either directly or through new "Internet intermediaries" with their customers. The direct links can be either direct individual links (e.g., between a particular hotel and a particular guest) or direct consortial or cooperative links (e.g., between an individual guest and a hotel chain's Web site, which then links to the individual hotel; or between an individual tourist and a regional tourism cooperative, and thence to the individual service provider) (Figure 3). The new Internet intermediaries can be new participants or consortia of existing participants (i.e., new slices of the tourism services value chain made by combining existing participants, or parts thereof, into new entities). The enormous potential for disintermediation in a value chain formerly built around intermediaries is the key to understanding the impacts of online delivery on tourism services.

## Drivers of Online Service Delivery

Evans and Wurster (2000) characterised the impact of the Internet as a movement out of the frontier of richness and reach. Richness refers to the depth and quality of information in an interaction, while reach refers to the number of entities that can be reached via the Internet. In the past, it was possible to share rich interactions with a limited number of suppliers or customers. A major impact of Internet-based communication and commerce is that it has greatly increased reach and increased the potential for richer, more customised and targeted interactions. Organisations can now broaden their supplier or customer base (better reach) and make relationships deeper and more effective (greater richness).

The evidence from surveys around the world suggests that the early and primary foci for the adoption of e-commerce, e-business applications and online delivery are indeed improved customer relationships and enhanced market reach. Cost savings and efficiency improvements have typically been lower in the initial consideration set of adopters (Accenture, 2001; APEC, 2002; CeBI, 2002, 2003; European Commission, 2004; Eurostat, 2003; Houghton, 2003, 2006; Kraemer, Dedrick, & Dunkle 2002a, 2002b; Palacios, 2003; SIKA, 2003, 2004; Tachiki, Hamaya, & Yukawa, 2004; Varian, Litan, Elder, Shutter, 2002).

Industry dynamics determine whether businesses focus on new customer attraction or the retention of existing customers (Dantuma & Hawkins, 2001), with sectors that lend themselves to recurring relations (e.g., business travel) tending to focus on building revenue from existing customers, and those that are characterised by one-off relations (e.g., tourism) tending to focus on extending their customer reach. Nevertheless, many tourism services providers use such means as "loyalty programs" to establish recurring relations and enhance their ability to provide tailored services (e.g., airlines and hotel chains). Industries also vary in terms of their focus and over time. The initial focus of e-commerce and e-business applications tends to be on marketing and sales (i.e., a customer focus). For tourism businesses, this is especially true. Over time, however, as experience with e-commerce and e-business grows, the focus shifts towards processes and costs (i.e., an efficiency focus).

## Potential and Levels of Adoption of Online Services Delivery

Tourism services are by their nature highly amenable to online delivery—they are information intensive and target customers who are typically not local. All the features that define the Internet for business, its richness (i.e., information intensity) and its reach (i.e., 24/7, worldwide accessibility) are essential for tourism. Moreover, the people most likely to be business travellers and tourists also are likely to be high level Internet users (i.e., the same age, professional, and salary groups). Hence, the potential is enormous and current level of adoption of online service delivery is relatively high in tourism compared to other sectors. While there are significant differences between countries in levels adoption and use of online delivery in tourism services, those differences appear to relate primarily to the general levels of ICT adoption and use.

The developments that now characterise the Internet also are crucial for the online delivery of tourism services. The take up of broadband is now rapid and widespread, and tourism services will benefit from the ability to use still and video images of facilities and locations to enhance their information provision and entice would-be customers. Languages other than English are now becoming a more established part of the online landscape, with local and multi-language Web sites enhancing the ability of tourism services providers and their intermediaries to communicate their offerings to would-be customers. Mobile technologies and a range of mobile and hand-held devices are now connecting to the Internet through Wi-Fi hotspots and other mobile communications technologies, providing tourism services providers with new opportunities to communicate with their customers whilst they are travelling.

On the demand side, users have taken to online search and reservation systems (i.e., looking and booking). Tourism services, especially airline ticketing and hotel reservations, are among the most popular and widely used B2C e-commerce applications (European Travel Commission 2004; KNSO 2004; Macussen 2003, 2004; McGann

*Box 1. Amenability of services to online delivery (Source: Houghton, 2003)*

Important factors influencing the amenability of services to online delivery include: the significance of the role of information exchange in the service concerned; the level of standardisation; the complexity of the tasks involved; the nature of the knowledge involved; the nature of the "problem" addressed by the service; and the context of delivery.

The level of **standardisation** of processes is an important determinant. Services that can be standardised and delivered in online form (e.g. research reports, statistical updates, images, etc.) and services that can be standardised and ordered via the Internet (e.g. courier delivery services, advertising space, airline tickets, etc.) are most amenable to online delivery. Those that resist standardisation tend to be less amenable.

The **complexity of the tasks** involved is one of the factors retarding standardisation and online delivery. Morris (2000) pointed out that many have underestimated the complexity of the work environment, and noted two related concepts that shed light on these complexities: articulation and emergence. Articulation is the way in which people arrange and co-ordinate activities to mesh with colleagues. Emergence refers to actions that are often difficult to articulate too far in advance. Complexity makes remote delivery more difficult, although bandwidth increases enable greater richness of interaction and can support remote delivery of more complex services.

The **nature of the knowledge** involved also affects the amenability of services to online delivery. It is common to make the distinction between codified and tacit knowledge. Codified knowledge is knowledge that can be written down and readily transmitted from one person to another (e.g. standard operating procedures, policy manuals, legislation, taxation formulae, etc.). Tacit knowledge tends to resist codification and remain a part of the knowledge and skills of individuals—it is more fluid and interpretive. Knowledge that can be codified is more amenable to online delivery than tacit knowledge. The transmission of tacit knowledge often requires face-to-face interaction in the negotiation of meaning and in learning. This makes online delivery more difficult. Again, however, high bandwidth networks can enhance the richness of mediated communications and enable the online delivery of more knowledge intensive services.

The **nature of the problem** involved also effects amenability to online delivery. Rittel and Webber (1973) noted that there are major differences between different kinds of problems and hence strategies to solve them. A "tame" problem can be expressed independently of its solution. In engineering, for example, one can specify what needs to be designed independent of any particular design solution. In contrast, a "wicked" problem cannot be explained without its solution. In working out a solution one understands the problem more clearly and can redefine it if necessary, which in turn leads to a better solution, and so on. Tame problems are easier to distribute in space and time, because they can be more accurately specified, and worked on independently, drawing on codified knowledge bases.

The **context of delivery** also affects amenability. In high context work, significant (informal) interaction is needed between co-workers to get the job done, whereas in a low context activity workers can proceed relatively independently. High context work tends to require a high degree of awareness of co-workers and of clients. Low context work is more amenable to online delivery than high context work.

2004; METI 2002; MoCIE 2003). Not only are online travel search and reservation widely used, but consumers have confidence in them—relative to other purchases. For example, one survey of online purchasers in Europe showed that consumers who had purchased via Internet were most confident doing so for: theatre and train tickets (48% of EU-15 respondents); hotel bookings (46%); airline tickets (45%); books, CDs and DVDs (39%); and car rental (35%) (European Commission, 2004). Growth also is rapid, driven by cost cutting on the supply side (e.g., budget airlines) and the development of fully online alternatives (e.g., e-ticketing). Promotion of tourism at national and regional levels is providing an important coordinating force, enabling tourism SMEs (also known as SMTEs) to adopt e-business and online delivery alternatives and, thereby, further encouraging adoption.

On the supply side, it is clear that the tourism services industry has adopted the Internet as a marketing and sales tool to a greater extent than most other sectors, and is one of the leaders of online delivery of services (ABS, 2004; E-Business Watch, 2002, 2003, 2004a, 2004b; Eurostat, 2003; MoCIE, 2003; SIKA, 2004; Statistics Canada, 2004; Tachiki et al., 2004; US Census Bureau, 2004; WTO, 2004). Tourism enterprises also use online procurement extensively, with smaller differences between large and small enterprises than might be expected. Supply chain integration is comparable to other sectors. Nevertheless, considerable potential remains (e.g., CRM and multi-language Web sites). The overwhelming impression is that in the tourism services sector the Internet is primarily and widely seen as a channel for marketing and sales (i.e., online delivery), although increasing attention also is now being paid to e-procurement.

Moreover, developments in the tourism services industry are propelling further adoption of online delivery. Perhaps the most obvious example is electronic ticketing, with e-tickets now the norm for air travel within some countries, and becoming increasingly established practice internationally. Less conspicuous developments, such as customer relationship management systems (CRM) and a range of related special offer, loyalty and merchandising programs operating through service provider Web sites, now also are enriching the relationship between service providers and their customers.

Online delivery and e-business offer tourism services enterprises opportunities, but there also are risks. E-Business Watch (2003) suggested that online delivery and e-business offered opportunities for enhancing customer relationships through the implementation of innovative CRM systems (e.g. airline frequent flyer clubs), which can provide customer databases that can be exploited for marketing purpose. As price competition is becoming fiercer, e-procurement is likely to become a more important factor in cost management and containment. In the meantime, online promotion and sales appear to offer particular opportunities, as they can be a means to increase the volume of sales, the number of customers, and the quality of customer service. Hence, while take-up and use of online delivery is already high in tourism, enormous potential remains.

## Impacts of Online Service Delivery

"The tourism industry has been profoundly and fundamentally affected (and to some extent already redefined) by the Internet" (E-Business Watch, 2004a). One major impact is disintermediation of travel agents, as hotels, airlines, and other service providers go direct to customer, in order to save costs and enable them to benefit from CRM systems and build customer loyalty. Disintermediation of agencies is being exacerbated by the cutting of commissions by airlines and, increasingly, hotel chains. However, there also are new participants (e.g., in the form of portals) and existing participants are expanding into other areas (e.g., easyjet.com expanding its offerings through easycar.com, easyhotel.com, etc.) (E-Business Watch, 2004a).

There is little evidence of the supplier streamlining sometimes seen in manufacturing occurring in tourism services, but there is evidence of integration and consolidation among participants in the value chain, as they seek to achieve economies of scale, ensure the availability of services from suppliers, and gain control of the whole process and thereby of prices and margins (E-Business Watch, 2002, 2004a). Klein and Loebbecke (2001) noted three major effects of the Internet on the air travel industry:

- The convergence of global strategies, with business models susceptible to almost immediate imitation
- The emergence of numerous cross-cutting alliances, with participants seeking new combinations of competencies and offerings
- An increase in concentration, with the Internet tending to encourage a "winner takes all" market, with thin margins and relatively high set-up costs

Pappas (2001) noted the impacts of disintermediation of travel agencies and the increased ability of services providers, such as airlines, to sell direct to their customers. He also noted the emergence of new "functional consortia" in the airline industry seeking to aggregate selling and sourcing capabilities—effectively taking Internet-based slices of the traditional value chain and aggregating them across competitors. Examples include such regional selling consortia as Orbitz in the United States and Zuji in the Asia Pacific.

*Table 1. Benefits of e-commerce and online delivery for European tourism SMEs (Source: E-Business Watch, 2004a)*

| Component | Benefit |
|---|---|
| Product promotion | Direct and indirect advertising |
| New sales channels | Easy access to potential customers<br>Online sales and transactions<br>Ability to reach out to international markets |
| Direct savings | Increase in market share of products/services<br>Low cost communication<br>Savings in communication costs<br>Savings in advertising costs<br>Increased productivity |
| Time to market | Lower cost margins for products and services |
| Customer service | Lower cost of obtaining suppliers |
| Brand image | Product delivery<br>Greater customer satisfaction |
| Technological and organisational learning | Company image enhancement<br>Create an up-to-date corporate image |
| Customer relations | Obtain know-how through discussion with others on Internet |
| New business models | Form and extend business networks<br>Competitor's performance benchmarking<br>Create new business opportunities<br>Speedy and timely access to information from Web sites<br>Communication efficiency improvement<br>Effectiveness of information gathering<br>Availability of expertise regardless of location<br>Better service and support from suppliers |

For tourism enterprises a Web site is a marketing and sales channel that can be used 24 hours a day. Given that travellers and tourists are by definition located elsewhere, this aspect of the Internet is crucial—liberating tourism enterprises from their native timezone and making them readily available to would-be customers around the world. Combined with low communications costs and the ability to browse richer information than might be possible by telephone or facsimile, this makes a Web presence an enormously powerful tool for extending the reach of tourism sector enterprises and the potential richness of customer interactions. From the consumer perspective, the availability of information online allows greater comparison of prices, increasing market transparency and competition (E-Business Watch, 2004a).

E-Business Watch (2002) noted that, in Europe, the tourism sector has been a forerunner in the widespread usage of ICT. Operations and transactions have been carried out electronically for decades. The industry was, therefore, a rapid adopter of the Internet, both for information and commercial purposes. They concluded that the effects of the widespread use of the Internet in the tourism value chain include:

- Disintermediation due to the possibility of selling most of the services directly to the final customer by using the Internet as a complementary and/or substitute channel, with positive effects on the costs of the intermediation

- Re-intermediation, and the entry of new Internet intermediaries (e.g., travel portals)

- Opportunities for enhancing customer relationships through the implementation of innovative systems, such as customer relationship management (CRM)

- New challenges for the participants who are more directly threatened by the process of disintermediation, with traditional intermediaries (e.g., travel agencies) having to enhance their ability to provide tailored services, and SMEs pushed towards niche activities and/or the establishment of co-operative structures (E-Business Watch, 2002)

One possible impact on the intermediaries sector (i.e., travel agents and tour operators) is polarisation, with the losers being those businesses that do not either grow to become scale participants or remain small enough to adopt niche business strategies (e.g., business travel and/or conferences and conventions). Taller (2002) noted that the retail tourism services business was evolving and industry members responding to the new business environment. Some travel retailers are using e-commerce technology and the Web, while others are creating niches within market segments. Some are selling complementary products and services through traditional retailing, while others are experimenting with new ways to generate or supplement revenue streams.

Taller (2002) also noted that business-to-business (B2B) and business-to-consumer (B2C) applications are driving industry efforts to reduce costs through the use of online business tools and the increased use of automation. After investing and then offsetting their costs of development, travel suppliers have increasingly adopted a business strategy that encourages B2B and B2C sales. Brochures, catalogues, e-procurement, and other ordering mechanisms are being made available on the Internet by most tourism supply chain participants. New technologies have allowed many to rationalise reservation and purchasing.

Increasingly, service providers are focusing on minimizing their distribution costs. At the same time, many firms (e.g., airlines) are using the direct Web site sales systems to broaden their revenue bases by, for example, merchandising a range of

*Box 2. Implications for tourism industry structures (Source: E-Business Watch, 2003)*

**Internet Intermediaries Emerge as New Participants in the Tourism Sector:** The Internet has given birth to new participants in the sector. Besides online agencies, new intermediaries such as travel portals and regional and local tourist portals play an important role. Travel portals offer tourist products which can be quite complex and require know-how and bargaining power. The Internet intermediaries have reached a state of maturity with mergers taking place (e.g., lastminute.com bought holidayautos.com). In the future, other intermediaries such as GDS and tour operators will have to justify their role and ability to add value.

**New Forms of Interaction Between Customers and Suppliers Through the Internet:** The Internet has become the new medium for interactions that were previously carried out through different means. For example, hotels and their customers may now communicate via e-mail or Web-based forms, supplementing or replacing communication by phone or facsimile. The Internet also has allowed direct interaction between customers and suppliers (e.g., between travellers and tour operators) and is leading to disintermediation. There is a strong movement towards ICT-enabled services, such as e-tickets, in order to enhance or complete the transition to online delivery.

**Possible Benefits for Enterprises Through More Direct Communication With Customers:** By facilitating direct communication between customers and suppliers, the Internet can have a significant impact on "do-it-yourself" tourism. This may offer particular opportunities to SMEs. Unlike larger tourism organisations, such as hotel chains and holiday villages, small enterprises need to draw on a wide range of local support services (e.g., restaurants, entertainment, sport and leisure facilities). These are usually provided by other small enterprises. Independent travellers who search for information about destinations, accommodation, travel conditions and prices may benefit from SME networks, local tourism organisations and destination management organisations that promote, market and disseminate information on local tourism enterprises through destination-related portals.

complementary and related products (e.g., carry-on luggage). Similar examples can be seen in the hotel industry—with, for example, Westin Hotels allowing customers to buy elements of furniture and fittings found in their rooms (Taller, 2002). How successful these strategies will be, and what impacts they may have on the tourism sector remains to be seen.

# Barriers to Online Service Delivery

Much of the content handled by tourism services providers is readily amenable to online delivery. Hence, unsuitability of product or service for online delivery is of less significance in this sector than others. However, trust and confidence are vital, raising issues of trust, security, and privacy to the forefront.

*Table 2. Barriers to e-commerce and e-business applications for European tourism SMEs, 2003 (Source: E-Business Watch, 2004a)*

| Category | Barrier |
|---|---|
| Awareness of SMEs / access to infrastructure | Costs (start-up costs) |
| | Unfamiliarity with the Internet |
| | Lack of guidance and competence in how to start the process |
| Critical mass among business partners | Suppliers are not online. |
| | Customers are not online. |
| Confidence in legal and regulatory framework / security | Security hazards |
| | Guarantee of message delivery |
| | Tampering with network messages |
| | Unauthorised access to internal networks |
| | Interception of network messages |
| | Verification of authorship of messages |
| Adaptation of business processes | Decreased productivity through frivolous use |

Many tourism businesses are small. Hence, the particular barriers facing SMEs are important—particularly in such areas as accommodation, food, and entertainment. Table 2 outlines some of the barriers facing tourism SMEs, highlighting the issues of scale, access to and affordability of ICT systems, infrastructure, and skills. These concerns are echoed around the world (E-Business Watch, 2003; European Commission, 2004; Eurostat, 2003; Heung, 2003; Kreamer et al., 2002b; MoCIE, 2003; Palacios, 2003; Tachiki et al., 2004).

On the demand side, concerns relate primarily to trust—relating to the credibility of information found and the solidity and honesty of the service provider or intermediary. One recent study found that 49% of respondents used offline services to confirm that their online reservation was booked, demonstrating that there is still some mistrust towards online booking systems. Another 32% used offline methods to update travel plans (Travelport, 2004).

Tourism services are a "confidence good"—one in which the consumer must feel confident in spending money for something to be delivered in a different place, by potentially unknown service providers at a future date. Having confidence, having trust in the service providers and intermediaries and having recourse to functional complaints and restitution mechanisms are vital. Hence, established brand names and scale will continue to be important and ensuring service (i.e., fulfilment) essential.

# Emerging Issues and Policy Challenges

Online delivery brings opportunities and challenges for tourism services. Consumer services can be delivered directly to the consumer (e.g., self execution of an online airline ticket reservation) or mediated by a services supplier (e.g., a travel agent). On the demand side the adoption of online delivery depends upon trust and confidence, price, flexibility, bandwidth and ease of access, and ease of use of online interfaces. On the supply side adoption depends upon the relative cost per transaction of online vs. face-to-face alternatives, as well as the development and availability of new delivery applications, ICT infrastructure availability and quality. New modes of delivery open up possibilities for disintermediation and new forms of mediation, new business models and new entrants (Table 3).

There are both challenges and opportunities. Online delivery brings a number of opportunities for tourism services enterprises. The richness and reach afforded by the Internet enable service providers to establish direct relations with their custom-ers, with significant implications for both reducing distribution costs and enhancing customer relationships through the capture and use of information and through the provision of greater information about their offerings. In turn, these information flows enable a better matching of demand and supply, with the possibility to more rapidly fine tune offerings in terms of both content and price, and thereby increase the possibility for better capacity utilisation (e.g., airline seats and hotel rooms). At the same time, there are many challenges. Tourism services have, historically, been mediated, with services providers (e.g., airlines and hotels) relying on intermediaries (e.g., travel agents and tour operators) to sell to customers. The very opportunities offered by the Internet for service providers are a threat to the intermediaries.

New alliances, consortia and new players are emerging to take advantage of oppor-tunities and the situation is fluid. It is, as yet, unclear which of the many businesses

Table 3. Consumer services: Impacts of online delivery on mediation (Source: Houghton, 2006)

|  | Disintermediation | New mediation |
|---|---|---|
| **Service supply** | Lower costs per transaction<br>Scale and market reach<br>Richness of customer interaction | New business opportunities<br>Provision of service information, information navigation, collecting and processing online transaction information |
| **User demand** | Better quality information (e.g., prices)<br>Reduced search costs<br>24/7 access to information and services | New travel support services<br>Increased choice<br>Price and quality comparisons |

*Table 4. ICT-related opportunities, challenges, enablers, and obstacles for tourism SMEs, 2003 (Source: E-Business Watch, 2004b)*

| Opportunities |
| --- |
| Direct access to potential customers |
| Cutting marketing and sales costs |
| Optimising lead-time and instant adjustments of supply according to demand |

| Challenges |
| --- |
| Minimising setup costs by developing systems and applications more suitable for SMEs |
| Creating standard ICT and e-business solutions for SMEs |
| Employing multi-channel strategies |

| Enablers |
| --- |
| The formation of network relations among SMEs |
| Customer-driven demand for e-business products and services |
| Large enterprises leading the way for SMEs |

| Obstacles |
| --- |
| SME reluctance to invest in ICT and e-business |
| The business case for SMEs to grasp the potential of implementing e-business |
| Lifestyle SMEs and management motivations |

and business models will thrive and which fail, and what the longer-term impacts will be on the tourism services value chain. Alignments of various enterprises are likely to be important. Currently, there are a number of regional selling consortia involving major players (e.g. the new airline-led Internet intermediaries, such as Orbitz and Zuji). There also are new opportunities for smaller players, with the emergence of national, regional, and local destination management systems (DMSs), which are often operated by or on behalf of destination marketing/management organisations (DMOs), national, or regional tourism offices. These create an online "front-end" or shop-front for many small businesses in a particular location. Such developments appear to offer new opportunities for service providers, perhaps even a vital life-line for tourism SMEs in such areas as specialist tourism activities, accommodation, and food services, galleries, museums, and historical sites. The future path of traditional intermediaries is less clear. What also is unclear is the extent to which corporate or political control of key search engines and portals and the willingness or ability of services providers to participate in them might effect competition.

There are a number of areas in which governments can assist in enabling adoption and diffusion and easing the transition and adjustments involved. These include: fostering innovation and increasing diffusion and use; ensuring the availability of infrastructure and establishing an environment in which there is trust online; and ensuring that the business environment is both conducive to the take up of innovations and is not compromised by the structural changes involved.

## Fostering Innovation, Increasing Diffusion and Use

Moving to online delivery requires new specialist skills (e.g., IT and change management skills) and internal retraining and re-skilling in support of business transformation. Governments play a major role in the provision of education and can influence the emphasis given to specific areas through information provision and target setting. Governments can promote lifelong learning through direction setting, funding and other incentives. Governments also can encourage deregulation of labour markets in order to make it easier for organisations to more flexibly manage their activities. Various initiatives specifically targeting casual and seasonal workers also might be considered, given the importance of such workers in the tourism sector.

The small scale of many tourism services providers affects their capacity to implement online delivery and e-business solutions (e.g., they lack vision, strategic leadership, and skills) and the affordability of doing so (e.g., the solutions available in the marketplace tend to be designed for and scaled to larger organisations). Governments might consider ways to publicise existing commercially available solutions, especially those appropriate for small businesses (e.g., by reviews, competitions, and awards). There also may be potential to encourage the development of new, less expensive solutions on the supply side, and foster consortial development and/or purchasing of such solutions on the demand side (e.g. by working through industry and professional associations, or local and national destination marketing/management organisations).

The Internet affords a major opportunity for tourism SMEs to develop collaborative networks. These are most likely to be based around a location and could be fostered through existing or new destination marketing/management organisations (DMOs). SMEs can promote their business and increase sales through such organisations. There also is the opportunity to reap the benefits of collective e-business applications—where, for example, customer relationship management (CRM) is linked into destination management systems (DMSs). There also may be opportunities to develop parallel procurement consortia, building from the base of the DMO/DMS-based selling consortia.

Governments can play an important part, through their involvement in national and regional tourism organisations, by playing a lead role in the co-ordination necessary for ensuring success or simply encouraging and supporting the development of network relations between SMTEs (E-Business Watch, 2004a). Where involved in destination marketing/management directly, governments also might consider the development of collaborative activities as an opportunity to demonstrate leadership in the use of online delivery and e-business solutions and/or as an opportunity for lead project demonstrations.

# Infrastructure and Trust Online

Bandwidth availability, network responsiveness, and competitive communications costs are the foundations for the online delivery of services. Much progress has been made in respect to liberalisation and the introduction of competition in telecommunications in many countries. Nevertheless, there is scope for further improvement in this rapidly evolving environment. Governments cannot afford to allow slow reform in one sector to adversely effect the development of globally competitive firms in others. Every effort must be made to ensure that communications and converging content regulation do not retard the provision of low cost broadband services to the home and to small businesses, and that there is scope for the emergence of new competitors in the provision of communications and content services.

The use of e-business solutions at an advanced level requires a certain network capacity, with frustrations and negative experiences likely when attempts are made to operate complex systems, features and programs on low bandwidth networks (E-Business Watch, 2004a). Tourism services are information intensive. There is considerable potential to develop sophisticated still and video image presentations of the sights and facilities that can be found at particular locations. Hence, the widespread availability of broadband for users and for small businesses is important. The ability to access tourism information and reservation sites and systems from mobile/portable devices also is important. Be it in the availability of wireless, $3^{rd}$ generation cellular, and other networks, in their affordability or in the availability of content and payment systems tailored to portable devices, there is considerable scope to foster the development and use of innovative technologies.

Tourism services feature the exchange of information and payments. Information security and trust are central. UNCTAD (2001) characterised tourism services as a "confidence good"—one for which the customer typically pays, in part or whole, in advance, to an intermediary or supplier located at a distance, and often in another country, for a promise to provide a service in the future and at a remote location. Hence, issues of trust, security, and risk loom large. Government, industry associations and other industry stakeholders can do much to build trust through awareness raising activities and ensuring that there are clear systems for information, payments, and dispute resolution. Efforts to increase the level of secure online payments—for example, by, educating services providers about the use of secure sockets layer servers and encouraging their use by Internet-based intermediaries—also could be helpful (E-Business Watch, 2003).

# Business Environment and Regulation

It is a characteristic of the sector that larger firms have taken the lead in the development and deployment of ICTs. Historically this lead was due to the development of large scale, proprietary reservation, and distribution systems, but even as Internet-based e-business solutions are emerging larger firms are still taking the lead. With a high share of SMEs in the tourism sector, enabling smaller firms to adopt e-business solutions is crucial (E-Business Watch, 2004b). This requires attention to a range of access, infrastructure and standards issues, and the setting and maintenance of a business environment that fosters competition and innovation.

As noted, there is evidence of integration and concentration among players in the value chain, of polarisation among intermediaries and the emergence of new "functional consortia" among some of the major players. There are obvious regulatory issues in the operation of major national and international consortia. There also is a range of cross-cutting regulatory issues, such as the partial deregulation of airlines and airports, management and operation of airline routes, management of the consolidation of airlines, and so forth. All of these raise complex issues for governments that challenge regulatory agencies due to their international reach and integration with other areas of regulation. Governments need to monitor developments closely and be aware of the potential linkages and pitfalls.

One particular area of concern is the potential for powerful players to shape online offerings by either refusing to make services available through rival intermediaries or portals or by directing controlled portal traffic to particular favoured service providers (including themselves). Governments can play an important role in monitoring and acting against anti-competitive practices as and when they arise and ensuring the provision of balanced information. The latter could be done through such means as content regulation, the establishment and operation or oversight of government or industry self-regulation of content, and/or the operation of local, regional and national destination marketing/management organisations (DMOs), destination management systems (DMSs), tourism promotion organisations and information systems that link into the necessary supporting reservation systems, thereby providing a gateway that ensures a minimum level of access and participation for all service providers, regardless of affiliation or size.

Hence, the key foci for future tourism policy are likely to include careful monitoring and management of competition, with due regard to the complex Web of inter-related regulatory issues, and the development and promotion of destination management systems that integrate the many SMTEs and provide a single front-end and path to market.

# References

ABS. (2004). *Business use of information technology 2002-03* (Cat. No. 8129.0). Canberra: Australian Bureau of Statistics.

Accenture. (2001). *The unexpected eEurope: The surprising success of European eCommerce.* Accenture. Retrieved January 2003, from www.accenture.com/eEurope2001.

APEC. (2002). *Application of e-commerce strategies to small and medium sized tourism enterprises in the APEC region.* Seoul: Korean Tourism Research Institute.

CeBI. (2002). *Net impact study Canada: The SME experience.* CeBI, Ottawa: Industry Canada. Retrieved May 2004, from http://www.cebi.ca/Public/Team1/Docs/net_impact.pdf

CeBI. (2003). *Net impact study Canada: The international experience.* CeBI, Ottawa: Industry Canada.

Cohen, S., Zysman, J., & Cowhey, P. (2001). *Tracking a transformation: E-commerce and the terms of competition in industries.* Washington, DC: Brooking Institute Press.

Dantuma, L. M. Y., & Hawkins, R. W. (2001). *E-commerce in the logistics sector: Assessing the effects on the logistics value chain* (TNO Report No. 01-41). Delft: TNO.

E-Business Watch. (2002, October). *ICT and e-business in the tourism sector* (Report No. 13). Brussels: European Commission. Retrieved November 2004, from http://www.ebusiness-watch.org

E-Business Watch. (2003, July). *ICT and e-business in the tourism sector* (Report No. 13/II). Brussels: European Commission. Retrieved November 2004, from http://www.ebusiness-watch.org

E-Business Watch. (2004a, May). *Electronic business in tourism* (Report No. 07-I). Brussels: European Commission. Retrieved November 2004, from http://www.ebusiness-watch.org

E-Business Watch. (2004b, August). *Electronic business in tourism* (Report No. 07-II). Brussels: European Commission. Retrieved November 2004, from http://www.ebusiness-watch.org

E-Business Watch. (2005, September). *ICT and electronic business in tourism,* (Report No. 07). Brussels: European Commission. Retrieved November 2005, from http://www.ebusiness-watch.org

European Commission. (2004). *European public opinion on issues relating to business to business e-commerce* (Eurobarometer Report). Brussels: European Commission. Retrieved November 2004, from http://www.e-bsn.org/

European Travel Commission. (2004). *New media review.* Brussels: European Travel Commission. Retrieved November 2004, from http://www.etcnewmedia.com/review/default.asp

Eurostat. (2003). *E-commerce and the Internet in European business* (Cat. KS-54-03-889-EN-N). Brussels: Eurostat. Retrieved June 2004, from http://europa.eu.int/comm/eurostat/

Evans, P. & Wurster, T. S. (2000). *Blown to bits: How the new economics of information transforms strategy.* Boston: Harvard Business School Press.

Heung, V. (2003). Internet usage by international travellers: Reasons and barriers.*International Journal of Contemporary Hospitality Management, 15*(7), 370-378.

Houghton, J. W. (2003). *Online delivery of business services.* Paris: OECD. Retrieved June 2004, from http://www.oecd.org/dataoecd/40/5/31818723.pdf

Houghton, J. W. (2006). *Online delivery in travel and tourism.* Paris: OECD.

Klein, S. & Loebbecke, C. (2001). Web impact on the air travel industry. In S. Cohen, J. Zysman, & P. Cowhey (Eds.), *Tracking a transformation: E-commerce and the terms of competition in industries* (pp. 112-127). Washington, DC: Brooking Institute Press.

KNSO. (2004, November 16). *Cyber shopping mall survey in September and in the third quarter 2004.* Seoul: Korean National Statistical Office. Retrieved November 2004, from http://www.nso.go.kr/eng/

Kraemer, K. L., Dedrick, J. & Dunkle, D. (2002a). *E-commerce: A mile wide and an inch deep.* CRITO, Irvine: University of California. Retrieved May 2004, from http://www.crito.uci.edu/

Kraemer, K. L., Dedrick, J. & Dunkle, D. (2002b). *E-commerce in the United States: Leader or one of the pack?* CRITO, Irvine: University of California. Retrieved May 2004, from http://www.crito.uci.edu/

Marcussen, C. H. (2003). *Trends in the US online travel market 2000-2002.* Denmark: Centre for Regional and Tourism Research. Retrieved November 2004, from http://www.crt.dk/

Marcussen, C. H. (2004). *Trends in European Internet distribution of travel and tourism services.* Denmark: Centre for Regional and Tourism Research. Retrieved November 2004, from http://www.crt.dk

McGann, R. (2004, November 10). US online travel market to soar. *Click Stats.* Retrieved November 2004, from http://www.clickz.com/stats/sectors/travel/article.php/3433881

METI. (2002). *Market survey of e-commerce 2001.* Tokyo: Ministry of Economy, Trade and Industry. Retrieved March 2004, from http://www.ecom.jp/ecom_e/report/survey/3.29.02.B1.0ECmarket.pdf

MoCIE. (2003). *E-commerce in Korea.* Seoul: Ministry of Commerce, Industry and Energy. Retrieved May 2004, from http://www.moci.e.go.kr/eng/policies/ecommerce/ecommerce1.asp

Morris, P. (2000). *World wide work: Globally distributed expert business services* (Emerging Industries Occasional Paper 4). Canberra: Department of Industry, Science and Resources.

Pappas, G. (2001). *The impact of the Internet on the airline industry.* Boston Consulting Group. Retrieved November 2004, from http://www.bcg.com

Palacios, J. J. (2003). *Globalization and e-commerce: Diffusion and impacts in Mexico.* CRITO, Irvine: University of California. Retrieved May 2004, from http://www.crito.uci.edu/

Rittel, H. & Webber, M. (1973). Dilemmas in a general theory of planning. *Policy Studies, 4*(1), 155-169.

SIKA. (2003). *Facts about information and communications technology in Sweden 2003.* Sweden: SIKA Institute. Retrieved October 2003, from http://www.sika-institute.se

SIKA. (2004). *Facts about information and communications technology in Sweden 2004.* Sweden: SIKA Institute. Retrieved October 2004, from http://www.sika-institute.se

Statistics Canada. (2004, April 16). Electronic commerce and technology 2003. *The Daily.* Ottawa: Statistics Canada. Retrieved November 2004, from http://www.statcan.ca/Daily/English/040416/d040416a.htm

Tachiki, D., Hamaya, S., & Yukawa, K. (2004). *Diffusion and the impacts of the Internet and e-commerce in Japan.* CRITO, Irvine: University of California. Retrieved June 2004, from http://www.crito.uci.edu

Taller, M. (2002). *A guide to the Canadian retail travel services industry.* Ottawa: Industry Canada.

Travelport. (2004). *Business travellers still use off-line travel services.* Retrieved November 2004, from http://www.emarketer.com/Article.aspx?1003126.

UNCTAD. (2001). *E-commerce and development report 2001.* UNCTAD/SDTE/ECB/1. New York & Geneva: United Nations.

US Census Bureau. (2004, April 15). *E-Stats.* Washington DC: US Census Bureau. Retrieved June 2004, from http://www.census.gov/estats

Varian, H., Litan R. E., Elder, A., & Shutter, J. (2002, January). *The net impact study* (V2.0). Retrieved November 2004, from http://www.netimpactstudy.com

WTO. (2004). *Survey of destination management organisations.* Madrid: World Tourism Organisation. Retrieved November 2004, from http://www.world-tourism.org

Chapter II

# A Framework for Ontology-Based Tourism Application Generator

Roopa Jakkilinki, Victoria University, Australia

Nalin Sharda, Victoria University, Australia

## Abstract

*This chapter provides an overview of tourism ontology and how it can be used for developing e-tourism applications. The Semantic Web is the next generation Web; it uses background knowledge captured as an ontology and stored in machine-processable and interpretable form. Ontologies form the core of the Semantic Web and can be used to develop intelligent applications. However, generating applications based on ontology still remains a challenging task. This chapter presents a framework that provides a systematic process for developing intelligent e-tourism applications by using a tourism ontology.*

# Introduction

Tourism is one of the most successful and dynamic industries in the world, and it is constantly evolving because of technological advancements. Information technology is being used to enhance tourism services such as travel bookings, itinerary planning, destination marketing, and information sharing. These services use dynamic Web applications.

The current tourism applications rely on static information sources such as Web sites to create tourism products and services. These applications lack intelligence; for example, an itinerary planner in the current scenario will allow the tourist to make bookings, but it cannot suggest an itinerary based on the travellers preferences. A Semantic Web application using an ontology, generic profiling, and semi-structured query tools can overcome the technical limitations of the current systems, and help build intelligent e-tourism tools, or applications.

This chapter discusses the purpose of developing a tourism ontology and proposes a model to develop intelligent tourism applications based on the same. The second section presents the background knowledge, followed by a proposed model for developing e-tourism applications, the following section demonstrates the working of an itinerary planner, and we finish with the conclusions.

The main objective of this chapter is to present a framework for developing ontology based e-tourism applications. The specific foci of the chapter are:

- To provide an understanding of the Semantic Web and ontologies
- To introduce various existing travel ontologies and applications based on the same
- To describe a process model for developing e-tourism applications
- To present a case study using an intelligent itinerary planner

# Background

## Semantic Web

The Semantic Web was thought up by Tim Berners-Lee as a mesh of information linked up in such a way so as to be easily processable by machines. It is not intended to be read by people, as it describes relationships between data that software will interpret (Palmer, 2001). Figure 1 represents the Semantic Web stack which has a layered architecture, it is based on a hierarchy of languages, each language both exploiting the features, and extending the capabilities of the layers below (Butler, 2003). A brief introduction to the Semantic Web layers is presented in the following:

- **Uniform resource identifier (URI):** The Web naming and addressing convention, like the strings starting with "http" or "ftp"; they are short strings used to identify resources on the Web. Anyone can create new URIs. Example: http://melba.vu.edu.au/roopa.txt.

- **Unicode:** A replacement for the older ASCII code and can cope with multiple languages. It is a 16-bit code that can be used to represent the characters in most of the world's scripts.

- **Extensible Markup Language (XML):** A standard format for serializing data using tags; XML file can contain data like a database, it is derived from Standard Generalized Markup Language (SGML) and is somewhat similar to Hypertext Markup Language (HTML). XML schema is a schema language used for describing XML data as well-defined schemas or data models. XML namespaces (NS) is an extension to XML for managing a collection of names identified by URIs.

- **Resource description framework (RDF):** This allows users to add metadata to describe the core data; RDF Schema is a language for describing RDF vocabularies (Bray, n.d.); in other words, RDF schema provides a way of organizing a large set of RDF vocabulary.

- **Ontology vocabulary:** A data model that represents the terminology used in a domain; it also is used to reason about the objects in that domain and the relations between them. Web Ontology Language (OWL) and Darpa Agent Markup Language + Ontology Interchange Language (DAML+OIL) are some of the languages used to describe ontologies.

- **Logic:** The Logic layer allows carrying out reasoning on a set of data, based on pre-defined rules, in order to draw conclusions. Inference engines or reasoners (Inference Engine, n.d.), such as, Racer, Fact, and Pellet work at this layer.

- **Proof and trust:** The proof and trust layers are still nascent. In most applications construction of proof is done by using some rules, the other party can use these rules to see whether or not a statement is true. Trust layer allows the creation of digital signatures for authentication and encryption.

*Figure 1. The Semantic Web stack, and its layers covered in this chapter*

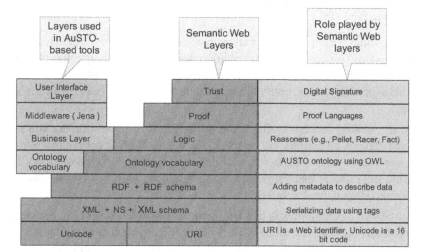

| Layers used in AuSTO-based tools | Semantic Web Layers | Role played by Semantic Web layers |
| --- | --- | --- |
| User Interface Layer | Trust | Digital Signature |
| Middleware ( Jena ) | Proof | Proof Languages |
| Business Layer | Logic | Reasoners (e.g., Pellet, Racer, Fact) |
| Ontology vocabulary | Ontology vocabulary | AUSTO ontology using OWL |
| RDF + RDF schema | | Adding metadata to describe data |
| XML + NS + XML schema | | Serializing data using tags |
| Unicode | URI | URI is a Web identifier, Unicode is a 16 bit code |

## What are Ontologies?

An ontology is a data model that represents a domain; it can be used to reason about the objects in that domain and the relations between them. Ontologies represent knowledge about the world or some part of it, they consist of: classes, collection of objects; attributes, properties an object can have and share; relations, represent the way the objects are related; and individuals, which are instances of the class (Chandrasekaran, Josephson, & Benjamins, 1999).

An ontology can be a domain ontology and theory ontology (Swartout, Patil, Knight, & Russ, 1997). A domain ontology models a specific domain; it represents the particular meanings of terms as they apply to that domain, for example, tourism. A theory ontology provides a set of concepts for representing some aspect of the world, such as time and space.

### *Need for Tourism Ontology*

Ontologies are especially useful where multiple entities such as researchers and organisations are active in the same domain, but each entity uses their own data model for that domain. For example, in the tourism domain, different entities such as travel agents, hotel chains, national, and regional tourism organisations have their own way of representing their services to the consumer (accommodation, events, attractions, services, etc.) using different data models. Furthermore, these data models maybe represented using different software technologies. This leads to interoperability problems, that is, software developed for one system cannot access data on another.

If tourism entities need to communicate with one another, a common data representation is needed. This common representation needs to represent both the concepts in the domain, and the relationships between these concepts. In addition, it should be possible for each tourism entity to map its data models to that used in a common ontology.

Having an ontology is very useful in this situation; as it models the domain in a structured manner, all entities will be able to use the ontology to communicate with all other entities, by mapping their source data model to the common ontology and then using the existing mappings between the ontology and the other destination data models (Clissmann & Höpken, n.d.).

Another benefit of ontologies is that they make it possible to carry out reasoning on the domain, they also act as back ends for intelligent applications, that is, they provide the ability to derive domain knowledge for developing intelligent applications. These applications, with the help of a reasoner, can infer facts from the domain ontology. Creating an ontology for tourism will allow knowledge sharing between different tourism organizations, and also will allow for the creation of intelligent e-tourism tools such as search engines and tour planners.

## Travel Ontologies

A variety of tourism ontologies have been developed to date. In this section we give an overview of a number of tourism related ontologies. The Harmonise ontology is not only a minimun standard ontology, but also a means of reconciling various ontologies.

### OTA Specification

The Open Travel Alliance specifications have been designed to serve two purposes, namely to act as a common language for travel related services, and to provide a mechanism for information exchange between travel industry members (The Open Travel Alliance, n.d.). It is possible to view the OTA specifications as a comprehensive ontology, defining concepts such as AirSchedule, GolfCourseReservation, HotelContentDescription, HotelPreferences, and so on. The OTA specification has already been utilised in a travel related project called Agentcities (Gordon, Kowalski, Paprzycki, Pelech, Szymczak, & Wasowicz, 2005).

## MONDECA

MONDECA's tourism ontology defines tourism concepts based on the World Tourism Organization (WTO) thesaurus (MONDECA, n.d.). These include among others, terms for tourism object profiling, tourism and cultural objects, tourism packages, and tourism multimedia content. MONDECA has created a proprietary system called the Intelligent Topic Manager (ITM) that is used to manage its travel ontology.

### TAGA Ontology

The Travel Agent Game in Agentcities (TAGA) is an agent framework for simulating the global travel market on the Web. Its purpose is to demonstrate the capabilities of Agentcities (Agentcities, n.d.) and Semantic Web technologies. TAGA works on the Foundation for Intelligent Physical Agents (FIPA) compliant platforms within the Agentcities environment (The Foundation for Intelligent physical agents, n.d.). In addition to the FIPA content language ontology, TAGA defines two domain ontologies to be used in simulations. The first ontology covers basic travel concepts such as itineraries, customers, travel services, and service reservations. The second ontology is devoted to auctions and defines different type of auctions, roles the participants play in them, and the protocols used. TAGA ontologies are limited in their usability, and are rather unrealistic due to the nature of the TAGA simulations.

### Harmonize Ontology

Harmonize is an attempt at ontology-mediated integration of tourism systems following different standards (E-Tourism, n.d.). Its goal is to allow organizations to exchange information without changing their data models. The Harmonize project also involves sub-domains that are partially related to the world of travel: geographical and geo-spatial concepts, means of transportation, political, temporal, and gastronomy, and so forth. These sub-domain concepts can be used within the travel system.

Numerous ontologies have been developed for the domain of tourism. Defining and agreeing on the right ontology is a difficult task. One could argue that the choice of the right ontology is purely subjective, because the meaning of various terms differs across domains, users, and situations. Each of these ontologies have been developed with a specific task in mind and specialises in a particular aspect of the tourism domain; for example, a tourism ontology that specialises in tourism events can be used to develop an event planner. Most of the ontologies have been developed with a tool in mind, and their scope is limited to that tool. We have developed an abstract ontology called the Australian sustainable tourism ontology (AuSTO) which covers all the general concepts used in tourism, both from the customer perspective and from the enterprise perspective; subsequently several intelligent tools such a tour planner, search engines and travel recommender systems are planned for development based on the AuSTO ontology.

## Applications Based on Travel Ontologies

A number of intelligent applications such as search engines, tour planners, and location-based tour guides have been developed using ontologies. These applications
help the traveller as well as tour operator to plan trips and find information about
destinations. In this section we describe two such applications and their usage.

### On Tour

On Tour can be considered as an intelligent search engine. The main objective of the
On Tour system  is to connect isolated pieces of information, that is,  to assist the
user in finding information from a variety of sources, and to allow individualized
use of the same (Daniel, 2005). As a search engine, On Tour allows for the querying of distributed data as well as considering the semantics of discovered concepts
and instances. It allows the user to specify preferences like maximum budget and
minimum comfort, and define further constraints such as personal schedule. This
system helps the user to plan a vacation from the beginning to the end. In later
phases of development On Tour will act as a recommender system by giving advice
on best restaurants, venue for musicals, and so on. It also will provide support for
mobile devices. On Tour approach is to extract pieces of information from structured
Web pages and conduct constraint based reasoning for the integration of multiple
information sources.

### Talea

Talea is a platform aimed at supporting the development of Web-based tourism
applications (Levi, Vagliengo, & Goy, 2005). This software was designed and developed within the Diadi 2000 (Dissemination of Innovation in Industrial Decline
areas) project. The Diadi 2000 project aims at applying ICT technologies to small
and medium enterprises (SMEs) to increase the value of their businesses. Talea
provides for multi device access, where customers and suppliers can use PDAs or
smart phones to buy and offer tourism services. This software acts as a matchmaker
by matching service provision with request; tourism suppliers can advertise their
services such as room availability, car rentals, and so on, and customers can perform
a search for a particular service.

### Dynamic Packaging System

An important type of e-tourism application that has evolved in recent years is a
dynamic packaging system (Cardaso, 2005). It is used by airlines, hotels, tour operators, and travel agencies to create customised packages for individual consumers.
Dynamic packaging can be defined as the combining of different travel components,
bundled and priced in real-time, in response to the request from a consumer or a

booking agent. They have created an e-tourism ontology that allows interoperability through the use of shared vocabulary and meanings for terms. Semantic mediators are used to support a virtual view that integrates semantically annotated e-tourism information sources. Final dynamic package processes are created using conditional planning ranking and selection. Once the dynamic package processes are evaluated they are presented to the tourist and the tourist can select the package that he finds most appealing or suitable according to his preferences.

## Tourism Application Generator Architecture

Figure 2 presents the underlying model for generating ontology based e-tourism applications; called the e-tourism application generator architecture (e-TAGA). The e-TAGA model consists of three layers: the ontology layer (OL), the business logic layer (BLL) and the graphical user interface layer (GUIL). The OL provides persistence for the tourism ontology; the business logic layer includes two common components and parts of the tourism applications themselves. The two common components in the BL are the inference engine (IE) and the custom logic (CL). The GUI layer includes the graphical user interface (GUI) components of individual tourism applications and some common GUI elements.

*Figure 2. A tourism application generator architecture (e-TAGA)*

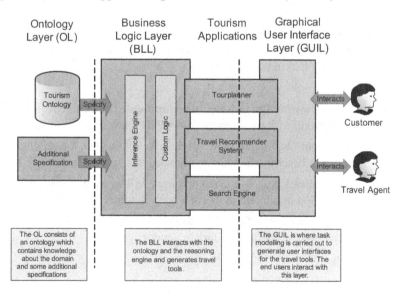

# Ontology Layer (OL)

The ontology layer consists of the ontology which embodies knowledge about the domain and some additional specifications. This layer is the core of all Semantic Web systems. We will use the AuSTO ontology to exemplify the operation of the various layers.

## Tools for Ontology Development

In any ontology development project one needs to begin by selecting an ontology development tool. In the AuSTO project three different tools were compared in order to decide which one of these would be most suitable for our tourism ontology development. The three tools considered were Protégé 2000, Ontolingua, and OntoEdit free. This comparison was based on ontological aspects and usability aspects. Our study indicated that Protégé 2000 is far superior in usability and ontology aspects as compared to Ontolingua and OntoEdit free (Jakkilinki, Sharda, & Georgievski, 2005), hence Protégé2000 was selected. Protégé2000 (Protégé, n.d.) comprises an open architecture that allows programmers to insert arbitrary components into the tool. This feature can be exploited during the development of Semantic Web applications based on the ontology. An additional benefit of Protégé 2000 toolkit is developers can package the implementation of the application as a Protégé plug-in and test how the system behaves in response to any changes in the ontology.

## Methodology Followed to Develop AuSTO Ontology

Ontology development methodology includes tools, techniques and process followed in order to develop the ontology. The methodology followed to develop the AuSTO ontology is as follows (Jakkilinki et al., 2005).

1.  **Identify the purpose behind ontology development:** The pertinent questions are listed here, along with their answer for AuSTO development.
    *   Why is the ontology being built? In the case of AuSTO, the ontology is being built to describe the tourism domain.
    *   What is its intended use? AuSTO ontology will be used as a knowledge base to develop intelligent tools such as an itinerary planner.
    *   Who are the users? AuSTO will be used by operators in tourism domain, such as the tourist operators, tourism vendors.

2.   **Ontology capture mechanism** consists of three different stages:

   - **Determining the scope of the ontology:** This involves identifying all the key concepts and relationships in the domain.

   - **Selecting a method to develop the ontology:** The method we followed to develop AuSTO is the top-down approach.

   - **Defining the concepts in the ontology:** This involves taking closely related terms and grouping them as classes.

3.   **Coding the ontology:** Coding refers to representing the ontology in some formal language. A suitable ontology editor has to be selected, in the case of AuSTO the ontology editor used is Protégé. Once the ontology editor is selected the classes have to be entered as concepts and their attributes are entered as slots.

4.   **Refinement:** This consists of two phases, namely intra-coding refinement and extra-coding refinement. Intra-coding refinement refers to the refinement done during the coding phase, whereas extra-coding refinement refers to the changes made to overcome the errors uncovered during the testing and maintenance stages.

5.   **Testing:** The testing process uncovers any defects in functional logic and implementation. Testing should be carried out during all stages of development.

6.   **Maintenance:** This can be corrective, adaptive or perfective. Corrective maintenance involves correcting the ontology to overcome the errors discovered by users while querying the ontology. Adaptive maintenance involves modifying the ontology to fulfil new requirements. Perfective maintenance involves improving the ontology by further refining it, in order to enhance its functionality (Pressman, 1997).

*Brief Description of Classes in AuSTO*

Creating an ontology involves delineating concepts into a class hierarchy. Three important approaches to develop class hierarchies are top-down, bottom-up and a combination approach (Uschold & Gruninger, 1996). In the top-down approach the development process starts with the definition of the most general concepts in the domain, followed by specialised concepts. In the bottom-up approach the development process starts with the definition of the most specific classes, which form the leaves of the class hierarchy tree, with subsequent grouping of these classes into more general concepts. The combined approach uses a combination of top-down and bottom-up processes. The approach followed for AuSTO is the bottom-up approach. This approach is usually driven by the need for having a workable vocabulary quickly and then enhancing it as the project progresses. AuSTO is written in

OWL (Web Ontology Language), Figure 3 is a screen shot of AuSTO ontology in Protégé. The AuSTO ontology consists of a class hierarchy shown on the left, each class has properties and one can create individuals, or instances of a class, using the instance tab in the Protégé interface.

AuSTO being tourism ontology it contains classes from the tourism domain. Following list gives some of the important classes in AuSTO:

- **Involved party** can be traveller, vendor, operator, and so forth.
- **Requirement** refers to travel requirements
- **Offering** includes travel products and services.
- **Solution** refers to systems outputs such as itineraries.
- **Resource** can be reserved or rented items.
- **Specification** allows for both offering specifications and requirement specifications
- **Preference** includes traveller's preferences such as date, time, location, or price range.

Each of these classes can represent a plethora of tourism information. For example, requirement represents diverse travel requirements such as accommodation, entertainment, transport, and offering represents the wide range of travel products and services that vendors make available to the traveller, often as part of a packaged solution.

*Figure 3. A screen shot of the AuSTO ontology*

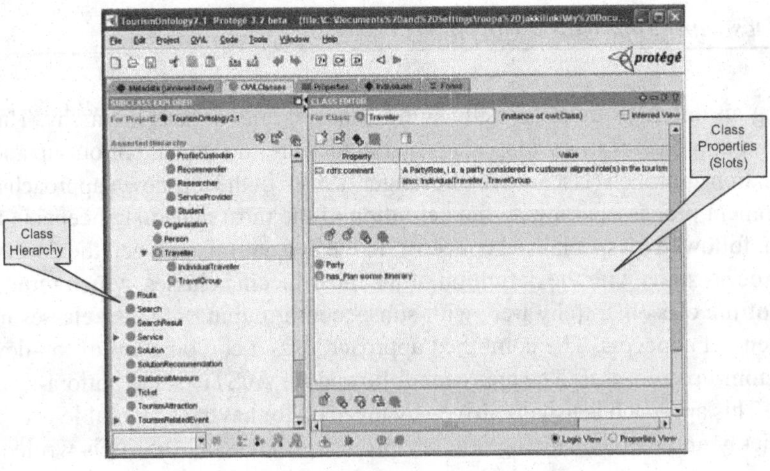

# Business Layer

The business logic layer (BLL) uses an inference engine and custom logic, and is responsible for generating outcomes; that is, it returns results based on user interactions. Figure 4 describes the BLL for the applications based on AuSTO. A user specifies his travel requirements in the ontology and the tourism vendor advertises his offerings which are tourism services in the ontology. The offerings and requirements are loaded into the ontology model of the Jena subsystem. Pellet reasoner matches the travel requirements to the vendor offerings and sends it to the travel application manger. Travel tools such as tour planners can query the travel application manager and produce the travel solution, which in this case is an itinerary.

*Figure 4. Architecture for the business layer*

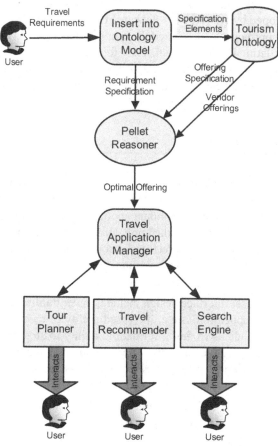

*What are Reasoners?*

The reasoner is a software that applies logic to the knowledge embodied in the ontology for arriving at some conclusions (*Inference Engine*, n.d.). We generally recognize two types of inferencing, namely forward chaining, and backward chaining. In forward chaining one proceeds from a given situation towards a desired goal by adding new assertions along the way; whereas, in backward chaining one starts with the desired goal and then attempts to find the method for arriving at the goal. A number of reasoners are available, such as Racer, FaCT, Pellet, and F-OWL. Pellet is the reasoner used in the AuSTO project, it  is an open-source Java-based OWL DL reasoner developed by the Maryland Information and Network Dynamics Lab Semantic Web Agents Project (Mindswap, n.d.).

*Role Played by Jena*

Jena is a Java framework for building Semantic Web applications, it is open source and has been developed by HP (Hewlett Packard) Labs. Jena acts as a middleware which connects the ontology, reasoner and the user interface. In Jena all operations are done by manipulating the Jena model. Therefore, to manipulate an ontology it needs to be loaded into the Jena model first. Jena has four subsystems: query engine, database interface, reasoning engine, and ontology management. Jena's architecture allows external reasoners to be plugged into the Jena models.

# User Interface Layer

One of the most difficult aspects of building an application is designing the user interface. User Interface design is the design of the graphical elements on the computer screen with which a user interacts to conduct application tasks. The user interface is as important as the functionality of the application, and plays an important role in the success of any product. User interfaces accomplish two fundamental tasks: communicating information from the computer to the user and communicating information from the user to the computer.

The benefits of a good user interface design include: lower training costs, less user stress, consistency in application usage, increased ability to recover from errors, better user control, less clicks to find information, ability to store more information per screen, easier to use the software, selection amongst many choices using limited space, see all selections at all times, better understanding of the software, save screen space, and higher data entry speed (Miller, n.d.).

Task analysis and modelling techniques are increasingly being used in designing user interfaces, they form an important part of user interface design process and help design more intuitive interfaces.

## What are Task Analysis and Task Modelling?

Task analysis involves the study of a system functionality as a collection of tasks. Generally the systems function is divided into a set of top-level tasks, and each one of these is further divided into sub-tasks, and so forth to develop a task-tree. This process can be used to guide the design of new systems beginning with user requirement capture. One of the most important applications of task analysis is designing user interfaces, in which menus are based on the task trees. The top level menus can be labelled after the top level tasks and the sub menus after the next level tasks (Dix, Finlay, Abowd, & Beale, 1998).

After an informal task analysis where the main tasks and their attributes have been identified, task modelling is used to understand the relationships among the various tasks in order to better address the design of interactive applications.

As task modelling is used to model the behaviour of a system from user's perspective, it captures the system requirements and actions defined as a set of tasks, and models the behaviour of the system as a scenario of tasks. This allows the designers to improve the human computer interaction aspects when designing a system's operation (Georgievski & Sharda, 2003). Although task models have long been considered in human-computer interaction, only recently have user interface developers and designers realized their importance to obtain more effective and consistent solutions (Giulio, Paterno, & Santaro, 2002). Task models play an important role because they represent the logical activities that should support users in reaching their goals, and knowing the tasks necessary to attain a goal is fundamental to any good design (Paterno, 2002).

There are two types of task models: user task model and system task model. A user task model states the problems to be solved by the system, and thus consists of overlapping user scenarios (Georgievski & Sharda, 2003). Actors involved in a user task model are generally human; however, it may include external systems and the environment. A system task model forms the basis for specifying a solution in the form of system requirements. Actors involved in a system task model are generally subsystems, interfaces, and, at times humans.

## Tools for Task Modelling

One of the main problems in task modelling is that it is a time-consuming and sometimes tedious process. To overcome this problem interest has been increasing in tools that support task analysis and modelling. However, current tools are outcomes of research projects, and are used mainly by groups that have developed them.

The concur task tree environment (CTTE) is a Java Applet based tool developed by Human Computer Interaction Group – ISTI (Pisa). CTTE provides the ability to build task models from a visual perspective where the user can define and structure the tasks in a logical fashion using the graphical editor provided in the tool. CTTE enables the user to focus on the activities of their model and thus allowing the user to identify the requirements of the model and organize them into a logical hierarchy of task and subtasks (Georgievski & Sharda, 2003).

The main features of the CTTE tool are (Giulio et al., 2002):

- **Focuses on activities:** Allows designers to concentrate on the activities that a user has to perform, rather than programming details.
- **Hierarchical structure:** Provides a wide range of granularity allowing large and small task tree structures to be developed and reused.
- **Graphical syntax:** Facilitates easy interpretation of the logical task structure using graphical representation.
- **Concurrent notation:** Provides rich set of possible temporal relationships that can be used to specify the relationship between the tasks.
- **Distinct task representations:** Uses distinct icons to represent user task, application task, interaction task, and abstract task

CTTE provides the ability to build two types of task models: single user task models and cooperative task models. Single user task models are used to represent systems that a single user controls. A cooperative task model is similar to a single user task model; however it includes tasks executed by two or more users.

Other useful features of CTTE tool are model comparison, reachability analysis, and interactive task model simulator (Giulio et al., 2002).

## Itinerary Planner Case Study

In this section we describe the task model created to represent the user interface for the itinerary planner. This task model guide the development of the user interface by focusing on the various functions the user interface needs to perform.

CTTE allows the following types of tasks to build the entire task model:

- **Abstract tasks** define a set of subtasks to be performed at a conceptual level
- **User tasks** denoted the operation/tasks executed by the user
- **Interaction tasks** represent tasks that carry out communication between entities within the task model.

*Table 1. Temporal operators used in CTTE*

| Syntax | Notation | Description |
|---|---|---|
| T1 [] T2 | Choice | A choice between two or more tasks |
| T1>>T2 | Enabling | T1 enables T2 when T1 is terminated |
| T1[]>>T2 | Enabling with Information Exchange | T1 provides some information to T2 besides enabling it |
| T1\|> T2 | Suspend/Resume | T2 can interrupt T1, and when T2 is terminated T1 can be reactivated from the state reached before the interruption |
| T* | Iteration | Tasks performed repetitively |

- **Application tasks** are of tasks executed by the system or application entities in the process model

CTTE uses transition notations to describe the temporal relationships between tasks and the execution sequence for the task model. The temporal operators used in CTTE are described in Table 1.

We have implemented the task model for itinerary planner as a single user task model that represents the overall function of the user interface from a user perspective. We represent these tasks as tree diagrams in Figures 5 to 11. In the task tree diagram we define the execution sequence for each task using the temporal operators described in Table 1.

**Figure 5:** This shows the itinerary planner abstract task model. It illustrates the tasks the user can perform on connecting to the itinerary planner Web site. Task 5

*Figure 5. Itinerary planner abstract model*

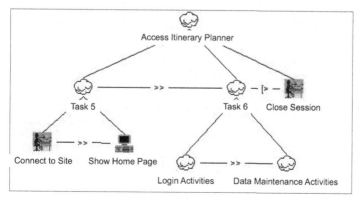

*Figure 6. Login activities*

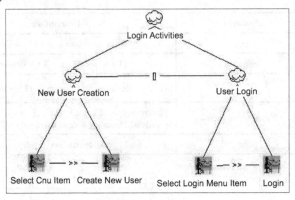

*Figure 7. Data maintenance activities*

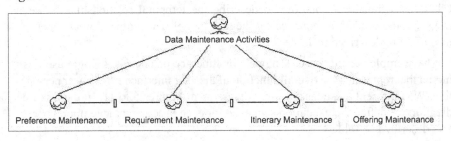

*Figure 8. Preference maintenance activities*

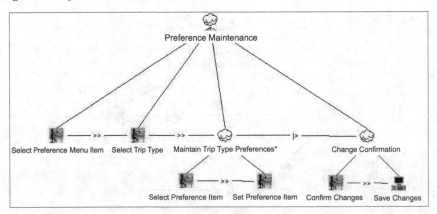

*Figure 9. Requirement maintenance activities*

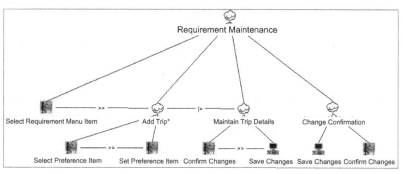

*Figure 10. Itinerary maintenance activities*

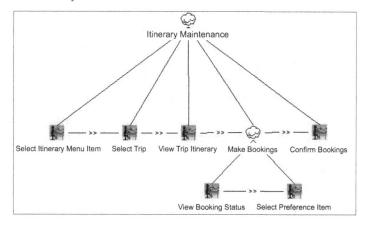

*Figure 11. Offering maintenance activities*

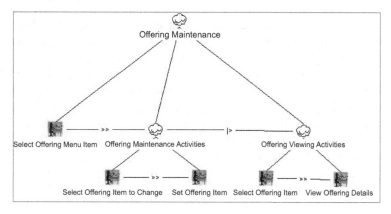

consists of connecting to the Web site and viewing the home page. Task 6 involves logging into the Web site and then carrying out the data maintenance activities. Figures 8 to 13 expand on these activities.

**Figure 6:** This shows the task model that expands the Login Activity task. Login Activities describe the tasks to be performed for the user to login, it allows for an existing user, as well as new user.

**Figure 7:** Data Maintenance Activities task tree, which provides a choice between four abstract tasks: Preference Maintenance, Requirement Maintenance, Itinerary Maintenance, and Offering Maintenance.

**Figure 8:** Preference Maintenance Activities task tree, which consists of the tasks involved in maintaining the preferences of the traveler. Here preferences refer to what of the traveler likes, with regard to various facilities such as accommodation, transport, and so forth.

**Figure 9:** Requirement Maintenance Activities task tree, which describes the tasks involved in maintaining the traveler requirements. Requirements refer to the travelers demands for the tour, for example the traveler may want 5-star accommodation and a business class flight.

**Figure 10:** Itinerary Maintenance Activities task tree, which describes the tasks involved in creating an itinerary for the traveler. An itinerary is generated by matching the traveler's requirements with the offerings available.

**Figure 11:** Offering Maintenance Activities task tree, which describes the tasks involved in maintaining the offerings being provided by various travel vendors. Tourism vendors can advertise their services such as room availability, tickets availability through this option.

## Working of an Itinerary Planner

In this section we describe the operation of a travel itinerary planner; this itinerary planner has been developed based on the application generator framework. It consists of AuSTO ontology, a user interface created using ASP.net, and a business logic layer, which acts as a connector between the ontology and the user interface. The AuSTO ontology is populated by a tourism domain expert, the application allows tourism operators to advertise their offerings in the offerings page, and the offerings are stored in the ontology. The end user or the tourist can specify his requirements in the requirements page, these requirements are stored in the ontology, and the tourist also can specify his preferences which also are be stored in the ontology. The itinerary planner matches the requirements with the offerings, and produces an itinerary; the end user can either reject the itinerary offerings or accept these and confirm bookings in the itinerary page. The user interface for the itinerary planner has been developed based on the task model described in the previous

*Figure 12. New user screen*

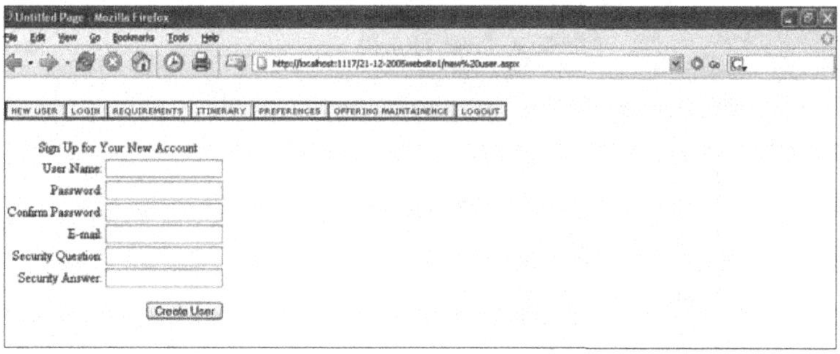

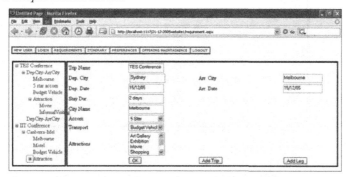

*Figure 13. Login screen*

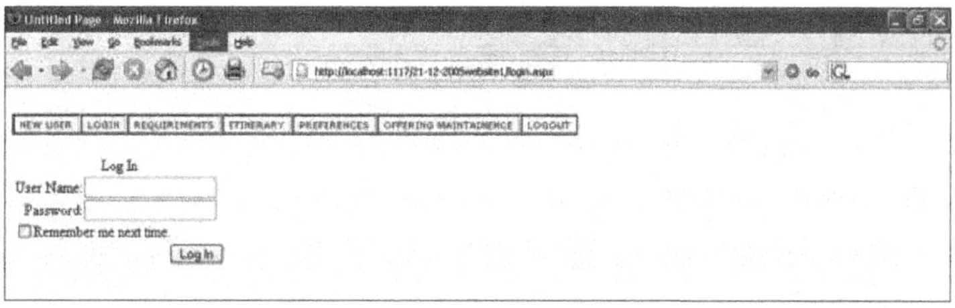

*Figure 14. Requirements screen*

section. This application is explained in some more detail with the help of screen shots in the following.

**Figure 12:** This shows the new user screen, which allows the creation of a new user. It is necessary to have an account in order to use the application.

**Figure 13:** This shows the user login screen where an existing user can login into the application. Once the user logs in, he has access to facilities such as storing preferences or specifying requirements.

*Figure 15. Itinerary screen*

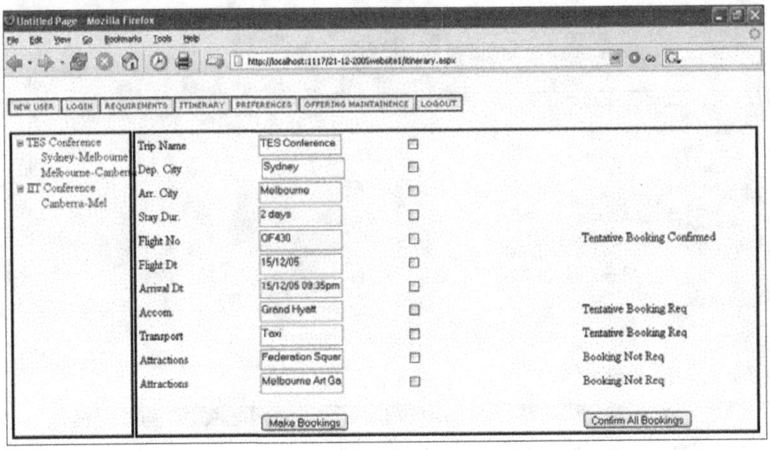

*Figure 16. Preferences screen*

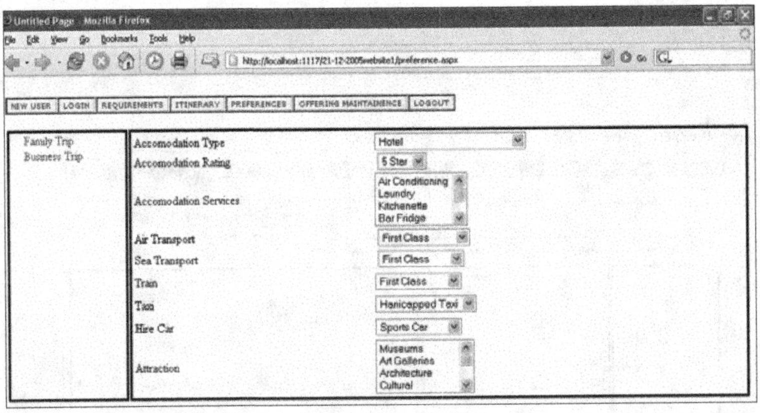

**Figure 14:** This shows the requirements screen where a tourist can enter his require-ments for a trip. Once the requirements are entered the tourist clicks the Add Trip button and a new leg can be added.

**Figure 15:** This shows the itinerary screen, the tourists' requirements are matched with the vendor offerings and an itinerary is produced. The tourist can accept offer-ings in the itinerary with the help of the checkboxes, and make booking by clicking on the Make Bookings button and then confirm bookings.

**Figure 16:** This shows the preferences screen, which allows the user to store his preferences for accommodation, transport facilities and other such services. Dif-

*Figure 17. Offerings maintenance screen*

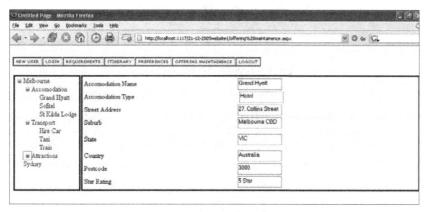

ferent preferences for different kind of trips can be stored, such as family trip and business trip.

**Figure 17:** This shows the offerings maintenance screen, tourism vendors such as hotels or transport providers can advertise their offerings on this page. For example, hotels can advertise their room availability, and transport providers can advertise their vehicle availability.

# Conclusion

There is a need for standardisation of definitions and concepts in the field of tourism; the solution is to develop travel ontologies. Number of travel ontologies have been developed in recent times, each with an application in mind; we have developed an Australian sustainable tourism ontology (AuSTO), specifically for the Australian tourism sector. This AuSTO ontology reuses the knowledge from some of the existing ontologies. Ontologies enable the development of Semantic Web applications, but ontology driven application development is still a nascent field. We are developing an intelligent travel application generator based on the AuSTO ontology. The application generator framework enables the production of different intelligent travel tools such as Itinerary planners, and recommender systems. We are building an itinerary planner by using this framework, and this intelligent itinerary planner can match the user requirements specified in the ontology with vendor offerings specified in the ontology and produce an itinerary as a solution. This chapter presented an overview of the Semantic Web, introduced different tourism ontologies and some applications based on tourism ontologies, and describes in detail a framework for developing e-tourism applications based on ontologies.

# Acknowledgments

We would like to thank Sustainable Tourism Cooperative Research Center (STCRC), Australia, for the funding this research. We also would like to thank Henk Meijerink and Paul Mohinyan for their help in this research.

# References

Agentcities. (n.d.). Retrieved August 15, 2005, from http://www.agentcities.org

Bray, T. (n.d.). *What is RDF*. Retrieved May 31, 2006, from http://www.xml.com/pub/a/2001/01/24/rdf.html?page=2

Butler, M. H. (2003). *Is the Semantic Web hype?* Retrieved May 31, 2006, from http://www.hpl.hp.com/personal/marbut/isTheSemanticWebHype.pdf

Cardaso, J. (2005). *E-tourism: Creating dynamic packages using Semantic Web processes.* Paper presented at the W3C Workshop on Frameworks for Semantics in Web Services.

Chandrasekaran, B., Josephson, J. R, & Benjamins, V. R. (1999). What are ontologies, and why do we need them? *IEEE, 14*(1), 20-26.

Clissmann, C., & Höpken, W. (n.d.). *Harmonise ontology user manual.* Retrieved from www.harmo-ten.info/harmoten_docs/D2_2_Ontology_User_Manual_V3.2.0.3.doc

Daniel, B. (2005). *On tour, the Semantic Web and its benefits to the tourism industry.* Retrieved May 25, 2006, from http://etourism.deri.at/ont/docu2004/OnTour%20%20Semantic%20Web%20and%20its%20benefits%20to%20the%20tourism%20industry.pdf

Dix, A., Finlay, J., Abowd, G., & Beale, G. R. (1998). *Human-computer interaction.* Prentice Hall.

E-tourism. (n.d.). Retrieved August 16, 2005, from http://deri.at/research/projects/e-tourism

Foundation for Intelligent Physical Agents, The. (n.d.). Retrieved August 15, 2005, from http://www.fipa.org

Georgievski, M., & Sharda, N. (2003). *Task modelling for a holistic quality of service model—TRAQS.* Paper presented at the IEEE India Council Annual Convention and Exhibition, India.

Giulio, M., Paterno, F., & Santaro, C. (2002). CTTE: Support for developing and analyzing task models for interactive system design. *IEEE Transaction on Software Engineering, 28*(9), 1-17.

Gordon, M., Kowalski, A., Paprzycki, M., Pelech, T., Szymczak, M., & Wasowicz, T. (2005). Ontologies in a travel support system. *Internet 2005,* 285-300.

Inference engine. (n.d.). Retrieved May 15, 2006, from http://www.emclab.umr.edu/consortium/Whatis/node17.html

Jakkilinki, R., Sharda, N., & Georgievski, M. (2005). *Developing an ontology for multimedia design and planning pyramid.* Paper presented at the International Symposium on Information and Communications Technologies, Petaling Jaya Malaysia.

Levi, G., Vagliengo, A., & Goy, A. (2005). *Talea: An ontology-based framework for e-business applications development.* Paper presented at the 2nd Italian Semantic Web Workshop on Semantic Web Applications and Perspectives, Trento, Italy.

Miller, R. H. (n.d.). *Web interface design: Learning form our past.* Retrieved May 25, 2006, from http://www.cs.rutgers.edu/~shklar/www4/rmiller/rhmpapr.html#background

Mindswap. (n.d.). Retrieved May 15, 2006, from http://www.mindswap.org/2003/pellet/index.shtm

Mondeca. (n.d.). Retrieved August 15, 2005, from http://www.mondeca.com

Open Travel Alliance, The. (n.d.). Retrieved August 15, 2005, from http://www.opentravel.org

Palmer, S. B. (2001). *The Semantic Web: An introduction.* Retrieved May 25, 2006, from http://infomesh.net/2001/swintro/

Paterno, F. (2002). *Task modelling: Where we are, where we are headed.* Paper presented at the First International Workshop on Task Models and Diagrams for User Interface Design, Tamodia, Bucharest, Romania.

Pressman, R. S. (1997). *Software engineering, a practitioner's approach* (4th ed.). McGraw-Hill.

Protégé. (n.d.). Retrieved May 25, 2006, from http://protege.stanford.edu/

Swartout, B., Patil, R., Knight, K., & Russ, T. (1997). *Towards distributed use of large scale ontologies.* Paper presented at the Symposium on Ontological Engineering of AAAI, Stanford, CA.

Uschold, M., & Gruninger, M. (1996). Ontologies: Principles, methods and applications. *Knowledge Engineering Review, 11*(2).

## Chapter III

# ICT and the Travel Industry:
## Opportunities and Challenges for New Zealand Travel Agents

Vladimir Garkavenko, Waiariki Institute of Technology, New Zealand
Simon Milne, Auckland University of Technology, New Zealand

## Abstract

*This chapter focuses on the impact of the ICT on the travel industry with a focus on the New Zealand travel agent (TA) sector. We present key findings from a longitudinal study of TA businesses conducted during 2000-2004. These findings are compared and contrasted with information gathered from in-depth interviews with consumers. The study explores major pressure factors on TA businesses: direct airline-consumers sale, introduction of the Internet, and the emergence of the well-informed consumer. The research also establishes that there is great variation in the extent to which travel agents use the advantages associated with new technology and how New Zealand travel agents perceive ICT. We argue that in such a crucial moment of disintermediation and the fight for the consumer, TA will need to implement more aggressive advertising policies with a strong emphasis on their professional advice, personal financial reliability, and time-saving attributes for clients.*

# Introduction

The evolution and impact of information and communication technologies (ICT) is a dominant issue in the tourism business today. Tourism is an information intensive industry. There are three main waves of technological development that have characterised ICT influence in tourism enterprises: computer reservation systems (CRS), global distribution systems (GDS), and the Internet. The Internet makes information accessible to consumers, and therefore establishes a direct link between the consumer and the supplier. As a result, the traditional travel distribution channel is changing rapidly. A major feature of this change is described as disintermediation: when the principal bypasses intermediaries such as travel agents. A lot of researchers and business experts suggest that the threat of disintermediation is imminent and that the trend is irreversible (Bloch & Segev, 1996; Harrington & Power, 2001; O'Brien, 1999; Prideaux, 2001).

Travel agents (TAs) are considered to be particularly vulnerable to disintermediation. ICT replaces the core competencies of the intermediaries which include transaction processing (ticketing and settlement) and information provision (raw product information as provided by suppliers). The disintermediation phenomenon is particularly pronounced in the relationship between airlines and travel agents. To minimize the risk of disintermediation and to improve business performance, travel agents need to reposition themselves and review their core strategies to compete efficiently in the changing business environment. It is argued that an intermediary will only survive in a distribution channel to which it adds value. The overall tendency can be described as a shift towards consumers rather than the principals. Some newly created travel agencies act purely in cyberspace while others try to act as the new intermediaries—infomediaries—aiming to help consumers to analyse and integrate information. Research into the travel agency sector by academics has focused on the need for travel agents to adopt strategies that enable them to compete in an ever-changing technological environment. There has, however, been little research outside European and North American settings.

The main objective of the chapter is to analyze the impact (challenges and opportunities) of ICT and the Internet in particular on the New Zealand travel agent sector as an example. The specific foci of the chapter are:

- What do New Zealand travel agents (TAs) perceive to be major impacts on their businesses?

- An analysis of the disintermediation process as a result of ICT introduction and adoption using the example of travel agents relationships with airlines

- How do TAs perceive ICT?

- How does the consumer perceive the role of a travel agent in the Internet era?

• How should New Zealand travel agents reposition themselves to compete successfully?

We present the results of a five year study of the New Zealand TA market. Consecutive in-depth interviews were held with TAs from the Auckland region in 2000 and then in 2003. The main issues and problems of the modern TA business environment were identified and conceptualised. The theoretical assumptions formulated on the basis of the received data were tested in a national online survey of TA businesses in 2004. To verify the congruency of the TA and consumer perception of the TA role in the modern environment, in-depth interviews were held with consumers.

# Background

Tourism is an information-intensive industry. For each traveler there are numerous messages and pieces of information to be exchanged: itineraries, schedules, payment data, destination and product details, and passenger information. Fast, efficient exchange of information between the players in the industry is essential for efficient distribution, sales and customer service (Figure 1).

*Figure 1. Model of tourism information flows (Source: Werthner & Klein, 1999, p. 8)*

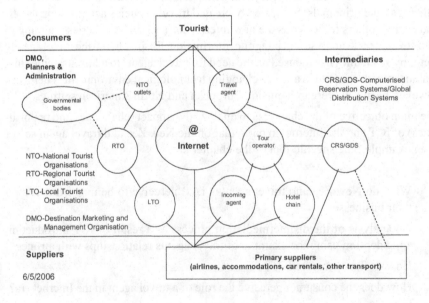

This information dependence has placed the industry at the forefront of ICT adoption (Mason & Milne, 2002). A most dramatic change for the tourism industry came in the1980s with the introduction of central reservation systems (CRS). CRS increased the power of the airlines in the distribution channel and dramatically altered the balance of power in the wholesale travel market (Poon, 1993). The Internet and electronic commerce is the next major wave of technological change which is influencing the industry.

## Tourism Industry: Changes in Distribution Channels

The Internet and electronic commerce developments in the late 1990s, and the adoption by tourism of the prime business to business (B2B) and business to consumer (B2C) applications, has changed the industry and has shifted the traditional way tourism and travel products are distributed (Buhalis, 1998; O'Connor, 1999; O'Connor and Frew, 2002). Increasingly, consumers can undertake their entire tourism product search and booking online and, therefore, the role of intermediaries has been changing dramatically. The Internet is widely used as a means to deliver up-to-date content. As a result, it has created the conditions for the emergence of a wide range of new tourism eMediaries. Tourism suppliers (particularly airlines, car rentals, and hotel chains) have taken advantage of the new opportunities and developed e-commerce applications by allowing users to directly access their reservation systems. This includes single supplier provisions, such as British Airways, Marriott Hotels, and Avis, as well as multi-supplier Web pages that have emerged to support airlines in their efforts to reach the consumer directly (e.g., www.orbitz.com).

In addition, several destinations have developed destination management systems to distribute their smaller properties and to present the destination as a holistic entity. A number of Web-based TAs also have emerged (Expedia.com, Travelocity.com) whilst off-line agencies have developed their online provision. Internet portals (Yahoo, Altavista, Excite) and vertical portals (or vortals) also have developed online travel distribution, often by sourcing their travel contents from external online agents and suppliers. Media companies, including newspapers and television networks, have gradually integrated their off-line with their online provision and have expanded to include e-commerce capabilities on their sites. Online last minute agencies have emerged to enable distressed inventory to be distributed efficiently.

According to Palmer and McCole (1999), the "most important structural change that could be brought about by the Internet is disintermediation wherein principals bypass the intermediary and sell directly to end-users" (p. 37). This phenomenon is especially pronounced in the relationship between airlines and travel agents. Travel agencies have always played a key role in the outsourcing of airline sales. The passage of the Airline Deregulation Act of 1978, accompanied by liberalization of many of the bilateral aviation agreements between the U.S. and other countries during the 1980s, brought about more competition and increasingly complex fare structures (Tretheway & Oum, 1992). Both of these changes favored the use of travel agents by prospective passengers. In 1976, 40% of the airline tickets issued in the USA were written by travel agents; by 1985 this proportion had increased to more than 80% (Tretheway & Oum, 1992).

Traditionally, the travel distribution role has been performed by outbound travel agencies, tour operators (TOs) and inbound travel agents or handling agencies (Buhalis & Laws, 2001) (Figure 1). They have been supported by computer reservation systems, global distribution systems or tour operators' videotext systems (leisure travel networks (Bordat, 1999; Karcher, 1997). These traditional electronic intermediaries, particularly GDSs, progressively consolidated their position to four major systems, namely SABRE, AMADEUS, GALILEO, and WORLDSPAN (Karcher, 1996; WTO, 1995).

## ICT Adoption by Airlines

The development of the World Wide Web represents a major opportunity for airlines (American Airlines, 2000; Buhalis, 2000a, b; Smith & Jenner, 1998). Airlines quickly have adapted to the potential opportunities associated with e-commerce (both B2B and B2C). Since the mid-1990s most airlines have offered Web sites, which not only inform consumers about basic fare and schedule information, but also enable itinerary building, fare construction, and reservations. This enables the development of marketing strategies focused on building direct relationships with customers (Buhalis, 2000b; French, 1998).

The Internet has revolutionised the airline business. Online booking revenue is forecast to rise to over 11% of the total in Europe by 2008 from just over 4% in 2003, according to Jupiter Research (*The New Zealand Herald*, 2004).

As a result of airlines ability to communicate directly with consumers, several structural changes in the industry have emerged. Airlines have reduced their commission rates significantly (i.e., from 10-12% to 7%), while they also have introduced "commission capping" (e.g., $10 per ticket). In addition, electronic ticketing and ticketless travel have gradually reduced both distribution and labour costs.

Airlines are increasingly dealing directly with their corporate customers, bypassing the agency entirely. For example, Continental, which derives over 50% of its revenues from business travellers, has established net fares for its corporate customers. Such fares, which are widespread in the USA, involve major discounts on published tariffs paid directly to the corporate customer. In these arrangements, carriers bypass the corporation's agency entirely, paying it no commissions. The agency is then left to derive its income from travel management service fees it charges the corporation.

There is also a rapid increase in Internet-generated bookings amongst U.S. and European low cost carriers. The majority of low cost carriers' online sales are on their own Web site whereas the full-service carriers' rely more heavily on online travel agents such as Travelocity and Expedia (Alamdari, 2002).

## ICT Impact on the Travel Agent Sector: Challenges and Opportunities

ICT have enabled travel agencies to build complicated itineraries in minutes, while they provide up-to-date schedules, prices and availability data. The proliferation of CRSs and GDSs has also provided an effective reservation mechanism which supports travel agencies in obtaining information, making reservations and issuing travel documents for the entire range of tourism products efficiently and at a fraction of the cost if these processes were undertaken manually (Vasudavan & Standing, 1999; Wardell, 1998).

It has been noted by some researchers that despite having used ICT for some time now, the vast majority of travel agents have not yet managed to take full advantage of ICT capabilities (Buhalis, 1999, 2000b). This is the result of a certain shortage of strategic vision in ICT usage as well as a reluctance to invest in new technology. Low profit margins and a traditional reluctance to invest in assets have deprived agencies of a wide range of critical tools that have prevented them from taking full advantage of emerging ICT. This results in a relatively low level of technology integration, and thus less information is available to support strategic and tactical decision-making. In addition, it results in a low level of management and operational integration, which does not allow agents to capitalise on information for efficient operations, integrated customer service and development of partnerships with suppliers and institutional buyers (Buhalis, 1999, 2000b).

The Internet has introduced challenges for travel agencies. Agents not only have to match the availability of information and reservation capabilities of the Internet, but they also need to provide great value when serving consumers who have access to available information. In addition, traditional travel agencies need to compete with several ICT-based newcomers, such as Expedia, Travelocity and the Internet Tourism Network, which enable consumers to have access to information and make online bookings (Buhalis, 1999, 2000b; Modahl, 2000; O'Connor, 1999).

The high dependence of travel agencies on information and communication in order to perform their role, in combination with their reluctance to take advantage of emerging technology, places traditional agencies in an extremely vulnerable position (Bloch & Segev, 1996; Garkavenko, Bremner, & Milne, 2003; Garkavenko & Milne, 2004; Poon, 1993; Richards, 1995). A "threatened intermediaries (or disintermediation) hypothesis" was introduced by Malone, Yates, and Benjamin

(1987) who used the term "electronic brokerage effect" for the phenomenon. The hypothesis essentially describes the reduction or elimination of the role of retailers, distributors, brokers and other middlemen in transactions between the producer and the customer (Atkinson, 2001). One common vision of the electronic marketplace is an ideal electronic market in which consumers interact directly with producers, as manufacturers internalize activities that traditionally have been performed by intermediaries (Sarkar, Butler, & Steinfield, 1995, 1998). Although entire channel layers may not be eliminated, there could be significant shifts in power from one channel layer to another (Vassos, 1996). According to Porter (1999), the Internet is going to lead to the demise of a lot of intermediaries.

There also is a threat to travel agents' "standard products": the processing of trans-actions (ticketing and settlement) and the supply of raw product information from suppliers (O'Brien, 1999). These roles will increasingly be replaced by technology as suppliers provide standard product information, electronic ticketing, and electronic funds transfer services directly to the customer. For instance, some traditional travel agents in the U.S. have reported a 10 to 20% decline in business as customers switch to online ticket purchasing (Taylor, 1998).

There are different opinions regarding the plausibility of disintermediation in the context of the travel industry. Most commentators would probably agree that the pre-Internet position of TAs is unsustainable (UNCTAD, 2000), and that TAs who fail to take advantage of the Internet are faced with a real threat. Yet, it has been pointed out that there is little empirical evidence to support any arguments and predictions relating to the future role of middlemen in the travel distribution channel (Anckar, 2003; Palvia & Vemuri 1999).

Drawing on data from surveys of managers and travel consultants of Australian travel agencies, Standing, Borberly, and Vasudavan (1998) and Vasudavan and Standing (1999) forecast that many high street retail TAs will be eliminated over the next few years. However, in a series of exploratory studies using survey data it was found that even experienced Internet users have trouble producing satisfactory travel arrangements through self-booking services (Anckar & Walden, 2000, 2002), so there may be a delayed effect in the take-up of alternatives to high street retailers.

Based on an exploratory survey among industry experts, Licata (2001) presented findings indicating that more conventional forms of distribution, such as global distribution systems (GDS) and high street shops, are likely to be bypassed or that their roles will change dramatically: Nearly all (97%) of the respondents in Licata's study agreed or strongly agreed with the statement that the Internet will be the most prominent distribution channel in five years; the corresponding figures being 20% for high street shops and 27% for GDS. Yet, the majority (70%) of the respondents also agreed that the disintermediation of the traditional distribution channel is avoidable, and that reintermediation is a more probable outcome (Licata, 2001).

Schmitz (2000) also pointed out that the disintermediation hypothesis is too simplistic, seeing its interpretation of intermediation as a single service rather than a number of different services. Sarkar et al. (1995, 1998) argue that the case for the elimination of intermediaries as a result of e-commerce is based on a questionable assumption, concluding that more, rather than fewer intermediaries (mainly new players, cybermediaries) will be involved in electronic markets (Giaglis, 1999).

Chircu and Kauffman (1999) propose an "IDR cycle," a recurrent pattern of intermediation, disintermediation, and reintermediation, arguing that traditional non-technological middlemen will be able to reintermediate in the long run. Werthner and Klein (1999) argue that evidence of a reintermediation process can already be seen as traditional intermediaries adjust their services offering to the needs and opportunities of an electronic sales channel. Giaglis (1999) envisaged three major scenarios for electronic intermediaries: disintermediation, reintermediation (the emergence of online subsidiaries of traditional intermediaries), and cybermediation (the emergence of new entrants with intermediary functions). The authors call attention to the fact that electronic markets are still far from reaching a state of maturity, and maintain that it is extremely difficult to predict the market structure of the future and the type of intermediation that will dominate in any given market.

Internet booking is not a panacea for the whole tourism industry (WTOBC, 2001). By retaining the human touch and specialising wisely, smaller offline travel agencies can reach a reasonable level of profitability. In the agents favour are a number of unique services that dot.com travel companies and airline Internet portals have difficulty offering. These include:

- The person-to-person nature of retail travel agency businesses
- The ability of agents to offer and explain complex fare options to clients
- Agents are able to discuss the advantages and disadvantages of destination selection.
- Clients have the option of developing long-term personal relationship with agents.
- Agents can develop specialist knowledge of specific destinations. (Prideaux, 2001, p. 224)

TAs must analyse what strategies they can follow to sustain their role as middlemen. There are two directions that agents can take in this quest (Tse, 2003). The first is to improve their efficiency by repositioning themselves as low-cost agents through the Internet. Another alternative is to develop a different business model that adds value to a travel experience. Providing travel advice, enhancing customer satisfaction, and building bookings with other related services are just some of the many options travel agents need to consider to fight this trend of disintermediation.

To survive, the agents should reintermediate themselves as being able to provide personal services. TAs must invest in deep learning about their target customers' preferences to find out what would most satisfy them (Tse, 2003).

## The New Zealand Travel Market

The New Zealand tourism market is certainly not immune to the changes outlined above. The Travel Agents' Association of New Zealand has stated that never before has the industry experienced a period of such turbulence and change (TAANZ, 2001b). In addition to the growth of the Internet, shifts in airline ownership, the disappearance of some carriers from the New Zealand market, commission cuts, and evolving consumer demand and expectations are fundamentally altering the ways in which NZ TAs conduct business (TAANZ, 2001b).

Tension between travel agents and Air New Zealand has been growing. The airline has poured large sums of money into creating a new Web site which was designed to increase the number of Internet based bookings and sales (www.airnz.co.nz). The airline has adopted the concept of paperless travel throughout its domestic network (Kennedy, 1997). In July 2002, Air New Zealand cut its fares by up to 28% for its one-class, no-meal Air NZ Express. The price to the consumer is lower if booked over the Internet. Air New Zealand has removed a 4% commission for each domestic ticket sale (Aronson, 2002a). Travel agents have responded by launching a campaign against Air New Zealand commission cuts (Aronson, 2002b; *The New Zealand Herald*, 2002).

The impact of these changes is not hard to see. According to TAANZ, 60% of processing by New Zealand TAs is airfare related (TAANZ, 2001a) and the bulk of this involves Air New Zealand. Over the past four years, the number of travel agents in New Zealand has plummeted. TAANZ noted that the number of travel agents within their organisation dropped to 470 by 2004 from the 1999 figure of 626 (*The New Zealand Herald*, 2000). By some estimates, around two agencies were closing their door each week in 2000 (Scherer, 2001).

New Zealand agents also face challenges from principals other than Air New Zealand. In a move similar to the North American Orbitz initiative, Zuji.com launched its Web site in the Asia Pacific region in 2001. Zuji.com has 16 members, including Japan Airlines, Qantas, Singapore Airlines, United, and China Airlines. Utilising the technology of the major GDS, SABRE, the portal allows the consumer direct access to systems that were previously the domain of travel agents alone. It also should be noted that there are, like the Orbitz case, serious legal challenges to the operation (Griffin, 2002).

With very high use of Eftpos and ATM technology, as well as with high Internet connection and Hi-Tech electronic ownership, New Zealand seems to have all the advantages for successful online business development. However, according to Deloitte Touche Tohmatsu (2000), New Zealand businesses, including those in the travel industry, are laggards in ICT adoption.

Although there are no firm figures on the total number of establishments in the NZ TA sector the total number of current TA employees can be estimated at 4800 with approximately 800-900 shops around New Zealand. TAANZ members employ 3610 staff in 533 locations. The biggest NZ travel agencies are TAANZ members except for Flight Center (approx. 1000 employees), Travel Centers (22 shops, 120 staff), Harvey World Travel (53 shops, 150 staff), STA travel (15 branches, 70 employees).

## Research on the NZ Travel Agent Sector

The investigation of the New Zealand TA sector and its changes in response to ICT introduction are identified as the purpose of this study. Primary data collection started with semi-structured interviews with TA and industry specialists to identify the main issues facing the New Zealand TA sector. The research then proceeded with a follow-up of semi-structured interviews to refine the findings regarding the main issues and to investigate the evolution of TA perceptions, attitudes and re-lationships. This allows us to formulate theoretical assumptions regarding the TA business environment in the information era. A fully-structured online questionnaire was designed and implemented to verify the assumptions made on the basis of the in-depth interviews.

The presented study adopts qualitative methods. Qualitative analysis is part of the naturalistic method of inquiry, which assumes that reality is continually changing and that human social phenomena are so complex that it is impossible to discover anything approximating a scientific law (Oppenheim, 1992; Silverman, 2004). A goal of qualitative research is to locate the understanding of a phenomenon within the context of other phenomena.

In-depth interviews with TA and industry specialists were adopted as a means of collecting data. It is well accepted that in-depth interviews are applied to enhance the knowledge of just-emerging, under-researched phenomenon (Oppenheim, 1992). Until the researcher is relatively clear on what is to be studied and how, the objective of the interview should be discovery and enhanced understanding of the phenomena. Such an understanding is derived from data grounded in the infor-mants' experience—what they say about what they did, how they felt, or what they thought. Such a theory development objective demands an emergent design for the research process—one that is fluid and adaptable as concepts and relationships are revealed in the course of data collection, analysis, and interpretation. Unlike survey or experimental research that demands the investigator's intervention prior to data collection through the precise creation of a questionnaire, qualitative methods such as in-depth interviews involve the researcher as an interpreter mostly during and after data collection (Oppenheim, 1992).

## In-Depth Interviews 2000-2001

Interviews were held with 20 senior management or owners of TA in the Auckland region by the New Zealand Tourism Research Institute during 2000-2001. A sampling method was adopted that enabled the researchers to include a cross-section of travel agent operations, including corporate/business, leisure specialists, franchise/chain retail operations, small independent enterprises, and wholesalers. The Auckland region was chosen because the city is New Zealand's major entry and departure point for tourists. Interviews with TAs were designed to elicit information on an agent's particular market, key competitive pressures, evolving relationships with airlines, the use of ICT, relationships with consumers, and main survival strategies. Interviewees were asked whether they thought that their customers have changed with time, and if they believe consumers are ready to buy travel products online.

Research conducted in 2000 on New Zealand TA revealed that processes of disinter-mediation, especially driven by the national carrier Air New Zealand, were a major concern (Garkavenko et al., 2003; Garkavenko & Milne, 2004). Commission cuts by the national carrier Air New Zealand were a major focus of attention for most of those interviewed along with direct sales through the airline's upgraded Web site. The major pressure factors were identified by TAs as commission cuts and direct sale of principals to consumers (Figure 2).

*Figure 2. Major pressure factors on TA businesses and TA responses (Source: 2000 survey interviews by authors)*

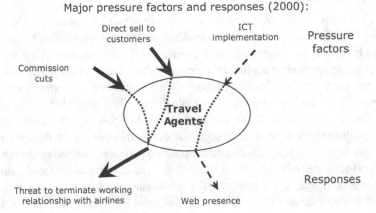

# In-Depth Interviews 2003-2004

The aim of the follow-up interviews was to refine the formulation of the main issues of the New Zealand travel agent market and formulate theoretical assumptions regarding the changes and main pressure factors facing this sector. In common with the 20 interviews held in 2000, a sampling method was adopted in 2003-2004 that included a cross-section of travel agent operations. Interviews were carried out with 25 retail travel agents, owners, wholesalers, senior management, and travel sector experts in the greater Auckland region to investigate their perceptions of the effects of the changing business environment.

Interestingly, neither commission cuts, nor direct Web-based sales by airlines, were on the list of major threats in the 2003 follow-up in-depth interviews with Auckland region TAs. Given that 60-85% of profits of those interviewed are still air-fare related it appears that New Zealand TAs have begun to find ways to build a healthier relationship with the majority of airlines.

Although no single concept underpinned respondents' views of ICT importance, there were a number of recurrent themes. The Internet and other ICT are considered as commodities rather than strategic means for survival. Only one interviewee mentioned the Internet and intelligent agent software in particular as tools for adding value. No other respondents mentioned ICT as an enabling factor. Further discussion identified that interviewees don't particularly know how ICT can add value to their product, or how specialised software can make their work more efficient.

The 2003 interviews with New Zealand TA also revealed that ICT in general and the Internet in particular are not perceived as a major threat to TA businesses. One of the interviewees said: "Consumers research on the Internet, and then they come to us to do bookings. It will come that they will be confident to book, but not at this stage. At this stage it is not a huge impact on what we do." Indeed, a Travel Agents Association of New Zealand representative recently said that travellers who book through the Internet are a different clientele from those who use an agent (*Newstalk ZB News*, 2004).

## *National Online Survey 2004*

When main issues of the TA sector and their evolution were identified and refined, a fully-structured national online questionnaire was designed and implemented. Over 120 TA businesses participated in the survey, the main aim of which was to check the following assumptions that were formulated from the analysis of in-depth interviews with New Zealand TAs:

- Commission cuts by airlines, suppliers selling directly to the consumer, the Internet and emergence of the more knowledgeable consumer have a great impact on the TA market in NZ
- ICT and the Internet in particular are not perceived as a strategic tool by NZ TAs
- Main survival strategies are: alliances, shift to consumers, niche marketing

The national online survey of TA businesses in 2004 refined the notion of how TAs perceive major pressure factors and ICT impact on the industry (Figure 3). The findings showed that TAs perceive commission cuts, direct principal sales to consumers, the Internet, and the emergence of a new more informed consumers, as well as terrorism and health threats as major pressure factors on their businesses. In general there is much more recognition of ICT as a pressure factor after 2003.

These data reveal that there is great variation in the extent to which TAs exploit the advantages of new technologies. As has been pointed out by Gamble, Chalder, and Stone (2001) and other researchers, the major barrier in relation to new technologies seems not to be technological capacity, but uncertainty surrounding the demand for online travel and the possible resultant disintermediation effects on the traditional travel agent. The national online survey established that TAs in big cities, especially Auckland, perceive ICT as a strategic tool. They invest in ICT earlier and that is why they do not perceive the emergence of the informed customer as a threat to their businesses.

*Figure 3. Major pressure factors on the TA businesses and TA responses (Source: National Survey by authors)*

Major pressure factors and responses (National Survey, 2004):

As with Tse's work (2003), two key tendencies in TA survival strategies are identified. One tendency is a low-budget orientation, especially pronounced in franchises
with high turnover (called by one interviewee "the McDonalds of travel") and small
TAs catering for specific ethnic and social groups. One interviewee noted that the
latter sell tickets with as little as a 2% margin to establish themselves on the market.
A second business model is to focus on adding value to travellers' experiences. For
example, some businesses add value to the travel product by providing expert advice
regarding destinations, bundling airfare bookings with other related services such as
visa support and organizing overseas working experience. One of the interviewees
noted: "We will become smarter. The days of sitting in your agency and waiting
for people to come in are gone."

Perhaps most importantly, the national survey revealed a greater emphasis on the
competitive problems associated with the emergence of better-informed and more
ICT savvy consumers. It is interesting to follow the evolution of TA perceptions
of consumers during the 2000-2001and 2003-2004 studies. This evolution can be
described as a progression from a perception of the consumer as "non-skilled," "not
ready to buy online" to "more informed," "more sophisticated." A lot of TAs now
find that consumers come to them with a solid knowledge of their destination and
ticket/hotel prices retrieved from the Internet.

The general feeling remains that the consumer is still not quite ready to buy travel
products through the Internet (especially those which involve long-haul/complex
itineraries). It was acknowledged that the majority of arrangements for domestic
and one-point trips will be done online in the near future. However, it was emphasised that there will be still some categories of travellers that will use TAs even for
simple itineraries. Online services and information searching are still perceived as
very complex, chaotic and time-consuming.

In simple terms these findings reveal that the consumers themselves are, in many
respects, becoming the main 'competitors' with TAs, in terms of gathering information and searching for destination-related knowledge. One of the interviewees
noted that to survive "TA have to be able to have access information 'cleverer' and
'quicker' than they [consumers] do. Then we will be able to charge for this." There
is a general understanding that TAs should be orientated to consumers. However,
customer-relationship management strategies vary considerably. None of the respondents reported being 100% satisfied with the quality of their current customer
management data. Only one TA that works with several niche markets has a well-
developed customer relationship strategy and an established customer database.
This particular TA looks after individual customers' post-trip follow-up, as well as
sending newsletters plus providing personalised services and detailed knowledge
of specific destinations.

For one TA who specializes in Eastern Europeans living in NZ, success has been
based on an intimate knowledge of his clients' psychology and language, and thus

of their specific needs and demands. The specific product for such a group includes not just tickets, but visa support and other immigration services. In this case the TA does not have any functional customer database, relying on word of mouth in a small, relatively tight-knit, community.

TAs continue to play a vital role in the tourism distribution system. Research shows that TA are a more frequently utilised external information source by international travellers from almost all EU member states (Gursoy & Umbreit, 2004). The success of TAs relies on their ability to provide products that suits clients' needs and wants. An understanding of those needs and wants, coupled with deep product knowledge are implicit in this assertion.

Consumer expectations and perceptions of the modern travel agent are an important element in the complex TA business environment. This is a reality that often determines the success of a TA in the disintermediation context. Gursoy and Chen (2000) and Gursoy and Umbreit (2004) state that there are national-culture differences in consumer's search and booking of travel products. These authors established that the European Union consists of distinctive segments of consumers that prefer brochures and TAs in search and booking, or the Internet, TV/radio and minitel. It therefore is relevant to find some specific characteristics of the New Zealand travel product consumer to determine if this is so in the local market.

The Pacific Asia Travel Association (PATA, 2004) reported that TAs were the most popular information source for overseas-bound New Zealand travellers. The Internet is becoming more popular in information searching with 11% of respondents using this tool. TAs were the most popular booking channel for outbound tourists in New Zealand. Only 9% of travellers booked their trips online. Nevertheless New Zealanders are frequent and skilled computer users. The Computer Industry Almanac estimates that there were 2.34 million Internet users in New Zealand in 2004 (European Travel Commission-New Media Review, 2004). In August 2001, Nua reported that 44% of New Zealand's Internet users went online to plan or book overseas holidays, up from 23% in 1999. The percentage was lower for online planning of domestic holidays, however 28% of online New Zealanders did go online to plan or book domestic holidays, up from only 10% in 1999.

## Subsequent Research

While there have been some studies on the demand side of the New Zealand TAs market (Gamble et al., 2001; Oppermann, 1998) these have not adopted an in-depth approach to understanding consumer perspectives. To embrace the complexity of the multifaceted characteristics of the TA business environment, the present research adopted a qualitative approach based on a "double-sided" analysis of TA services that included both TA and consumer's in-depth interviews. Twenty in-depth interviews with consumers were conducted.

A convenience sample was used for the consumer interviews. Rather than following a random selection routine, professionals and white-collar workers who travel regularly (two to three times a year) were approached. When selecting consumers, respondents were pre-screened and only those who use the Internet on a regular basis were asked to participate. The argument for pre-screening is that those customers who are familiar with the Internet and use it on the regular basis would have a choice between using the Internet or a travel agent in their trip preparation. The interviews mainly focused on the use of the Internet in trip planning and preparation, the (dis)advantages of using a TA for trip preparation, and the consumer's perceived role of TAs in the modern era.

The aim of the in-depth interviews with consumers was to identify their attitude towards TAs in the modern Internet era. It was found that travellers are pragmatic in choosing which channel to book through—looking for where they can get the best deal (Tse, 2003). This reflects previous findings on service attributes of travel agencies in New Zealand (Oppermann, 1998). Oppermann pointed out that differences in perceptions of the importance attached to service vary between TAs and clients/potential clients. Attributes rated highly by consumers were not considered in the same light by travel agents. The most highly rated service attribute for consumers was that the "agents give clients the best deal" and for travel agents it was "agent is courteous and friendly." Similarly, in our study there was a discrepancy between TA and consumer perceptions of quality service: during in-depth interviews TAs mentioned more "personalised service," "specific product catering," and consumers were talking more about a "better deal," and "flexibility," or "financial responsibility."

The research findings also reveal that there is a gap between customer expectations and customer perceptions of the services provided by travel agents. The ideal travel agent is expected to be a professional who gives the best deal in term of prices, and has intimate destination-related knowledge. The perceived role of TAs is as a transaction facilitator and not as an information source or adviser. There is a tendency among consumers to look for information online and use a TA only for bookings and financial transactions.

The findings further show that consumers perceive competitive pricing, flexibility in arrangements and personal financial responsibility as being crucial factors when choosing/using a TA. If TAs are to survive—and thrive—in the years to come, it is important that they address the issue of what matters most to consumers. Interestingly, another study regarding online relationships examined the importance of trust in accommodation bookings in New Zealand (Fam, Foscht, & Collins, 2004).

Perceptions of the main service attributes by TA and by consumers are compared and summarized in Table 1.

It appears that considerably improved computer and Internet skills are expected by consumers from TA, and at the same time the national survey revealed that most TA

*Table 1. Congruency and discrepancies in consumers' and TAs' perception of quality services (Source: Authors)*

| Coincidences | Discrepancies |
|---|---|
| • TA should be more skillful in computer usage <br> • Consumer is the main TA competitor for the travel information | • Main attributes of the quality service <br> • Role of TA <br> • Fees for TA services |

respondents realise that these factors are very important for their business progress and survival. Similarly, both consumers and TA recognise that consumers are often very knowledgeable about the travel product. On the other hand, consumers named "personal financial responsibility," "finding a better deal" and "flexibility" as the main service attributes they look for in a TA. TAs however were talking more about "personalised service," and "added value" as the main attributes. Consumers also see the role of TAs in the Internet era almost exclusively as "transaction facilitators." They also were quite suspicious regarding the professionalism of TAs. While many TAs are ready to charge their customers for the services they provide there, was a great deal of hesitation regarding TAs fees among interviewed consumers.

It appears that the mainstream consumer is hesitating and can be convinced by aggressive marketing to buy travel products either online or through TAs. These findings have very important implications for TAs. If the Internet becomes more user-friendly there is no doubt that more and more consumers will purchase online. TAs will need to implement more aggressive advertising policies with a strong emphasis on their professional advice, personal financial responsibility (including the bond system), time-saving attributes, and intimate knowledge of destination. TAs also need to develop their Internet skills to compete with their customers when searching for information/best deals.

# The "Success Mix" for
# New Zealand Travel Agent Businesses

The New Zealand travel agent sector is represented mainly by SMEs; almost half of them are independent or family operated. It appears that ICT adoption by New Zealand TAs is less advanced than in the USA or Europe. There is a great deal of hesitation regarding the use of ICT as a strategic tool. While the Web presence of New Zealand TAs increased considerably from 2001-2004, many are still more interested in using cyberspace for marketing rather than as a core component of overall business strategy. There are no giants in New Zealand cyberspace like Expedia or Travelocity. Indeed, online travel has proved a difficult business for local operators venturing on the Web. Local provider Travel.co.nz lost more than $2 million in revenue of $20 million in the year 2003.

Overall, it appears that the reintermediation process is the reality for the average New Zealand travel agency. First of all, the national survey of 2004 revealed the considerable heterogeneity of NZ TA businesses in perceived pressure factors, attitudes towards technology, relationship with the consumer, and business success. The major differences were found not between franchises and independent TAs as was expected, but between TAs from Auckland and other major cities, and those from small towns. Early recognition of the ICT impact on their businesses, and recognition of the fact of emergence of the "new" consumer gave some TA business, especially in Auckland a market advantage.

TAs that perceive their business situation as better or much better compared with three years ago point out that excellent customer service is a big part of their advantage. They recognised reasonably early that with ICT accessibility to all parties in the distribution channel the way to survive is to become a customer representative and to add value to services. TAs recognise that there is a need to improve their computer/Internet skills to deliver a service. Successful TAs are catering to specific niche markets trying to deliver a personalised service with added value. These findings allowed the formulation of a "success mix" for TAs in New Zealand (Figure 4). The research has established that businesses which recognised the emergence of a new, more sophisticated consumer, embraced ICT as a strategic tool, and/or began to cater for niche markets are better off now than three years ago. At the same time there is another feature specific to the New Zealand TA market—all outbound travel is long haul, and much of this is complex with several stop-overs and costs a considerable amount of money. Interviews with consumers show that although they largely perceive TAs as simple transaction facilitators, they still hesitate to trust the Internet with their money and are still not quite confident to complete complex travel arrangements online in this situation. In simple terms this means that New Zealand consumers still need TAs, results replicated elsewhere (Anckar, 2003).

Nevertheless, the data reveal an intention by a growing number of consumers to abandon high street travel agencies when booking travel. Approximately half of the existing and prospective Internet bookers intend to use direct distribution approaches, whereas half intend to use the Internet merely as a communication channel to human travel agents, thereby primarily fostering reintermediation.

Although the Internet undoubtedly has the potential to revolutionize the travel distribution chain, it should be noted that many hindrances to the mass adoption of online services in travel still exist. The lack of travel agent expertise and advice is one of the greatest consumer disadvantages of electronic travel distribution. "Buy direct from the factory and save money" may be good advice for some types of products, but is

*Figure 4. "Success mix" for New Zealand TA businesses*

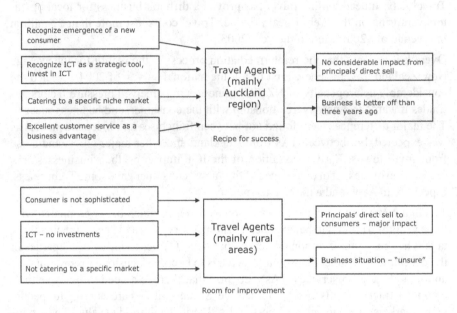

generally not true for travel products. Anckar (2003) has pointed out that there are several categories of barriers for consumers booking and purchasing online. These barriers are: lack of knowledge or experience with the Internet, technical problems, system limitations, and poor Web services, as well as difficulties in locating Web sites. Furthermore, making price comparisons is time-consuming.

Although the demand for online arrangements exists, the supply side has to be more mature and offer easy-to-use reliable ways of travel booking. It can be hypothesized that the next step in the evolution of distribution in the travel industry will be the development of special software that assists consumers in online bookings of their trips. TA will again be put in the position of adding value to their services, repeating once again the disintermediation-re-intermediation cycle.

# Conclusion

ICT has changed the competitive environment for travel agents in the New Zealand travel market. Tourism industry principals and technology providers in New Zealand are entering the market—bypassing TAs and selling directly to consumers.

This study on the New Zealand travel agent market revealed that commission cuts, suppliers selling direct to the consumer, the Internet, and the emergence of a new more informed consumer are the main pressure factors on travel agent businesses in New Zealand.

This research has also established that there is great variation in the extent to which travel agents use the advantages associated with new technology and how New Zealand travel agents perceive ICT. It seems that the major barrier in relation to new technologies is not the technological capacity of TAs, but the uncertainty surrounding the demand for online travel. The research also reveals great variability in attitudes towards ICT as a basis for sustained competitive advantage. The majority of the study participants have decided not to invest in ICT and do not perceive ICT as a strategic tool. So, while it appears that the level of ICT adoption among New Zealand travel agents is high, the use of ICT is limited to e-mailing and information searching. The majority of NZ travel agents have Web sites, but the role of these Web sites is mainly for information and marketing rather than for e-business.

The Internet has provided several challenges for travel agents. Agents not only have to match the availability of information from off the Internet, but they also need to provide great value when servicing consumers who already have access to most of the available information.

It has been established in this chapter that the New Zealand consumer perceives travel agents mainly as "transaction facilitators" rather than a source of information or a person who intimately knows a destination or provides an unbiased deal for an airfare. At the same time, consumers pointed out that "flexibility" and "financial responsibility" are definite advantages in using travel agents. Consumers also pointed out the often chaotic nature of online information.

The New Zealand consumer is currently "hesitating" in their preference to use the Internet or a travel agent in purchasing travel products. Travel agents can use this critical time to promote their businesses more assertively, putting the emphasis on their personal financial responsibility and skills in the construction of complex itineraries as well as flexibility in changing travel arrangements to suit their clients.

# References

Alamdari, F. (2002). Regional development in airlines and travel agents relationship. *Journal of Air Transport Management, 8*, 339-348.

American Airlines. (2000). *American Airlines Web site.* Retrieved April 3, June 14, August 20, 2000 from the World Wide Web: http://www.aa.com/

Anckar, B. (2003). Consumer intentions in terms of electronic travel distribution: implications for future market structures. *E-Service Journal, 2*(2), 68-86.

Anckar, B., & Walden, P. (2000). Destination Maui? An exploratory assessment of the efficacy of self-booking in travel. *Electronic Markets, 10*(2), 110-119.

Anckar, B., & Walden, P. (2002). Self-booking of high- and low-complexity travel products: exploratory findings. *Information Technology & Tourism, 4*, 151-165.

Aronson, C. (2002a, June 12). *Travel agents boost pressure on Air NZ.* Retrieved July 5, 2002, from http://www.nzherald.co.nz/storydisplay.cfm?thesection=news&thesubsection=&storyID=2046185

Aronson, C. (2002b, August 1). Price war as Qantas hits back. *The New Zealand Herald,* p. A1.

Atkinson, R. D. (2001). *The revenge of the disintermediated: How the middleman is fighting e-commerce and hurting consumers.* Washington, DC: Progressive Policy Institute. Retrieved from http://www.ppionline.org

Bloch, M., & Segev, A. (1996). *The impact of electronic commerce on the travel industry: An analysis methodology and case study.* The Fisher Centre for Information Technology and Management. CA: University of California.

Bordat, P. (1999, January 20-23). Repositioning a GDS for future electronic markets. In D. Buhalis & W. Schertler (Eds.), *Information and Communication Technologies in Tourism 1999. Proceedings of the International Conference,* Innsbruck, Austria (pp. 318-327). Wein: Springer-Verlag.

Buhalis, D. (1998). Strategic use of information technologies in the tourism industry. *Tourism Management, 19*(5), 409-421.

Buhalis, D. (1999). The cost and benefits of information technology and the Internet for small and medium-sized tourism enterprises. In D. Buhalis & W. Schertler (Eds.), *Information and Communication Technologies in Tourism 1999. Proceedings of the International Conference,* Innsbruck, Austria (pp. 218-227). Wien: Springer-Verlag.

Buhalis, D. (2000a). Conference report: Distribution channels in the changing travel industry. The Dorchester, London, 9-10 December 1998. *International Journal of Tourism Research, 2*(2), 137-139.

Buhalis, D. (2000b). Tourism and information technologies: Past, present and future. *Tourism Recreation Research, 25*(1), 41-58.

Buhalis, D., & Laws, E. (Eds.). (2001). *Tourism distribution channels: Practices, issues and transformations.* London: Continuum.

Chircu, A. M., & Kauffman, R. J. (1999, January 5-8). Analyzing firm-level strategy for Internet-focused reintermediation. In *Proceedings of the 32nd Hawaii International Conference on System Sciences,* Maui, HI (pp. 5035-5045). Los Alamitos, CA: IEEE Computer Society Press.

Deloitte Touche Tohmatsu. (2000, Summer). Understanding the impact of e-business. Deloitte Touche Tohmatsu Publications. *Insights: For Innovative Business Enterprises, 10*. Retrieved May 15, 2000, from http://www.deloitte.co.nz

European Travel Commission—New Media Review. (2004). *Markets by country—New Zealand*. Retrieved June 9, 2004, from http://www.etcnewmedia. com/review/default.asp?SectionID=11&CountryID=78

Fam, K. S., Foscht, T., & Collins, R. D. (2004). Trust and the online relationship: An exploratory study from New Zealand. *Tourism Management, 25*, 195-207.

French, T. (1998). The future of global distribution systems. *Travel & Tourism Analyst, 3*, 1-17.

Gamble, P., Chalder, M., & Stone, M. (2001). Customer knowledge management in the travel industry. *Journal of Vacation Marketing, 7*(1), 83-91.

Garkavenko, V., Bremner, H., & Milne, S. (2003). Travel agents in the "information age": New Zealand experiences of disintermediation. In A. J. Frew, M. Hitz & P. O'Connor (Eds.), *Information and Communication Technologies in Tourism. Proceedings of the International Conference, ENTER 2003*, Helsinki, Finland (pp. 467-476). Wien: Springer-Verlag.

Garkavenko, V. & Milne, S. (2004, June 27-30). *Travel agents and disintermediation: Exploring the complex competitive environment*. Presented at the International Conference: Tourism—the State of the Art II, Glasgow.

Giaglis, G. M., Klein, S., & O'Keefe, R. (1999, June 7-9). Disintermediation, reintermediation, or cybermediation? The future of intermediaries in electronic marketplaces. In *Proceedings of the 12th Bled International Electronic Commerce Conference*, Bled, Slovenia (pp. 389-407).

Griffin, P. (2002). *Travel giant casts shadow*. Retrieved 10 September 2002, from http://www.nzherald.co.nz/storydisplay.cfm?thesection=technology

Gursoy, D., & Chen, J. S. (2000). Competitive analysis of cross-cultural information search behavior. *Tourism Management, 21*(6), 583-590.

Gursoy, D., & Umbreit, W. T. (2004). Tourist information search behavior: cross-cultural comparison of European union members states. *International Journal of Hospitality Management, 23*, 55-70.

Harrington, D., & Power, J. (2001). Quality issues in tourism distribution: practices and prospects. In D. Buhalis & E. Laws (Eds.), *Tourism distribution channels: Practices, issues and transformations*. London: Continuum.

Karcher, K. (1996). The four global distribution systems in the travel and tourism industry. *Electronic Markets, 6*(2), 20-24.

Karcher, K. (1997). *Reinventing the package holiday business: new information and telecommunications technologies*. Gabler, Germany: Deutscher Universitats Verlag.

Kennedy, G. (1997). Air NZ's electronic tickets are winning the paper war. *National Business Review,* 27.

Licata, M. C., Buhalis, D., & Richer, P. (2001, April 24-27). The future role of the travel e-mediary. In P. J. Sheldon, K. W. Wober & D. R. Fesenmaier (Eds.), *Information and Communication Technologies in Tourism. Proceedings of the ENTER 2001 Conference,* Montreal, Canada (pp. 139-149). Wien: Springer-Verlag.

Malone, T. W., Yates, J., & Benjamin, R. I. (1987). Electronic markets and electronic hierarchies. *Communications of the ACM, 30*(6), 484-497.

Mason, D., & Milne, S. (2002). E-Commerce and Community Tourism. In P. C. Palvia, S. C. Palvia & E. M. Roche (Eds.), *Global information technology and electronic commerce: Issues for the new millenium* (pp. 294-310). Marietta, Gerogia: Ivy League Publishing Ltd.

Modahl, M. (2000). *Now or never: How companies must change today to win the battle for Internet consumer.* New York: HarperCollins.

*Newstalk ZB News.* (2004). Net no threat say travel agents. Retrieved February 27, 2004, from http://xtramsn.co.nz/business/0,,5112-3124930,00.html

*New Zealand Herald, The.* (2000, December 17). p. C9.

*New Zealand Herald, The.* (2002, August 12). *Editorial: Beating the net threat.* Retrieved August 28, 2002, from http://www.nzherald.co.nz/storydisplay. cfm?thesection=news&thesubsection=&storyID=2348908

*New Zealand Herald, The.* (2004, April 28). Security crackdown predicted on Internet flight bookings.

O'Brien, P. F. (1999). Intelligent assistants for retail travel agents. *Information Technology & Tourism, 2*(3/4), 213-228.

O'Connor, P. (1999). *Electronic information distribution in tourism and hospitality.* Wallingford: CABI Publishing.

O'Conner, P., & Frew, J. (2002). The future of hotel electronic distribution: Expert and industry perspectives. *Cornell Hotel and Restaurant Administration Quarterly, 43*(3), 33-45.

Oppenheim, A. N. (1992). *Questionnaire design, interviewing and attitude measurement* (2nd ed.). New York: Continuum.

Oppermann, M. (1998). Service attributes of travel agencies: A comparative perspective of users and providers. *Journal of Vacation Marketing, 4*(3), 265-281.

Palmer, A., & McCole, P. (1999). The virtual re-intermediation of travel services: A conceptual framework and empirical investigation. *Journal of Vacation Marketing, 6*(1), 33-47.

Palvia, S., & Vemuri, V. K. (1999). Distribution channels in electronic markets: A functional analysis of the "disintermediation" hypothesis. *Electronic Markets, 9*(2), 118-125.

PATA. (2004). *Online travel agents cast their web wide by Deloitte*, from http://www. pata.org/mbrarea4.cfm?pageid=167speechid=69&datatable=currentissues.

Poon, A. (1993). *Tourism, technology and competitive strategies.* Oxford: CAB International.

Porter, M. (1999, October 25). The net won't transform everything. *Inter@ctive Week.* Retrieved from www.zdnet.com

Prideaux, B. (2001). Airline distribution systems: the challenge and opportunity of the Internet. In D. Buhalis & E. Laws (Eds.), *Tourism distribution channels: Practices, issues and transformations.* London: Continuum.

Richards, G. (1995). Retailing travel products: bringing the information gap. *Progress in Tourism and Hospitality Research, 1*(1), 17-31.

Sarkar, M. B., Butler, B., & Steinfield, C. (1995). Intermediaries and Cybermediaries: A continuing role for mediating players in the electronic marketplace. *Journal of Computer-Mediated Communication, 1*(3), 1-9.

Sarkar, M. B., Butler, B., & Steinfield, C. (1998). Cybermediaries in electronic marketspace: Toward theory building. In J. Sheth, A. Eshghi & B. Krishnan (Eds.), *Internet marketing* (pp. 252-261). Orlando: Harcourt College Publishers.

Scherer, K. (2001, December 20). Travel flies to the Net. *The New Zealand Herald.*

Schmitz, S. W. (2000). The effects of electronic commerce on the structure of intermediation. *Journal of Computer-Mediated Communication, 5*(3).

Silverman, D. (Ed.). (2004). *Qualitative research: Theory, method and practice* (2ⁿᵈ ed.). London: SAGE Publications.

Smith, C., & Jenner, P. (1998). Tourism and the Internet. *Travel & Tourism Analyst, 1*, 62-81.

Standing, C., Borberly, S., & Vasudavan, T. (1998). Re-engineering travel agencies with the World Wide Web. *Electronic Markets, 8*(4), 40-43.

TAANZ. (2001b, July). TAANZ Actions. *Industry News, 19.*

TAANZ. (2001a). Handbook 2001. In *Travel industry directory & information guide 2001.*

Taylor, P. (1998, October 27). Middle men deleted as word spreads. *The Financial Times.*

Tretheway, M. W., & Oum, T. H. (1992). *Airline economics: Foundations for strategy and policy.* Vancouver, BC: Centre for Transportation Studies, University of British Columbia.

Tse, A. C.-b. (2003). Disintermediation of travel agents in the hotel industry. *International Journal of Hospitality Management, 22*, 453-460.

UNCTAD. (2000, July 27). *Electronic commerce and tourism: New perspectives and challenges for developing countries* (United Nations Publication TD/B/COM.3/EM.9/2). Retrieved 15/10/2005, from http://www.eyefortravel.com/papers/ecomtour.pdf

Vassos, T. (1996). *Strategic Internet marketing*. Que Corporation.

Vasudavan, T., & Standing, C. (1999, February 10-13). Web technology diffusion and service offerings by travel agencies. In *Tourism & Hospitality: Delighting the Senses 1999. Proceedings of the 9th Australian Tourism and Hospitality Research Conference*, Adelaide, South Australia. Canberra: Bureau of Tourism Research.

Wardell, D. J. (1998). The impact of electronic distribution on travel agents. *Travel & Tourism Analyst, 2*, 41-55.

Werthner, H., & Klein, S. (1999). *Information technology and tourism: a challenging relationship*. Wien: Springer-Verlag.

WTO. (1995). *Global distribution systems in the tourism industry*. Madrid: World Tourism Organisation.

WTOBC (World Tourism Organisation Business Council). (2001). *Internet poised to take a quarter of tourism sales*. Retrieved December 18, 2001, from http://www.world-tourism.org/newsroom/Releases/more_releases/October2001/011023.htm

# Section II

# Transformation of the Tourist Industry

## Chapter IV

# The Transformation of the Distribution Process in the Airline Industry Empowered by Information and Communication Technology

Patrick S. Merten, International Institute of Management in Technology, Switzerland

## Abstract

*This chapter reviews the historical evolution of the airline market and its first-generation airline reservation and distribution systems. The development and diffusion of computer reservation systems (CRS) and global distribution systems (GDS) is discussed extensively in order to provide a comprehensive overview of the state of business in the 2000s. Based on this evaluation, the influence of modern information and communication technology (ICT) on the airline distribution system environment is discussed. The traditional distribution chain has been transformed into an electronic multi-channel distribution environment. This (r)evolution of the airline market is analysed for the different market participant groups, as the competitive and cooperative situation increases in this cross-influence network industry.*

# Introduction

The information revolution has dramatically reshaped global society and is pushing the world ever more towards an information-based economy. Tourism is one of the industries which is able to generate enormous synergy effects from the use of the Internet. This technology is a potential instrument to implement change in the structure and processes of the entire sector. In particular, the airline market environment has experienced significant changes in the recent decades, induced by the different generations of information and communication technology (ICT). Consequently, this chapter deals with the fundamental transformation of the airline industry—with a focus on the technologies in the distribution process.

Since its emergence, the tourism industry has experienced continuous and sustainable growth, not only in terms of increasing customer numbers, but also in the acquisition of new markets. These developments have been coupled with the expansion of travel intermediaries in response to an increasing demand for travel. While airlines first sold their products separately and on their own, they soon became an integral part of the tourism industry, which in turn gained complexity in terms of distribution. Therefore, and not surprisingly, the airline industry is one of the first business sectors that introduced and relied on information and communication technology to cope with the challenges of rising complexity, notably in distribution. Accordingly, the first main part of this chapter reviews the historical evolution of the airline market and its first-generation airline reservation and distribution systems. This provides a comprehensive overview of the state of business in the latter part of the 1990s.

The following and key part of this chapter focuses in particular on the current reshaping of distribution processes, caused by and based on the development of new information and communication technology. The exponential growth of online platforms and Internet usage has led to the appearance of numerous alternative distribution channels and new intermediaries. Having already established their positions on the market, the new electronic distribution channels now co-exist alongside traditional channels. As a result, the market structure and balance of power between airlines, distributors and customers is rapidly changing. To understand this multi-channel distribution environment, an in-depth analysis of today's airline market is required. Therefore, in the second part of this chapter, the (r)evolution of the airline market is examined from diverse perspectives, that is, those of the different market participants. Furthermore, the evolution towards second-generation airline core environments is investigated, in order to understand the forces behind the emerging paradigm shift.

Figure 1 gives an introductory overview of this chapter's structure.

*Figure 1. Overview of chapter structure*

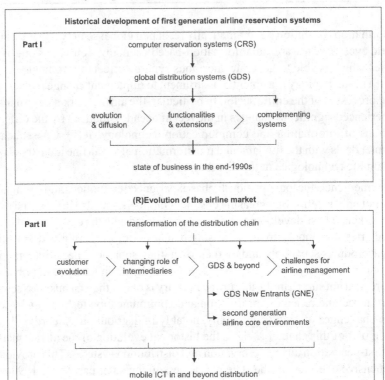

# First-Generation Airline Reservation Systems

Today's airline industry is a product of post-World War II prosperity. Civil aviation took off in the second half of the 20<sup>th</sup> century with the introduction of many new technologies including jet engines, new lightweight metals, radar systems, and computers—making air transportation faster, more comfortable, and above all safer (Prideaux, 2001). In the early years of commercial air flights, bookings were made via telex, telephone, and postal services. These methods were labour intensive, relatively slow, and expensive. However, there were no options to paper-based storage and retrieval systems. Usually, a "request and reply" system was used, collecting all the information and inquiries at a central location. Other airlines used wall-sized availability boards, which had to be updated manually (Sheldon, 1997). This situation changed radically with the emergence of information technology and the diffusion of modern telecommunication networks. The ensuing evolution of first-generation airline reservation systems is discussed in the following sections. For a more detailed description of the historical development leading to computer reservation systems see Copeland and McKenney (1988).

## The Emergence of Computer Reservation Systems (CRS)

Since the 1950s, when air travel became a mass phenomenon, airlines have had to deal with large amounts of diverse information (Sheldon, 1997). The enormous increase in demand (passenger numbers) in the 1950s and 1960s brought management and operational challenges for airlines and airports. In particular, the complexity of all passenger related processes increased dramatically (Buhalis, 2003). Sheldon (1997) stated, that "it is a daunting task to keep track of thousands of flights, fares, seat inventories, crew, passengers, cargo and baggage without automation" (p. 15). Hence it is not surprising that from the outset the airline industry has been one of the most technologically advanced sectors in the field of tourism. The need to formalise the exchange of booking related information led to the introduction of computerized reservation systems (Werthner & Klein, 1999). A harbinger of such systems in the 1950s was a mechanical system called Reservisor used by American Airlines. It performed arithmetic algorithms with the aid of random access memory drums (Sheldon, 1997).

The concurrent computing revolution paved the way for the following first technology driven reservation and distribution systems. However, as no standard platforms and solutions were available at that time, first *computer reservation systems* (CRS) had to be developed in a "hand coded" manner (Werthner & Klein, 1999). For this reason, American Airlines initiated cooperation with IBM in 1953, finally developing the first computer reservation system after years of research and investments of over US$40 million (Sheldon, 1997). This significant breakthrough system was initially called SABER (Semi-Automated Business Environment Research) and has been trailblazing ever since.

The immense technological requirements for the introduction of automated reservation systems ranged from real time and simultaneous transaction processing to an airline specific message code for transmitting information. In addition, the system had to be designed for permanent operation with high reliability (Werthner & Klein, 1999). This necessity resulted in the advancement of new technological concepts such as hardware redundancy, backup generators and uninterrupted power supplies (UPSs). The fully functional SABER was launched by American Airlines and IBM in 1963/64, consisting of two IBM 7080 mainframes for real time and batch processing, an online storage of six magnetic drums and terminal connections at 2,400 baud (Copeland & McKenney, 1988) and met the demanding requirements.

The first requirement for real time and simultaneous transaction processing was fulfilled by the introduction of a new operating system, the Transaction Processing Facility (TPF). Originally this real time inquiry-response system had a response time of less than three seconds and is still the core of most of today's airline reservation systems. But as the TPF is a 6-bit processing first-generation computer language, it requires large investments in human resources to keep the system running and updated; for example, in the 1990s an airline employed an average of 1,200 programmers, each paid approximately US$100,000 to keep the system up to speed (Feldman, 1994).

The second requirement for an airline specific message code for transmitting information led to the introduction of the Airline Line Control (ALC), a full-duplex, synchronous communication protocol, which is still used today (Sheldon, 1997). However, the real challenge at the time was the design of an extensive data communication network across the U.S. and "eventually" across the world (initially offering a 2,400 bits per second transmission rate). This pioneering goal was reached in cooperation with telecommunication companies, in particular the ARINC network (Aeronautical Radio Incorporated) and the SITA network (Société Internationale Télécommunications Aéronautique).

After SABER's completion, IBM used its know-how to create the Programmed Airline Reservation System (PARS) which incorporated application software into the TPF operating system (Sheldon, 1997). Capitalising on their experience with state-of-the-art mainframes, IBM offered PARS to other airlines such as Delta, Continental, Northwest, PanAm, and United Airlines, enabling them to create their own systems similar in function to SABER. In response to IBM's move, American Airlines renamed the original system as SABRE. While the evolution of CRS described so far mainly refers to developments in the U.S., in Europe and Asia airlines also computerised their reservation systems, but did so using videotext technology to perform queries and bookings.

Figure 2 shows the typical configuration of an airline reservation system environment, keeping the mainframes, storage devices, and front-end communication processors (FECPs) on a central site, under high security because of its immense value to the airline, and designed to withstand natural disasters such as fire, flood or earthquake in addition to bomb attacks (Sheldon, 1997).

Implemented as illustrated in Figure 2, the first terminals were installed at airports and airline offices in the late 1960s. These terminals enabled agents to check airline schedules, seat availability and prices from their desktop, allowing them to make confirmed bookings at the time of first inquiry. Until the mid-1970s, computer reservation systems were used only for proprietary airline information, that is, every airline had to have its own system running (Sheldon, 1997). To conclude, CRS can be "regarded as a critical initiator of the electronic age, as they formulated a new travel marketing and distribution system" (Buhalis, 1998, p. 412).

*Figure 2. Configuration of an airline reservation system environment (Source: Sheldon, 1997)*

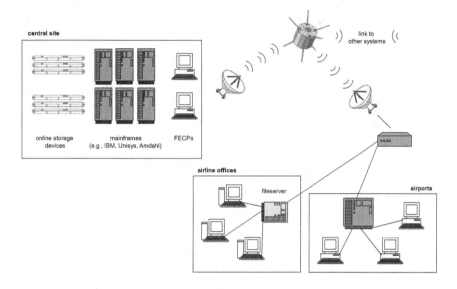

## The Development of Global Distribution Systems (GDS)

The distribution of products and services—available through the CRS—became the next unique challenge for the industry in the 1970s. At an early stage, the distribution of flights was handed over from the airlines (at airports and offices) to travel intermediaries (Werthner & Klein, 1999). As travel intermediaries needed access to more than one CRS, but more than one terminal on an agent's desk did not make sense, an initiative was started in 1975 to create a single industry reservation system. In the same year, the Joint Industry Computer Reservation System project took place, bringing together the major carriers to plan a system which could enable travel intermediaries access to all major airline information. However, despite intense discussions, the effort failed and no agreement was reached (Sheldon, 1997). The situation remained unchanged: the different CRS were each in the possession of single airlines and used exclusively by them.

However, due to the increasing number of airlines and respective CRS, vice versa, combining the different CRS became mandatory in the 1970s. Consequently, some of the CRS, such as SABRE, opened their systems to other airlines. As a result of a continuous concentration process, different CRS were combined and became known as global distribution systems (GDS) (Inkpen, 1994). From this point on, airlines were able to store their information either directly in a GDS or in their own CRS and link it to one or more GDS. This choice basically depended on whether an airline was affiliated with a GDS company or not (Sheldon, 1997). Despites the affiliations, GDS suppliers became generally independent market participants. Therefore the term GDS denotes both the systems as well as the companies operating these systems. Their shareholders are mainly airlines, since the management of airline inventories and their distribution constitute their origin (Werthner & Klein, 1999).

Despite the systems' evolutionary differences, the two terms CRS and GDS are often used synonymously in the literature. This can be legitimated by the overlapping functionalities and complexity of the systems. Henceforth, in this chapter, the systems also are referred to as first-generation airline reservation systems. In general, the CRS/GDS:

- Contain and handle flight schedules, seat inventories, availability and prices
- Enable airline reservations and ticketing
- Store passenger name records (PNRs)

Thus, CRS/GDS have provided airlines with a powerful database that enabled new efficiencies in inventory control and other fields, for example through the introduction of yield management methods (Prideaux, 2001). As GDS contained all necessary distribution information of a growing number of airlines, the GDS suppliers have leased their systems to travel intermediaries. This move led the GDS providers to become the key link between the airlines and travel intermediaries (Prideaux, 2001). The consequential basic distribution structure is shown in Figure 3.

*Figure 3. Distribution structure of first-generation airline reservation systems (Source: Werthner & Klein, 1999)*

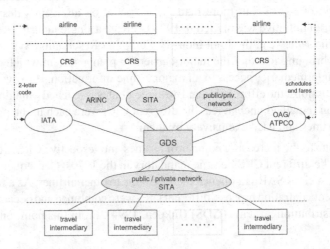

The complex structure of first-generation airline reservation systems can be justified by "the huge number of interconnected companies, both on supply as well as the demand side" (Werthner & Klein, 1999, p. 186) and the existence of numerous different communication channels. Although the underlying architecture can be simply displayed as a star, as illustrated in Figure 3, over time the network has expanded due to new business needs, technological progress and also legal interventions. Companies or institutions such as the Official Airline Guide (OAG) and Airline Tariff Publishing Company (ATPCO) have maintained databases of flight schedules and fares (Werthner & Klein, 1999). For instance, a new airline must be first certified and assigned a two-letter code by the International Air Transport Association (IATA). Subsequently, the airline has to deposit its fares at the ATPCO and its schedules in the OAG, or appropriate institutions (if not based in the U.S.). The transfer of all these files, containing approximately 40 million fares and schedules, over private or public networks is handled by the Aeronautical Radio Incorporated (ARINC) or Société Internationale Télécommunications Aéronatutique (SITA). Founded in 1949, SITA is owned by over 600 airlines and air transport related companies and offers support connections in over 220 countries worldwide (SITA, 2006).

## The GDS Worldwide Evolution and Diffusion

A cause and effect of the emergence of global distribution systems were the travel intermediaries, by taking over the business of distribution of airline products to the end customer. For this reason, travel intermediaries, also often referred to as travel agents, though not including tour operators and speciality providers, were equipped with CRS/GDS terminals in the mid-1970s. Not taking telephone, fax and telex into account, these originally "dumb" terminals were the first kind of information technology in travel offices, providing a connection to the host mainframes and an interface to the airlines. For instance, they replaced the printed Official Airline Guide (OAG) for schedule and fare information. Over time, more and more computer terminals were installed to facilitate airline bookings.

Due to the deregulation of the U.S. airline market in 1978, the number of terminals installed increased tremendously, reaching a penetration of over 85% in the early 1980s (Werthner & Klein, 1999). As prices, schedules and routes were liberated, airlines were able to change them indefinitely, that is, they could be flexible in adjusting pricing, and in setting the medium range schedules and adapting routes to the actual demand. This led to increasing complexity as well as a lack of transparency in fares, which again increased the computing and communication needs for airlines as well as travel intermediaries (Boberg & Collison, 1985). In addition, "until the late 1970s, airlines relied on the International Air Transport Association (IATA) to negotiate international fares on behalf of airlines. IATA mediated between airlines and regulators on the determination of bilateral air service agreements and operation of distribution systems. Domestic fares were often subject to government regulation" (Prideaux, 2001, p. 215). However, with the deregulation and the challenge to IATA's fare regime by non-IATA airlines in South East Asia (Singapore Airlines, Thai and MAS) the importance of IATA as a price regulator subsequently declined.

As a further consequence of deregulation, the American Civil Aeronautics Board issued the first regulation on CRS/GDS in 1984. This directive forced the CRS/GDS providers to display all airline offers in a neutral order, sorted by flight numbers. Until then, SABRE for example always listed American Airlines flights on top (so-called biased listing). This was a lucrative approach for their owner, as it generated as much as 40% extra income (Werthner & Klein, 1999). Following Boberg and Collison (1985) flights of the first screen were booked in 90% of the time, in 50% even of the first line of the first screen. According to Williams (1994), airline-owned GDS allowed a small number of carriers to achieve positions of market dominance through the airline's ability to control the sale of their products via travel agencies. Despite the U.S. Department of Transportation regulations, in 1984, sorting algorithms for flights were often still not fully unbiased, as other variables such as displacement time, non-stop, direct, or connecting flights and elapsed time of the journey were "legal" variables to be used.

Looking at the GDS providers themselves again, SABRE remained affiliated with American Airlines during this period, while Apollo belonged to United Airlines. Other airlines such as Delta Airlines, Eastern Airlines and TWA followed with GDS called DATAS II, SystemOne and PARS respectively. By the 1980s travel intermediaries wishing to automate had a choice of these five systems. A merger between DATAS II and PARS created a new system called Worldspan and reduced

*Figure 4. History of CRS/GDS (Source: Kärcher, 1997)*

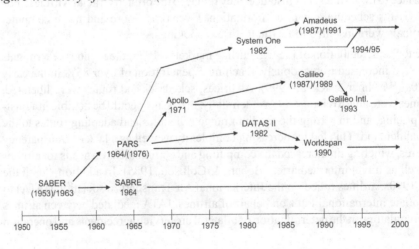

the number to four by the early 1990s. Figure 4 shows the start-ups and merges within the CRS/GDS market, leading to four main systems, holding over 98% of the total market in 1992.

Having reviewed the historical evolution and diffusion of GDS in terms of the systems themselves, the terminals for travel intermediaries and the merges of suppliers in the U.S. market, the following sub-sections reflect on the development of airline reservation systems in other parts of the world.

## The European and Asian Markets

The European idea of nationally developed systems and the subsequent goal of later on dominant GDS was the creation of systems representing multiple carriers—learning from problems in the U.S., where systems were originally affiliated with only one airline. Overall, the European market developed differently from the U.S. market. In the beginning, airline reservations could be made through videotext terminals of the national airline's computer systems (Sheldon, 1997). In the UK, for example, TRAVICOM, a multi-access reservation system owned by the national carrier British Airways, was used primarily; another videotext system was called Prestel (Bennett, 1988). However, in Germany a system called START was designed and implemented jointly by travel agencies, the national carrier Lufthansa as well as German Rail and a tour operator. START subsequently merged with Amadeus (Sheldon, 1997). Finally, in Europe two systems: Amadeus and Galileo appeared and dominated the market. Merging with SystemOne (Amadeus) and Apollo (Galileo) respectively, these GDS expanded the global reach of the systems (Sheldon, 1997). But unlike in the U.S., the Europeans and Asians designed their systems to be unbiased from the beginning. This choice was made by the European Commission and the management of Abacus after seeing the controversy created by biased systems in the U.S. (Sheldon, 1997).

In the Asian market (the next most automated area after the U.S. and Europe), a system called Abacus was established by an independent company; however, it has not operated its own GDS. It initially used the system Worldspan, but in March 1998 signed a cooperation agreement with SABRE and switched its operations to this platform (Werthner & Klein, 1999). In addition to Abacus other GDS vendors, represented by so-called national marketing companies (NMC), have established a 40% market share of GDS in Asian travel agencies.

Tables 1 and 2 give an overview of the airline affiliations and the huge market value of the major GDS Amadeus (including SystemOne), Galileo (including Apollo), SABRE and Worldspan in the 1990s.

*Table 1. Airline affiliations with GDS in the 1990s (Source: Sheldon, 1997)*

| GDS | Airline | Affiliation |
|---|---|---|
| Amadeus | Lufthansa | 29.2% |
|  | Air France | 29,2% |
|  | Iberia | 29,2% |
|  | Continental Airlines | 12.4% |
| Galileo | United Airlines | 38% |
|  | British Airlines | 15% |
|  | Swiss Air | 13% |
|  | KLM Royal Dutch Airlines | 12% |
|  | US Air | 11% |
|  | Alitalia | 8.7% |
|  | Olympic, Air Canada, TAP Air Portugal, Austrian Airlines | 2.3% |
|  | Aer Lingus | |
| Sabre | American Airlines | 100% |
| Worldspan | Delta Airlines | 38% |
|  | Northwest Airlines | 32% |
|  | TransWorld Airlines | 25% |
|  | Abacus | 5% |

*Table 2. Estimated market value of major GDS in the 1990s (Source: Green, 1996)*

| GDS | Million US$ |
|---|---|
| Abacus | 650 |
| Amadeus (System One) | 600 (500) |
| Galileo (Apollo) | 400 (1100) |
| Sabre | 1500-2000 |
| Worldspan | 500 |

*Table 3. GDS scope and penetration (Source: Original by the author)*

| GDS | Scope | Major markets |
|---|---|---|
| Abacus | Southeast Asia | Southeast Asia |
| Amadeus | Worldwide | Europe, South America, USA |
| Apollo | USA, Canada | USA and Canada |
| Galileo | Worldwide | Australia, Europe, New Zealand |
| Sabre | Worldwide | Canada, Europe, USA |
| Worldspan | Worldwide | Europe, Middle East, USA |

## Other Regions Worldwide

In Australia NMC again took over the promotion of the GDS: Sabre is distributed by Fantasia and Southern Cross has the marketing rights to the Galileo system, which hold 53% of the Australian market. The distribution of the GDS in Australia is carried out under the auspices of TIAS (Travel Industries Automated Systems, Ltd.). In New Zealand, all four major GDS are represented but Galileo and SABRE cover 80% of the agencies and 95% of the bookings (Sheldon, 1997).

Finally, in some lesser developed countries, the GDS vendors are aggressively trying to capture the market. In India, for example, the SABRE system is being marketed under the name SITAR and in Latin America, SystemOne from Amadeus is well represented with two national airlines (Varig and Aerolineas Argentinas) being part of the Amadeus consortium. Still, due to the lack of telecommunication infrastructure, numerous countries do not have GDS access (Sheldon, 1997).

Although GDS act on a worldwide basis, they have regionally dominant positions in specific markets (see Table 3), for example the nearly exclusive position of Amadeus in Germany. Overall, however, the four GDS providers Sabre, Amadeus, Galileo and Worldspan hold a worldwide dominant market position as distribution partners of airlines, and intermediaries between airlines and travel intermediaries (Sheldon, 1997).

A comprehensive overview of the historical GDS development and their role in distribution is given by Sloane (1990) and Truitt, Teye, and Farris (1991).

## GDS Functionalities and Extensions

Having discussed the appearance, evolution and diffusion of global distribution systems, this section concentrates on their functionalities and extensions, again focusing on the travel intermediaries, as their agents are the main end users of the systems.

"Even though all GDS have much in common, there are variations in the product and in the contract that must be considered" (Sheldon, 1997, p. 45). A travel agents' choice of GDS involves the consideration of many factors. In general, the system of choice should provide easy access to the most relevant and updated information on the one hand, and a most flexible contract with low costs and excellent service on the other hand.

## GDS Product and Contracts

The first aspect mentioned above refers to direct access links, quicker communication, faster confirmations, and access to last seat availability, as well as an unbiased display of data. Then again the aspects of the contract itself are much more complicated. Historically, contracts issued by the GDS supplier were very restrictive and were often referred to as a "golden handcuff." However, very tight contractual clauses became more flexible over time as, prior to the deregulation, contracts had an infinite length with no option to discontinue or switch systems without paying damage costs. In addition, the GDS had to be used exclusively and required a certain minimum usage level. Finally, productivity pricing was part of the contract, meaning that travel agencies with larger volumes of transactions were charged less by the GDS supplier (Sheldon, 1997). The latter point is still part of most contracts while the other aspects have undergone some change over time. For example, in 1984 the maximum length of contracts was limited to five years, and again reduced to three years in 1992. The U.S. Department of Transportation also decided that exclusivity was illegal (Sheldon, 1997).

It is thus clear that the complexity of GDS contracts is a huge challenge for travel agency managers, and the need for careful analysis of contractual clauses cannot be overemphasized. More room for negotiation lies in the level of service and training provided by the GDS suppliers. For a long time, this aspect has been of some importance, as the GDS have traditionally been command-driven, requiring the use of formats and codes to process inquiries and perform transactions. Compared with menu-driven systems, they are often faster for expert users and are still widely used (Sheldon, 1997). Nevertheless, the dominant Microsoft Windows environment forced the GDS to offer a graphical user interface, this in turn reducing the need for expert training. In addition, as most systems today have computer-aided instruction modules, training issues have become less critical. Finally, the service aspect or rather the repair or replacement of hardware as well as software problems are mostly solved on-site (often by a national service company) or online.

As the handling of information is critical to business for the travel intermediaries, not only the contract and service level agreements, but also the range of functions of the GDS product is of fundamental importance. Sheldon (1997) stated that "indeed, information on travel products, destinations, schedules, fares, rates, and availabilities is their most important product and defines their existence. The more information the travel intermediary can access electronically, the more timely, accurate and efficient service can be provided to the client" (p. 42). Consequently, the entire airline distribution process should be supported by the system. Starting with the request of flight information (schedules, availability and prices) and followed by reservations and bookings, the system also should include a payment and ticketing engine as well as diverse management functionalities (Sabathil, 2002).

## GDS Extensions

As GDS became the first and most important interface and database to be used widely, other industries from the fields of tourism became interconnected with the GDS. Hence the systems contain or connect to various sets of other information, for example concerning transport and accommodation as well as tour operator products. This information is integrated by links to the respective reservation system. For instance, the hotel industry established a system called THISCO (The Hotel Industry Switch COmpany) in 1989 to link major hotel chains. It is owned by 70 major hotel chains and provides common electronic booking interfaces for hotel reservation systems worldwide. The core of this system is called the UltraSwitch, which performs the switching and translation of data formats necessary for the communication of different systems; see Figure 5 for illustration (Werthner & Klein, 1999). In fact, it has been recognised and obviously accepted that GDS networks represent the main distribution channel.

Following Hart (1997), THISCO processed 600 million messages and made 18 million net reservations per year in the mid-1990s. It covered 60% of the worldwide market share and generated US$3.2 billion in room revenue. THISCO also has subsequently adjusted its strategy to the Internet and launched an Internet system travelWeb.

*Figure 5. THISCO system basic structure (Source: Hart, 1997)*

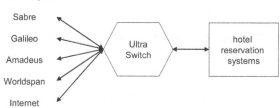

Wizdom, owned by Avis Rent-a-car, is a similar system with access to the GDS world (Sheldon, 1997). It serves a client base of car rental companies and other travel businesses.

## GDS Widespread Functionalities

Having discussed aspects of the GDS products and contracts, as well as their extensions, the overall functionalities can now be recapitulated. In general, Buhalis (1998) described the role of GDS as horizontally integrating airlines and vertically integrating all other tourism suppliers in a system that can be described as the circulation system of the tourism industry. By 1995 the coverage of GDS had expanded to such an extent that they could be termed 'global travel and tourism information and reservation systems' (O'Conner, 1999). Therefore, the widespread functionalities of GDS systems and terminals can be summarised according to Sheldon (1997):

- Flight information: schedules, inventories, availability, fares, fare rules, bookings
- Passenger information: create, modify and store passenger name records (PNRs), itineraries, frequent flyer information, and special requests
- Document printing: facilities to print tickets, boarding passes, and itineraries
- Car rental, hotels, cruises, rail, and tour packages booking*
- Theatre & event ticket and foreign currency ordering*
- Accessing Department of State travel advisories*
- GDS subsection TIMATIC provides information on visas and passports, health, customs, currency controls, and departure taxes*
- Communication service: fax & e-mail*

*Non-airline functions mostly available through today's GDS*

In general, business applications such as word processing and spreadsheets but also data communication programs (e.g., e-mail clients) represent the standard of today's computer infrastructure of travel agents—independently from the GDS.

## GDS Complementing Airline and Airport Systems

Due to their historical evolution, their functionalities and extensions as well as their worldwide spread and dominance, the GDS have become the core systems of operational and strategic airline management. In general, a wide range of business functions of tactical and strategic management are supported: revenue analysis and forecasting, yield management, competition monitoring, maintenance of historical data to predict demand or to design desirable products, and finally management of business models. In addition, numerous information management and decision support systems are used to support core business processes. The operational management requirements for airlines include check-in procedures, allocation of seats, generation of reports and orders, such as flight paths, weather forecasts, load and balance calculations, manifests for airports, in-flight catering orders, and crew rotas (Buhalis, 2003).

However, as management needs and processes have increased in complexity, different distribution and distribution related tasks had to be supported or executed by additional systems. So far in this paper, distribution has been equated with the GDS, but as Figure 6 shows, the understanding of the term "distribution" has to be expanded to cover enlarged management and process challenges. Figure 6 shows different views on distribution, taking airline, airport, intermediary and customer aspects into account.

To deepen the view of Figure 6, the following paragraphs briefly consider some special systems; as described extensively in Buhalis (2003). For example, special flight schedule management systems have been introduced to optimise network performance, taking technical and operational characteristics into consideration, including, for example, equipment, human resources, availability of seats, regulations, demand for traffic, or air traffic control rules. Following the flight scheduling, station control systems monitor all kinds of connections on a hub in an airline's network, including passenger and crew connections. The handling of crew planning processes is supported by crew management systems. These assist in the creation and maintenance of duty rotas, ensuring that they are efficient, complete, legal, economical, and fair.

*Figure 6. Different views on the distribution process (Source: LufthansaSystems, 2006)*

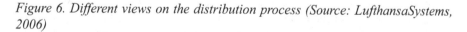
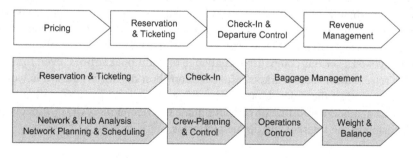

Due to the multiplicity and complexity of all these systems, a separate operations control system is often included to generate alert messages and update all other operational systems, such as flight scheduling, reservation, maintenance, and crew control systems.

In addition, all airlines need airport infrastructure for their operations. Different systems cope with the challenges of requesting landing slots and docking gates, informing about arrivals and departures, altering slots in case of delays, declaring flight paths and coordinating their operations. Other activities at the airport, such as maintenance, refuelling, catering and cleaning as well as the loading and dispatch of aircraft are carried out by different cooperating organisations. The latter interacts closely with the baggage handling and monitoring systems, ensuring that baggage is distributed correctly and no baggage is transported without its owner, as per the International Civil Aviation Organisation (ICAO) regulations.

## The GDS and Airlines State of Business in the 1990s

To round off the historical analysis of first-generation airline reservation systems the airline distribution situation in the 1990s is more closely examined in this section. Economically, the 1990s were challenging for the airlines. Even though the overall passenger numbers increased, ticket prices had to be lowered constantly and profits deteriorated due to growing competition. The challenge of keeping up or even improving current market shares led to different worldwide operations and marketing alliances. Competition between alliances replaced the rivalry between single airlines—introducing an intra-alliance-coopetition, a mix of cooperation and competition. A good example of this new strategy seems to be the combination of different frequent flyer programmes (FFP), which were introduced by airlines earlier, due to the new possibilities of the digitalisation of all reservation based information. These kinds of new marketing strategies represent one possible instrument of cooperation. However, in the beginning, alliances were initiated in terms of code sharing agreements to overcome air traffic regulations, for example concerning departure and touch down slots restrictions. Another key aspect of strategic cooperation has been the stabilisation of the market environment, as competitors became partners and gained bargaining power within a network. These network effects could not only be identified in back office activities but, above all, have been clearly visible and advantageous to the customers. In contrast to today's three large strategic airline alliances (StarAlliance, OneWorld, and SkyTeam) the emergence of low-cost airlines evoked a serious competitive challenge to traditional airlines, even forcing them to retreat from some markets, especially on short distance routes. It is worth noting that most of these developments would not have been possible without the emergence of modern information and communication technology (ICT), especially the diffusion of the Internet and online platforms.

In fact, traditional airlines suffered from their dependency on the GDS supplier throughout the decade. The cost of GDS representation and distribution increased considerably in the 1990s, when it was estimated that average airline expenditure on distribution represented 25-30% of their turnover. Basically, the GDS income rested upon usage based fees, which were rather high compared to the respective costs. In addition, suppliers and intermediaries also had to pay to link their systems to a GDS. Furthermore, airlines relied on travel agencies to distribute their products in exchange for a commission payment, which was usually between 5 to 10% or more. During this era, distribution costs were regarded as a fixed cost (Prideaux, 2001). Doganis (1991) estimated ticketing, including commission and promotion costs, comprised 18% of the total operating cost. The different fees and commissions are represented in detail in Figure 7.

Thus it becomes clear that the fees and commissions (illustrated in Figure 7) in the traditional airlines' distribution chain represented a growing threat to the existence of many airlines. The rising costs of distribution were additionally accompanied by stagnating market segments. Still, until the end of the decade, GDS suppliers represented major players in the tourism value chain, since they provided the main (electronic) link between a huge supplier group and the travel intermediary community. As illustrated throughout this first main part of this chapter, Figure 8 summarises the traditional distribution chain on the airline market.

*Figure 7. Fees and commissions in the airline distribution chain (Source: GAO, 2003)*

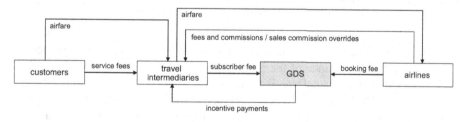

*Figure 8. Traditional distribution chain (Source: Original by the author)*

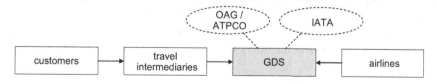

By the mid-1990, this traditional distribution chain had already existed for almost three decades, being a constant in an ever-changing environment. Although the basic structure remained the same, the underlying processes altered over time, concerning all market participants. But, due to the emergence of new information and communication technology the entire distribution process is now almost turned upside down. With the rapid growth of the Internet in the late 1990s, the second stage of information and communication technology (ICT) evolution in the airlines industry ended. The third phase of growth of airline distribution systems is discussed in the following part.

# (R)Evolution of the Airline Market

In the early years of the new millennium the airline industry is facing major challenges subsequent to the privatisation of many national airlines and the establishment of partnerships and global alliances. The airline free market economy has become highly volatile in recent years, especially after facing an economic and psychological crisis in the light of the terror attacks using passenger aircrafts in the United States on September 11, 2001. Furthermore, economic factors such as deteriorating revenues, the fluctuating health of several major national economies, and new competitors such as low-cost carriers have further exacerbated the situation. Thus, deregulation and globalisation forces have brought both new challenges and threats to airline management. These include, for example, over-capacity, high investment pressure, and rising cerosin prices. Consequently, the influence of such wide-ranging factors on the airline business frequently demands rapid adaptations or even a change of business models (Merten & Teufel, 2006).

Above all, the emergence of modern information and communication technology (ICT) has led to a fundamental transformation of the airline market environment. In particular, the appearance of the Internet and the diffusion of the World Wide Web have radically reshaped the distribution environment. This alteration of the distribution structure and processes is examined in the following sections. For this analysis the impact on each market participant group will be considered separately, using the relationships outlined in Figure 8 and starting with the customer. After looking at customer evolution, the changing role of travel intermediaries will be studied. Subsequently, the main section of this chapter analyses the transition from first-generation airline reservation systems (CRS/GDS) to the introduction of second-generation airline core environments. To round off the discussion, the consequences of modern information and communication technology are reviewed from an airlines perspective, including future scenarios, even beyond the distribution systems themselves.

# Customer Evolution

The rapidly increasing popularity of the Internet in the 1990s and its penetration into private households as well as business environments pushed airlines to launch their first Web sites in the mid-1990s. By 1998 most airlines already offered Web sites, which primarily informed visitors about schedules, prices and itineraries as well as other flight and airline-related information. Over time the interaction potential of these platforms grew and the adoption of modern technologies brought new opportunities. Indeed, the Internet provided airlines with the potential to open direct channels to their customers, offering their whole range of services, from flight information (schedules, availability and prices) to reservations and ticketing (including payment options), as well as further value-adding services. As a rapidly increasing number of flights are booked over the Internet, more and more information is being made available to the end consumer. By bringing all necessary booking information right to the customer, online booking engines have enlarged product availability and price transparency.

In this newly created online distribution environment, customers are increasingly using the Internet to obtain travel information and book online. Thus, their behaviour has become more individual, heterogenic, mobile, sovereign, and time-sensitive, as they can take advantage of a far wider range of options than it was previously the case. Furthermore, a broad shift of bookings from classical distribution channels back to the airlines themselves can be observed, while customers seem to swap between channels during the buying process. Therefore, in future, a multi-channel distribution environment will be the most likely scenario (Schmidt, 2004). Figure 9 underlines these trends.

*Figure 9. Trends of online distribution on the airline market (Source: von Götz, 2005)*

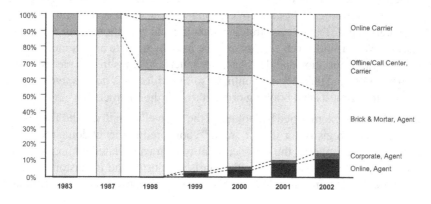

So far, the discussion focused on the customer as an individual. However, customers as a category also can be subdivided into leisure customers as well as unmanaged and managed business travel customers. The business analyst PhoCusWright Market Research forecasts that the online part of leisure and unmanaged business travel bookings would double in size in the period from 2003 to 2006, being worth some US$78 billion in the U.S. In addition US$36 billion is predicted to be spent online on the managed corporate market (N.N., 2005). On closer examination of the latter point, it can be noted that in particular large-scale businesses hold strong framework agreements with single airlines. However, in the corporate market, companies more and more allow their employees to make their own bookings online, but within the rules set by their employer. These online booking services are thus proving extremely popular. Moreover, low-cost airlines encourage, and in most cases require, customers to buy their tickets online. In addition, America's and Europe's market-shaking shift to online travel services and bookings is yet to take off in the huge Asian market, for which an enormous potential also is forecast. These trends, along with ever-changing customer behaviour and new airline strategies represent a threat to travel intermediaries, to be considered in the next section.

## The Changing Role of Travel Intermediaries

Obviously, the establishment of direct channels to customers also marked a turning point in the relationship between airlines and travel intermediaries. As the Internet allowed airlines to bypass travel agencies, commission payments from airlines were lowered or even cancelled. Indeed, tensions peaked when airline management embarked on its policy of reducing or eliminating the existing commission structure. In turn, this zero commission forced travel agencies to move to charging customers a fee for products and services offered (Prideaux, 2001).

Since electronic connectivity brings air travel products directly into the hands of the consumer, this poses a potential threat to the existence of travel intermediaries. But in the same way, information and communication technology is threatening the agencies; they also mitigate the threat by creating value-added products and services, and by integrating ICT into their strategic planning and operational processes. For instance, the World Wide Web can not only be used by them to access more information about transportation and destination products, which is in turn passed on to the customer. Offering their services online also can widen their geographical range when receiving requests and booking orders through the Internet.

These trends can be exemplified by looking at the ".travel" initiative. The Tralliance Corporation is the registry for these ".travel" sponsored top level domain names. Its major aim is to improve the Internet identity of travel-related companies and to increase the level of trust between the tourism industry and its customers. For this, the initiative features an authentication of a registrant's industry credentials and name(s) eligibility by an independent third party. With this confirmed identity, a registrant lifts its business out of anonymity of today's Internet. Beyond this, a first of its kind central online directory has been established, based on a unique vocabulary to match providers travel products and services precisely with consumers needs worldwide (www.directory.travel). The success of this initiative is however yet to be confirmed as the whole system was only launched on January 2, 2006 (Tralliance, 2006).

Beyond the external opportunities offered by the Internet, modern ICT also can be used to optimise, simplify and extend current internal business processes, for example, by sending tickets or booking information via e-mail. Finally, online platforms from airlines, which enable the bypass of travel intermediaries from an airlines point of view, of course also can be used by the travel agents themselves. In doing so, they in turn bypass GDS, no longer relying on a terminal infrastructure and tight contracts with the GDS.

## GDS and Beyond

Due to their historical development, the GDS providers have established supremacy in the airline industry and its traditional distribution chain. They have proven to be reliable, they succeeded in standardising the products included and still hold a dominant market position (see Figure 10) (Merten & Teufel, 2006).

Although the GDS provide airline managers with powerful management tools, for example to identify new market segments and maximize yields, the use of GDS

*Figure 10. GDS air bookings year-on-year percent growth at month end (Source: Sattel, 2005)*

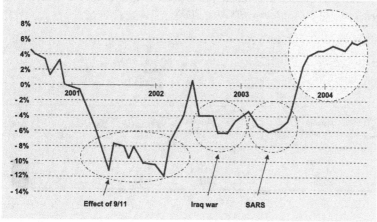

adds to the overall distribution costs (Prideaux, 2001). On the one hand, the systems themselves have become more and more expensive in terms of maintenance and upgrades, with respect to finance and personnel (Werthner & Klein, 1999). On the other hand, fees and commissions increased over time as already shown in Figure 7. As Graham Atkinson, a United Airlines Senior Vice-President, noted, "The company spends about US$250 million on GDS fees annually" (Tedeschi, 2005). In fact, the margin of airline market participants correlates with their relative dominant market position and is especially high for the GDS companies, as shown in Figure 11.

Similarly, Atkinson (ibid.) remarked, that "there has been awareness in the industry for some time that the price-value relationship there is out of sync. Anytime that happens, you will ultimately find someone with a better solution to the business problem. That is what has happened" (Tedeschi, 2005).

In consequence, airlines and travel agencies have sought for possibilities to bypass the GDS as distribution intermediaries, not least because GDS fees amount to approximately $12 per ticket (LufthansaSystems, 2006). Parallel to this development and due to rapid technological progress, alternative distribution platforms have achieved maturity and market penetration in recent years, which has enabled airlines to compete directly with the traditional distribution channels. Still the airlines' backend systems are the GDS, but new technologies opened up new opportunities with alternative front ends for new distribution channels, which therefore not directly involve the GDS companies any more. This competition has placed increasing pressure on the GDS suppliers.

To give an example, in 2004, Northwest Airlines cancelled, with immediate effect, a new fee charged to travel agencies for a round-trip domestic ticket booked through global distribution systems. Northwest hoped the move would drive customers and travel agents to its Web site to buy tickets, which did not include ticketing fees. In

*Figure 11. Margins of air travel participants in correlation with their relative dominant market position (Source: von Götz, 2005)*

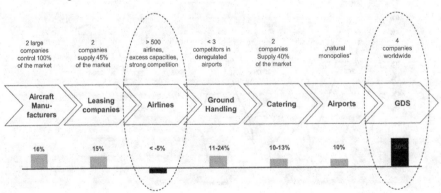

response, Sabre said they would no longer prominently display Northwest fares on the schedules they provided to travel intermediaries. In consequence, Northwest sued Sabre for changing the way it displayed fares on its reservation system and Sabre sued the carrier for alleged violation of contract (von Götz, 2005)

This example shows that the Internet enables airlines to regain control over the distribution of their products by bypassing the travel intermediaries and enforcing a zero-commission. Likewise, travel agencies use these online platforms to become more independent from the GDS suppliers. These distribution platforms were first set up by airlines by adapting the front end of their distribution systems. As airlines are not only trying to bypass the GDS in the distribution chain, but also search for opportunities to replace the existing GDS as backend systems themselves, the GDS suppliers have to reflect on their own strategy. The first step for GDS suppliers has been, not surprisingly, to counter with their own online booking engines like amadeus. net. However, having to deal with the problem of brand (non)recognition, they also have started to offer their complete range of services under new brand names, as they have developed or bought special alternative Internet platforms such as opodo. com (Amadeus) or lastminute.com (Sabre). Further, GDS providers have reacted by expanding the functionality of their old platforms using modern technologies—but still having old legacy technology in the centre of their systems. Consequently, and in addition to the adoption of front ends of GDS, also the backend systems were due for redesign.

In addition, in July, 2004, the U.S. Department of Transportation formally phased out all GDS regulations. This deregulation empowered suppliers to re-evaluate their participation in the four major global distribution systems. Finally, GDS became fully independent and no longer airline owned. Airlines were thus able to selectively distribute inventory at different levels in the four systems. Therefore, with the deregulation of GDS, it was no longer possible to rely upon a single GDS as the sole source of all air travel information. As a single source information distribution model, the GDS were no longer sufficient to ensure total content availability. Therefore new platforms were needed to aggregate disparate content and enable comparative shopping from multiple sources of fares and inventory. These platforms should seamlessly provide content from traditional distribution sources (GDS), direct connections to emerging suppliers and Web-based inventories as well as private fares and Internet fare sources.

These developments clearly show that the GDS suppliers have to fear for their traditional core business. As Holger Taubmann, CEO of Amadeus Germany, admitted in 2005, due to growing online bookings the whole classical GDS market will stagnate or even decrease in the long run as increasing cost pressure and declining margins are foreseeable (Genger, 2005). Therefore GDS providers today have to re-evaluate their business strategy. Nevertheless, airlines will still rely on the traditional distribution system at least for some years.

In the light of these challenges and threats, GDS companies turn their business strategy from travel distribution system and content providers to travel IT solution providers with new technologies (Merten & Teufel, 2006). For example Amadeus changed its name to Amadeus IT Group SA and identified three future business fields (Amadeus, 2006): the travel distribution business area covers all aspects related to the traditional GDS (more and more building on modern technologies), including additional tools and services. Second, Amadeus e-travel provides online travel technology and corporate travel management solutions for airlines, corporations, travel agencies and other online travel businesses. Next to this e-commerce division, the airline IT services business area offers a new second generation IT platform: Amadeus Altéa Customer Management Solution (CMS). It is built on open system technology and consists of three different modules: Amadeus Altéa Reservation (sell), Amadeus Altéa Inventory (plan) and Amadeus Altéa Departure Control (fly). This CMS platform has been designed scalable for airlines, low cost carriers and as well as airline networks or alliances (Amadeus, 2006).

Despite all these developments, decisions and improvements, GDS suppliers have been struggling for some years, as new companies appeared on the market and offered simpler and cheaper solutions—so called GDS new entrants (GNE). Although, as start-up companies, GNE could not effectively compete the GDS in all fields, they increased the competition and enabled airlines and travel agencies cheaper access to the market and new opportunities.

## GDS New Entrants (GNE)

Due to the GDS deregulation and the emergence of alternative platforms for direct sales, the limits of the original GDS and their underlying technologies became more and more obvious in the last years. Additionally, as the number of alternative platforms for direct sales grew, GDS became unable to cover the full range of services on the market. Consequently, different kinds of work around systems, combining the "legacy" GDS with new technology appeared on the market and called themselves GDS new entrants (GNE; also known as global new entrants). GNE providers used modern technologies to allow airlines to close this gap and pool the offers from GDS and other distribution platforms. Table 4 gives a short overview of the leading GNE players on the market, listing some highlights of the different companies.

All of these companies target low cost distribution with their systems, while recognizing the need to aggregate content from all kinds of different sources. FareLogix is exemplarily in its approach and will therefore be examined more closely. The company currently provides solutions with multiple source content to some of the largest travel companies in Canada and the United States, including Navigant International, American Express, and Carlson Leisure Group Services. The centrepiece of the FareLogix system environment is the FareLogix FLX platform, as illustrated

*Table 4. GDS new entrants (GNE) credible players (Source: Lewitton, 2005)*

| GNE Company | Highlights |
|---|---|
| ITA Software | Founder: Jeremy Wertheimer, PhD (MIT)<br>Established in 1996, privately held.<br>Built industry-leading shopping engine.<br>Supplied code for Orbitz launch.<br>Clients include agencies, suppliers and GDS. |
| G2SwitchWorks | Founder: Alex Zoghlin,<br>built 3 sucessful tech. companies, including Orbitz.<br>Privately held start-up (2004).<br>Employing existing direct connects to<br>AA, CO, NW, UA and others. |
| FareLogix INC. | Founder: Rick Gossage<br>CEO: Jim Davidson, ex-CEO Amadeus US<br>Established in 1998, privately held.<br>Built industry leading contract management system<br>and call centre travel booking applications.<br>Clients include major agencies and consolidators. |

in Figure 12. Following FareLogix (2006), it represents a multi-GDS gateway that connects to all four GDS, using structured data streams that normalize the communication in a common application programming interface (API). The multi-GDS gateway provides independence from the single-source GDS model and allows the integration of multiple GDS inventories at an individual-itinerary level. In addition, direct connections to supplier systems can be established for real-time availability. And finally, as new Web-based direct distribution platforms have diffused, content from low-cost carriers and online travel sites is integrated via appropriate interfaces. Consequently, FareLogix banks on advanced Web search technology to capture and aggregate content from different online portals to provide travel agents and travellers with a comprehensive integrated inventory solution.

As illustrated in Figure 12, the FareLogix FLX platform consists of a set of different systems. First of all, the Distribution Manager (DM) is a business rules engine, which controls the supply and handling of source information. The sources are the different GDS, direct supplier connections and Web inventories. The Master Itinerary (MI) integrates the supplied source information into a so called super-PNR (passenger name record), which acts as a single record repository for all travel itinerary information. Furthermore, the Virtual Fare Store (VFS) incorporates fares from the Airline Tariff Publishing Company (ATPCO) and private fares from the Fare Management System (FMS) to calculate the lowest fare for each itinerary. The FMS itself provides a new flexible platform to store private fares from airlines, no

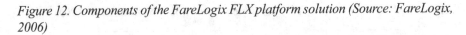

*Figure 12. Components of the FareLogix FLX platform solution (Source: FareLogix, 2006)*

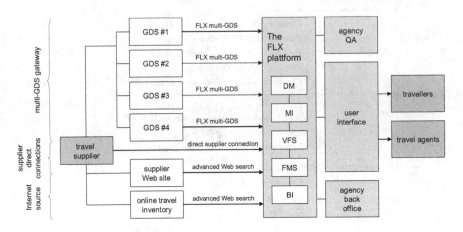

longer requiring the cumbersome reliance on traditional ATPCO fare filing. This independent faring and pricing engine allows airlines a new level of distribution channel management that did not exist in the ATPCO-driven, GDS-centric environment. Finally, the business intelligence (BI) module primarily serves reporting purposes on operational performance and vendor analysis. For a more comprehensive description of the FLX platform, see FareLogix (2006).

Going one step further, travel intermediaries and customers can either access the FLX platform by a standard certified user interface or use an existing neutral agent point-of-sale (POS) application. Based on an API technology, it also allows simple interfaces to agency quality assurance (QA) and back office accounting systems. Obviously, the FLX platform is built on open standards using Web technologies such as "the Extensible Markup Language (XML), simple object access protocol (SOAP), Web Services Description Language (WSDL), and the universal description, discovery, and integration (UDDI) open standards over an Internet protocol (IP) backbone. This robust open architecture enables seamless integration of disparate inventory sources. Furthermore, the platform uses standard Open Travel Alliance (OTA) XML schemas and traditional EDIFACT communication protocols to provide suppliers with familiar communication methodologies" (FareLogix, 2006).

In conclusion, referring to the CRS/GDS as first-generation airline distribution systems, the GNE platforms can be seen as a transitional solution, which will presumably have a growing importance in the airline distribution market in forthcoming years. The GNE platforms provide airlines with a sophisticated and cheaper solution and the possibility to circumvent the GDS companies as distribution intermediaries;

still the GDS remain the systems in which airlines store all their business critical data. But, as airlines are offering more and more information and functionalities via direct connections (for example the FLX platform), they increasingly have to develop their own systems, often with the aim of becoming totally independent from the GDS. With regard to the growing complexity of airline systems, not only in terms of distribution, but also with regard to internal and external processes and management, it can be foreseen that second-generation airline core environments will emerge (also including new systems of the GDS providers). Of course, airline distribution will remain their central focus. As system development is generally not part of the airlines' core competences, the need for airline IT providers has risen. These providers can either position themselves as a full service provider of airline systems and supporting IT solutions, the latter going beyond airline core processes (so-called value added services), or they can be a specialised supplier of only these value adding systems.

## Second-Generation Airline Core Environments

In the current changing market environment, airlines are offering their products through a wide range of distribution channels. Nevertheless, although circumventing the GDS in the distribution chain through direct channels (for example online platforms), the airline system environment still relies on the GDS. Therefore, if airlines are to regain total control over the whole distribution process they will be forced to undertake a radical shift towards completely new airline core system environments. Regaining control means not only cutting costs and eliminating commissions. The new systems also can provide new kinds of management information, while supporting a much broader range of operational and management processes.

In addition to new IT platforms of traditional GDS companies, new airline IT full service providers offer these new systems and promise flexible solutions for quick reactions in a fast paced market environment. In general, the requirements for a second-generation core environment range from multi-channel distribution and distribution cost control to immediate adjustment possibilities of core processes to keep the system in line with the business strategy.

Different new airline full service IT providers have emerged on the market recently and have developed completely new information system environments. An example of such a system in terms of the fundamental change from first to second-generation systems is that of Lufthansa Systems, whose new system is called FACE: Future Airline Core Environment. The struggle of global distribution systems will inevitably "be an opportunity for flexible and cost-effective solutions to move into spotlight", predicted Wolfgang F.W. Gohde, CEO of Lufthansa Systems, at a press conference in Frankfurt/Germany on June 24, 2005 (LufthansaSystems, 2006). Lufthansa Systems is currently investing 40 million euros in the future development of its

*Figure 13. FACE—Future Airline Core Environment by Lufthansa Systems (Source: LufthansaSystems, 2006)*

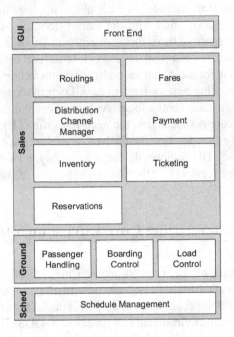

airline systems—regarding FACE as the cornerstone of the new information based landscape (LufthansaSystems, 2006).

The FACE platform uses a modular approach, enabling a suitable fit for different business models: from classic network carriers with global route networks, to low-cost airlines with point-to-point transportation. Furthermore all business models can be used simultaneously within a single airline or airline group. FACE supports the classic core processes of passenger airlines, from inventory, schedule distribution, reservations, ticketing and departure control, to passenger service processes as classified in Figure 13.

"FACE enables airlines to freely choose their favourite distribution channels," stated Gohde (ibid.). "This makes airlines more flexible and allows them to respond faster to market changes. FACE provides open interfaces, thus ensuring seamless data communication between different technology platforms—including airlines using different systems" (LufthansaSystems, 2006). The modular approach further enables airlines to adopt different parts of the system over time and adapt them to their business processes and requirements. The different parts or functional areas introduced in Figure 13 support the following business processes (LufthansaSystems, 2006):

- All schedule management processes support the creation of schedules and the conversion into marketable offers, thus allowing the distribution to all relevant partners.

- Passenger ground handling processes maintain the passenger handling from check-in to boarding, including additional customer care activities. The management of flight-related processes involved in loading an aircraft and preparing it for departure also is included.

- Sales processes range from the management of the inventory via reservation and sale to the issuing of and payment for a ticket. Special emphasis is placed on enabling airlines to actively manage and effectively control sales through the various traditional and upcoming distribution channels in a deregulated, competitive, and agile market environment.

- Finally, the FACE front-end graphical user interface (GUI) provides the business process logic with workflow orientation and a high degree of automation.

Beside the fact that FACE is GDS neutral, it operates under the IATA code L1 so that it can be run as a computer reservation system by Lufthansa Systems, and therefore represents a potentially fully equivalent system to replace the GDS backend. Of course, connections to GDS, GNE, and Internet sources will still be possible; to keep the backdoors open for all intermediaries and customers still relying on these kinds of information sources. Enabling airlines to combine different distribution channels, FACE also is designed for use in airlines alliances, and will therefore be marketed both inside and outside of the StarAlliance.

## New Management Challenges for Airlines

At the beginning of this part of the chapter, general airline management challenges relating to economic factors were already discussed. This section therefore concentrates on the opportunities and threats for airlines with regard to distribution. In fact, distribution is increasingly regarded as one of the most critical managerial aspects, as it can determine the competitiveness and profitability of organisations.

In the airline business, distribution has always been ICT driven, in the past heavily relying on the first-generation of airline reservation systems (CRS/GDS). However, modern information and communication technology has provided airlines with a completely new set of diverse opportunities. Today, airlines can take advantage of such opportunities by using the Internet as a distribution channel, starting with airline-owned Web sites, alliance booking engines, electronic intermediaries and other kinds of sales tools, including electronic auctioning of unsold seats. Airlines have managed to bypass intermediaries and to enforce zero commission, and also regained control over distribution. All of these different options represent a potential threat to travel intermediaries and GDS suppliers, as examined throughout the previous sections. As a result, the airlines' distribution chain has undergone a fundamental transformation. An overview of these transformations is given in Figure 14.

In this highly competitive market environment, airlines of all sizes have to react swiftly to market trends and constantly cut costs. In fact, increased cost pressure seems to have become a constant. In the past, management often concentrated on cost cutting while improving efficiency and effectiveness—traditionally targeting fields such as engineering, engine efficiency, air traffic control systems, administration, wage costs, and improvement in the design of aircrafts and related systems. With the emergence of the Internet, however, airline managers were enabled to shift the emphasis from these previous fields to a focus on reducing distribution costs. To round off the analysis of today's distribution environment from the different perspectives throughout the previous section, Figure 15 reflects on the different stages of distribution technologies and providers.

Overall, modern information and communication technology has led to a fundamental reshaping of the airlines' distribution, internal processes as well as the market structure and balance of power. As the ICT induced opportunities for airlines become obvious in terms of distribution processes, the possible use of modern information and communication technology beyond the distribution rises. The following section concentrates on these new efforts and future developments, going one step further beyond distribution.

*Figure 14. Transformation of the distribution chain (Source: Original by the author)*

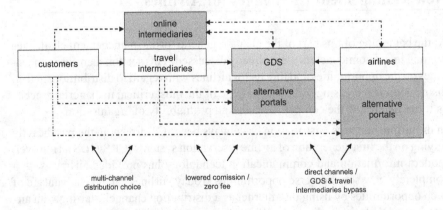

*Figure 15. Stages of evolution in distribution technologies and providers (Source: LufthansaSystems, 2006)*

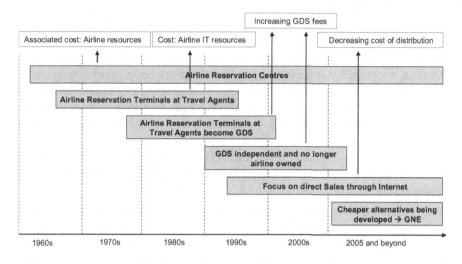

## Mobile ICT in and Beyond Distribution

In recent years, not only "traditional" information and communication technology have developed rapidly. Increasingly, also the impact of mobile technologies has to be considered when planning and developing business solutions and system environments. For companies as well as private and business customers, mobile networks and end devices represent new opportunities and are becoming widely used standards. Clearly both airlines and other distribution channel providers are thinking about means of transferring and integrating existing online booking engines to mobile platforms. As successful general mobile platforms (for example, i-mode or Vodafone live!) vary markedly depending on providers and countries/continents, it seems difficult to identify a representative solution among those available. Except for some information services, so far mobile ticketing is the only available mobile distribution service going beyond the booking process itself. Principally, it is based on a similar assumption to electronic ticketing, that is, clients who book online also possess an e-mail address and a mobile end device respectively, to receive their booking confirmation. This mobile ticket could replace not only the printed invoice and booking confirmation, but also the whole paper-based ticket. In addition, the electronic ticket is the basic precondition for most available self-check-in procedures at airports. Again, the check-in procedure marks today's end of a seamless electronic distribution process, due to the necessity of passport control and registration of baggage.

To return to the discussion on the use of mobile end devices, it can be observed that a growing number of passengers are carrying their notebooks, organisers or mobile phones on to the aircraft. On the ground, that is, at airports, these devices can be widely used, encouraging airports to ensure good network coverage or even install wireless access points, so far often been restricted to business and first class lounges. Furthermore, a survey from WirelessCabin (2006) shows that business customers in particular, increasingly demand on-flight connectivity. The survey identified 30% of these customers as potential frequent users. The demand for services on-board ranges from news (84%), e-mail (78%), Internet (73%) and virtual private network (VPN) access to the company's intranet (66%) to mobile telephony (60%) and video conferencing (16%).

For these reasons different interest groups of industrial and scientific background work on new technological and business solutions for a new generation of in-flight entertainment and communication systems (IECS). For example, as part of the European initiative (European Union contract no IST 2001 37466) the WirelessCabin project has been launched with the aim to clarify a possible system and business structure. Based on these elaborations and different scientific publications on numerous mobile technology conferences the basic network architecture can be displayed as shown in Figure 16.

Following Jahn et al. (2002a, 2002b), a future IECS will consist of three different parts: the cabin segment, space or transport segment, and the ground segment. Passengers are offered mobile access with their own notebooks, PDAs, or mobile phones via different wireless technologies, which are combined in a so called col-

*Figure 16. Network architecture of in-flight entertainment and communication systems (Sources: Jahn, Holzbock, & Werner, 2002a; Jahn, Holzbock, Diaz, & Werner 2002b)*

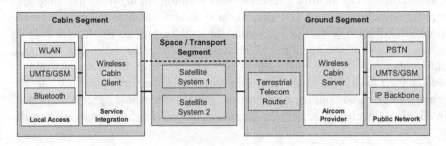

*Figure 17. Parties and relationships involved in the new business model (Source: WirelessCabin, 2006)*

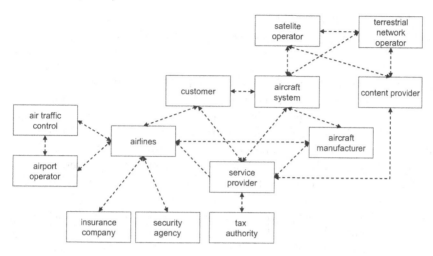

lectively mobile heterogenous network (CMHN). After the service integration, the wireless cabin client establishes a satellite connection to the terrestrial server, which in is handled by the aircom provider. As part of the ground segment, this server also provides links to fix-line and mobile networks as well as the Internet and other networks as for example corporate intranets or virtual private networks (VPN). The complexity of establishing such new systems can be generally underlined by showing an abstract diagram of the parties involved as well as their relations in Figure 17.

Due to customer expectance and the complexity of these new systems, it is not surprising that Boeing and Airbus as the major aircraft companies are investing in the development of innovative new on-board systems. The current communication and entertainment infrastructure in airplanes is planned to be completely replaced within this decade by new systems called "Connexion by Boeing" or "OnAir", the latter being a joint venture system of Airbus, SITA, and Tenzing. In both cases, the business model involves a large number of parties as pointed out in Figure 17 and represents a major challenge to all participating players. This shows on a more general level that the entire distribution process, including all related processes, is a complex phenomenon—inter alia caused and affected by information and communication technology.

# Conclusion

Throughout this chapter, it has been shown that information and communication technology (ICT) has always been a driver of change in the airline industry. For over four decades, ICT has repeatedly affected and determined the way of airline business. In turn, the airline industry also has been a driver of evolution for the ICT sector. First, ICT helped the airline industry to lift-off in the 1950s and 1960s, by providing new methods of handling the rising flood of passenger related information. Indeed, ICT soon became critical to business in the distribution process. As a result of ongoing system enhancements and due to the influence of deregulation on the airline market, original computer reservation systems (CRS) slipped into a concentrating process, which led to an interconnected network of different systems, calling themselves global distribution systems (GDS). Over several decades, the GDS suppliers grew to be major players on the airline market, handling the distribution of products for the airlines, with the aid of travel intermediaries as main access to the end consumer. Finally, modern information and communication technology has led to a fundamental reshaping of the airlines' internal processes as well as the market structure and balance of power, resulting in a need for completely new airline core system environments. In this process the traditional distribution chain has been transformed into a form of multi-channel distribution environment as illustrated in Figure 18.

In this, all different market players form an interconnected network, where every action directly influences the entire network and vice versa. Due to this cross-linking the complexity of management decisions increases, and enforces a much stronger competitive situation. As a result, a duality of competitive and cooperative relationships coexists. Therefore future research ought to examine the network effects and challenges of the so-called coopetition in the airlines industry's cross-influenced network. A particular focus should be on the different market players

*Figure 18. The airline industry's electronic multi-channel distribution environment (Source: Merten & Teufel, 2006)*

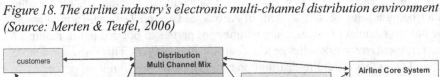
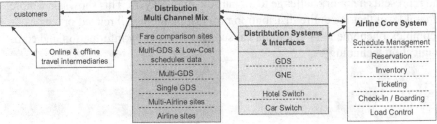

in this multi-channel distribution environment. For further details see Merten and Teufel (2006).

This chapter aimed to provide a comprehensive overview of the transformation of the distribution process in the airline industry empowered by information and communication technology. Today, airlines, old and new intermediaries as well as the customers are all affected by changes made possible through the Internet. While airlines are successfully using the opportunities provided by the Internet, travel agents quarrel with lowered commissions and are forced to charge customer fees as they have not yet identified the potential of the World Wide Web for their sector. Customers, on the other hand, drift off to online services using the new diversity of distribution channels, exploring and exploiting the possibilities of their newly gained independence.

# References

Amadeus. (2006). *Amadeus: Your technology partner*. Retrieved March 31, 2006, from http://www.amadeus.com/

Bennett, M. (1988). Information technology and the travel agency. *Geographical Papers, 105*, University of Reading, p. 42.

Boberg, K., & Collison, F. (1985). Computer reservation systems and airline competition. *Tourism Management*, 174-183.

Buhalis, D. (1998). Strategic use of information technologies in the tourism industry. *Tourism Management, 19*(5), 409-421.

Buhalis, D. (2003). *Etourism: Information technology for strategic tourism management*. Harlow, UK: Financial Times Prentice Hall.

Copeland, D., & McKenney, J. L. (1988, September). Airline reservation systems: Lessons from history. *MIS Quarterly*, 353-370.

Doganis, R. (1991). *Flying off course: The economics of international airlines*. London: Routledge.

FareLogix. (2006). *The new multi-source environment*. Retrieved March 31, 2006, from http://www.farelogix.com/solutions/index.html#ebt

Feldman, J. (1994, August). Airline distribution under siege—at last. *Air Transport World*, 35-43.

GAO. (2003). Airline ticketing—impact of changes in the airline ticket distribution industry. *United States General Accounting Office, Washington, Report to Congressional Requesters*. Retrieved July 20, 2005, from http://www.gao.gov/new.items/d03749.pdf

Genger, J. (2005, June 21). Amadeus fürchtet um sein kerngeschäft. *Financial Times Deutschland,* 6.

Green, D. (1996, March 9). Airline ticket shops bridge the atlantic. *Financial Times.*

Hart, P. (1997). *Tourism industry innovation in securing online sales.* Paper presented at the 4th ENTER Conference, Edinburgh.

Inkpen, G. (1994). *Information technology for travel and tourism.* London: Pitman Publishing.

Jahn, A., Holzbock, M., & Werner, M. (2002a): *Dimensioning of aeronautical satellite services.* Paper presented at the 53rd International Astronautical Conference.

Jahn, A., Holzbock, M., Diaz, N. R., & Werner, M. (2002b): *Passenger multimedia service concept via future satellite systems.* DGLR Jahrbuch.

Kärcher, K. (1997). *Reinventing the package holiday business.* Wiesbaden: Deutscher Universitäts-Verlag.

Lewitton, D. (2005). Emerging changes in travel distribution economics and technologies: Letting the gne out of the bottle. *Travel Technology Congress.* Berlin: ITB.

LufthansaSystems. (2006). *FACE module concept.* Retrieved January 21, 2006, from http://www.lhsystems.de/en/resource/document/pdf/br/br_face_einleger.pdf

Merten, P., & Teufel, S. (2006). *Co-opetition in an electronic multi-channel distribution environment: The airline industry case.* Paper presented at the EURAM, 6th Annual Conference: Energizing European Management, Oslo, Norway.

N. N. (2005, October 1). Flying from the computer. *The Economist.*

O'Conner, P. (1999). *Electronic distribution technology in the tourism and hospitality industries.* New York: CABI Publishing.

Prideaux, B. (2001). Airline distribution systems: The challenge and opportunity of the Internet. In D. Buhalis & E. Laws (Eds.), *Tourism distribution channels: Practices, issues and transformations* (pp. 213-227). London: Continuum.

Sabathil, S. (2002). *Lehrbuch des linienflugverkehrs* (4th ed.). Frankfurt/Main: Schule für Touristik Datz und Weigand.

Sattel, J. (2005). New opportunities in travel it and sales, *Travel Technology Congress.* Berlin: ITB.

Schmidt, I. D. (2004). *Kunden in mehrkanalsystemen—eine prozessorientierte analyse des kanalwahlverhaltens von kunden in der reisebranche.* University of St.Gallen, Switzerland.

Sheldon, P. J. (1997). *Tourism information technology.* Oxford, UK; New York: CAB International.

SITA. (2006). *Sita corporate profile*. Retrieved 31 March, 2006, from http://www.sita.com/News_Centre/Corporate_profile/default.htm

Sloane, J. (1990). Latest developments in aviation crss. *EIU Travel & Tourism Analyst, 4*, 5-15.

Tedeschi, B. (2005, January 31). *E-commerce report*.

Tralliance. (2006). *Tralliance.Travel registry*. Retrieved January 21, 2006, from http://www.tralliance.info/

Truitt, L., Teye, V., & Farris, M. (1991). The role of computer reservation systems. *Tourism Management*, 21-36.

von Götz, G. (2005). Flexibility—it all boils down to the right choice, *Travel Technology Congress*. Berlin: ITB.

Werthner, H., & Klein, S. (1999). *Information technology and tourism: A challenging relationship*. Wien; New York: Springer.

Williams, G. (1994). *The airline industry and the impact of deregulation* (revised ed.). Aldershot: Avebury Aviation.

WirelessCabin. (2006). *Advanced communications for aircraft passengers*. Retrieved January 21, 2006, from http://www.wirelesscabin.com

## Chapter V

# Design and Implementation Approaches for Location-Based, Tourism-Related Services

George Kakaletris, University of Athens, Greece

Dimitris Varoutas, University of Athens, Greece

Dimitris Katsianis, University of Athens, Greece

Thomas Sphicopoulos, University of Athens, Greece

## Abstract

*The globally observed recession of mobile services market has pushed mobile network operators into looking for opportunities to provide value added services on top of their high cost infrastructures. Recent advances in mobile positioning technologies enable services that make use of the mobile user location information, offering intuitive, attractive applications to the potential customer. Mobile tourism services are among the primary options to be considered by service providers for this new market. This chapter presents the key concepts, capabilities, and considerations of infrastructures and applications targeted to the mobile tourist, covering data and content delivery, positioning, systems' interactions, platforms, protocols, security, and privacy as well as business modelling aspects.*

# Introduction

During the last decade of the 20th century, wireless data networks have invaded everyday life and have gradually started taking over areas traditionally considered as being only suited to wired applications. Due to their versatility, wireless telecommunications systems have become a widespread standard, leading to hardware price drops and radical quality increases. Today there exist a bunch of technologies that allow the delivery of information to mobile or wireless devices and their users, all presenting different characteristics in performance/quality, autonomy and cost. These technological advances accompanied by the reach of the saturation level (Ellinger, Barras, & Jackel, 2002; Gruber, 2005; Gruber & Verboven, 2001) in the mobile telephony market pushed hardware vendors and network and service providers into looking for new business opportunities. The needs of tourism-related information provision and services were amongst the first to be considered for new applications in the field of communication devices.

In traditional fixed systems, the location of a terminal and its user was a part of its identity and remained constant for a long period during its lifetime. In this new mobility era, this observation no longer holds: the physical position of the user might be highly variable, introducing a whole new range of issues and opportunities to be taken into account. The use of intelligent systems that exploit the positional information of the client, accompanied by the ability to provide feedback over a wireless medium, can lead to the provision of innovative highly intuitive services that were not available in the near past (Grajski & Kirk, 2003; Kakaletris, Varoutas, Katsianis, Sphicopoulos, & Kouvas, 2004; Rao & Minakakis, 2003; Staab & Werthner, 2002; Yilin, 2000).

But, although mobile telephony networks offer maximum mobility, they are not the only means for providing location-based services (LBS) for tourism. Local fixed wireless networks in their various forms are another of the modern and popular technologies facilitating relevant services. In addition to telecommunication systems and from a technological perspective, there are a wide range of other systems such as global positioning system (GPS) (Dana, 1994; ETSI, 2006; GARMIN, n.d.), or ID tags (Bohn & Mattern, 2004; Tarumi, Morishita, & Kambayashi, 2000) which might have a significant role in the development and deployment of e-tourism applications based on location information.

This chapter presents the technological concepts associated with the provision of location-aware tourism-related services under a service-oriented approach capable of supporting open value chains and to lead financially viable open and powerful communication systems. The rest of the chapter is organised as follows: The "Background" section presents the technological and business background of location-based services; the "Technology Overview" section gets into details of the technological aspects and issues raised in the domains of positioning and data/content delivery, which are fundamental elements of the examined class of services; the section on "Mobile Tourism Services" captures the specific needs and opportunities in the specific application area and presents issues and considerations with respect to integrating the various parts into an open system capable of delivering such services. In the "Conclusion," technology and market conclusions and trends are presented. Finally, due to the large number of acronyms and the frequency of their appearance, a table of acronyms is provided at the end of the chapter in order to ease reading through it (see Appendix).

# Background

The application of the above-mentioned technologies and concepts in tourism gave birth to the ubiquitous tourism[1] concept (OTC, 2003), which refers to the existence and access of tourism related services at any place, any time. Although tourism-related services are mostly related to content provision, more applications can be identified. In its entirety, content provision for e-tourism covers a large number of thematic areas: culture, urgencies, transportation, events, and so on. Thus, content might be both temporally and spatially labelled (LoVEUS, 2002; M-Guide, 2002). In addition, information seeking and avalanche-like content provision might guide the user to areas quite outside her/his initial focus areas.

The information technology (IT), the Internet and the mobile telecommunications revolutions of the last decades of the 20th century made it possible for enterprises to enable massive access to their applications and data. Users are able to access applications and information through a variety of integrated "channels" including the Internet, mobile telephony, and voice interfaces and thus bring forward the concept of multi-channel architectures. Consequently, multi-channel content delivery and media-independent publishing have emerged in order to address the demand for personalised content that can adapt to the end-user device capabilities. Devices, such as PDAs, cellular phones, smartphones, and television set-top boxes, introduced the need for additional channels for publishing content. The approach of maintaining independent content sets per channel proved to be highly inefficient in terms of maintenance, until the wide adoption of eXtensible Markup Language (XML) and related technologies, such as eXtensible Stylesheet Language / XSL Transformation (XSL/XSLT), offered a standard solution to this challenge.

Technology is not the sole reason behind the emergence of the ubiquitous tourism concept. The existing 2/2.5G[2] mobile market has reached saturation as analysts have predicted, but its effects have only been acknowledged lately, due to the high expectations of the emerging 3G[3] markets. The costs of licensing (Andersson, Hulten, & Valiente, 2005; Katsianis, Welling, Ylonen, Varoutas, Sphicopoulos, Elnegaard, et al.,2001; Yan 2004) and deployment of 3G networks led mobile network operators[4] (MNOs) into a global recession era and a global pessimism for their adoption which actually reflects user attitudes towards the new standard. In order to confront that, business opportunities based on existing mobile and wireless networks have been further investigated (Katsianis et al., 2001; Varoutas, Katsianis, Sphicopoulos, Loizillon, Kalhagen, & Stordahl, et al., 2003). The provision of value added services over 2.5/3G networks not only allows providers and users to make the most out of the existing infrastructures, but also encourages usage and drives expectations for the next generation of mobile networks (Varoutas, Katsianis, Sphicopoulos, Stordahl, & Welling, 2006). To provide such services, the integration of various components and base-services is required, which breaks the current status of most MNOs that have traditionally been formed as almost monolithic self-contained service(s) providers.

This need for integration of various market stakeholders in complex business models aiming for the provision of high quality services has been indicated not only by mobile market analysts but also by information systems architects. The service-oriented approach (Brown, Johnston, & Kelly 2003; Colan, 2004), a whole new IT perspective which is rushing into the industry, underlies the concepts and offers the guidelines that render possible such complex collaboration schemes. In the LBS domain, mobile positioning protocol and mobile location protocol (Ericsson; OMA, 2002) already exercise concepts in-line with current service-oriented architectures (SOA) common practices. Nevertheless, the design of services, such as location-based ones, will always have to face domain specific challenges concerning technical, economical or even ethical and social factors of the service application (Daoud & Mohan 2002).

Nowadays it is possible and desirable to build open systems that can support the delivery of tourism-related location-dependent content to an end-user on top of the technological and business background already described, allowing:

- Seamless interoperability of systems and content provided by several market stakeholders towards providing a large range of high-quality location-based content delivery services, through standards and loosely coupled elements

- Exploitation of state-of-the-art and future technology in positioning, mobile devices, and network infrastructures

- Compliance with requirements and standards for personalisation and quality of service (QoS)

- Low-cost implementation and upgrade roadmap from 2/2.5G to 3G and other current and future mobile and wireless networks

- Guarantees of privacy

As already mentioned, provision of tourism-related content can be shown that covers a large portion of the information that is usually delivered through location-based services. A number of studies already exist that focus on various aspects of technologies, architectures and business models of this area (Devine & Holmquist, 2001; EMILY, 2002; M-Guide, 2002). This chapter presents the design aspects of such services in a generic way, capturing the needs of many location-dependent services since it assumes a highly heterogeneous network infrastructure leveraged by the Internet protocol (IP) layer. In this way, dealing with the details of mobile or other wireless network infrastructures is avoided yet interoperability and integration issues are been identified and investigated.

# Technology Overview

In the following sections the technologies involved in the provision of mobile tourism services are introduced. Connectivity, which essentially allows delivering data to a device, and positioning, which is the ability to locate a device and consequently its user in space, are the fundamental enabling technologies for the provision of location-based services. Assuming these, tourism related information could be delivered to devices capable of presenting it (e.g., mobile phones), with a multitude of options (quality, depth, size, etc.), derived from exactly the same content that would drive traditional applications (Web sites, printed elements, etc.). The driving force behind these is modern software platforms and system architectures that facilitate the creation of the various nodes of a complex structure of collaborating service elements.

## Wireless and Mobile Data Services

Since the last decade of the $20^{th}$ century and the beginning of the $21^{st}$, the mobile user has come to enjoy the provision of many technologies and services that were hard to even imagine several years before (Lin & Chlamtac, 2001). Besides voice, some of the most common ones are:

- **Information services** (News, Directories, Weather, Athletics, Financial, etc.)
- **Entertainment** (Chat & Flirt Services, Guess who, Alerts, Horoscope, ringtones, etc.)
- **Communication tools** (SMS, MMS, e-mail, instant messaging, etc.)

Apart from these common services, a series of other, more complex ones are being offered to the user like navigation, local news, SMS vote, microbilling, and so forth. Enabling these services is achieved through various means the most important of which being the Web, SMS, and MMS. These higher-level information exchange media are based on lower level communication channels offered by an infrastructure provider. The most important ones are briefly described below:

- **Global system for mobile telecommunications (GSM)** refers to $2^{nd}$ generation mobile telephony networks (Mouly & Pautet, 1995), which although digital, was designed with voice communications in mind, thus giving data rates of 9.6kbis/s, which is rather slow for multimedia applications. Additionally data transfer is not packet switched thus not optimised for computer type communications requiring circuits to be allocated even if no data are exchanged. Since its initial appearance, several enhancements where proposed as side-by-side technologies that enable higher performance data transfers (Korhonen, Aalto, Gurtov, & Lamanen, 2001).

- **General packet radio services (GPRS)** is a wireless communication protocol based on the same modulation as GSM, designed to be provided as a complementary medium to facilitate data transfers over GSM networks. It is packet-based and delivers data rates of approximately 40kbps[5] (Korhonen et al., 2001; Pahlavan & Krishnamurthy, 2002; Patil, 2003; Tisal 2001). It supports continuous connection to the Internet for mobile equipment users. Since GPRS radio resources are utilised only when devices have data to exchange, its end-user cost is lower in both terms of money and power consumption. Packet switching allows more users to be simultaneously connected to the Internet, yet performance drops on high load and no strict guarantees can be given.

- **Enhanced data rates for global evolution (EDGE)** facilitates high-speed mobile data transfer over which can reach a peak rate of 384kbps and is aimed to mobile network operators that might not be able to obtain UMTS (further information is provided below) spectrum but would not like to be left out the modern high speed data services (Halonen, Romero, & Melero, 2003; Rysavi 2005). Even higher speeds may be available in good radio conditions. EDGE provides the same benefits of GPRS (e.g., packet switching, always connected) however by using a different modulation schematic achieves much higher speeds.

- **High speed circuit switched data (HSCSD)** overcomes the limitation of GSM circuit switched data, which supports the allocation of one user per channel per time slot and allows multiple channels to be virtually merged thus offering higher data rates (Halonen et al., 2003; Korhonen et al., 2001). However the allocation of multiple channels raises the connection cost of the end-user, rendering the service rather inappropriate when compared to other modern techniques.

- **Universal mobile telecommunications system (UMTS)** utilises WCDMA (wideband CDMA) over a 5MHz bandwidth thus allows speeds the increase of mobile network speed in order to allow high-speed transfers. UMTS is one of the five types of 3G radio interfaces specified in the ITU[6]'s IMT-2000 recommendation. It allows various classes of service, ranging from more than 100kbps for a fast moving user up to a 2Mbps for a fixed client "lab" speed (3GPP, 2002; Lin & Chlamtac, 2001; UMTS, n.d.).

- **High-speed downlink packet access (HSDPA)** is deployed as an upgrade to UMTS networks and captures the observation that most end-user high-bandwidth demanding applications require one-way high-speed communications, downstream (i.e., towards the end-user). On-demand video, TV and data downloading are some applications that expose such a transfer pattern thus can benefit quite significantly from the speed offered by HSDPA which is up to 3.5 times faster compared to the maximum rate of 14Mbps of today's 3G UMTS (Holma & Toskala, 2004; Kaaranen, 2005; Rysavy, 2005).

- **Wireless fidelity (WiFi)** is a term that in general refers to the 802.11 family of wireless network protocols (Muller, 2003; Smith, 2003). A variety of protocols (e.g., 802.11b, 802.11g) that operate in 2.4GHz and 5GHz bands, being the most popular ones, belong to this family, offering nominal speeds of up to 108MBps (802.11.Super-g). WiFi networks are fixed, local-area, wireless networks thus do not offer the mobility capabilities provided by mobile networks. Additionally, although they can operate without an infrastructure (e.g., on a computer-to-computer way), yet another (usually fixed) connection to the Internet is required in order to obtain worldwide access.

- **Bluetooth (IEEE 802.15)** is a short-range, relatively low performance communications protocol. It is designed so that it allows low power consumption and it is very simple to implement so that it can be easily adopted by "dummy" devices such as headphones, computer mice, keyboards,and so forth. (Bluetooth. org, 2001; Miller & Bisdikian, 2002; Morrow, 2002; Muller, 2001; Xiao & Pan, 2005).

## Location-Based Services

Location-based services are an entire class of mobile services that utilise positional (mostly geospatial) information of the mobile user in order to provide intuitive, easy access to content and tools. The term covers a quite large group of services since it

Table 1. Typical wireless and mobile data networks

| Technology | Typical Performance[7] | End-user relative cost | Scope | Compatibility |
|---|---|---|---|---|
| GSM | 9.6Kbps | High | Global | Very high |
| GPRS | 40Kbps | Medium | Global | High |
| HSCSD | 64Kbps | Very High | Global | Low |
| EDGE | 115Kbps | Medium | Global | Low |
| UMTS | 220Kbps | Medium | Global | Medium (in deployment) |
| HSDPA | 750kbps | Medium | Global | Low |
| WiFi | 11Mbps[8] | Low | Local/indoors | High |
| Bluetooth | 500Kbps | Low | Indoors | High |

can range from global scale services to highly spatially constrained ones (within a room or a building, such as a museum or a conference center).

One of the main aspects of location-based services is positioning, that is, the estimation of the user position, a topic to be covered in detailed sub-sequent sections. Depending on the service class, the mobile equipment and the infrastructure, different approaches and accuracy levels can be applied (Dao, Rizos, & Wang, 2002; Northstream, 2001). In this chapter, the focus is on global scale services, but the elements and concepts presented are not restricted to this particular class of services (Kakaletris et al., 2004). Most location-based services can be categorised into four main business applications:

- **Tracking services (with two sub categories):** emergency services and fleet management services. In the case of emergency services (such as the E-911), the network has the ability to locate persons who are in danger or missing (with special interests for kids) and give them the necessary protection (Reed, Krizman, Woerner, & Rappaport, 1998). Emergency services are first priority for USA (FCC, 2001) and US companies focus on these class services. Road assistance and tracking of stolen equipment (cars, boats, etc.) are other similar services (Fritsch & Scherner, 2005). Fleet management services cover scenarios such as radio-taxi coordination, transportations, delivery, and so on, and in the general case, require high accuracy (Feng, Zhu, Mukai, & Watanabe, 2005; Iwasaki, Kawaguchi, & Inagaki, 2005).

- **Information services:** In this category of services content relative to the location of the user is provided to him/her. However in global scale services the focus is not on the accuracy of user's position acquisition but rather on the content and the way it is presented (Taylor & Ryan, 1995). Local news, cultural information, events highlighting, or even advertising are some of the applications of this category. Such services may be provided near sightseeing or within museums (Zimmermann, Lorenz, & Specht, 2003). In high granularity services (e.g., within museums) positioning has to be accurate and in many cases highly sophisticated since it might even need 3-dimensional location of the user and directional clues (Pateli, Giaglis, & Spinellis, 2005).

- **Fun and entertainment:** Player position-aware games are a new opportunity for service providers and the first flavors are already out. Despite the criticism, chat and flirt is another very popular type of service. In this area, location-aware systems will have the opportunity to refine partner matches within a certain distance (Gratsias, Frentzos, Delis, & Theodoridis, 2005; Karagiozidis, Markoulidakis, Velentzas, & Kauranne, 2003; Lee, Prabhu, & Park, 2002).

- **Billing:** Billing also can adopt location-aware schemes. Creating attractive options such as allowing users to exercise cheaper communications when in certain hot spots (such as home, etc.) is a possible scenario of location-based billing (Gratsias et al., 2005; Koutsopoulou, Panagiotakis, & Alonistioti, 2005).

## Positioning

Location-based tourist information requires positioning of the mobile user with a variable accuracy (Kakaletris et al., 2004; Yilin, 2000). Yet this does not imply that automated acquisition of positional information is always required or desired in order to consume such a service, as when checking available information by forehand, not being physically present in some area. It is obvious that locating the user requires that one is equipped with a module that has some kind of connection to a fixed infrastructure. However the elements of this composition might vary:

- **Equipment** can be a PDA, a 2G or 3G mobile phone, a personal computer, an ID tag, an IR Scanner, a GPS receiver, and so on.
- **Connection to the infrastructure** can be unidirectional or bidirectional utilizing systems such as WiFi, GSM, GPRS, UMTS, satellite antenna/receiver, IR receiver/transmitter, and so on.
- **Infrastructure** can be mobile or fixed network such as a satellite system, a mobile telephony/data network (GSM, GPRS, UMTS, etc.), a set of WiFi or Bluetooth access points, installed RF tags, fixed IR scanners, and so on.

Positioning can be categorised under two main classes:

- **Active:** The client is the only one responsible for the computational load of the position estimation.
- **Passive:** The client (user/mobile equipment) is being located without adding any logic to positioning by itself. Infrastructure obtains simple to extract information from client and calculates the position.

Hybrid methods also are very popular, allowing for high accuracy and availability systems. Exploitation of the positional information also can vary quite significantly:

- In **self-contained systems**, such as GPS enabled PDAs, the content might be already present on the mobile equipment and a local piece of software acts on them, thus no further connection to the outside world is required. The range of location-based services to be supported in this case is limited, navigation being the most popular one.
- In **always-connected systems** a medium for exchanging information with the infrastructure and usually the world (the Internet) is required. This can be done in order to acquire the position, or exchange information that will allow position estimation, or access the core service/content.

The rest of this section presents the details of some of the most important positioning methods, their requirements, and their characteristics. There are a number of ways for obtaining user's position and the following sections describe some of the current applied automated methods:

## The GPS

GPS positioning (ETSI, 2006; GARMIN, n.d.) is based on a network of 24 earth orbiting satellites. It was originally designed and implemented to cover the needs of the US military forces, however since the 1980's it has been used for wide spectrum of applications ranging from civil engineering to recreational systems. Communication is one-way; consequently clients only receive signals, thus guaranteeing privacy. A GPS client/device receives signals from several satellites with at least three satellites needed for 2-dimensional coordinate estimation (latitude, longitude) while four are required for three-dimensional positioning (latitude, longitude, and altitude). Signals are time-tagged, enabling the client to calculate distance from each satellite using the send/receive time difference. Accurate position estimation requires combining the aforementioned distances for multiple satellites. Bookkeeping of coordinates is a

*Figure 1. GPS operation*

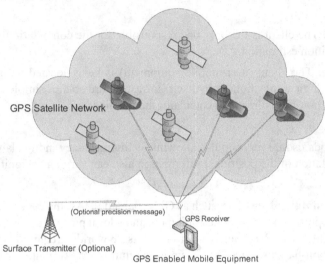

way to calculate the speed and direction of moving GPS devices, a facility provided by almost all modern receivers. In such systems end-user devices are quite small and due to low power consumption tend to be highly autonomous.

Civilian GPS satellite signal is low power (i.e., less than 50 watts in 1575.42 MHz). It penetrates glass and plastic, but cannot go through metal, ground or concrete, effectively preventing indoors GPS usage. Dense urban use also can be problematic in some cases. Additionally, the GPS signal is vulnerable to signal travel time errors that lead to false distance estimation. Reflection of signal on solid objects as well as other orbital/stratospheric phenomena can result to wrong time estimations. Utilizing more satellites is a way to deal with such problems.

One of the strongest points of GPS however is accuracy, which can range from 1 to 15 meters for civilian systems. This fact, accompanied by the simplicity of the relevant devices and the availability of the service which can be utilised at no cost (apart from equipment) makes it capable of driving major successful commercial applications, such as navigation for tourists. As already mentioned, GPS is controlled by the U.S. Department of Defence, nevertheless it is expected that the European Galileo system will be competing with it by 2008 (Di Fazio, Mocci, Rossini, D'Angelo, Lorelli, & Jarosh, 2004; El-Rabbany, 2002; Prasad & Ruggieri, 2005). GPS has to be accompanied by a supplementary network in order to drive interactive on line systems where satellite coverage is unavailable. Pseudo-GPS systems emulate the existence of satellites for indoors use without requiring any additional equipment, yet they are not widely adopted solutions (Schmid, Neubauer, Ehm, Weigel, Lemke, Heinrichs, 2005).

## GSM-Positioning

GSM positioning (ETSI, 2006; Mao & Douligeris, 2000; Spirito, 2001; Zhao, 2002) is a facility potentially provided by GSM mobile network operators. Its operation is based on the fact that there is always some type of raw information on the location of a certain GSM mobile device in order for the network to be able to deliver information to the user. Since it can be originated from the network, it is raising serious privacy and security concerns, which can be overlooked for emergency purposes but not without risk of misuse.

GSM positioning is always available in some form, as long as network coverage is provided. However depending on the network infrastructure and method utilised its accuracy might vary quite significantly ranging from 100m to more than 500m (even several kilometers) (Caffery & Stuber, 1998b; Drane, Macnaughtan, & Scott, 1998). Although due to this low level of accuracy GSM positioning is of little use for high accuracy demanding application, it is accompanied by a bidirectional communication channel (voice or data) thus enabling interactive applications. Its network-side activation, whenever applicable, makes it ideal for some special emergency and tracking cases.

- **Cell ID** is a location technology that utilises the well-known location of fixed network elements, that is, the base station transceivers (BTS), to identify the mobile equipment location (Figure 2). It can be easily combined with timing advance (TA) in GSM networks and round trip time[9] (RTT) information in WCDMA networks in order to improve accuracy. TA is a technique that utilises the timing advance information applied by the GSM network to determine the approximate distance a MS is from a base station.

*Figure 2. Cell ID/Cell ID + TA*

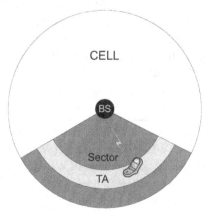

*Figure 3. E-OTD operation*

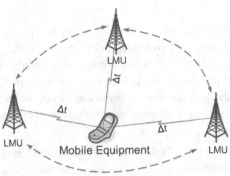

- **Enhanced-observed time difference (E-OTD)** is a more complex method for calculating device position (Caffery & Stuber 1998a, 1998b). It requires location measurement units (LMUs), a type of device used to provide precise timing information for asynchronous networks. Although this method can increase accuracy, it also increases infrastructure cost and it still suffers from issues with network density in rural areas. E-OTD and time of arrival (TOA) methods are very similar to GPS positioning already described. The location of mobile devices is calculated using the signaling time from two or more stations (see Figure 3).

Typically GSM-positioning would not always be enabled, since this requires significant resources from the operator's side. In the typical usage scenario, the user has to ask for locating him/her, either through an SMS or through a request over the standard Internet protocol (IP). Due to its privacy risk, GSM positioning is usually surrounded by rules of activation and bureaucratic procedures/agreements, which can be even harder to overcome in cross-MNO cases unless a standard user-driven mechanism is utilised. Unfortunately despite the existence of specifications, in mid 2001 decade there is still no standard for GSM positioning that is widely adopted by operators. A final restriction on its use is its cost, which can vary quite vastly depending on the level of consumption of the service.

## WLAN

Wireless local area network (WLAN) positioning (Wang, Jia, Lee, & Li, 2003) is a local type of positioning usable within range of WLAN hot spots, which is mostly restricted indoors or in quite constrained areas (e.g., building blocks, etc.).[10] It is the primary candidate technology for big buildings like airports, museums, market places and other sites where radio interference is not an issue and it should generally be accurate enough to guide a visitor through the coverage area. Positioning is very similar to GPS and GSM positioning, thus it uses the time difference between the signals from some known positions. This information can be corrected and improved with site calibration, a method which also can be utilised in some GSM positioning cases but not without significant difficulties. In the WLAN positioning case, information about the physical structure of the target area (walls, obstacles, etc.) is of crucial information in order to obtain reliable results.

According to systems' vendors, WLAN positioning can be quite accurate (one meter indoors according to Ekahau, 2006) yet site calibration is definitely required for such accuracy. Its cost is quite reasonable since infrastructure and equipment are quite cheap and it is well suited for interactive on-line applications since data network coverage is implied.

## Other Methods

Despite its peculiarity considered in the context of the e-services described above, observation accompanied by a traditional map (i.e., paper-printed) also could be a useful method of information dissemination for tourists even in the electronic age. This does not suffer from service unavailability, privacy, mobility, and autonomy issues, and its price is usually low. Using an electronic map instead of a printed one would add in detail and in some cases reduce in size while posing some restrictions on autonomy, however if not accompanied by a positioning system it would still require observation and manual operation in order to consolidate other information.

Positioning through mapping addresses to geographical coordinates is very similar to using maps since it requires observation and manual utilisation of information. However the location is obtained through lookups in appropriate databases, such as geographical information systems[11] (GIS). It is quite usable in urban areas and roadsides of rural areas and it can be both electronic and traditional (maps with indices).

There are several other methods, like local sensor networks, ID tags based on infrared or radio frequencies (IR or RF), gyroscopes, and statistical models (Hightower & Borriello 2001; Nellen, Bronnimann, Held, & Sennhauser, 2004; Spratt 2003). Out of these one could expect low-cost gyroscopes to be the most attractive mechanisms for mobile travelers in the future (whenever it becomes possible to build lightweight, low-cost gyroscopes) since they could drive the most fascinating classes of applications. For example taking into account the direction of sight of the user could even further enhance the simplicity of interaction with a service, especially in complex (with respect to location and quantity of content) environments such as museums or exhibitions. Further issues and opportunities can be found in the section on "Mobile Tourism Services."

## Summary

Each method presented has advantages and shortcomings. It seems that GPS is currently the primary means of reliable positioning when global positioning comes into play, however hybrid positioning (i.e., by blending of different location technologies) utilizing GSM and WLAN methods could be optimal. In the rest of this chapter "hybrid" will refer to combining GPS with other location techniques.

There are several whitepapers, guidelines, studies, and surveys showing the details of each positioning approach (Caffery & Stuber, 1998b; Hightower & Borriello, 2001), however a higher level evaluation of the ones applicable to tourism as it appeals to mobile network operators will be introduced below. Other types of systems like personnel/patient tracking in hospitals (Dao et al., 2002; Douglas, 2004), information delivery in museums (Sparacino, 2002) or emergency related ones (FCC, 2001; GSM, 2002) generally require more sophisticated means for delivering their services.

When designing an open infrastructure then, positioning should not have any strong relation to the implementation of services for the mobile traveler. Realisations of different services should leave methods of getting positioning information open, allowing the end-user to choose among them: GPS, GSM and map outdoors, WLAN and GSM inside. Services should be prepared to receive coordinates as bunches of

Table 2. LBS summary of performance, implementation, and cost trends (Sources: EMILY, 2002; Hightower & Borriello, 2001; Moureu, 2000; SnapTrack, 2001)

| Metric | CELL-ID + TA | E-OTD | GPS | A-GPS | Hybrids |
|---|---|---|---|---|---|
| Accuracy | 100m 10km | 100m 500m | 10m undefined | 10m 100m | 1m 100m |
| Kick-off time | Low | Low | High | Very high | Very high |
| Dimensions | 2 | 2 | 3 | 2/3 | 2/3 (+direction) |
| Mobile Equipment Requirements | None | Low | High | High | High |
| Applicability | Good | Poor | High | Medium | Good |
| Infrastructure Cost | None | High | None | None-to-high | High |
| Best area applicability | Dense urban | Urban / Dense urban | Suburban | Suburban, urban | Outdoors, Indoors |
| Coverage | High | High | Partial | High | High |
| Overall Quality | Poor | Medium | High | High | Excellent |
| Compatibility | Medium | Poor | Full | Medium | Poor |

*Figure 4. Indicative LBS technologies quality per area  (accuracy, availability, cal-culation time)*[12]

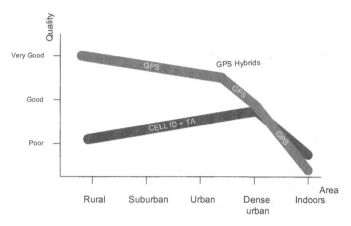

numbers in the three-dimentional + direction space accompanied by definition of coordinate-standard and accuracy.

Such an approach would leave all possibilities open for the user. Also this method would keep service providers' monetary costs down, because service provider can leave all costs of positioning to be decided by the traveler.

*Figure 5. LBS technologies services and accuracy*[13]

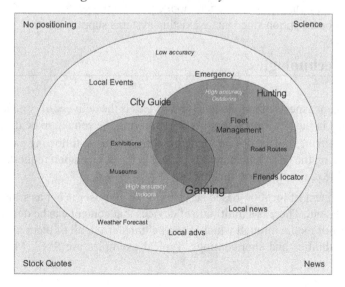

When building services for the mobile traveler, designers should ideally therefore forget the actual positioning method and provide a service in a way that it would be able to cope with any degree of accuracy or availability of positioning information. Obtaining the position would then be a task to be carried out by external parties such as equipment manufacturers or infrastructure providers, both of them working on low details of the software that manages the "networking" hardware.

## Positioning Standards

An attempt to standardise positioning has been carried out during the past few years. Solutions and best practices have been proposed by vendors, associations and individual researchers (Adams, Ashwell, & Baxter, 2003; GSM, 2002; Rao & Minakakis, 2003). As a consequence the terms mobile positioning center (MPC) and gateway mobile location center (GMLC) systems emerged in order to label the entities of the infrastructure that where used in order to extract positioning information and estimate end-user locations. The mobile location protocol (MLP) is an application protocol developed by the location interoperability forum (LIF) that specifies the messages to be exchanged over standard Internet technologies in order to obtain coordinates from a positioning center. It is focusing on network based positioning and has its origin in proprietary commercial protocols. OpenLS (OpenGIS location services [OGS]) defines the interfaces to an open location-based services platform, such as the GeoMobility server. Utilizing XML for location services (XSL) defines the data exchanged in the interactions with the geographic information system (GIS) for various classes of services that capture facilities such as routing (navigation), position extraction, lookup (directory), map drawing (presentation), and so on.

Popular, yet proprietary protocols such mobile positioning protocol (MPP) (Ericsson) also can be an option since many existing systems support these.

# Content Technologies

One of the major aspects of mobile tourism services is the delivery of content to the end-user. This in the general case involves identifying the content to be displayed, (optionally) moving it to the device[14] and presenting it. In the following paragraphs focus is given on the case that content is passed to the device upon request, that is, does not reside pre-installed on the device.

Delivering content of location-based services to the end-user is not as simple as it seems at first sight. There is a multitude of devices that content can be delivered to and a number of media through which it can be transferred, all of them presenting different capabilities and shortcomings. Typical examples are SMS, MMS, and WAP:

- **SMS** market penetration is significantly higher than the penetration of WAP. The majority of the location-based systems implemented by MNOs, use the SMS for exchanging data. However presentation and interaction facilities are severely limited over this transport medium; furthermore SMS can be extremely expensive per byte of data exchanged

- **MMS** significantly increases the quality of presentation and reduces the price per byte of exchanged data. Yet its penetration is significantly lower than SMS, it suffers the same interaction restrictions and finally its cost can be significant over SMS for simple text information exchange

- **WAP** adds to presentation and interactivity quite significantly. However its penetration is quite limited and it is not expected to be widely adopted unless significant convergence to Web technologies is achieved

Research on service types show that the SMS/MMS solution might be more appropriate, while WAP/Web is the only way for others (Bennett, 2001; Heijden & Taylor 2000). Taking into account that current end-user mobile terminals have limited displays and end-users are not accustomed to consuming interactive services through the mobile phone interface, SMS/MMS may be a commercially viable solution for a wide range of location-based services. Special sub-sections of tourism related services such as directory lookups can be ideally served through simple SMS exchanges.

Positioning also is influenced by device capabilities. The majority of mobile phones are not equipped with GPS devices, which could have a significant impact on their autonomy, size, and weight since the cost of a GPS receiver is insignificant compared to the cost of the rest of the device. Even PDAs or laptops do not usually come out of the box accompanied by GPS receivers, making it a requirement to purchase one separately. The primary option is a Bluetooth GPS device that can be easily connected to portable computing devices such as latest mobile phones, PDAs, or laptops; however despite the small size of these devices this scenario requires that the user carry one extra component.

## Mobile Terminals That Support LBS

The development and full deployment of high quality location-based services for tourists assumes the existence of terminals with extended capabilities in battery capacity, processing power, main memory, application capabilities, size, and weight. Such devices may be categorised according to an incremental rating of the applications they can support. Today, four categories of terminals can be found in market:

- **Standard GSM mobile terminals**

- **GPRS/UMTS phones:** There are two categories of GPRS/UMTS phones. The WAP based and the HTML based ones. The former category offers facilities for consuming WAP information sources (WAP sites) while the latter one exchanges information in Web standard formats such as HTML, JPEG, etc. The require a Web server, which will host the mapping applications and will be responsible for routing requests to external systems.

- **PDAs/Smartphones:** Smartphones are latest generation mobile phones equipped with enhanced displays, more powerful processors and capabilities of carrying out tasks that were formerly responsibility of computer systems. PDAs are devices in some extent similar to the smartphones, stressing on presentation and application capabilities rather than communications. Latest generation devices are usually equipped with an HTML browser able to interface with standard Web sites. PDAs offer built in or expandability options for GPS, GSM, WiFi, and so on.

- **Laptops with communication facilities:** These offer all the advanced options of computers in terms of computational and storage capacity, yet they have limited mobility features.

## Multi-Channel Content Delivery

Multi-channel content delivery is a very important aspect of the content provision system. Infrastructure and content should be suitably constructed so that they allow delivery of information through various media and means, be it SMS message exchanges, GPRS, or fixed networks connections, computers/PDAs/phones, and so on. Nowadays there is a whole suite of technologies and a large number of systems that enable multi-channel content delivery, under the *author once—publish many* approach, where the same source content is used for several targets ranging from printed media to mobile devices.

Nowadays the most widely applied solutions for this approach are based on a set of standards and tools build around XML, a simple text language developed by the World Wide Web Consortium (W3C) that has its roots on SGML. XML can be used with a wide range of applications, such as authoring tools, content display engines, translation tools, and database applications (Anderson 2000; Bosak 1998; Bosak & Bray 1999). However, its major use in the context of mobile tourism services is for structuring the tourism related content in a form that it becomes meaningful for a series of software elements and operations. More precisely, the various parts of a document are labeled in a special manner (tagged) so that can be extracted by various applications to fulfill their own needs (Anderson, 2000). A relevant technology is the well-known HTML which uses a somewhat similar tagging mechanism yet it neither enforces structure nor allows for application specific labeling that would facilitate a customised use of the document. HTML uses a fixed set of tags and describes only formatting instructions for the Web. On the other hand XML is completely extensible since it does not have predefined tags, unless it explicitly conforms to a schema. Various schemas exist in order to capture industrial and domain specific needs and as long as two systems comprehend the same schema they can use XML documents to exchange information. News Industry Text Format (NITF) and News Markup Language (NewsML) are two examples of markup languages that could be of some use to tourism related services, since they enable the sharing of syndicated news articles from alternative news providers.

In addition to XML, the combination of XSL/XSLT is one of the fundamental parts of the described content delivery chain. A stylesheet is a declaration that describes how to display a document and XSL is a language for expressing stylesheets for XML documents. By keeping content and its presentation information separate in the XML document and the XSL stylesheet respectively, display of the same original document on different media and preferences sets is achieved by simply modifying the stylesheet.[15] However modifying presentation might not be enough in several cases; transformation of the source document might be required and this is where XSLT comes into play. Although XSLT transformation was originally intended to perform complex styling operations, like the generation of tables of contents and indexes, currently it is often used as a complete general-purpose XML transformation language. In that manner it is the standard means for transforming the source XML document (e.g., tourism content) into presentable forms such as HTML or WML[16] pages, or other XML schemas or even into other more complex formats.

Apart the content structure, a number of features are exploitable in the context of establishing advanced, reliable multi-channel content delivery services, such as mobile tourism related ones:

- **Security**, in order to authenticate users and authorise access to sections of the system and potentially charge usage, required in order to safeguard mobile user's privacy and content/service providers resources
- **Session management**, in order to drive stateful applications driven by a series of user actions, a feature required for almost every type of modern interactive Web application
- **Automated device/channel detection**, in order to enable adaptation to device capabilities, with minimal user intervention that drive better application experience
- **Client and/or server form processing and validation** that allows meaningful interaction with the system while minimizing message exchanges

- **Content rendering**, that adapts to the device capabilities and user preferences (personalisation), required for delivering content to a multitude of heterogeneous devices
- **Support for off-line operation of devices**, able to drive different application and connectivity scenarios, especially useful in several forms of application in the mobile tourism area[17]

Unfortunately, it can be shown that with today's applied technologies, depending on the device/channel, almost all requested features have to be achieved by a different set of technologies and interactions each time. Approaching this problem through the Model-View-Controller design pattern (Gamma, 1995) offers a potential design solution to the challenge, by breaking an application into modules so the logic can be dealt separately from the interface. This allows developers to maintain a single code base for all channels and face each device/channel as a different view for a given transaction. The Model-View-Controller pattern can have as many views as desired and isolates the request handler (aka the Controller) and enterprise system (the Model) from any knowledge of the view. Achieving the desired features (e.g., security, session management, form validation, and content rendering across all devices and channels) is case/device/channel specific.

In the proposed multi-channel approach considering the Web as the primary channel allows an all-in-one solution for already established Web content provision services. The value of a multi-channel content delivery enabling platform is that it provides to the hosting enterprise a single interaction model for all external systems or users and leverages security, session management, and content rendering.

Commercial, freeware and open source software markets offer a wide range of tools that relate to the multi-channel content delivery process. One can easily locate a series of software tools that transform rich content into tailored formats mainly for adopting Web content to mobile devices or vice versa, or systems that offer some degree of support for multi-channel content delivery. These systems mostly belong to one of the following categories:

- **Content management systems (CMS)**
- **Authoring and publishing tools**
- **Wireless application gateways (WAG)**

Platforms such as enterprise portals and e-commerce suites also might be offering some degree of support for multi-channel content delivery, however they are considered of rather little use in the case of rich mobile tourism services by themselves, since they are capturing this aspect under the perspective of their specific application domain. Such facilities also can be offered by application servers, however at a much lower level. Currently there is no product that provides a full solution that can take raw content and transform it automatically to multiple formats for any requesting device taking into account all the aspects of multi-channel content delivery referenced in the previous section.

## Content Types

There are various types of content that can be delivered and displayed by end-user devices. Text is the easiest to handle, however it is relatively less attractive compared to the others due to its nature, which only uses vision through the channel reading. On the opposite side, rich multimedia content such as Flash[18] (Against the Clock [Firm], 2002; Kozak, 2002) is highly attractive, however its current support by mobile devices is not global, yet it is expected to increase in the near future, as convergence of technologies dictates. Direct execution of "binary" code on the devices through industry standards also can be referenced, however support is relatively limited and minimal or no cross device compatibility is provided.

## The Semantic Web

The Semantic Web (W3C, 2001) comes into the scene in order to cover, among others, many of the issues met in the multi-channel content delivery area. It is led by W3C and provides a whole framework so that data obtain a well defined meaning and can be reused under different cases potentially leading to quite different end-user experiences and content compositions. The key-enabling concept is the resource description framework that is heavily dependent on XML contracts. The

*Table 3. LBS content types (Source: M-Guide, 2002)*

| Content class | Compatibility | Features | Size | Power requirements | Sample technologies |
|---|---|---|---|---|---|
| Text | Very high | Poor | Very Low | Very low | HTML, Plain text |
| Audio | High | Medium | Low | Medium | MP3, MIDI |
| Image | High | Medium | Low | Medium | JPEG, WBMP, GIF |
| Video | Medium | High | High | Very high | MPEG, 3GP[19] etc |
| Integrated interactive multimedia | Poor | Very high | Medium | Very high | Macromedia Flash |
| Executable entities | Very poor | Very high | Medium | Very high | Applets / ActiveX Components |

Semantic Web can be considered as the next step of the current World Wide Web (Berners-Lee & Hendler, 2001; Berners-Lee et al., 2001).

## Software in Control

All of the above mentioned technologies are provided through software elements which might be either proprietary, bound to a specific device and/or case or generic enough to fit several scenarios or even totally irrelevant services. Commercial or open source platforms do exist that can support almost all of the stages of mobile tourist content delivery, with little or even no need for integration development.[20] Nevertheless, provisioning of custom services will most probably demand explicit development of custom software elements.

In scenarios that several market players are involved for the provision of a rich service, such as the case of mobile tourism ones, the traditional component oriented architecture, which modularises software in order to be reused among various cases, needs to be enriched by concepts that allow independence among the various stakeholders.

The concept of service-oriented architecture (SOA) captures architectural style that aims to achieve loose coupling among interacting software entities (Erl, 2004, 2005; Newcomer & Lomow, 2005). In this context a service is a unit of logic and data provided by the service provider that is assigned to provide the appropriate results for its consumer. In this framework the provider and consumer are both software agents that act behalf of their owners. As a concept SOA is quite abstract and can be utilised both for B2B and B2C interactions. Typically lots of protocols and operations fall under its meaning, however in mid-2001, more concrete forms of service oriented paradigms are being applied, accompanied by relevant protocols and enabling platforms.

The model of publisher/subscribers, assisted by a directory service over a transport consisting mostly of XML and Internet based protocols is the current roadmap for applying the SOA:

- **Service publishers** (might) announce their characteristics in a directory service (e.g., UDDI, 2004).

- **Service consumers** can either look in the directory service and locate the service that meets their requirements and obtain a reference to the access point of the service or they directly obtain this through other media.

- **Consequently consumers** use the access point reference to directly communicate with the server.

- **SOAP over XML over HTTP** (i.e., TCP/IP) are the most common protocols for consumer/provider interaction, yet message details are service dependent.

Recent extensions of the initial concept of Web services for the SOA approach add state management, thus allowing a standardised way to access resources hosted by suppliers (Czajkowski, Foster, Ferguson, Frey, Graham, & Snelling, 2004; Foster, Frey, Graham, Tuecke, Czajkowski, & Ferguson, 2004; Huber & Huber 2002; Snell, Tidwell, & Kulchenko, 2002). Typically consumers have no internal knowledge of the operation of the service provider and a particular service in question. The provider might revise implementation, as well as other characteristics of a service without explicitly notifying clients.[21]

One level below the overall software architecture is the software technology, which in the case of location-based services has two facets: infrastructure and client. Developing on the infrastructure side is facilitated by numerous technologies and platforms and is of little interest from the mobility perspective. All Web service enabling technologies, assisted by technologies to deliver reach content are quite applicable for the purposes of tourism location-based services. Dozens of open-source free or fully commercial platforms exist in the today's software market, making it available for anyone to adapt its infrastructure to their own needs and capabilities. However, due to its relatively recent appearance, development on the device has somewhat limited options. For the time being, the most common platforms for mobile device development are the two described bellow and come from commercial software vendors, however they are both freely available to the development communities:

- **The micro edition of the Java 2 platform** is the port of Java to portable devices that have minimal capabilities of processing and storage. It is a runtime environment that provides on one hand a subset of the facilities offered by the typical desktop java engines, yet it provides microdevice-specific capabilities access, potentially assisted by vendor specific libraries. J2ME is very common in latest 2G and 3G mobile phones as well as non PocketPC PDAs (SUN).

- **The Microsoft .NET compact framework** is a subset of the Microsoft .NET framework, the Microsoft technology for desktop and Web application on the Windows platform. Although meant to be platform independent through standardisation (ECMA[22]), currently .NET compact framework is only available for PocketPC and other flavours of the Windows platform. Due to its requirements it is not suitable for current low-end devices, yet its performance is very promising in addressed devices (Microsoft).

# Mobile Tourism Services

"Tourism-related" content refers to any content that might be of interest to the visitor of a location (Beatty 2002; Kakaletris et al 2004; Karagiozidis et al 2003; Kim, Kim, Gautam, & Lee, 2005). This content, be it static (e.g., maps, routes), of low refresh rate (e.g., scheduled or periodic events), highly dynamic (e.g., traffic), cultural (e.g., museums, exhibitions, local historical info), informative (e.g., weather, local news) or commercial (e.g. restaurants, commercial fun parks, etc.), has an increased degree of interest to the "consumer", especially when he/she is in particular locations. The term "location" is a varying-"size" descriptor which might range from the actual spot where one is standing in a room, to just a rough approximation of a country. In this context of course, the term "tourist" is very loosely related to the typical "tourist" and mostly fits the definition of "mobile equipment user". It is obvious that a very large number of services related to content delivery fit this definition, such as map delivery, archaeological information delivery, events announcements, emergency, or health services, transportation information acquisition, even in-doors museum exhibition presentations. These are all forms of this type of location-based tourism-related content delivery service.

When designing an infrastructure able to support such services, requirements that have to be met come from various sources:

- **Technical issues** that have to be exploited and addressed in order for it to be applicable
- **Regulatory and social/ethical restrictions** that have to be met in order for the supplied services to be publishable
- **End-user expectations and requirements** that have to be considered in order to achieve successful commercialisation, and so on.

The requirements presented here arise from a careful study of the 2/2.5G and 3G mobile network technical specifications, location-based services related whitepapers and applied paradigms (Laitinen, 2001; Ludden, 2000; Northstream, 2001; Searle, 2001), modern IT system architecture concepts (Varoutas, Katsianis, Sphicopoulos, Cerboni, Kalhagen, Stordahl, et al., 2002; Varoutas et al., 2006), regulations & standards (FCC, 2001; GSM, 2002; IST-REPOSIT, 2001; LIF-IOT, 2002), and finally, market and end-user surveys (Beatty, 2002; Dao et al., 2002; Katsianis et al., 2001; LoVEUS, 2002; M-Guide, 2002). This comprehensive study led to the identification of the following key points that require careful consideration when implementing a location-aware service that aims to provide tourist information content:

- **QoS in quantifiable technical terms** (response time, throughput, availability, scalability, coverage, accuracy; etc.)

- **QoS in non-quantifiable terms** (quality of content e.g coverage, depth, media, multilinguality/multiculturality, etc.)

- **Integration capabilities** (relevant services support and integration capabilities)

- **Security** (authentication, authorisation, privacy, etc.)

- **Service related procedures** (e.g., activation / de-activation, billing, pricing, personalisation, stakeholders interoperability, etc.)

- **Service specific features** (e.g., notification, positioning triggering)

- **Content related issues** (e.g., ontology)

- **Present and emerging technology capabilities** (positioning, presentation, mobile networks, etc.)

Having carefully examined alternatives and the potential impact of decisions on the above-mentioned key points, several interesting conclusions can be identified as referenced below. Although technology enthusiasts would think otherwise, end-users are not generally amazed by high accuracy positioning mechanisms or very high data rate demanding services. The already referenced user surveys show that they rather prefer low cost intuitive services that will satisfy their expectations, within reasonable quality limits. In the same context, widely used equipment lacks high interactivity capabilities (i.e., means of passing information to the service and presenting content to end-users). Although emerging devices are expected to vastly improve this particular aspect, average users are not enticed by such capabilities.

High accuracy in positioning is not always a real concern either. For example delivering some sort of transportation information or providing a local directory service, requires only a rough approximation of the position. On the other hand, presenting information in an actual exhibit, which the visitor is looking at, requires not only precise position as to where one is located but also information about the direction of sight, and even that detail of information may not be adequate. At this point, the conclusion is that "less accuracy" does not render LBS useless but rather restricts the range of services that can be provided. Therefore, although almost identical content might be available for presentation to each end-user visiting a museum or an open archaeological site, equipment differentiation (e.g., display capabilities, channel usage, positioning mechanism, and capabilities), can drive a completely different degree of content exploitation.

Another issue is that some requirements, for example accurate positioning and enhanced content, come with some extra "cost" to the end user. Cost is not only in financial terms, which are mostly obvious, positioning accuracy (e.g., through a GPS module) and advanced display capabilities for example, might have a severe impact on device autonomy and size. Enhanced content (video, virtual reality representations, etc.) will require more bandwidth and even more powerful equipment (having indirect impact on autonomy and size).

When to locate a user is yet another confusing issue. User-requested positioning requires an extra step to be taken by the end user, who actually has to request to be located or explicitly state his/her location at the moment. Alternatively, the user can be continuously located (tracked) by the system. Continuously positioning the mobile user is not usually required, even in the case when the undoubted demand it implies in terms of infrastructure and equipment resources is not a problem. A typical example is a highly mobile user who is accessing some location-based directory of content, related to a specific position he/she has been some time earlier. While the user may be attracted to these particular sites of interest, mobility might cause the delivery of quite different content in subsequent requests for information, which could come to be quite irritating. Thus the user should have the possibility to allow either continuous or on-request triggered positioning. A good practice would be to totally avoid automatic positioning instead of temporarily ignoring new position information, however certain applications could require two positional indicators ("live" position and "querying" position). The issue of delay also needs to be taken into consideration when locating the user. In on-demand positioning schemes, the system might introduce quite significant delays due to high load or computational issues which might render some applications rather unattractive.

Finally, a very important observation that guides the proposed approach is network convergence; xxML/HTTP/TCP/IP "stacks" tend to provide a uniform roadmap for offering a very large range of services to each-and-every consumer oriented device type.

## System Concepts

In the rest of this chapter various concepts of an open architecture, capable of providing rich mobile tourism services, are pointed out. Although an architectural approach is introduced, the intention is not to propose a single solution that could be identified as the best in one way or the other for the tourist; the purpose of the analysis to follow is rather to position the enabling technologies and identify the issues, shortcomings and strong points of various approaches. Depending on the particular application one has to provide, different roadmaps can be followed. An hypothetical structure of an LBS provision system targeting tourism content delivery is shown in Figure 6. In this scenario, the elements are separated in three conceptually different clusters:

- **End-user devices**, be it mobile or fixed ones. For simplicity, it will be considered that mobile ones have some sort of positioning capabilities either on their own (e.g., GPS) or network assisted/provided.

- **Network infrastructure**, which is either a mobile network or a fixed wireless local area network, or a combination of both. In case of mobile equipment that lack positioning capabilities, it is necessary that the network provide the ability to locate the user through connection information, spatial information and potentially the user's previous behavioural data. The network might provide various means of submitting information to the user, such as MMS/SMS (GSM, 2003).

*Figure 6. Example of layout of LBS system (Based on Kakaletris et al., 2004)*

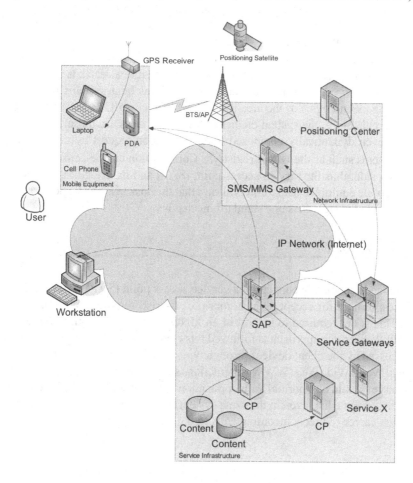

- **Service infrastructure**, which relates to the systems that delivers information and facilities to the user utilizing as one of its implied inputs, the positional information of the user.

The mobile/wireless network details such as access points, MSCs, VLRs, HLRs and so forth are almost totally hidden and only interactions of higher-level components are being referenced. Additionally SOA constructs which obey to specific patterns are omitted (Brown et al., 2003; Colan, 2004; UDDI, 2004). The following sections highlight important structural and operational aspects of such a system.

## Service Interactions

In the presented architecture, the main element is the "service" (i.e., to tourists). Under the modern understanding of realizing a service-oriented architecture, services are implemented under the WebServices paradigm, utilizing in almost 100 percent of the cases the SOAP/XML - HTTP - TCP/IP route. Thus messages are exchanged in a very standardised manner which can be found to be fully supported by vendors' major server systems (content management systems, relational database management systems, runtime environments, etc.), and mobile/client systems as stated by the leading technologies of the area (provided by Microsoft, SUN, IBM, etc.). Under this architecture, the system elements such as services are loosely coupled and can be even dynamically composed upon interaction/request by using SOA enabling systems such as the UDDI registry.[23] Composition can be entirely left to the servicing side, thus the service access point (SAP) and its delegates, however exploring mobile equipment capabilities allows that this task also can be performed at the client side through the same standard mechanisms.

## Service Access Point

In the proposed scheme the concept of a service access point (SAP) is introduced, which is responsible for accepting customer (i.e., tourist) requests for a bunch of services. This is not required to be part of an MNO infrastructure, but in the case that the full Webservice approach is followed this element is a Web service hosting server, accessed by the client devices through typical WS addressing constructs. In case typical World Wide Web (WWW) interactions are performed through a browser then this server would be a normal Web/application server. A unifying approach can be that both servers exist (even in the same system) in the provider's infrastructure and the Web server redirects incoming calls to the same SAP that the Webservice consuming capable clients access. This point can be responsible for a series of actions, which among others include:

- Authenticating end-user even beyond typical username/password challenges by utilising sophisticated network provided authentication mechanisms
- Orchestrating service interactions in an application specific scenario when an end-user delivered service requires invocation of a series of services
- Providing facilities for dynamic service composition allowing the end-users, devices or services to seek and locate suitable content and service provided that match their needs with regards to quality, cost, availability, and so on; delegating lookups to registries such as UDDI is performed at this level
- Providing a repository for open-schema persistent end-user profiles that can be selectively partially offered to subsequent request handlers. Alternatively a distributed profile schema could be used however this would raise interoperability issues and would increase the risk of compromising user privacy. Updating profiles could be triggered by users and other services to the extent allowed by their role in the system
- Providing a "service-side triggered" positioning acquisition point, in case end-user equipment is incapable of autonomously handling positioning which is the main the case when SMS/MMS channels are utilised. In this case requesting services would address this element in order to obtain user position upon and special security concerns have to be handled
- Providing a mechanism for content lookup in registered content providers acting as a content broker, so that content that meets specific minimal structural requirements can be delivered to end users without additional processing nodes
- Maintaining session state on top of stateless protocols
- Acting as a front-end for non-IP network connected channels, such as SMS/MMS ones, to coordinate requests and replies between channel gateways and content/sub-service providers
- Providing presentation transformation layer to adapt content to client device/channel needs

Optimisation features as a caching of aggregated content are application specific ones that can be considered as part of the SAP. Advanced value added services on top of positioning such as movement prediction also can be considered however they should preferably be implemented as a typical Web service to be accessed on demand.

## Homogenisation of Positioning

Examining the details of user positioning, be it network driven, client driven, or even manual, shows a significant heterogeneity not only in the area of the actual position estimation, but also in the process of obtaining this information which is a rather quite important aspect of the system design. Even the relatively simple case of manual positioning might have various implementations: manually supplying the coordinates of the location or indirectly acquiring them out of location information (e.g., road intersections, etc.). The following graph shows various potential interactions among equipment, software, and data that could be utilised to drive user positioning.

*Figure 7. Positioning interactions (Based on Kakaletris et al., 2004)*

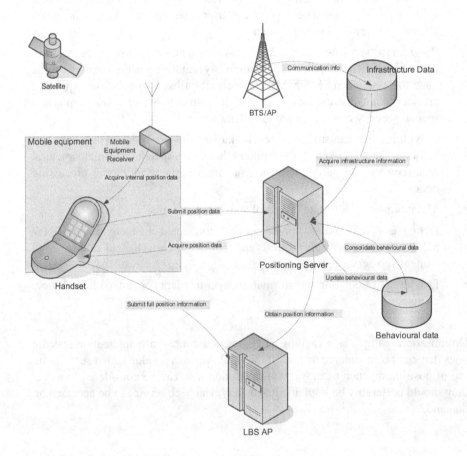

It is desirable to hide as much as possible of this heterogeneity from the ASP point of view. A potential solution would be as to separate positioning into three distinct layers as follows:

- One layer is concerned with the actual calculation of the position. This layer is quite different in each and every implementation, not only due to the various alternatives of positioning mechanisms but also due to differentiation to details of the actual algorithms and infrastructures. Very little can be done in order to unify this layer other than defining the appropriate interfaces
- The second layer is the SAP positioning layer, which has to provide the actual end-user position to the application layer. This layer is separated in a server-side and a client-side part (components to extract device data where applicable) and its purpose is to determine the actual position supplier and extract information data, or provide a means for manually identifying position
- The top-level layer is the application layer, which has to determine whether new positioning is required, reuse of previous information is adequate or actual position is known (e.g., within query), forward a request to SAP layer and ultimately return location information back to the end-user (within response)

The aforementioned layers might make use of components (e.g., coordinates translators) or services (e.g., GIS). A subset of the previous interactions, through eliminating the direct message exchange of the positioning server and SAP could potentially minimize the risk of building privacy holes in the system.

## Push & Pull Services

There are two ways one can consider delivery of content to the end user. In both cases, it assumed that the user has posed a request for content and they are not entirely network driven, since this would raise several regulatory issues. In each case the user interaction pattern is somewhat different:

- A **pull** service is the one that delivers request to the user upon his/her explicit request within a reasonable interaction time;
- A **push** service is one that submits information to the user when special criteria are met and there seems to be no explicit binding of a request to a response in the form of interaction. These criteria could be location, time or more advanced ones like matched lookups for information and so on.

Over the typical HTTP/TCP/IP stack found in advanced mobile equipment one can consume such services by various mechanisms. The simplest approach would be by periodically polling through a proprietary client for any kind of pushed information to be presented to the user. Triggering polling by identifying significant positional change also could be considered for appropriate devices. This solution introduces network usage even when no information is to be delivered to the user, and is actually a mixture of pushing and concepts services. Traditional mobile devices could be contacted through typical gateways (SMS/MMS) whenever network-monitoring procedures decide that interesting information is available. Push services on location criteria can however become a potential scalability and performance threat for an LBS infrastructure, because of the computational and bandwidth demands required for scanning vast collections of data on each and every end-user move.

## User Authentication and Identification

A very important part of the service is user identification, authentication, and authorisation (Gajparia, Mitchell, & Yeun, 2005; Soppera & Burbridge, 2005). The SAP is proposed for taking over the responsibility of authorizing end-users. Authentication is actually optional since it is considered that just identifying the user can be quite enough in several application scenarios, such as free-of-charge information delivery. Simple identification might be utilised for some personalisation facilities. A basic scenario for authentication would be based on a username/password challenge scheme, which will be verified against a user directory. Client certificates are a more advanced option. Using secure channels for performing authentication is required to avoid common security penetration cases, yet not all devices might capable of all common types of secure information exchange. SAP is the responsible for maintaining the user directory where users (via their credentials) are mapped to unique identifiers and authorisation information.

Authentication is of crucial importance when positioning takes place under a network provided positioning mechanism. Acquiring end-user's location relying on simple username/password challenge opens a wide opportunity for service misuse. Taking advantage of the "spying effect,"[24] an unauthorised user can attach a typical mobile device related to a specific user account on a person to be "watched," and request positioning information through a secondary device (e.g., fixed PC or other mobile equipment [ME]) on behalf of the above-mentioned account. If no network session data are being used, location information will potentially be delivered to the "spy". This might be a well-accepted feature of some implementations but the typical perspective of privacy forces counter measures for avoidance of such situations. In the SMS/MMS channels case this information is being incorporated in the state of the gateway/SAP session that is being established to fulfil a client request. On the

TCP/IP typical channel the situation is a bit more complicated. Since the client is requesting position over an HTTP request, the MNO typically receives the request for locating the user by the SAP. Thus some user identifier must be presented (other than the username). Fortunately, the SAP already has the TCP/IP session information (source address/port) that is being used in order for the user to be serviced. Typically end-user mobile equipment is behind a NAT gateway and this address is not a real one, thus the port number must also be used in order for the related MNO to locate the correct user. The SAP can select the correct MNO either by the internal directory service (the source address of the request directly or indirectly identifies the MNO) or by the end-user information record being used. The MNO can therefore identify the actual user through NAT layer information and GPRS IP address assignment records.

Nevertheless a highly secure approach could be restricting positioning information exchange internally to the MNO infrastructure, by having positioning servers to replying only to requests raised internally by MNO subscribers, and more specifically only by the mobile device being located. In this scenario, the client device acts as an autonomously positioned piece of equipment, at least as this can be understood from the SAP point of view.

## Content Structure

Limiting delivered content to "tourism" related categories might not be a significant restriction for the location-related content to be provided, but certainly poses some requirements on the structure this content must meet. There exist rich schemas for describing "tourism" content (TourML 2003), which attempt to fully capture the corresponding ontology. However from our point of view forcing "over" structuring of content is usually a source of problems for the content producers and providers. It is a strategic decision that content providers expose content compliant with a minimal set of requirements. These requirements could include position information (in various forms, e.g., rectangles, series of points, etc.), language identifiers, labels, multiple classifications in a two level hierarchy (though not a hard constraint) and a content rating scheme. Content classifiers are open to extension by CPs and are being aggregated by the SAP. The first level is mainly proposed to be a means to define end-user content selection preferences, but a more sophisticated scheme can make use of a free hierarchy. Content rating is being required in order for free of charge, simple or rich content to be differentiated by the SAP, in order for it to be delivered to various clients, although the actual content manipulation is to be performed by the content provider (CP). Internally CPs might realise a more complex structure, but the SAP is concerned only about the above-mentioned tags. Usage of extra tags can be handled by additional user preferences, for which an extensible mechanism should be provided.

## Presentation

A final, but quite important issue is that eventually data must be presented to the end-user. Presentation can be realised by a wide series of equipment, which might range from high quality multimedia laptops to simple SMS capable mobile phones. As already mentioned the XML/XSL/XSLT set of standards and related tools provide a powerful mechanism for implementing an *author-once-publish-many* times scheme, capable of covering a wide range of end user preferences and equipment. At this point, it can be identified that these are two level transformations in order to achieve maximum content reusability:

- The first level is internal CP transformation and renders original data into a form that will comply with the SAP required minimal structure;
- The second level of transformations is the one that will transform the content in a way that it will fully exploit the capabilities of the end user device and user preferences. Such rendering can result into simple text fragments to be posted over SMS, MMS fragments, WML, HTML, DHTML pages, and even advanced SMIL[25] presentations.

Presentation transformation should not be considered as a Web-only requirement; even if data are accessed through proprietary Web service clients such transformations would be of use.

## Application Gateways

The assumed infrastructure of these models of service delivery is heavily based on the assumption of a homogeneous underlying network—on HTTP/TCP/IP layers. It is obvious that this is not a realistic assumption especially when mobile networks come to play. In order to hide the diversity of the underlying infrastructures, gateways are required that allow for the translation of non-SAP native requests to be fulfilled. These gateways receive client requests and deliver them to the SAP in a form they can be understood. At this point it is obvious that in order for uniform interaction to be achievable by all CPs, translation of requests is being handled by a specific reception point of the gateway that analyses the content of the incoming message and forms the appropriate request to the SAP. When requests are being replied, the data are being appropriately packaged and delivered to the actual network operator infrastructure components that will push it back to the requesting equipment through the appropriate "channel." Typically channels that require gateways are the SMS,

EMS, MMS ones, while the functionality of such gateways also is significant for implementation of alerting services.

## *Pricing/Billing*

Authorizing users is not only required for enabling access to the services and content authentication but also for charging and billing. When requests and responses are being exchanged among the various parties, the SAP user identification is being utilised in order for the CP or application service provider (ASP) to authorise and charge the appropriate subscriber. Alternatively ASPs or CPs perform no user identification and deliver data on behalf of the SAP, which is the actually charged partner. This would cover the CP/ASP/SAP part of the service usage. On the other hand the network operator will charge network usage, potentially posing a premium on top of the traffic which is being delivered to specific ASP/CPs/SAPs, and so on. Another scenario is that ASPs/CPs might vary the charges depending on user location or user preferences (such as content quality, type, or location-based advertising allowance), thus allowing for quite complex pricing/billing schemes.

# Conclusion

Making use of standards and protocols (e.g., LIF, XML, and HTTP), avoiding proprietary solutions and limiting interoperability requirements to a minimum renders architecture capable of integrating various stakeholders with limited cost and implications. The technologies being proposed allow interoperability and redirection among various sub-service providers and the integration of services in order to provide a homogenous application to the end-user.

Although the proposed solution for tourists has been tested[26] on a single network operator elsewhere, support for location-based services is not restricted to a single network provider, even when positioning is performed by the mobile network operator. Despite its "tourism content delivery" orientation, the infrastructure in this testbed can be made capable of providing more complex services with minimum impact on service providers, by making use of state-of-the-art client equipment features, such as Java, DHTML, and so on. In this regard, utilizing a directory service under a standard protocol, within the SAP, is mostly adequate for creating a totally uniform platform for in-doors and outdoors LBS and quite heterogeneous positioning methods and capabilities (e.g., RFID, wireless access point identification, etc.). Since the motivation behind location-based services is its potential beneficiary commercial exploitation, a preliminary technoeconomic evaluation based on hypothetical deployment and commercialisation scenarios has been attempted by the authors and can be found in M-Guide (2002). The study presents basic financial indicators that showed the viability of the proposed solution as well as a full description of the evaluation scenarios and results. The details of the methodology used in technoeconomic evaluation can be found in IST-TONIC (2000).

There are various aspects of the presented approach where potential improvements will lead to further benefits for the end-user and the content/network providers. These largely involve standards identification and adoption, as well as refinements of current implementations. An essential improvement would be to fully fit the design discussed here to the open service-oriented architecture initiative, thus providing dynamic service discovery. Introducing the attributes and rules that will enable the creation of a universal directory service to support each and every relevant information and service lookup is a step that should be made.

Although business-to-customer (B2C) information interchange is sufficiently faced under our perspective, business-to-business (B2B) is partially dealt with. B2B data exchange is limited to areas where information is essential for servicing a particular user request, for example, positioning, authentication, and so on. However B2B collaboration can be further exploited in subjects such as content modifications due to relocation, caching, restructuring service organisation, and so on. Further work on this area would potentially enhance scalability of "push services," another area that has not been fully exploited.

Work also needs to be done on roaming-user scenarios in order for the infrastructure to fully comply with market requirements, since handling and network positioning of roaming users is currently performed inefficiently. Moreover, a more detailed technoeconomic study is needed, based on specific deployment scenarios, taking into consideration up-to-date technological and financial data in order for a more precise profit/loss prediction of relevant service deployment to be made possible.

# Acknowledgments

A part of this work has been performed with the support of the E-Content M-Guide Project, which was partially funded by the European Union. The authors would like to acknowledge the support and contributions of their colleagues from M-Guide project, namely Exodus SA, Vodafone-Panafon SA, University of Athens, Municipality of Athens, Adaptia and Iternet. The authors would also like to thank the two anonymous reviewers for the fruitful comments.

# References

Adams, P. M., Ashwell, G. W. B., & Baxter, R. (2003). Location-based services: An overview of the standards. *BT Technology Journal, 21*(1), 34-43.

Against the Clock (Firm). (2002). *Macromedia flash 5: Animating for the Web.* Upper Saddle River, NJ: Prentice Hall.

Anderson, R. (2000). *Professional XML.* Birmingham, UK; Chicago: Wrox Press.

Andersson, P., Hulten, S., & Valiente, P. (2005). Beauty contest licensing lessons from the 3G process in sweden. *Telecommunications Policy, 29*(8), 577-593.

Beatty, C. (2002). Location-based services: Navigation for the masses, at last! *Journal of Navigation, 55*(2), 241-248.

Bennett, C. (2001). *Practical WAP: Developing applications for the wireless Web.* Cambridge, UK; New York: Cambridge University Press.

Berners-Lee, T., & Hendler, J. (2001). Publishing on the semantic Web: The coming Internet revolution will profoundly affect scientific information. *Nature, 410*(6832), 1023-1024.

Berners-Lee, T., Hendler, J., & Lassila, O. (2001). The Semantic Web: A new form of Web content that is meaningful to computers will unleash a revolution of new possibilities. *Scientific American, 284*(5), 3.

Bluetooth.org. (2001). *The bluetooth membership site.* Retrieved from http://www.bluetooth.org/

Bohn, J., & Mattern, F. (2004). Super-distributed RFID tag infrastructures. *Ambient Intelligence, Proceedings, 3295,* 1-12.

Bosak, J. (1998). Media-independent publishing: Four myths about XML. *Computer, 31*(10), 120-122.

Bosak, J., & Bray, T. (1999). XML and the second-generation. *Scientific American, 280*(5), 89-93.

Brown, A., Johnston, S., & Kelly, K. (2003). *Using service-oriented architecture and component-based development to build Web service applications*: IBM Corporation.

Caffery, J., & Stuber, G. L. (1998a). Subscriber location in CDMA cellular networks. *IEEE Transactions on Vehicular Technology, 47*(2), 406-416.

Caffery, J. J., & Stuber, G. L. (1998b). Overview of radiolocation in CDMA cellular systems. *IEEE Communications Magazine, 36*(4), 38-45.

Colan, M. (2004). *Service-oriented architecture expands the vision of Web services*: IBM Corporation.

Czajkowski, K., Foster, I., Ferguson, D. F., Frey, J., Graham, S., Snelling, D., et al. (2004). *The ws-resource framework*. Retrieved from http://www.globus. org/wsrf/specs/ws-wsrf.pdf

Dana, P. H. (1994). *GPS overview*. Department of Geography, University of Texas at Austin.

Dao, D., Rizos, C., & Wang, J. (2002). Location-based services: Technical and business issues. *GPS Solutions, 6*(3), 169.

Daoud, F., & Mohan, S. (2002). Strategies for provisioning and operating VHE services in multi-access networks. *IEEE Communications Magazine, 40*(1), 78.

Devine, A., & Holmquist, S. (2001) *Mobile internet content providers and their business models*. The Royal Institute of Technology, Sweden.

Di Fazio, A., Mocci, G., Rossini, E., D'Angelo, G., Lorelli, A., & Jarosh, A. (2004). Gauss satellite solution for location-based services. *International Journal of Satellite Communications and Networking, 22*(1), 55-85.

Douglas, E. (2004). Indoor positioning system can track equipment and people. *Anesthesiology News*.

Drane, C., Macnaughtan, M., & Scott, C. (1998). Positioning GSM telephones. *IEEE Communications Magazine, 36*(4), 46+.

Ekahau. (2006). Ekahau Positioning Engine 3.1—Ekahau Site Calibration. Retrieved from http://www.ekahau.com/

El-Rabbany, A. (2002). *Introduction to GPS: The global positioning system*. Boston: Artech House.

Ellinger, F., Barras, D., & Jackel, H. (2002). Mobile phone market study. *TRLabs/ IEEE Wireless 2002*. Retrieved from http://www.ife.ee.ethz.ch/~ellinger/ Homepage/mp_rev.pdf

EMILY. (2002). *Business models: EMILY (IST-2000-26040) Project*.

Ericsson. *Mobile positioning system / mobile positioning protocol*. Ericsson.

Erl, T. (2004). *Service-oriented architecture: A field guide to integrating XML and Web services*. Upper Saddle River, NJ: Prentice Hall Professional Technical Reference.

Erl, T. (2005). *Service-oriented architecture: Concepts, technology, and design*. Upper Saddle River, NJ: Prentice Hall Professional Technical Reference.

ETSI. (2006). *ETSI telecom standards*. Retrieved from http://www.etsi.org/

Extensible markup language (XML). (n.d.). Retrieved from http://www.w3.org/ XML/

FCC. (2001). *FCC wireless 911 requirements*. FCC.

Feng, J., Zhu, Y. L., Mukai, N., & Watanabe, T. (2005). Search on transportation network for location-based service. *Innovations in Applied Artificial Intelligence, 3533*, 657-666.

Foster, I., Frey, J., Graham, S., Tuecke, S., Czajkowski, K., & Ferguson, D. F. (2004). *Modeling stateful resources with Web services.* Retrieved from http://devresource.hp.com/drc/specifications/wsrf/ModelingState-1-1.pdf

Fritsch, L., & Scherner, T. (2005). A multilaterally secure, privacy-friendly location-based service for disaster management and civil protection. *Networking ICN 2005, 2*(3421), 1130-1137.

Gajparia, A. S., Mitchell, C. J., & Yeun, C. Y. (2005). Supporting user privacy in location based services. *IEICE Transactions on Communications, E88B*(7), 2837-2847.

Gamma, E. (1995). *Design patterns: Elements of reusable object-oriented software.* Reading, MA: Addison-Wesley.

GARMIN. (n.d.). *GPS guide for beginners.* Retrieved from http://www.garmin.com/aboutGPS/manual.html

Grajski, K. A., & Kirk, E. (2003). Towards a mobile multimedia age—location-based services: A case study. *Wireless Personal Communications, 26*(2-3), 105-116.

Gratsias, K., Frentzos, E., Delis, V., & Theodoridis, Y. (2005). Towards a taxonomy of location based services. *Web and Wireless Geographical Information Systems, Proceedings, 3833*, 19-30.

Gruber, H. (2005). *The economics of mobile telecommunications.* New York: Cambridge University Press.

Gruber, H., & Verboven, F. (2001). The diffusion of mobile telecommunications services in the european union. *European Economic Review, 45*(3), 588.

GSM. (2002). *Location based services.* Retrieved from http://www.gsmworld.com/documents/lbs/se23.pdf

GSM. (2003). *MMS interworking guidelines.* Retrieved from http://www.gsmworld.com/documents/ireg/ir52310.pdf

Halonen, T., Romero, J., & Melero, J. (2003). *GSM, GPRS, and EDGE performance: Evolution towards 3G/UMTS* (2nd ed.). Chichester, West Sussex, UK; Hoboken, NJ: J. Wiley.

Heijden, M. v. d., & Taylor, M. (2000). *Understanding wap: Wireless applications, devices, and services.* Boston: Artech House.

Hightower, J., & Borriello, G. (2001). Location systems for ubiquitous computing. *Computer, 34*(8), 57+.

Holma, H., & Toskala, A. (2004). *Wcdma for UMTS: Radio access for third generation mobile communications* (3rd ed.). Hoboken, NJ: J. Wiley & Sons.

Huber, A. J., & Huber, J. F. (2002). *UMTS and mobile computing*. Boston: Artech House.

IST-REPOSIT. (2001). Real time dynamic bandwidth optimisation in satellite networks. *IST*. EU.

IST-TONIC. (2000). Technoeconomics of IP optimised networks and services. *IST*. EU.

Iwasaki, Y., Kawaguchi, N., & Inagaki, Y. (2005). Azim: Direction-based service system for both indoors and outdoors. *IEICE Transactions on Communications, E88B*(3), 1034-1044.

Kaaranen, H. (2005). *UMTS networks: Architecture, mobility, and services* (2nd ed.). Chichester, West Sussex, UK; Hoboken, NJ: J. Wiley & Sons.

Kakaletris, G., Varoutas, D., Katsianis, D., Sphicopoulos, T., & Kouvas, G. (2004). Designing and implementing an open infrastructure for location-based, tourism-related content delivery. *Wireless Personal Communications, 30*(2-4), 153-165.

Karagiozidis, M., Markoulidakis, Y., Velentzas, S., & Kauranne, T. (2003). Commercial use of mobile, personalised location-based services. *Journal of the Communications Network, 2*, 15-20.

Katsianis, D., Welling, I., Ylonen, M., Varoutas, D., Sphicopoulos, T., Elnegaard, N. K., et al. (2001). The financial perspective of the mobile networks in europe. *IEEE Personal Communications [see also IEEE Wireless Communications], 8*(6), 58-64.

Kim, J. W., Kim, C.S., Gautam, A., & Lee, Y. (2005). Location-based tour guide system using mobile gis and Web crawling. *Web and Wireless Geographical Information Systems, 3428*, 51-63.

Korhonen, J., Aalto, O., Gurtov, A., & Lamanen, H. (2001). *Measured performance of GSM, HSCSD and GPRS*. Paper presented at the IEEE International Conference on Communications (ICC'01).

Koutsopoulou, M., Panagiotakis, S., Alonistioti, A., & Kaloxylos, A. (2005). Customised billing for location-based services. *Distributed Applications and Interoperable Systems, 3543*, 27-37.

Kozak, B. (2002). *Macromedia flash MX freehand 10: Advanced training from the source*. Berkeley, CA: Macromedia Press.

Laitinen, H. (2001). *Cellular location techniques*. Paper presented at the MLW.

Lee, Y., Prabhu, N., & Park, E. K. (2002). Middleware for location based information services in mobile environment. *Developing and Infrastructure for Mobile and Wireless Systems, 2538*, 173-182.

LIF-IOT. (2002). *Location services (LCS) inter-operability test (IOT) specification in GSM*. Location Interoperability Forum (LIF), Interoperability Testing Group.

Lin, J. Y.-B., & Chlamtac, I. (2001). *Wireless and mobile network architectures*. New York: Wiley.

LoVEUS. (2002). *User requirements of the LoVEUS system* (LoVEUS IST-2000-30155).

Ludden, B. (2000). *Location technology*. Vodafone.

M-Guide. (2002). *User needs—market analysis* (Deliverable D2.1).

Mao, Z., & Douligeris, C. (2000). A location-based mobility tracking scheme for pcs networks. *Computer Communications, 23*(18), 1729-1739.

Microsoft. (n.d.). *Microsoft.Net compact framework 2.0*, Retrieved from http://msdn.microsoft.com/mobility/netcf/

Miller, B. A., & Bisdikian, C. (2002). *Bluetooth revealed* (2nd ed.). Upper Saddle River, NJ: Prentice Hall PTR.

Morrow, R. (2002). *Bluetooth operation and use*. New York: McGraw-Hill.

Mouly, M., & Pautet, M. B. (1995). Current evolution of the GSM systems. *IEEE Personal Communications, 2*(5), 9-19.

Moureu L. (2000), Impact of location-based services on the mobility market. *Alcatel Telecommunications Review 2nd Quarter 2000*.

Muller, N. J. (2001). *Bluetooth demystified*. New York: McGraw-Hill.

Muller, N. J. (2003). *WiFi for the enterprise*. New York: McGraw-Hill.

Nellen, P. M., Bronnimann, R., Held, M., & Sennhauser, U. (2004). Long-term monitoring of polarization-mode dispersion of aerial optical cables with respect to line availability. *Journal of Lightwave Technology, 22*(8), 1848-1855.

Newcomer, E., & Lomow, G. (2005). *Understanding soa with Web services*. Upper Saddle River, NJ: Addison-Wesley.

Northstream. (2001). *Location based services: Considerations and challenges*. Retrieved from http://www.northstream.se

OGS. (n.d.). *Opengis location services, open geospatial consortium*. Retrieved from http://www.opengeospatial.org/functional/?page=ols

OMA. (2002). *Mobile location protocol, location working group*: Open Mobile Alliance.

OTC. (n.d.). *Open tourism consortium*. Retrieved from http://www.opentourism.org/

Pahlavan, K., & Krishnamurthy, P. (2002). *Principles of wireless networks: A unified approach*. Upper Saddle River, NJ: Prentice Hall PTR.

Pateli, A. G., Giaglis, G. M., & Spinellis, D. D. (2005). Trial evaluation of wireless info-communication and indoor location-based services in exhibition shows. *Advances in Informatics, Proceedings, 3746*, 199-210.

Patil, B. (2003). *IP in wireless networks*. Upper Saddle River, NJ: Prentice Hall Professional Technical Reference.

Prasad, R., & Ruggieri, M. (2005). *Applied satellite navigation using GPS, Galileo, and augmentation systems*. Boston: Artech House.

Rao, B., & Minakakis, L. (2003). Evolution of mobile location-based services. *Communications of the Acm, 46*(12), 61-65.

Reed, J. H., Krizman, K. J., Woerner, B. D., & Rappaport, T. S. (1998). An overview of the challenges and progress in meeting the e-911 requirement for location service. *IEEE Communications Magazine, 36*(4), 30-37.

Rysavy, P. (2005). *Data capabilities: GPRS to HSDPA and beyond.* Retrieved from http://www.3gamericas.org/pdfs/rysavy_data_sept2005.pdf

Schmid, A., Neubauer, A., Ehm, H., Weigel, R., Lemke, N., Heinrichs, G., et al. (2005). Combined Galileo/GPS architecture for enhanced sensitivity reception. *Aeu-International Journal of Electronics and Communications, 59*(5), 297-306.

Searle, M. (2001). *Location base services.* Paper presented at the InSig.

Smith, R. J. (2003). *WiFi home networking*. New York: McGraw-Hill.

SnapTrack. (2001). *Location technologies for GSM, GPRS and WCDMA networks*. White paper.

Snell, J., Tidwell, D., & Kulchenko, P. (2002). *Programming Web services with soap* (1st ed.). Sebastopol, CA: O'Reilly & Associates.

Soppera, A., & Burbridge, T. (2005). Wireless identification: Privacy and security. *Bt Technology Journal, 23*(4), 54-64.

Sparacino, F. (2002). *The museum wearable: Real-time sensor-driven understanding of visitors' interests for personalized visually-augmented museum experiences.* Paper presented at the Museums and the Web.

Spirito, M. A. (2001). On the accuracy of cellular mobile station location estimation. *IEEE Transactions on Vehicular Technology, 50*(3), 674-685.

Spratt, M. (2003). An overview of positioning by diffusion. *Wireless Networks, 9*(6), 565-574.

Staab, S., & Werthner, H. (2002). Intelligent systems for tourism. *IEEE Intelligent Systems, 17*(6), 53-55.

SUN. (n.d.). *Java 2 platform, micro edition (j2me).* Retrieved from http://java.sun.com/j2me/

Tarumi, H., Morishita, K., & Kambayashi, Y. (2000). Public applications of spacetag and their impacts. *Digital Cities, 1765*, 350-363.

Taylor, J. H., & Ryan, J. (1995). Museums and galleries on the internet. *Internet Research-Electronic Networking Applications and Policy, 5*(1), 80+.

3GPP. (2002). *3rd Generation Partnership Project—3GPP.* Retrieved from http://www.3gpp.org/

Tisal, J. (2001). *The GSM network: GPRS evolution: One step towards UMTS* (2nd ed.). Chichester; New York: J. Wiley.

TourML. (2003). *TourML.* Retrieved from http://www.tourml.org/

UDDI. (2004). *Enabling service-oriented architecture*, Retrieved from http://www.uddi.org/

UMTS. (n.d.). *The UMTS forum.* Retrieved from http://www.umts-forum.org/

Varoutas, D., Katsianis, D., Sphicopoulos, T., Cerboni, A., Kalhagen, K. O., Stordahl, K., et al. (2002, June 16-19). *3G MVNOs financial perspectives.* Paper presented at the IST Mobile and Wireless Telecommunications Summit, Thessaloniki, Greece.

Varoutas, D., Katsianis, D., Sphicopoulos, T., Loizillon, F., Kalhagen, K. O., Stordahl, K., et al. (2003). Business opportunities through UMTS—WLAN networks. *Annales Des Telecommunications-Annals of Telecommunications, 58*(3-4), 553-575.

Varoutas, D., Katsianis, D., Sphicopoulos, T., Stordahl, K., & Welling, I. (2006). On the economics of 3G mobile virtual network operators (MVNOs). *Wireless Personal Communications, 36*(2), 129-142.

W3C. (2001). *The Semantic Web.* Retrieved from http://www.w3.org/2001/sw/

Wang, Y., Jia, X., Lee, H. K., & Li, G. Y. (2003). *An indoors wireless positioning system based on wireless local area network infrastructure.* Paper presented at the SatNav 2003, the 6th International Symposium on Satellite Navigation Technology Including Mobile Positioning & Location Services, Australia.

Xiao, Y., & Pan, Y. (2005). *Wireless lans and bluetooth.* New York: Nova Science Publishers.

Yan, X. (2004). 3G licensing in Hong Kong: The debate. *Telecommunications Policy, 28*(2), 213-226.

Yilin, Z. (2000). Mobile phone location determination and its impact on intelligent transportation systems. *IEEE Transactions on Intelligent Transportation Systems, 1*(1), 55.

Zhao, Y. L. (2002). Standardization of mobile phone positioning for 3G systems. *IEEE Communications Magazine, 40*(7), 108-116.

Zimmermann, A., Lorenz, A., & Specht, M. (2003). User modeling in adaptive audio-augmented museum environments. *User Modeling 2003, Proceedings, 2702*, 403-407.

# Endnotes

[1]    Being redefined for the electronic era.

[2]    2nd generation (2G) of mobile telephony is widely known as GSM, while the term 2.5G is used for the 2G networks with data and Internet access capabilities mainly based on GPRS.

[3]    The 3rd generation of mobile telephony is mainly known as UMTS.

[4]    Also labelled as "operator" when no ambiguity is introduced.

[5]    Speed might vary upon device capabilities, reception quality, network load, and so forth.

[6]    International Telecommunication Union whose standardisation sector is ITU-T, known as CCITT up to 1993 (CCITT originates back to 1865).

[7]    Performance highly varies upon network load, infrastructure specifications, reception and mobile equipment capabilities.

[8]    Nominal speed varies from 11 (802.11b) to 108MBps (Super-G).

[9]    The time required for a signal (or minimal data element) to be send by the source, transmitted back by the target and received back at the source.

[10]    Outdoors WLAN access is becoming more and more popular since year 2005.

[11]    Basic geographical information systems are data repositories that offer storage and retrieval facilities suited to the type of information in focus (geospatial) accompanied by appropriate management and visualisation tools.

[12]    Source: Derived from Searle (2001)

[13]    Source: Derived from Searle (2001)

[14]    There are cases that content might be preinstalled on a device.

[15]    The XSL Formatting Objects (XSL-FO) vocabulary is designed in order to facilitate content display on a wide variety of media such as screen, paper, or even voice.

[16]    Mark-up language technologically similar with HTML for use with WAP and 2G/2.5G Web-enabled mobile phones.

[17]    In advance downloading of the content to the mobile device and consequently displaying it to the tourist by utilizing combined user-interaction and equipment (such as a GPS device) provided information.

[18]    Flash technology (introduced by MacroMedia Inc. in 1996) is mainly used for creating interactive multimedia presentations on the Web.

[19]   3GP is a format defined by 3GPP as a simplified version of MPEG-4 Part 14 for multimedia objects exchange and playback on 3G mobile phones.

[20]   Development effort required to achieve systems' inter-working when no sufficient configuration/customisation capabilities exist in the involved software entities.

[21]   Special concerns apply to this assumption.

[22]   An initially European standardisation organisation, currently named as ECMA International.

[23]   The UDDI registry is essentially a "yellow pages" like service for locating Web services capable of serving a particular request.

[24]   The term has been proposed by Antti Damski, Adaptia Ltd. in M-GUIDE Project (M-Guide, 2002)

[25]   A markup language of similar technology to HTML that allows display and playback of interactive multimedia content adding special features for synchronisation/presentation, partially supported by some of the well-known Web browsers.

[26]   The solution has been developed and tested as part of the M-Guide Project, which has been partially funded project by EU under the eContent initiative, during 2002-2004.

# Appendix: Acronyms

| Acronym | Description |
| --- | --- |
| 2 G | 2nd generation mobile telephony (e.g., GSM) |
| 2.5 G | 2nd generation mobile telephony (e.g., GSM + GPRS) |
| 3GPP | 3G Partnership Project |
| A-GPS | assisted GPS |
| AOA | angle of arrival |
| ASP | application service provider |
| B2B | business to business |
| B2C | business to client |
| BS | base station |
| BTS | base transceiver station |
| CCITT | International Telegraph and Telephone Consultative Committee |
| CDMA | code division multiple access |

*continued on following pages*

| | |
|---|---|
| CMS | content management system |
| COO | cell of origin |
| CSS | cascading stylesheet |
| DHTML | Dynamic HTML |
| ECMA | European Computer Manufacturers Association |
| EDGE | enhanced data GSM environment |
| E-OTD | enhanced observed time difference |
| GIS | geographical information system |
| GMLC | gateway mobile location center |
| GPRS | general packer radio service |
| GPS | global positioning system |
| GSM | global system for mobile communication |
| HSCSD | high speed circuit switched data |
| HSDPA | high-speed downlink packet access |
| HTML | Hypertext Markup Language |
| HTTP | hypertext transfer protocol |
| ICT | information and telecommunication technology |
| IEEE | Institute of Electrical and Electronics Engineers |
| IP | Internet protocol |
| IR | infrared |
| IS | information systems |
| IT | information technology |
| ITU | International Telecommunication Union |
| JPEG | Joint Photographic Experts Group' |
| LAN | local area network |
| LBS | location-based services |
| LIF | location interoperability forum |
| LMU | location measurement unit |
| ME | mobile equipment |
| MLP | mobile location protocol |
| MMS | multimedia messaging service |
| MNO | mobile network operator |
| MPC | mobile positioning center |
| MPEG | Motion Picture Expert Group |
| MPP | mobile positioning protocol |

| MSID | mobile subscriber ID |
|---|---|
| NAT | network address translation |
| OMA | Open Mobile Alliance |
| OpenLS | OpenGIS location services |
| PDA | personal data assistant |
| QoS | quality of service |
| RDF | resource description framework |
| RF | radio frequency |
| RTT | round trip time |
| SAP | service access point |
| SMS | short message system |
| SOA | service oriented architecture |
| SOAP | simple object access protocol |
| TA | timing advance |
| TCP | transport control protocol |
| TDMA | time division multiple access |
| TOA | time of arrival |
| UDDI | universal description, discovery, and integration |
| UMTS | universal mobile telecommunications system |
| URI | uniform resource identifiers |
| URL | uniform resource locator |
| W3C | World Wide Web Consortium |
| WAG | wireless application gateway |
| WAN | wide area network |
| WAP | wireless access protocol |
| WCDMA | wideband CDMA |
| WiFi | wireless fidelity, any type of 802.11xx network |
| WLAN | wireless LAN |
| WML | Wireless Markup Language |
| WSRF | Web services resource framework |
| XLS | XML for location services |
| XML | eXtensible Markup Language |
| XSL | eXtensible Stylesheet Language |
| XSL-FO | XSL formatting objects |
| XSLT | XSL transformation |

## Chapter VI

# Developing Visual Tourism Recommender Systems

Mohan Ponnada, Victoria University, Australia

Roopa Jakkilinki, Victoria University, Australia

Nalin Sharda, Victoria University, Australia

## Abstract

*Tourism recommender systems (TRS) have become popular in recent years; however, most lack visual means of presenting the recommendations. This paper presents ways of developing visual travel recommender systems (V-TRS). The two popular travel recommender systems being used today are the TripMatcher™ and Me-Print™. Tour recommendation using image-based planning using SCORM (TRIPS) is a system that aims to make the presentation more visual. It uses SCORM and CORDRA standards. Sharable content object reference model (SCORM) is a standard that collates content from various Web sites, and content object repository discovery and registration/resolution architecture (CORDRA) aims to locate and reference SCORM repositories throughout the Internet. The information collected is stored in the form of an XML file. This XML file can be visualised by either converting it into a Flash movie or into a synchronized multimedia integration language (SMIL) presentation. A case study demonstrating the operation of current travel recommender systems also is presented. Further research in this area should aim to improve user interaction and provide more control functions within a V-TRS to make tour-planning simple, fun and more interactive.*

# Introduction

Recommender systems have become popular with the advent of e-commerce. The development of this technology is being strengthened as more people start using the Internet for making purchases. Recommender systems are used by Amazon.com (Linden, Smith, & York, 2003) to recommend books, and movies are recommended on MovieLens (Miller, Albert, Lam, Konstan, & Riedl, 2003). In recent years there has been much work done to improve recommender systems. With increasing Internet adoption, business transactions on the Internet are likely to grow substantially; this encourages vendors to add recommendation capabilities to their Web sites (Peddy & Armentrout, 2003). Tourism is one of the most successful and dynamic industries in the world, and is constantly evolving with continuous technological advancements that include Internet based systems. One such advancement is visual travel recommender systems (V-TRS).

Travel recommender systems (TRSs) are increasingly being adopted to support the tourism industry, some examples of this include Triplehop's TripMatcher™ (Delgado, 2001; Starkov, 2001), and VacationCoach's expert advice platform Me-Print™ (VacationCoach, 2002). A TRS allows tourists to access an informed recommendation for travel planning via an artificial intelligence-based engine. However, current TRSs do not provide tourists with the facility to visualise their complete holiday itinerary, integrating location, transportation, accommodation, attractions, and entertainment. The tourist has to browse through individual Web pages to build a mental picture of the planned tour. In this chapter we introduce the concept of a visual TRS, which can overcome this limitation.

The main objectives of this chapter are:

- To understand recommender systems
- To provide an insight into current application of recommender systems in the tourism industry
- To gain an understanding of services provided by TRS systems, their benefits and limitations
- To present the framework of a visual travel recommender system
- To present a case study demonstrating the operation of current travel recommender systems
- To discuss the future trends in travel recommender systems

# Background Information

## Recommender Systems

"Recommender Systems are an attempt to mathematically model and technically reproduce the process of recommendations in the real world" (Berka & Plößnig, 2004). Recommender systems are being used by e-commerce Web sites to make suggestions to their customers (Schafer, Konstan, & Riedl, 1999). These recommendations can be made on various factors such as demographics, past buying behaviour of the customers, and prediction of the future buying behaviour.

Recommender systems enhance sales in three different ways (Schafer et al., 1999):

- **Browsers to buyers:** A good Web site can turn visitors of the site into buyers by helping them find the products they wish to purchase.

- **Cross-selling:** Well linked Web pages can improve cross-selling by suggesting additional products for the customer to purchase.

- **Loyalty:** Recommender Systems can improve loyalty by creating a relationship of trust between the Web site and the customer.

### Classification of Recommender Systems

The process of recommendation varies depending on the application and the system in question. However, the general concepts underpinning recommender systems are the same. Recommender systems can be classified into four recommendation paradigms (Stabb et al., 2002), namely:

- **Content-based recommender systems**
- **Collaborative-filtering recommendation systems**
- **Knowledge-based recommendation systems**
- **Hybrid recommender systems**

### Content-Based Recommender Systems

In content-based recommender systems, the users express their needs, desires and constraints. The recommender system makes a recommendation by matching the user profile with the product information, using information retrieval techniques. The system understands the user's desires and preferences based on the characteristics and ratings provided, and by looking at past user preferences.

However, this system has a number of limitations (Balabanovi, 1997; Shardanand, 1995):

- Firstly, the "new user problem" comes into play since the user has to rate a sufficient number of items before a content-based recommender system understands the user's preferences.

- Secondly, the number of features associated with an item influences this type of system. To extract sufficient features, the content must be in a text form, or features should be assigned to items manually. Such feature extraction is difficult for graphics, audio and video streams.

- A third disadvantage is that a content-based recommender system recommends items that match against the user profile, this provides little opportunity to the users to experience the item being recommended (Shardanand, 1995).

### Collaborative-Filtering Recommender Systems

Collaborative-filtering recommender systems are the most widely used recommender system, where user feedback, reviews and rating given by other users are relied upon to recommend an item (Hill, Stead, Rosenstein, & Furnas, 1995). For example, suppose if a user is looking for a book on the Java language in an online book store, the system recommends books which have high ratings based on the feedback from readers who have read various Java books. These systems work well if there is a large volume of ratings for each item.

Reliance on these types of systems is problematic for the recommendation of new items or where the number of reviews is low. Also, it does not account for divergence in preferences between new and previous users. Pazzani (1999) suggests one way of overcoming this limitation via the use of a hybrid recommender system, that combine collaborative, content-based, and demographic filtering approaches.

### Knowledge-Based Recommendation Systems

Knowledge-based recommender systems combine the knowledge about the user and the products and services on offer to make a recommendation. If a user visits an online book store, the system recommends other books in related topics. The system knows what the user is looking for, and based on this the system recommends additional products (Burke, 2000). These systems do not need extensive knowledge about an item to make a decision, but like the content-based recommender systems, they require knowledge about the user and his/her buying patterns, which can be acquired by a series of queries.

## Hybrid Recommender Systems

Hybrid recommender systems combine two or more recommendation methodologies. These systems were developed in order to overcome the limitations of each of the individual systems. Most often, collaborative-filtering is combined with some other methodology. Decisions are made by combining two or more techniques, including artificial neural networks (Pazzani & Billsus, 1997), information retrieval techniques (Hull, 1998), and Bayesian classifiers (Mooney, Bennett, & Roy, 1998).

In the modern Internet world, recommender systems have the ability to act as key tools that influence the success of a business. "Recommender systems are changing from novelties used by a few e-Commerce sites, to serious business tools that are re-shaping the world of e-Commerce" (Schafer et al., 1999), these systems are supporting many Web sites that help customers find the right product.

## Current Travel Recommendation Systems

Since the mid 1990s, tourism Web sites have flourished, allowing users to plan and view their holiday locations online. As tourists began using online tourism information, TRSs were developed to recommend holiday locations and activities. The two most popular recommender systems for tourism and travel presently in use are TripMatcher™ (Delgado, 2001; Starkov, 2001) used by Ski-Europe, and Me-Print™ (VacationCoach, 2002) used by Travelocity.

## TripleHop's Trip Matcher™

Traditionally, when a person wanted to go on a holiday, they visited a travel agent and had a counselling session. After having analysed the requirements and specifications of the customer, the travel agent made recommendations as to what would be an ideal place for them to visit. TripleHop's Trip Matcher™ tries to mimic the counselling scenario by allowing the users to search for advice on available destinations. The technical process behind the system is designed so that when the user specifies his/her requirements and constraints, the system matches the specified preferences with the services and items on the catalogue, or the database. This system is being used by Ski-Europe.com.

Ricci (2000) explains, "TripleHop's matching engine uses a more sophisticated approach to reduce user input. It guesses importance of attributes that the user does not explicitly mention. It then combines statistics on past user queries with a prediction computed as a weighted average of importance assigned by similar users."

The system then advises users about potential destinations they may book, based on their interest and browsing pattern. The software learns about user preferences by remembering navigation patterns each time he/she browses through the Web site, enabling it to provide useful recommendations. From an algorithm perspective, it uses contextual filtering and attribute-based collaborative filtering.

### VacationCoach Me-Print™

Me-Print™ relies on three important components to give personalised travel advice, namely, intelligent profiling, expert knowledge base, and robust advice engineering. Me-Print™ uses profiling of users to categorize them. It exploits user profile such as their unique lifestyle and leisure preferences in relative terms. For example, if a user likes golf, the algorithm considers user's preference for golf in comparison to other sports such as tennis, or swimming. These multiple preferences are used to provide advice based on priorities and interests.

## Services Offered by Current TRS

A travel recommender system allows users to choose their holiday while sitting in front of a computer. A simple user interface provided by the recommender system offers an interactive and simple means of communicating with the system. These systems aim at making the interaction time brief, by reducing the time needed for visiting various Web sites to gather information. At times the system has to deal with issues relating to under, or, over specification of user requirements. The system suggests appropriate repair actions such as "constraint relaxation" if the user has over-specified the requirements, and "tightening," if details have been under specified. The framework for this system is based on case-based reasoning (Ricci, 2002).

The system has the ability to formulate queries and offer various examples to users if they are not experienced enough to come up with a proper query. Ricci (2002) states that an effective TRS should not only support active preference construction, but also should allow users to explore the different options available.

## Benefits of Integrating TRS in Today's Business

A TRS system can be very helpful in tourism business, as it displays a list of products retrieved by a query to the system, and allows the user to make an informed selection. After the choice has been made, the initial query is saved along with the selected destination, this enables the system to identify and suggest a better set of products in the future. An information feedback technique such as Rocchio's method (the relevance feedback technique) is used to add new terms and constraints into the original query based on the selections made (Ricci, 2002). Research shows that an accurate recommendation, even if not taken up by the customer, can increase the user's trust in the system, which is necessary for future recommendation acceptance.

Some TRSs interact with the users in multiple stages and pose a sequence of questions, each question raised as a result of previous interaction. If these systems are designed to manage the human-machine interaction effectively they help to grow the business, as the users are not expected to be familiar with the system to begin with. This draws in more potential buyers who need help in making decisions.

## Limitations of Current Travel Recommender System

Recommendations from a TRS aim to help the tourist in making informed decisions about their travel plans. However, current TRSs deal only with the first stage of planning a trip, that is, destination selection. Present TRSs are unable to generate a complete travel itinerary which includes information such as accommodation and tourist attractions. Furthermore, a tourist is unable to visualise the planned holiday by using the current TRS technology. New information presentation models are required to increase user's confidence in the selected destination, such as providing the user a view of his/her trip, and allowing comparison between different options on a given trip.

# Visual Travel Recommender Systems (V-TRS)

Visual travel recommender system (V-TRS) is a TRS that uses visual information, along with audio, to enhance the presentation of the recommendations made to the user. Two models aiming to develop the V-TRS are presented in the following.

## Tourism Recommendation Using Image-Based Planning (TRIP)

Most of the TRSs available today don't provide a complete itinerary, but rather focus solely on the destination selection. This forces travellers to spend a lot of time browsing the Internet, looking for different attractions at their chosen destination. In addition to the suggestions provided by the recommender system, there can be a number of factors that effect the tourist's decision. Generally, tourists seek a second opinion from their acquaintances (relatives and friends). Often, many changes, and some backtracking is required before a travel itinerary is finalised. All of these factors make travel planning a complex undertaking.

As more people rely on the Internet to book their travel plans, it is important for travel Web sites to not only provide textual information, but also visual information. This will further help travellers in their decision-making process. A recommender system with more visual presentation and reasoning enables tourists to get a feel of the destination. The tourism recommendation using image-based planning (TRIP) proposed by Kimber, Georgievski, and Sharda (2006) aims to achieve this.

## TRIP Overview

Before booking a holiday package, the traveller would want to have an idea of what he/she is going to experience on the trip. "How am I going to organize my trip?" and "How can I get the maximum value for my time and money?" are the major questions that occur at that point in time. Most of the time, it is difficult to find the right details about the trip, and one has to go though the time consuming process of visiting Web sites, gathering chunks of information and then sorting the details. The TRIP system aims to overcome this drawback by presenting the details visually. The presentation can be customised based on the user's requirements. This will enable the user to have a clear idea as to what he/she is going to experience on the trip. The presentation provided by the visual travel recommender system will include details about the user's selection such as hotels, the services offered by the hotels, the places that he/she is going to visit, and other major activities.

Tour planning is influenced by experiences, thus, the recommender system should provide the tourist with visual clues to assist them in decision making. Planning a complete tour involves various components and decisions, which can be categorised into travel, accommodation, interesting places to visit and hospitality considerations. Some hindrances to decision making can be the time required to gather and analyse information about the destination, balancing schedules with other activities, and ensuring that the travel experience is satisfying.

Keen and Rawlings (2004) have proposed a system which facilitates the decision making process by using a visual language. Their prototype demonstrates tourism products available in Northern Tasmania, Australia. Users are provided information on a wide range of tourism products in the form of images and videos. As the user explores the information, the system keeps track of their browsing pattern, and a logic-based statistical profile is constructed. The profile building is a continuous process—the more the user uses the system, the better the profile becomes. This profile influences the system's interaction with the user in the future and any information of interest to the user is stored in an electronic scrapbook (e-scrapbook).

The e-scrapbook is a personalised area in which the user can place information about items of interest. Typical information could be travel schedule, accommodation booking, and recreational activities. The user can place different products in the e-scrapbook, for example, cost of accommodation at various hotels. The user can easily delete items from the e-scrapbook, and also save items in it for future use. This gives flexibility to the user, and helps in gathering information over a period of time.

The system also allows past users to post their e-scrapbooks on a Web site, thereby allowing new searchers to import partial or entire e-scrapbooks from experienced users. This facility gives new users a demonstration of how to plan a trip, and gives valuable feedback. Once the user is happy with all the information in the e-scrapbook they can purchase the products. This method of travel recommendation using image-based planning helps user to narrow their choices until they are satisfied, and, at the same time, provide a graphical overview.

## *Tour Recommendation Using Image-Based Planning with SCORM (TRIPS)*

In the present Internet environment, tourists have to visit a number of Web sites in an attempt to visualise their tour. The proposed tour recommendation using image-based planning with SCORM (TRIPS) system, will allow tourists to visualise their entire vacation by collating content from various Web sites. TRIPS uses the sharable content object reference model (SCORM) to store tourism information on various Web servers. If tourism Web sites post their information based on the SCORM standard, the proposed system could assemble relevant multimedia content from different sites and present it to the user to create a virtual experience. The SCORM standard has originally been developed as a reference model for Web-based e-learning technology. It is possible for us to adapt this standard for creating a visual experience generator for tourists.

The SCORM standard was proposed by The Department of Defence (DoD) and Advanced Distributed Learning (ADL) laboratories in 1997 to standardise the format of e-learning contents on the Web. The SCORM model aims to improve performance and reduce costs of e-learning systems. It was created by collating various e-learning specifications used by the Institute of Electrical and Electronics Engineers (IEEE). The main objectives of SCORM standards are to define reusable learning objects and to develop content and assessment models. SCORM, as an e-learning standard, enables portability of learning contents, thereby allowing content to be used across different courses. In addition to SCORM, an extension is being developed to enable content registration and resolution of all relevant information throughout the Internet, this is called the content object repository discovery and registration/resolution architecture (CORDRA).

## CORDRA

The CORDRA model also is an undertaking of the Department of Defense (DoD) and Advanced Distributed Learning (ADL), and aims to extend the current SCORM standard. This model is being developed so that one can locate and reference SCORM repositories throughout the Internet. Figure 1 presents a conceptual model of how CORDRA will achieve this. CORDRA searches the World Wide Web, much the same way current search engines do. Once the required resources are discovered, their location is resolved; making the resources accessible to SCORM based systems as the sharable content objects (SCOs). Even though SCORM and CORDRA standards have been developed for e-learning systems, these can be used to create visual TRSs. If the tourism Web sites store information using SCORM, then based

*Figure 1. Finding and delivering content as SCOs*

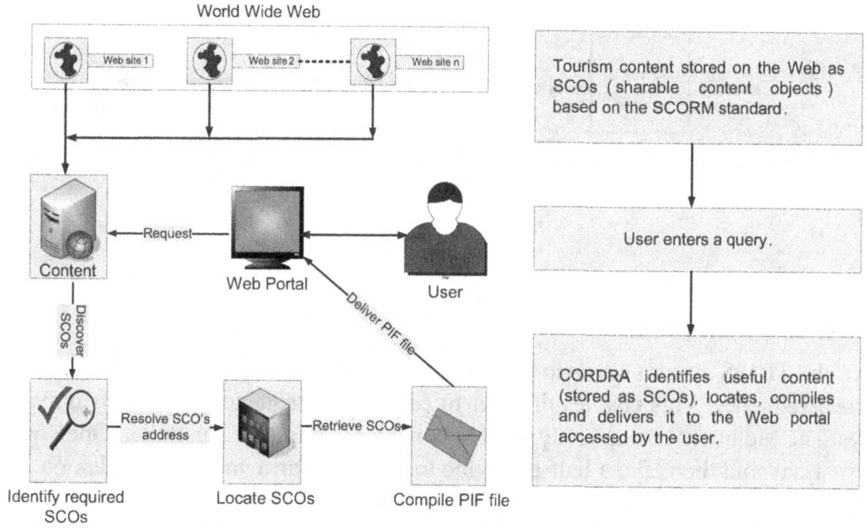

on a user query, the CORDRA system can collate all related information from the Web. However, the collated information needs to be combined into presentations that the user can view in a controlled manner.

## Visual Tour Planning Using TRIPS

The TRIPS system uses sharable content objects (SCOs); these are Web information objects such as pictures, videos, and descriptions of places. Once a traveller's destination is finalised, further options need to be explored. For example, if a traveller is travelling to Melbourne (Australia) in January, options could include watching the Australian Open (tennis), visiting beaches, cruising over the Yarra River, or visiting historic sites. Depending on the number of days available, the tourist can visit all the places mentioned, or visit a selection of places based on priorities. The TRIPS system contains information about the tourist's destination and their interests, and gathers SCOs related to the tourist's interests. Once the tourist finalises his/her selection, TRIPS can create an activity tree of the itinerary, and deliver the useful content (SCOs) as a package interchange file (PIF). The PIF contains an XML file (imsmanifest.xml) with all control files and resources referenced in the contents pages. The PIF, therefore contains information about the activities available to the tourist, structured in a hierarchy.

*Figure 2. Conversion of PIF file to Flash movie file using ActiveSWF software*

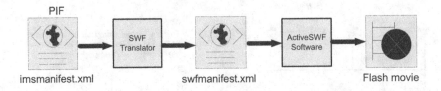

## Conversion to Flash Movie

Next, the TRIPS system needs to provide options for delivering content in a user-defined sequence. This enables the user to control the sequence of on-screen displays. The Melbourne tourist may want to consider visiting the Australian Open on the first day and then take a half-day wine tour of the Yarra valley, and relax on a beach in the afternoon, followed by a dinner cruise on the Yarra River. SCOs with information relating to these activities will be collated in the PIF file. The aim is to present to the tourist a short presentation of the travel itinerary being considered. One way to do this is to convert the imsmanifest.xml file to a format compatible with ActiveSWF (Activeswf, 2005) tool which can convert an XML file to a Flash movie. The duration of the movie can be selected by the user bearing in mind the number of options to be viewed. Figure 2 shows the conversion of imsmanifest.xml file to swfmanifest.xml (ActiveSWF readable xml file), and then to a Flash movie.

## Conversion to SMIL Movie

The conversion of PIF file into a presentation also can be achieved by using the SMIL standard, as shown in Figure 3. The synchronized multimedia integration language (SMIL) is a W3C recommendation that makes use of XML for creating descriptive multimedia presentations. It defines different mark-ups such as timing mark-up, layout mark-up, animations, and visual transitions. The translated SMIL file can be sent to any user device, such as a Web browser on a computer, or on a portable device. The program checks for parameters such as screen resolution, bandwidth, and customises the SMIL presentation to match the system parameters. This process can optimise the presentation suitable for display on the specific user device.

*Figure 3. Conversion of PIF file to SMIL file using a translator*

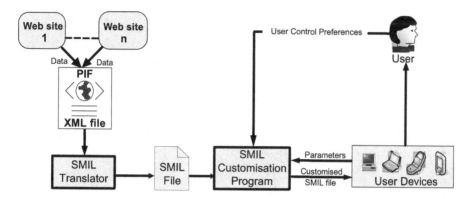

As shown in Figure 3, SCOs from various Web sites are collected and stored into the PIF file, this file is sent to a translator which translates the file into a SMIL file, and the SMIL file is then sent to a customisation program which checks the parameters on the user device. The SMIL file is modified according to these parameters and then sent to the user device for viewing.

## TRIPS Architecture

Based on the characteristics of SCORM, a new model has been developed for creating the TRIPS system. This new model allows tourism information to be converted into reusable content packages. These packages will be searchable and accessible through the local SCORM repositories, as well as through the CORDRA enhancement. The advantage of this is that all information stored using the SCORM standard will be more interoperable, accessible, reusable, maintainable and adaptable. The overall architecture of the TRIPS system is shown in Figure 4.

The process of converting imsmanifest.xml to a presentation file (swfmanifest.xml or .smil) takes place on the server-side. On the client-side, a graphical user-interface is used to browse potential destinations and their components.

The TRIPS architecture can be broken down into five main components: visual-TRS Web portal, learning management system (LMS) using SCORM, dynamic tourism information repository, repository access, and CORDRA. This system has three types of users: tourist, system administrator, and content producers.

174   Ponnada, Jakkilinki, & Sharda

*Figure 4. Tour recommendation using image-based planning with SCORM (TRIPS) model*

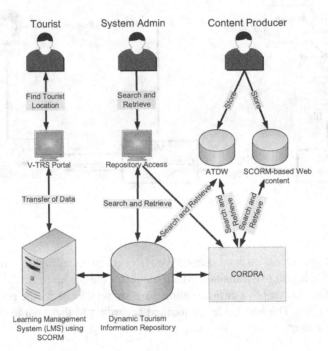

## V-TRS Web Portal

The tourist interacts with the system via the V-TRS portal. This portal works with a SCORM-based learning management system (LMS).

## Learning Management System (LMS)

As SCORM is a standard designed for e-Learning, the system designed to use it are called learning management system (LMS). The TRIPS system can use any of the standard LMSs available, and adapt it to work as a V-TRS.

## Dynamic Tourism Information Repository

Dynamic tourism information repository is a central storage system. This repository can be set up as a single server or a network of shared resources. The primary function of this repository is to store all the sharable content objects (SCOs) that will be used for tour visualisation.

### Repository Access

Repository access is a console or a portal used by the system administrator to access the information within the repository. Unlike the tourist, who gains admittance through the LMS, the system administrator accesses the SCOs in their raw format and can even modify these, if required.

### Role of CORDRA

CORDRA, though currently under development, already shows great promise when considering the possibility of incorporating it into the TRIPS model. CORDRA will pave the way for a far superior search facility due to its access to the World Wide Web, which is an ever expanding resource of tourism information. Currently, the Australian Tourism Data Warehouse (ATDW) stores tourism product and destination information that relates to Australian tourism (ATDW, 2005). In order to implement the functionality promised by CORDRA, the ATDW's expanding database could be included. The data from various databases, when combined with information on the Web, creates a huge data source that can be accessed by TRIPS. This provides TRIPS the opportunity to become a universally accessible V-TRS.

# Future Trends

## How Visual TRS Can Enhance the Current TRS

Even though the current travel recommender systems make quality recommendations to the user, these recommendations are not presented in a way that lets the user visualise the entire trip. Future recommender systems will make use of audio-visual media to provide an in-depth view of the user's trip, where, the human-computer interaction is made more interesting by using audio and video in innovative ways. Dynamic text will be displayed along with the images to provide a description of each destination. Narration of this text in different languages also will be possible. TRIPS can be used in a distributed environment using CORDRA. If all tourism related Web sites are SCORM and CORDRA compliant, then information from any Web site can be retrieved and used to recommend a complete holiday plan, including travel, accommodation, and other activities. Tourists will then have an easy and effective way of planning their personal or business travel. This also will improve the credibility of the World Wide Web as an effective vehicle for travel planning.

## Case Study

Current recommender systems are not very interactive in terms of presenting the details of the tour. Even though the recommendations that they make are of a good quality, their presentation is more textual and rather unappealing. The system output does not give a feel of what the user is going to experience on the trip. In other words, the current recommender systems give a simplistic description of the different available destinations and offers.

For the purpose of this case study, we have developed a Web site that emulates how current TRSs work and make suggestions based upon user's choices and other criterion. We discuss this system and present screen shots of its user interface.

Figure 5 shows the input screen for the recommender system. First, one must answer some questions, such as the region, budget, desired length of vacation, type of vacation and other such preferences.

The user input is analysed and the system makes recommendations with brief details of different packages which match the user's preferences. In this case, if the user wants to know what is included in each package, he/she needs to visit different Web links. Figure 6 shows a screen capture of how recommendations are often displayed.

*Figure 5. Input screen of the travel recommender system*

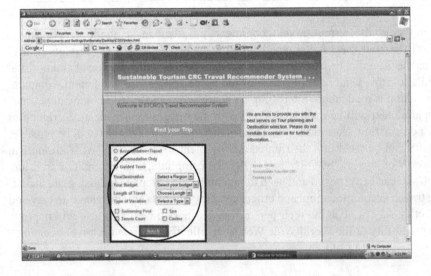

*Figure 6. Screen showing the recommendations made by the system*

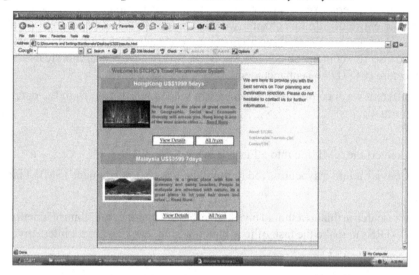

To some extent, recommendations made by such systems are useful; however, they fail to hold the user's attention. Our aim is to present these recommendations in a more appealing and attractive manner. We want to make the process of making recommendations more fun and interactive, by changing the way information is presented to the user. Rather than displaying the recommendations in the form of text, we are introducing audio, video and text narration, thereby taking the concept of travel recommender systems to the next level.

# Conclusion

The technology of recommender systems is improving constantly as more people use the Internet for making purchases. Vendors all over the world are encouraged to add recommender capabilities to their Web sites to attract more online business. This chapter discussed how the limitations of current travel recommender systems (TRS) can be eliminated by using visual travel recommender systems (V-TRS). Recommender systems are classified as content-based, collaborative, knowledge-based and hybrid. The most widely used travel recommender systems today are the TripMatcher™ and MePrint™. Current TRSs only deal with the first stage of tour planning, that is, destination selection, and are unable to provide a visual presentation of the entire tour. The proposed V-TRS aims to save time, while making the systems more interactive, and providing a visual presentation to give the tourist a feel of the entire trip. In this chapter we have proposed a sharable content object reference model (SCORM) based architecture to visualise the tour, and suggested ways to use the content object repository discovery and registration/resolution architecture (CORDRA) enhancement.

Two different ways can be used to generate a video presentation from the data in XML format:

- Convert the XML file into a Flash movie
- Convert it into a synchronized multimedia integration language (SMIL) file

Further research in this area should investigate the user interface and control functions of the V-TRSs to make the task of tour planning, fun, easy, and more interactive.

# References

Activeswf. (2005). *Software ActiveSWF Prof 1.9.3*. Retrieved December, 2005 from http://www.activeswf.com

ATDW. (2005). *Australian Tourism Data Warehouse*. Retrieved December, 2005 from http://www.atdw.com.au

Balabanovi, M., & Shoham, Y. (1997). Fab: Content-based, collaborative recommendation. *ACM Communication, 40*(3), 66-72.

Berka, T., & Plößnig, M. (2004). Designing recommender systems for tourism. In *Enter 2004*, Kairo.

Burke, R. (2000). Knowledge-based recommender systems. *Encyclopedia of Library and Information Systems, 69*(32).

Delgado, J. (2001). *Who's who in recommender systems*. Paper presented at the ACM SIGIR Workshop on Recommender Systems, New Orleans.

Hill, W., Stead, L., Rosenstein, M., & Furnas, G. (1995). *Recommending and evaluating choices in a virtual community of use*. Paper presented at the CHI-95 Conference, Denver, CO.

Hull, A. D. (1998). *The TREC-7 filtering track: description and analysis*. Paper presented at the Proceedings of TREC-7, 7th Retrieval Conference, Gaithersburg, US.

Kimber, J., Georgievski, M., & Sharda, N. (2006, January 18-20). *Developing a visualisation tool for tour planning.* Paper presented at the IFITT Global Travel & Tourism Technology and eBusiness Conference, Lausanne, Switzerland.

Mooney, R., Bennett, P., & Roy, L. (1998). *Book recommending using text categorzation with extracted information.* Paper presented at the AAAI Workshop on Recommender Systems, Madison.

Pazzani, J. M. (1999). A framework for collaborative, content-based and demographic filtering. *Artificial Intelligence Review, 13,* 393-408.

Pazzani, J. M., & Billsus, D. (1997). Learning and revising user profiles: The identification of interesting Web sites. *Machine learning, 27*(3), 313-331.

Ricci, F. (2002). Travel recommender systems. *IEEE Intelligent Systems,* 55-57.

Schafer, J. B., Konstan, J. A., & Riedl, J. (1999). *Recommender systems in electronic commerce.* Paper presented at the ACM Conference on Electronic Commerce.

Shardanand, U., & Maes, P. (1995). *Social information filtering: Algorithms for automating "word of mouth."* Paper presented at the Proceedings of ACM conference on Human Factors in Computing Systems.

Stabb, S., Werther, H., Ricci, F., Zipf, A., Gretzel, U., Fesenmaier, D. R., et al. (2002). Intelligent systems for tourism. *Intelligent Systems, IEEE [see also IEEE Intelligent Systems and Their Applications], 17*(6), 53-66.

Starkov, M. (2001). *How to turn lookers into bookers—Recommendation engines in travel and hospitality,* Retrieved May 10, 2006, from http://www.hotel-online.com/News/PR2001_3rd/Aug01_EnginesinTravel.html

VacationCoach. (2002). *Using knowledge personalization to sell complex products.* Retrieved January 20, 2006, from http://crm.ittoolbox.com/pub/LK032002.pdf

## Chapter VII

# Virtual Reality
# Applications in Tourism

Călin Gurău, Groupe Sup de Co Montpellier, France

## Abstract

*Virtual reality represents one of the most promising digital technologies and offers significant benefits in various areas such as medicine, entertainment, training, teaching, and tourism. This study attempts to identify, analyse, and present the existing virtual reality applications in tourism, and to predict future possible developments. Based on an extensive literature review, as well as on the direct observation and use of virtual reality applications implemented on the Web, this chapter attempts a classification of the virtual reality applications in tourism, based on different phases of tourist experience. This classification can assist practitioners in developing more adapted virtual reality applications for tourist activities.*

# Introduction

Virtual reality can be described as the science of integrating man with information (Roberts & Warwick, 1993) or as a way for humans to visualize, manipulate, and interact with an alternative, artificial universe, using computers and extremely complex data (Aukstakalnis & Blatner, 1992). In summary, virtual reality application represent three-dimensional, interactive, computer generated environments. These environments can be models of real or imaginary worlds, and their purpose is to represent information through a synthetic experience. The virtual reality technology was born from the merging of many disciplines, including psychology, cybernetics, computer graphics, data-base design, real-time and distributed systems, electronics, robotics, multimedia, and telepresence (Wild, 1997).

At present, virtual reality represents one of the most promising digital technologies that offers benefits in various areas such as medicine, entertainment, training, teaching, and tourism. This study attempts to identify, analyse, and present the existing virtual reality applications in tourism, and to predict future possible developments. Based on an extensive literature review, as well as on the direct observation and use of the virtual reality applications implemented on the Web, this chapter attempts a classification of the virtual reality applications in tourism, based on different phases of tourist experience.

The chapter starts with a description of the present development of virtual reality technology and applications. The physical tools and the software programmes required to interact with virtual reality applications are presented, and on the basis of their description, various hardware/software systems of virtual reality are identified and discussed.

The chapter continues with an analysis of the main areas of application of virtual reality in tourism, supported by numerous examples. The main benefits and problems related with each of these applications are outlined and discussed. The main focus of this analysis is to identify the existing customer needs and to provide an understanding of the context in which virtual reality applications can enhance tourists' experience.

The chapter ends with a review of the main issues related with the development of virtual reality applications in tourism, and with a presentation of the safety and ethical challenges still raised by virtual reality applications.

# The Historical Development of Virtual Reality Applications

The idea of virtual reality emerged in the 1960s, when researchers began immersing human participants (operators) in visually-coupled teleoperated environments (Kalawsky, 1994). Virtual reality represents a major step in creating new ways to interact with an artificially-constructed environment via computers and to visualize information (Mahoney, 1999). Instead of using a mouse and keyboard or joystick, people can put displays over their eyes, gloves on their hands, and headphones on their ears in order to interact with the information. The head-mounted display submerges a person in a computer generated three-dimensional world. This world presents realistic images that instantly adjust and move, based on the direction in which the user's eyes are looking (Baker, 1993; Stevens, 1994). By combining the sights with realistic sounds, the illusion is further enhanced. The data gloves allow the user to manipulate items in a virtual environment such as open doors, pick up objects, or cut into virtual patients. By using these devices the computer transmits information to three of the five senses.

Although it is difficult to categorise virtual reality systems, most configurations can be ranked by the sense of user immersion in the virtual environment. From this perspective, we can consider virtual reality applications as non-immersive, semi-immersive and fully immersive (Costello, 1997). In non-immersive systems the virtual environment is viewed through a portal or window, by using a standard high resolution monitor. The user's interaction with the virtual reality application takes place using conventional tools, such as keyboard, mouse or trackball, but can be enhanced by using 3D devices such as SpaceBalls or DataGloves. The semi-immersive environments are developed using high performance graphics computing systems, which can control large screen monitors, screen projection systems or multiple television projection systems. Finally, the most complete experience of virtual reality is provided by fully immersive systems, which requires the use of head mounted displays or binocular omni-orientation monitors (Bolas, 1994).

Virtual reality systems comprise several components which are essential to create the virtual environment and to permit the user interaction with it. These components are: the hardware system, the virtual reality software (which runs on the hardware system), and the interface-interactive devices.

## The Hardware System

Probably the most important feature of the hardware systems used for virtual reality applications is processing power. In order to provide the experience of a realistic virtual world, computer systems have to provide high quality, real-time, interactive 3-D graphics, sound, touch and temperature sensations. This requires powerful processors with lots of memory. However, in the last 10 years the cost of processor power has been dropping steadily, the power of microcomputer chips has doubled every 18 months, and the cost of computer memory became affordable.

In the case of multi-user virtual applications (Capin, Pandzic, Magnenat-Thalmann, & Thalmann, 1999), when some of the participants might be located in different regions of the same country or even in different countries or continents, the capability of the data transmission network also is extremely important. The bandwidth required to transmit input/output data will be very large, necessitating glassfibre cables or satellite transmission.

## Virtual Reality Software

Virtual reality software differs from a traditional graphics programs in one specific way: it allows for interactivity between the viewer and the computer-generated environment. A good way to analyse this software is to present the various functions it has to perform (Stevens, 1994):

1.  To accept data input from input and control devices attached to the system. At present, the most used input systems are those familiar to any computer or video game user: keyboard, mouse, trackball, joystick, and steering wheel. Virtual reality programs may use more exotic devices, such as 3-D mice, head trackers, 6-D position trackers, data gloves, temperature gauges, voice (from a voice input system), video (from an image recognition system), or networked data from body suits.

2.  To create the simulation logic. The simulation engine must interpret correctly the meaning of various inputs, determine the properties of objects in the virtual reality world, and understand the consequences of any action, as the input data interacts with virtual objects. The simulation engine has to be fast because for each time frame the simulation process has to be repeated; the new input and new interactions have to be considered and new results have to be generated. If the virtual reality system has multiple users simultaneously, a simulation engine that coordinates the actions of all users (coordinating the simulation engines on each user's system) has to be included in the system.

3.  After the simulation engine creates the logic (the scenario of the virtual reality world), the system has to render it on the screen or head-mounted display for visual perception. The system also is responsible for creating the sound and for more complex applications, the feelings of smell, touch, temperature, and taste.

The virtual reality software will usually comprise the following elements (Stevens, 1994):

- **Object database:** All virtual reality systems include a database, which houses the descriptions of the virtual objects. The database may be generated using virtual reality software, but more often an external graphics program, such as AutoCAD, is used to create the files. The CAD database contains numeric data, which are used for modeling and rendering the objects on the screen of the head-mounted display.

- **Attribute database:** Many virtual reality systems also have a database of object attributes. These attributes, such as motion, orientation, colour, and sound, may be fixed or conditional, and are based on an external data source.

- **Sensor driver:** The job of the sensor driver is to monitor the tracking devices in order to define, at any given moment, the user's position.

- **Display driver**: This element updates the display based on the sensor driver, as well as the various databases.

- **The simulation manager:** This is the brains of the virtual reality system; its job is to coordinate the activities of all the components. The manager sends instructions to the generated graphics, tracks on-screen objects, and maintains the correct visual perspective;

- **Programming:** To program a virtual reality system, first it is necessary to create the object database; the next step is to specify the properties and the behaviors of each object; and in the last stage, the programmer has to codify the system's response to sensor data derived from the sensor driver.

## Interactive Devices

The interactive devices allow the user to actively interact with the virtual environment. The most important functions of these devices are listed below (Stevens, 1994).

### *Virtual Vision*

Virtual reality systems can provide various types of visual display. Some systems use a simple monitor; others, such as CAVE systems, project the image onto the entire wall, or on multiple walls (DeLeon & Berry, 1998). But, the majority of virtual reality systems, and all immersive virtual reality systems, provide users with vision through a head-mounted device.

Most head-mounted devices use two displays, eyeglass-sized screens, to offer stereoscopic imaging. In some cases they use a single large display. At present, most such devices suffer from low resolution, narrow range of field, poor or nonexistent stereoscopic vision, general awkwardness, and relatively high cost.

## Virtual Sound

Most virtual reality systems include an audio component. For the sake of economy, some devices use monophonic sound; but the majority of them use stereophonic sound. However, only a 3-D audio system can re-create a perfect sound illusion, allowing listeners to locate sound not only in the horizontal plane (as in stereo) but also in the vertical plane.

## Virtual Touch

Force feedback devices provide a sense of touch or feel, by relaying to the user the force exerted by a virtual object. Many different types of mechanisms are used to provide force feedback information to users: joysticks, steering wheels or robot arms have been programmed to simulate gross force feedback to the user's hand. Although it is possible to simulate spatial patterns of forces to the user's skin, current systems are still far from actually providing the feel of sandpaper or slate.

## Sense of Temperature

Although the sense of touch still cannot be replicated by virtual reality systems, a few devices have been developed that provide a sense of temperature. Temperature is important for the application in which the temperature of objects or room temperature is an essential part of the virtual world. Temperature also is necessary to provide clues to the type of object or material being touched, or simply to make the virtual world more realistic.

## Voice Input

A perfect immersive virtual reality system—one in which users communicate as naturally as they would in a real world—would incorporate voice input and control. The main goal of speech recognition software developers has been to create a system with functionally unlimited vocabulary and complete speaker independence, which allows for continuous speech, offering high accuracy rates. At present, though, there is no system that offers all these features.

## Manipulation and Control Devices

Input into a virtual reality system can be made through a variety of devices: keyboards, digitizers, joysticks, mice, trackballs, and lightpens, are often used on the simpler virtual reality systems (Pimentel & Teixeira, 1995). But the problem with all these devices is that they track position in only two dimensions. To track objects in a virtual world it is necessary a 6-D control: the three positional coordinates (X,Y,Z), and three orientation measures (roll, pitch, yaw). Accordingly, some manufacturers have developed mice, trackballs, and joysticks that work in a 6-D mode.

The best way to manipulate virtual objects is through the use of a glove that tracks the gestures, positions, and movements of the operator's hand. The main problem with hand-based input is the lack tactile or force feedback (Stevens, 1994).

Bio-controllers, which use biological factors as input, offer virtual reality developers a wide range of possibilities. In its most extreme form, a bio-controller may be able to "read" thoughts and act on mental commands, which is far beyond present capabilities. The possible alternatives are:

- **Myo-electrical devices:** A myo-electrical system maps muscle electrical activity. It can be programmed to recognize a large range of muscle signal intensities and durations. One application of this system is to control musical instrument digital interface (MIDI) devices. The amount of muscle exertion, for example, can be used to determine volume. The speed at which the muscle moves can control beat. Using this method, entire musical sequences can be played on an "air guitar" causing real music to be played on the synthesizer.

- **Eye movement:** Eye movement systems make use of vertical and horizontal eye movement to create a virtual joystick; they enable users to control video games using only their eyes. But this technology may have a more serious impact on the lives of physically disabled people or those who need their hands free while controlling a computer or another machine.

- **Cerebro-electrical signals:** A system that tracks the cerebro-electrical signals would enable users to visualize actions, which are then turned into code that controls a computer process. The user might be able to think a word that would then be typed or used as a command.

# Virtual Reality Applications

It is difficult to predict exactly where the greatest benefits will occur and in which field, simply because there are so many potential applications for virtual reality programs. Possible application areas are likely to include those shown in Table 1. The table is not intended to be exhaustive but merely illustrates the enormous possibilities offered by this technology.

However, before trying to apply virtual programs, it is more prudent to analyse exactly what are the problems and the benefits offered by this technology. At present, there are several technological and cost limits that can be restrictive to the use of virtual reality applications in many areas of activity. Despite this, the rapid technological and scientific development in computer and communication industries offer the possibility to increase the use and the quality of virtual reality applications in the near future, decreasing in the same time the cost of their implementation.

*Table 1. Possible applications of virtual reality (Source: Kalawsky, 1994, p. 14)*

| Application area | Description |
|---|---|
| Air traffic control | Improved situation awareness for air traffic controllers |
| Architectural design | Design and visualization of buildings and impact on city layout. The technology can allow a virtual walk-through to be made |
| Aircraft design | The paperless aircraft—the traditional drawing board could be replaced and the whole design process undertaken in an electronic form, from initial design through to rapid prototyping and system evaluation |
| Acoustical evaluation | Soundproofing and room acoustics |
| Computer aided design | Design of complex objects with a high degree of designer interaction |
| Education | Virtual science laboratories; Cost-effective access to sophisticated laboratory environments; Virtual planetariums |
| Entertainment | Wide range of immersive interactive games |
| Legal/police investigations | Re-enactment of accidents and crime |
| Medical applications | Radiation therapy treatment planning; medical training—virtual patients; ultrasound imaging; molecular docking—drug synthesis |
| Scientific visualization | Aerodynamic simulation; computational fluid dynamics; planetary investigations |
| Telepresence | Robot operations in hazardous environments |
| Training/simulation | Flight or fight simulation |
| Virtual manufacturing environments | Ease of assembly and performance evaluations |
| Virtual tourism environments | Virtual tours, marketing, heritage protection (as presented in this chapter) |

## The Application of Virtual Reality in Tourism

Considering the specific characteristics of the tourism industry, it is possible to identify three main uses of virtual reality applications.

### The Use of Virtual Reality Applications for Choosing an Unknown Destination

Traditionally, the selection of tourism destinations represents a sensitive problem for tourists. The complex nature of tourist activity, which incorporates many intangible elements, the influence of the climate, and the environment on tourism services quality, and the subjective needs and perceptions of individual tourists, all create the need for rich and relevant information even before the choice of a tourist destination. In the tourism industry, the services cannot be fully standardized because, on one hand, the needs and preferences of individual tourist are different, and on the other hand, because each service situation is unique, as it is created through the convergence of various tangible and intangible, material and human elements. In these conditions, the virtual representation of various tourist destinations and services can help the tourist to choose a destination that would better satisfy his/her needs and expectations. By directly experiencing some of the aspects of the tourist destination (landscape, accommodation, specific attractions) through the use of virtual reality applications, the tourist can make an informed choice, and adjust more realistically his/her expectations to the specific characteristics of the tourist destination.

Designed to help sales agents present visual information more effectively, these *virtual* tours are based on Apple's QuickTime VR software technology, which interactively displays spatial environments by enabling users to view any direction around a scene. Users also can zoom in for a closer inspection from any angle (Doyle, 1996). The free QuickTime VR player extension displays a movable viewing window around the *virtual* panorama, while hot spots programmed into the panorama allow users to click on a doorway to "enter" a different room.

A research group based in Switzerland has developed a specific virtual reality system, called Virtual Reality Tourist Information System (ViRTIS) that allows the potential customer to explore a possible tourist destination (Szabó, Stucki, Aschwanden, Ohler, Pajarola, & Wildmayer, 1995). In addition, this platform permits the user to interact with other real-time communication systems. For example, a user may log-in in order to experience the scenario of a possible holiday trip, asking simultaneously the advice of a local tourist guide about the most interesting sights that s/he can visualise in the virtual world.

The use of Internet-based virtual reality applications by more and more tourist organisation demonstrates that the adoption and mastering of new information and communication technologies can not only enhance tourists' experience, but also can create a significant competitive advantage for tourism agencies (Buhalis & O'Connor, 2005).

*Figure 1. The use of virtual reality applications as an additional source of information for tourists in choosing their destinations*

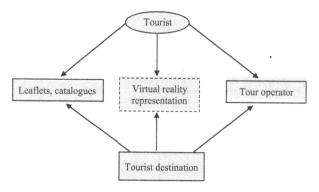

## The Use of Virtual Reality Applications as Specific Attractions of a Tourist Destination

Virtual reality applications can enhance the attractiveness of a tourism destination. Many theme parks are using this principle to attract lovers of virtual experiences or games. For example, virtual reality games represent the main attraction of the indoor interactive theme park organised by Disney in its Florida resort. The visitors can choose among a variety of virtual reality applications, such as CyberSpace Mountain, Virtual Jungle Cruise, Aladdin's Magic Carpet Ride, Ride the Comix, and others. For example, on the Virtual Jungle Cruise, the visitors sit inside an inflatable raft situated in front of a flat-panel projection display, they paddle down a real-time river where thin mists of real fog and water are splashed in their faces. This combination of virtual images and real elements creates a very intense and entertaining effect (DeLeon & Berry, 1998).

In this case the virtual reality applications will complement more traditional attractions, increasing the value of tourists' experience (e.g., a museum that displays virtual reality applications together with traditional artifacts [Ruiz, Weghorst, Savage, Oppenheimer, Furness III, & Dozal, 2004]), or, in some cases might represent even the main attraction of a destination (e.g., a theme park specialized in virtual reality games).

Another possible application of virtual reality technology to enhance the tourists' experience is the use of augmented reality (AR) systems for outdoor navigation and information browsing (Reitmayr & Schmalstieg, 2004). The augmented reality system permits the user to visualize the real environment, but complements the reality with additional information, that is displayed in parallel to the real image on a visual interface. Although the AR cannot be defined as pure virtual reality applications, they can help the tourist to identify and reach specific destinations or to obtain details about their history and characteristics.

*Figure 2. Virtual reality applications as additional or specific attractions of a tourist destination*

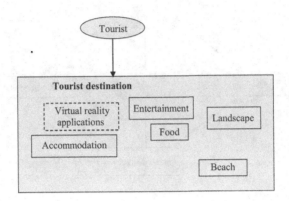

The augmented reality systems use head-mounted displays to present information either as graphical objects rendered to fit into the natural environment or as text, images, and 3-D objects. The graphical objects are drawn to enhance and complement the user's perception of the natural environment; they can represent abstract information, alternative representations of real objects or highlighted real structures. For example, the augmented reality system can provide the tourist with a visual representation of a building that has been destroyed and reconstructed several times, as it looked in various historical moments. Alternatively, specific virtual reality applications can be associated with this AR system, allowing the tourist to virtually visit a building that is closed or who was already destroyed. For example, the tourist visiting the Coliseum can access a virtual reality application, living the experience of a gladiators' fight in ancient Rome.

The head-mounted display also can provide an interactive interface that can be controlled by the user with a touchpad that is either worn on the belt or handheld. The user can use the interactive system to switch between different modes of the application such as navigation, information browsing and annotation. Each mode presents a number of individual panes to provide control of parameters and other options related to the current task. A small window located at the bottom of the display presents generic information such as the current location, selected target location, distance to the target, and an orientation compass.

Considering the large amount of data required in real-time by augmented reality applications, and the specific link between such data and a specific geographic location, the principles of ubiquitous computing can be used to simplify the use of the system. The information databases can be distributed in the explored environment, the user interface system accessing the necessary data in real time, to the specific request of the tourist.

## Virtual Reality Applications as Tourist Destinations

Virtual reality can be used to replace the physical travel to existing tourist destination, and to create novel, imaginary destinations. In this situation, the richness of the virtual world experience by the tourist will depend on the complexity of the virtual program, and on the technological sophistication of the interface used to access the virtual reality. The tourist can not only choose a specific virtual world, but has also the option to define his/her own persona (the characteristics of his/her avatar), and the type of interaction with other virtual personas or objects. For example, a male tourist can decide that he wants to experience a travel to Paris using a female avatar, or the persona of a cinema star. This kind of identity change is often used by the members of a multi-users dungeon (MUD), which represent shared cyberspace games played by people from various geographical locations. In this case, the virtual reality tourism can be combined with an "identity tourism", in order to live the experience of a completely different character (Nakamura, 2002).

This model opens extraordinary possibilities, offering an almost infinite choice of tourist destinations experienced through an immersion in a virtual reality world. For example, the use of virtual reality destinations can provide an opportunity to disabled persons to visit distant places without leaving their room, or to eliminate their disability in the virtually constructed avatar. There are already in use on the Web Virtual reality applications that permit to visit museums, exhibitions, or cities using a virtual programme accessed over the Internet. For example, a project developed Hugh McAtamney in conjunction with Dublin Institute of Technology has made available on the Web two virtual reality applications: a virtual reality walkthrough the National Gallery of Ireland, and a virtual walk down O'Connell Street in Dublin. These virtual reality applications can be viewed using CosmoPlayer 2.0 for Netscape users or Worldview for Internet Explorer 3 users. Another virtual reality project is proposed by the site http://www.arounder.com, which offers 360° panoramas of famous tourist places throughout the world.

Recently, a group of Brazilian researchers have developed a virtual reality program based on CAVE technology, that permits the tourist to fly over the city of Rio de Janeiro, using hang-gliding (Soares et al., 2004). During this virtual experience, the use can look at the landscape, and modify the direction of the flight by shifting his/her weight on a static hang-gliding structure. In order to increase the reality of the experience, the developers have even recreated the feeling of the wing blowing in user's face during the flight. This application permits any person to experience in total safety the unique sensation of flying over Rio de Janeiro, but also can be used for training purposes.

*Figure 3. Virtual reality applications as tourist destinations*

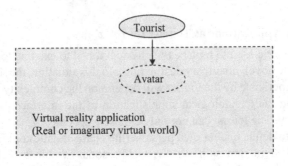

On the other hand, virtual reality can open access to imaginary, artificial destinations such as cybercities or cyberplanets, using and improving the computer technology already developed for interactive games. Some of these applications are already available on the Internet. As an example, Cybertown is a virtual reality program which supports the developing and functioning of a virtual community, using shared-state environments where the interaction with virtual objects will be seen simultaneously by people in the same environment from anywhere in the world (McGuire, 2003). To make this experience more credible, the avatar which represents each community member has a specific identity, can own properties inside Cybertown, and can earn cybermoney. The virtual city has even a constitution that outlines the rules of interaction within this online community. Another Web site, called Active Worlds, proposes to cybertravelers to explore more than 1000 virtual worlds, or even to build their own virtual reality space on the Internet. Some of the most popular cyberworlds are Yellowstone, Mars, or Atlantis.

These constructed alternative worlds progressively become increasingly attractive, as the evolution of information and communication technology permits the creation of highly complex virtual environments, often even more accessible than many real distant tourist destinations, because the costs of cybertravelling are dropping rapidly. The virtual experience of another world and identity offers the same benefits as a real trip—the access to another reality, which temporarily suspends the daily work routine and provides a different life context for the user. The existing virtual reality worlds offer one, or multiple specific theme scenarios, connected with tourism myths—such as the tropical island, or with foreign cultural destinations (Book, 2003). For example, the Active Worlds cybergame displays an International Teleport just outside the main welcome area, offering such destinations as England, Greece, Russia, and America. In order to enhance the illusion of a virtual tourist experience, many cyberworlds offer the option of taking screen shots, in which the users can decide to place their avatar in the middle of the virtual landscape.

However, the benefits are not only on the tourists' side. Using this option, highly popular sites can be protected from the damage incurred by huge numbers of tourists (DeLeon, 1998; Letellier, 1999; Cooper & MacNeil, in this book), and buildings or places that are unsafe for real-life visits can still be admired by virtual visitors. On the other hand, the historical or cultural sites that are destroyed by natural calamities can be reconstructed in a virtual reality application, as it was the case of the citadel of Bam in Iran, destroyed by an earthquake in December 2003.

## Potential Problems Associated with Virtual Reality Applications

The development of, and the interaction with, virtual reality environments is not problem free. Various studies have attempted to identify and outline some of these existing issues (Jackson & Cloete, 2000).

Some issues are technology-related. A simple browse of the virtual reality applications available on tourist sites shows problems of hardware and software compatibility. Sometimes the computer used to access these applications cannot open or execute them, or additional software has to be downloaded before the user can experience virtual reality programs.

Other areas of possible problems are related with the impact of virtual reality applications for real-life tourism. We can envisage a not so distant future in which virtual reality technology will be able to provide high-quality, highly-customised tourist experiences. Although this can have a positive impact for damaged sites, endangered species, or fragile natural environments (Boucouvalas), in other cases, the reduction of tourism activity can represent a significant loss of income for local and isolated communities, some of which do not have any other obvious source of revenues.

Experiments have shown that virtual reality applications also raise health and safety issues. The following table summarises the negative effects resulting from exposure to virtual reality environments. Obviously, the virtual reality applications cannot be commercialized on a large scale without first solving, or at least alleviating, these problems.

An additional challenge to the use of virtual reality in tourism has a strong philosophical and ethical dimension. By constructing, re-constructing or copying the reality in virtual reality applications, the specialist can distort the reality, simplifying or magnifying particular aspects. This raises the questions of how much can we know the reality by interacting with a virtual reality environment, and how much this can create a certain cultural bias towards the natural environment. A well-designed

*Table 2. Effects of exposure to virtual reality environments (Source: Costello, 1997)*

| Physical | Physiological | Psychological, Behavioural, Cognitive |
|---|---|---|
| Physical discomfort | Visual asthenopic symptoms | Stress |
| Hygiene | Postural instability | Perceptual shifts |
| Immersion injuries | Simulator sickness | Addiction and disorientation |
| Equipment fit | Dissociation of accommodation/ convergence | Isolation |
| Unnatural postural demands | Cardiovascular change | Changes in mood |
| | Gastrointestinal change | Changes in perceptual judgement ability |
| | Biochemical change | Change in psychomotor performance |

virtual reality program can present a cosmeticised version of the natural landscape, creating a tourist preference toward the artificial environment, or maybe even an addiction in relation to perfectly customized tourist experiences (Horsfield, 2003). A case study presented by Fencott (2002) explains the enhanced representation of a real tourist attraction. In order to increase the complexity and the attractiveness of users' virtual experience, a series of artificial, but well-planned elements were integrated in the virtual reality representation such as attractors, rewards, surprises and shocks. A list of some "attractors" used in this application includes: partially obscured/revealed objects, strange or unknown objects, closed and open doors and doorways, objects that belong to another world, strange symbols, spatialised sounds, vibrations, smells, objects of desire, objects of fear, and so on.

On the other hand, being customer-oriented, the virtual reality environment, can transmit a trivial/caricatured image of real places, people or situation, which can distort the reality and produce alienating effects (Hillis, 1999). Finally, the commercialized virtual reality can replace the existing reality with artificial narrative that are conceived and disseminated by dominant cultures or peoples. The widespread use of virtual reality applications can raise questions about power relations at social and individual level: who creates these applications and for what purpose, who has and who does not have access to this technology, and with what consequences (Horsfield, 2003)

# Conclusion

The successful implementation and use of virtual reality applications are determined by a balanced combination of three main elements: technology, applications and human dimensions. The technological evolution can solve some of the existing problems related to hardware and software components, platform compatibility, high graphics resolution, complexity of virtual reality environments, and the possibilities of users to experience and interact with virtual reality applications. However, on the other hand, the technology should be applied responsibly to situations in which can produce positive results, such as medicine, education, or sustainable tourism. Finally, the human dimension of this triad should not be neglected: the users of virtual reality applications should develop and actively apply ethical principles to this new technological development (e.g., to avoid problems related to induced addiction or mind control), and the negative impact of virtual reality applications of human health and safety should be completely eliminated.

The potential of social change that may occur because of virtual reality is enormous: "the future is still mostly fuzzy, but one thing is clear: how people use or abuse virtual reality technology will be based on both how technology is designed and what people get out of it" (Aukstakalnis & Blatner, 1992, p. 294). Virtual reality can change society, but is up to the individual to decide how helpful or detrimental this impact will be (Heim, 1993).

# References

Andaroodi, E., Ono, K., Kitamoto, A. Beheshti, S. M., Mokhtari, E., Adle, C., et al. (2005). *3Dimensional reconstitution and virtual reality, bam and its cultural landscape.* Retrieved February 2006, from http://dsr.nii.ac.jp/bam/virtual/Bam-VR%20reconstitution-NII-ICHTO-WU-UT.pdf

Aukstakalnis, S., & Blatner, D. (1992) *Silicon mirage: The art and science of virtual reality.* Berkeley, CA: Peachpit Press.

Baker, R. (1993). *Designing the future: The computer transformation of reality.* London: Thames and Hudson.

Bolas, M. T. (1994). Human factors in the design of an immersive system. *IEEE Computer Graphics and Applications, 14,* 55-59.

Book, B. (2003). *Traveling through cyberspace: Tourism and photography in virtual worlds.* Retrieved March, 2006, from http://www.cs.uu.nl/docs/vakken/vw/

literature/Traveling%20Through%20Cyberspace_%20Tourism%20and%20 Photography%20in%20Virtual%20Worlds.pdf

Boucouvalas, A. C. (2002, March 25-26). Plato, e-tourism and the search for knowledge. In *Proceedings of the E-Tourism Futures Workshop*, University of Surrey. Retrieved December 2005, from http://dec.bournemouth.ac.uk/staff/ tboucouvalas/plato.pdf

Buhalis, D., & O'Connor, P. (2005) Information communication technology revolutionizing tourism. *Tourism Recreation Research, 30*(3), 7-16.

Capin, T. K., Pandzic, I. S., Magnenat-Thalmann, N., & Thalmann, D. (1999). *Avatars in networked virtual environments*. John Wiley and Sons, Chichester.

Costello, P. (1997). *Health and safety issues associated with virtual reality: A review of current literature.* Retrieved December 2005, from http://www.agocg. ac.uk/reports/virtual/37/report37.htm

DeLeon, V. J., & Berry, H. R. (1998). *Virtual Florida Everglades*. Retrieved December 2005, from http://www.digitalo.com/deleon/vrglades/VDeleon-vrglades.PDF

Doyle, A. (1996). QUICKTIME VR enables 3D VR tours on net. *Computer Graphics World, 19*(5), 9-10.

Fencott, C. (2002) *Virtual Saltburn by the sea: Creative content design for virtual environments.* Retrieved December 2005 from http://vads.ahds.ac.uk/guides/ vr_guide/vlib3.html

Heim, M. (1993). *The metaphysics of virtual reality.* New York: OUP.

Hillis, K. (1999). *Digital sensations: Space, identity and embodiment in virtual reality*. Minneapolis: University of Minnesota Press.

Horsfield, P. (2003) The ethics of virtual reality; the digital and its predecessors. *Media Development, 45*(2). Retrieved December 2005 from http://www.wacc. org.uk/wacc/publications/media_development/2003_2/the_ethics_of_virtual_reality_the_digital_and_its_predecessors.

Kalawsky, R. S. (1994). *Virtual reality and virtual environments.* Wokingham: Addison-Wesley.

Letellier, R. (1999, October 3-6). Virtual reality ... A new tool for sustainable tourism and cultural heritage sites management. In *Proceedings of the CIPA International Symposium*, Olinda, Brazil. Retrieved December 2005, from http://cipa.icomos.org/fileadmin/papers/olinda/99c102.pdf

Mahoney, D. P. (1999). Better than real. *Computer Graphics World, 22*(2), 32-38.

McGuire, M. (2003). *PlayStation 2: Selling the third place.* Retrieved December 2005, from http://hypertext.rmit.edu.au/dac/papers/McGuire.pdf

Nakamura, L. (2001). Race in/for cyberspace: Identity tourism and racial passing on the Internet. In D. Trent (Ed.), *Reading social cultures* (pp. 226-235). Malden: Blackwell Publishers.

Pimentel, K., & Teixeira, K. (1995). *Virtual reality: Through the new looking glass, Second Edition*. New York: McGraw Hill.

Reitmayr, G., & Schmalstieg, D. (2004). *Collaborative augmented reality for outdoor navigation and information browsing*. Retrieved April 2006, from http://www. ims.tuwien.ac.at/media/documents/publications/reitmayrlbs2004.pdf

Roberts, D., & Warwick, K. (1993). *Virtual reality in engineeering*. In K. Warwick, J. Gray, & D. Roberts (Eds.), *Stevenage: The institution of electrical engineers*.

Ruiz, R., Weghorst, S., Savage, J., Oppenheimer, P., Furness III, T., & Dozal, Y. (2004). *Virtual reality for archaeological Maya cities*. Retrieved December 2005, from http://www.hitl.washington.edu/publications/r-2004-51/r-2004-51.pdf

Soares, L., Nomura, L., Cabral, M., Dulley, L., Guimarães, M., Lopes, R., & Zuffo, M. (2004). *Virtual hang-gliding over Rio de Janeiro*. Retrieved March 2006, from http://resumbrae.com/vr04/soares.pdf

Stevens, L. (1994). *Virtual reality now*. New York: MIS Press.

Szabó, K. I., Stucki, P., Aschwanden, P., Ohler, T., Pajarola, R., & Wildmayer, P. (1995). *A virtual reality based system environment for intuitive walk-throughs and exploration of large-scale tourist information*. Retrieved May 2006, from http://citeseer.ist.psu.edu/cache/papers/cs/2038/ftp:zSzzSzftp.inf.ethz.chzSz-doczSzpaperszSztizSzgrpwzSzEnter95.pdf/szabo95virtual.pdf

Wild, F. (1997). *Exploring multimedia*. London: Dorling Kindersley.

## Chapter VIII

# Virtual Reality Mapping Revisited:
# IT Tools for the Divide Between Knowledge and Action in Tourism

Malcolm Cooper, Ritsumeikan Asian Pacific University, Japan

Neil MacNeil, Ritsumeikan Asian Pacific University, Japan

## Abstract

*This chapter provides a brief overview of the available technologies and opportunities for the use of virtual reality in tourism marketing. It acknowledges that in almost all formulations of the tourism marketing model to date however, much has been made of the notion that tourism is unique because production and consumption occur not only at the same time but in the same place, and therefore that location or proximity is often a critical determinant of the take-up of tourism opportunities. The chapter then goes on to posit the question: what if the place variable could be removed from this equation through the further development of virtual reality techniques? The impacts of this might include: less requirement for travel per se (perhaps); better and more real information about the physical actuality of a destination for the potential consumer (likely); price and service quality information very much simplified and improved (definitely), and changed tourism promotion strategies would change (undoubtedly). At the barest minimum, the uncertainties involved in relying on unverified initial information for tourism travel decision-making could be considerably reduced.*

# Introduction

As consumers become more committed "Web surfers," their processes of decision making based on the information found there will become more sophisticated, particularly when purchasing products and services (Buhalis, 1998; Sheldon, 1997). In the early days of mass use of the Internet to contact potential clients, anyone with anything to sell or provide information on could develop a Web site to advertise their intention to trade; a process that was really nothing more than transferring print or television/cinema-based static visual information to the new medium (Buhalis, 1998). With respect to tourism and hospitality such users ranged from the major airlines and hotel/resort chains to the family with a holiday villa for rent in Europe, or to a bed and breakfast operator in Australia, or to an *Onsen* proprietor in Japan. By assisting the promotion of tourism services in this way the early e-commerce boom certainly dramatically extended the marketing reach of tourist operators (Buhalis, 1998). With maturity however, markets generally become more sophisticated and demanding, and require higher standards of interaction, particularly at the more expensive end of product cost (Weiermair & Mathies, 2004). As a result, the variety and scale of information the purchaser of tourism product now has in terms of making informed buying decisions, and the increasing sophistication of both consumers and tourism marketing organizations is leading to more creative applications of the Web as a channel to reach consumers in this industry (Sitepal, 2005).

Nevertheless, much of the information currently provided to tourism consumers remains 2-dimensional; if it is visual then it is at best generally only composed of good photographs with associated text, unless video capture is used. However, very high processor and memory demands on the destination computer make the latter less attractive to the average Internet user. So, in practice, consumer processing power constraints mean that operations on current tourism Web sites remain heavily dependent on text for their message delivery, with software robots used "behind the scenes" to retrieve text-based information for consumers (Ishida, 2002). Obviously this search and retrieve metaphor works well, even on a global basis, but if the Internet is to be used for real personal interaction with the tourism environment an immersive image-based *geographical* interface is ultimately going to be needed. One way to provide this is to construct a 3-D virtual image of a destination or travel route for the potential consumer; however there has to date only been limited adoption of virtual reality (VR) technology in the sales pitch of tourism organizations and businesses large and small, so despite the widespread availability of appropriate receiving media this form of message representation has not really entered the mainstream as yet (however, see Google Earth, http://earth.google.com/tour/).

# The Advent of New Technologies

This situation is likely to change in the near future as products like more sophisticated digital cameras become accessible to the wider consumer market, allowing tourists themselves to depict destinations in virtual reality terms to their friends and contacts. The technical sophistication of the Canon IXY is one example of what the next generation of digital cameras will be capable of. With a photo-stitch assistant built in, the photographer using one of these cameras (and others like them) is able to make seamless panoramic images over 360 degrees. The wider spread of technology of this nature will force producers of commercial promotional material in tourism to undertake more sophisticated use of VR to ensure that their products are visible in these ways to the more sophisticated user. In this context it is no surprise to see that immersive video and the ability to stream high quality video content to the Web consumer are now becoming increasingly acknowledged as an acceptable technology in promotional terms (Buhalis, 2002), and for this reason we argue in this chapter that such advances in technology will add to the VR impact of tourism marketing on the Web in the very near future.

Set against the development and general societal take-up of new technology is the extent and speed of its adoption by individual consumers, subjects of much interest to the marketing and tourism industries for many years (Bierman, 2002; Buhalis, 2002; Cetron, 2001; Hall, 2000; Inkpen 1998; Leiper, 1995; Prideaux, 2000, 2002; Weaver & Lawton, 2002; Witt & Moutinho, 1995). Most studies have found that there is a lag between the introduction of technological innovations and their widespread acceptance (Witt & Moutinho, 1995, pp. 273-284). Here, individual differences in learning and, indeed the whole human learning process come into play (Bednar, Cunningham, Duffy, & Perry, 1995). Effective learning derives from an individual developing a mixture of behavioural (new behavioural patterns being repeated until they become automatic), cognitive (the effects of changes in behaviour are observed and used as indicators to future useful behaviour), and constructive solutions to a given problem. This concept is based on the premise that we personally construct our own perspective of the world, especially with respect to problem solving in ambiguous situations, rather than have it done for us by an external agency (Schwier, 1995). As a result of this mechanism, because a human learner is able to interpret multiple realities depending on need, they are better able to deal with real life situations if they can actively problem-solve within them or before they occur. The actual circumstances surrounding the particular situation help us decide which approach to learning is most appropriate, but the process is intermediated by personal experience, cognitive and physical ability and other specific and non-specific situational variables. The end result is that some problems require highly prescriptive solutions outside the learner's control, whereas others are more suited to the control of his or her environment by that learner (Schwier, 1995).

From these, and earlier observations, a number of conclusions can be drawn about the likely learning behaviors and responses of the tourist to the type of almost total immersion environments (3-D) exemplified by virtual reality techniques (Bitgood, 1990; Psotka, 1995). The most general one is that users will still use specific environmental features as clues to behavior on entering a virtual space, just as they do in real space. Authentic environmental reproduction is therefore required to convey that sense of place. In fact, the inclusion of accurate renditions of artifacts and real environmental elements from the actual places being recreated is essential to effective immersion environments, even if initially the learners involved have very little directly transferable prior knowledge about the content area. What this means is that properly constructed virtual environments could quite easily and satisfactorily replace actual travel for some potential tourists, given the way in which human beings learn experientially, in theory at least.

Prideaux (2002) tested this theoretical conclusion in a small study carried out in 2001 of the reactions of tourism students to the likely impact of the virtual reality concept on the tourist experience, but instead found that while the benefits of virtual reality as an information and marketing tool were well recognized by such technologically-savvy groups, as a substitute for a real-life experience it had not gained any form of mass acceptance and was not in fact much welcomed as a replacement for this. In the light of this result, this chapter investigates the *potential* of virtual reality tools to describe tourist experiences and attractions (especially over the Internet) as a form of tourism marketing, and the current constraints on the full realization of this potential. Through an examination of the advantages of the Internet as a marketing tool and of the characteristics of the 21$^{st}$ century tourism industry and of the social, political, and natural environments in many countries, it is suggested that the use of virtual reality via this medium is likely to become very important for marketing and experiencing tourism for the general public in the near future, notwithstanding the conclusions of the earlier study.

The chapter also looks at some of the reasons why although it might be apparent that imaging technology can and will be able to help market tourism product at least to the experienced internet user and/or the user interested in specific sites, it currently remains underutilized in most other tourism applications. To provide a partial answer to this question, an online survey of VR imaging professionals was undertaken in early 2005. The results are outlined later in this chapter, but in essence suggest that marketing using fully VR enabled tools is as yet only partly accepted due to cost and perceived difficulty of use. Thus, VR is not yet an essential part of the marketing mix for any significant number of destinations, although its potential is well recognized, at least by the IT industry professionals that would be required by the tourism industry to make its use feasible.

# Tourist Destination Decision Making
# and the Internet

The critical components that determine the demand for a destination or product may be collectively characterized according to the 6P model (Weaver & Lawton, 2002, p. 222), and includes such items as place, product, price, packaging, promotion, and people, when applied to the service industries. In regard to marketing most emphasis is usually placed on the dimensions of product and place attributes, price, packaging and promotion. The additional people dimension within the overall model in this case includes tourists, service workers and residents and refers to consumer behavior, service quality and resident support for, or opposition to tourism and has been extensively studied in the tourism literature (Witt & Moutinho, 1995). Topics of interest to tourism market researchers have been how to better evaluate the predictors of destination and travel mode choice, or how to determine the best promotional campaign for a particular destination.

In almost all formulations of the demand-side model to date place has been included not only for its intrinsic value as the location in space of the desired tourism product, but also because it is generally asserted that tourists must *travel* to a destination in order to consume the tourism product (Weaver & Lawton, 2002, p. 223). Much has in fact been made in tourism marketing theory of the notion that tourism is unique because production and consumption occur not only at the same time but in the same place (Morrison, 2002; Ritchie, 1996), and that relative location (proximity) is often a critical determinant of the take-up of tourism opportunities. While place is of course as much influenced by accessibility (price and physical accessibility) as relative physical location in determining how effective any given connection between market demand and a particular destination actually is, insisting on the importance of relative physical location nevertheless reinforces the notion of the centrality of place and by implication a requirement for travel before tourism opportunities can be realized. But what if the physical nature of the place variable could be removed from this equation through the further development of virtual reality (VR)? There might indeed be less requirement for actual travel, but even if this did not happen at the very least the traveler could be better informed about the physical actuality of a potential destination before travel, assuming that the realities are fully described and adverse aspects not covered up by the VR equivalent of air-brushing. In this way the uncertainties involved in tourism destination decision making could be considerably reduced.

# The Internet as a Marketing Tool and Resource

Before examining the question of whether or not VR will contribute a great deal to future destination decision making, or indeed remove the need for actual travel entirely, it is useful to look at the current use of the Internet in the marketing and experiencing of tourism. Tourism has been amongst the top three commercial users of the Internet for some time and information and communications technologies (ICT) continue to rapidly change "spatial relationships" in society as a whole and in tourism in particular (Buhalis, 2002). For example, e-mail is pervasive, the Internet is everywhere despite some attempts at its control in some countries, there has been a massive uptake of broadband capability, and there has been a very high penetration of mobile devices as both information sources and as communication facilitators; indeed the use of ICT is pervasive in the workplace and the home. With respect to tourism, using the Internet to research, request and feedback information and to purchase is now "taken for granted" by tourists (Prideaux, 2002). It is probably therefore possible, even at this relatively early stage in our use of the Internet as a marketing tool to say, as do Buhalis, Jafari and Werthner (1997) that there is really no choice for many tourism operators but to include this new technology as a central part of their marketing repertoire in order to satisfy tourist demand and to survive in the marketplace in the long run. Organizations that fail to participate in the electronic marketplace in the future face severe competitive disadvantage and may lose market share (Buhalis, 1998).

The Internet also is very important on the supply-side of the market. It offers a means to sell to final consumers at a reasonable price without many overheads, allowing individual tourist operators to compete with wholesalers (agents), and to improve their distribution channels in many cases. It is a particularly important information source for international and domestic travelers, with the travel sector rated amongst the top three product/service categories purchased via the internet (Heung, 2003; Weber & Roehl, 1999). As Buhalis has noted, this could be very important for small and medium enterprises in a market traditionally dominated by larger firms (and their allies in government tourism organizations—Buhalis, 1998, 2002). By using the Internet their costs of marketing can be contained, the influence of often peripheral spatial locations reduced (Vich-I-Martorell, 2002), and/or the small firm's almost universal inability to effectively utilize local/regional business assistance and tourism promotional organisations offset (Cooper & Abubakar, 2004).

On the demand side how does the Internet currently impact on buyer behaviour? Models of consumer purchase decision making range from the very simple *need—information search—evaluation—decision—post purchase evaluation* type to more complex formulations for services that are based on a range of psychological and socio-economic factors (Palmer, 1994, pp. 116-120). These models incorporate the following elements:

- **Inputs:** Information about the range of competing services and products that may satisfy the immediate felt need
- **Behavioral determinants:** The individual factors in decision making, influenced by socialization, personality, culture, level of information, and so on
- **Perceptual reactions:** Interpretation of information inputs through personality and experience
- **Processing determinants:** The way in which a decision is made, incorporating motivation to satisfy felt needs, critical product requirements and attributes, past experiences of suppliers, ability to use and recognize available information, and so on
- **Inhibitors:** Ease of access, price, terms and conditions for delivery
- **Outputs:** The outcome of the decision process (proceed, defer, do not proceed)

Palmer (1994, p. 118) notes that most buyers of services do not act with total rationality—to be able to do so would require that all possible sources of information would be known to them and that their contents could be fully and logically evaluated. Of all the service industries, tourism is a confidence or experience good (Werthner & Klein, 1999), where product characteristics such as quality or price value are difficult to observe and can only be fully ascertained upon actual consumption (or from a reasonable facsimile of this provided by the much discussed 'word of mouth' phenomenon). Experience goods pose difficulties for consumers in accurately making consumption choices because at the moment of decision making only information about the product, but not the product itself, is available. Moreover, the role of experience in consumption decisions is only now being realized in effective marketing strategies for tourism (Gretzel & Fesenmaier, 2002). This is based on the fact that experiential learning, often assisted by friends and relations is not only entertaining and stimulating but also central to the travel decision making process because it lets consumers understand and evaluate the travel product in ways not bound by the need to describe such products in functional terms or in monetary values (Vogt & Fesenmaier, 1998). This is precisely why those VR technologies that allow experiential learning of an environment independently of travel to the actual destination should have a great future in the tourism industry.

But, beyond the use of evocative photographs there has been little virtual reality product in the tourism industry's commercial uses of the Internet to date. While consumers are becoming mature Internet users, in that they are more "cyber-savvy," more demanding, more willing to search, and more willing to provide community feedback to business, these "consumers with attitude" are not apparently demanding VR products in addition to text and 2-D image based information (see Chapter VII of this book). So, while the process of attracting, drawing-in, and retaining potential consumers of tourism product is becoming more challenging for operators and their agents, and consumers are talking to each other like never before on the Internet through blogs, review sites, opinion sites, user groups, chat, or other online communities, business is not yet taking the next step and providing virtual reality experiences for their potential customers, other than the 2-dimensional photograph or the video clip.

## Virtual Reality Tools
## to Enhance the Tourist Experience

As a marketing channel, the Internet is thus now a mature medium for the tourism industry. The travel and tourism sector blazed the trail of e-commerce in the 1990s (Buhalis, 1998). Even as long ago as 1999 "Travel" was the No.1 online product; considerably exceeding the combined online sales of books, software, computers, music, flowers, and toys, so why are the new VR technologies of the 21$^{st}$ century not being taken up in a similar fashion to develop the individual consumer's experience of tourism products? By being able to "walk through" or otherwise experience a more complete model of a destination for example before purchasing accommodation and/or tours surely the potential consumer would be able to gather more information than is available through 2-D photographs and the like. On this question Prideaux (2002) notes that, in an increasingly affluent world the pressure of numbers of tourists on particular environments may in fact encourage tourists to begin to demand this alternation between real and cyberspace experiences in a much more systematic way than at present. In other words, the use of virtual reality in tourism may be in fact more likely as a replacement for *travel* than as a more sophisticated tool for marketing destinations, under pressure from external factors like conservation of the environment. Thus while for some "tourists" the increasing possibility of becoming a voyeur in a personalized and private cyber-world may be strong (Williams & Hobson, 1995), for a greater number the chance to visit an otherwise *unattainable* location may be paramount in their decision to make use of such technologies in the future.

Nevertheless, VR has been a buzzword for over ten years now, and despite widely available VR imaging technologies such as QuickTime, Java, and other authoring tools, widespread use of the medium remains elusive in the tourism industry. In the next section we define virtual reality as it is currently used with respect to human experience of environments, and describe some of the tools for constructing such virtual realities that presently exist or may be developed in the near future to enhance the tourism experience.

## The Nature of Virtual Reality

Virtual reality is exactly that, a computer generated environment that seems real to the user (HarperCollins, 1996). Extensively used in computer gaming software, with increasing levels of "reality" as computing power has evolved, in the business world educational/instruction virtual reality-based tools are moving from highly specialized uses such as flight simulations to building business skills for sales and call centre reps and enhancing coaching and leadership skills for managers and executives. The use of simulations through immersion in virtual realities increases the efficacy of online teaching as much as 75% by involving employees for example in virtual job situations in which they gain experience without the risk of making mistakes (Psotka, 1995). Equally, IMAX and other large-format immersive experiences, from a realistic 360° panorama of objects and landscapes to a flythrough of an interactive virtual world on the Internet, aim to stimulate the senses of the user to get them as close to the real world as possible, virtually.

Alternatively known as Immersive Media (Bitgood, 1990; Psotka, 1995), virtual reality also can be used as a component of e-brochures, e-catalogues, Web sites, and other interactive presentations to provide a realistic look and feel of consumer products, hotels, cars, real estate, or other facilities. In addition, technologies such as *Immersive Television* that can engender in viewers a "sense of being there" in depicted scenes and 3D broadcast experiences may be widely available to the consumer in less than 10 years time. Immersive imaging is a technology that lets users experience 3D photographic scenes at if they were really there.

There are two types of immersive images that may be used for tourism experience and marketing purposes: panoramas and objects. *Panorama* (panospheric—panographic) type images are 360 degree views that allow users to look up and down, turn around, and zoom in to see the detail, or zoom out for a broader view. These are photographic images, presented in a software "player" that permits navigation on each of the x, y, & z axes. Multiple, overlapping images are stitched together with software tools and photos are taken using special tripod attachments or the multiple image features of digital camera software. As users change the view of a scene the correct perspective is maintained, giving the ability to look around just as in real life. Panorama images are currently used to provide realistic views and walk-throughs of real estate, outdoor scenes, and hotel resorts. Figure 1 is a 2-D static representation of a 360 degree panorama by Spinning-Eye, a specialist VR imaging company that can be experienced as 3-D on the Internet. Many other tourism and hospitality examples may be found on the Internet sites.

*Object* imagery on the other hand allows users to "pick up" and view an item from all sides using software tools. Its uses include being able to look more closely at consumer products, fashion, automobiles, and heritage items as if the consumer was really handling or otherwise experiencing them physically, and this applies as much

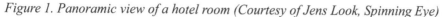
*Figure 1. Panoramic view of a hotel room (Courtesy of Jens Look, Spinning Eye)*

to the tourism facility (from airplane seats through attractions) as it does to any other item. Virtual manipulation of, to the observer, an apparently physical object has immediately obvious uses in heritage and cultural tourism for example, while its combination with panoramas would allow much richer sampling of potential environments before purchase of the "trip."

## Digital Preservation, Digital Visitation

For those lacking the desire or money to travel, or where there are restrictions on travel for environmental or political reasons, a virtual destination could provide an acceptable substitute for actual visitation (Sung, Lee, Kim, Kwon, & Jang, 2000). This may be especially so where the tourist's desire is actually for re-creation of history or heritage rather than in visiting the current physical remains of a past culture. Virtual reality special effects are already being used to great effect in the television documentary format and in "epic" film making such as the Lord of the Rings film trilogy, and these will ultimately allow the virtual tourist to visit a site during different (re-created) stages in its history. Along with this opportunity virtual guides or "avatars" also are available to provide expert commentary and feedback in a number of languages, a service that can be quite costly to provide in the real world (Weaver & Lawton, 2002). An important example of the use of this technology is the World Heritage Preservation Project, initiated by UNESCO in 2001, and designed to ultimately provide panoramic VR tours through the creation of a documentary image bank of panoramic pictures and virtual reality films for all sites registered as World Heritage by the United Nations Educational, Scientific and Cultural Organization (http://www.world-heritage-tour.org/list.html, 2005). At the time of writing, a *virtual* tourist can visit World Heritage Sites in Afghanistan, Bangladesh, Eastern Canada, China, Cambodia, Egypt, India, Indonesia, Iran, Korea, Laos, Malaysia, Nepal, Pakistan, Sri Lanka, Thailand, The Philippines, and Vietnam. This represents

15% of all 812 such sites, and covers 125 sites in 700+ panographies, a number of which are of sites that are in areas of political tension (for example in Sri Lanka, Afghanistan).

## Is the Potential of VR for Tourism Going to be Realized in the Near Future?

From this brief discussion it is readily apparent that imaging technology (the creation of virtual realities) could be of assistance in the marketing of tourism products to the internet consumer and/or the consumer interested in historical/heritage sites, but has not been taken up in any significant way as yet. The prevailing view amongst developers and users of existing VR technology is that it is ideally suited for these tasks because it is immersive, compelling, and the consumer is in control, even though it remains underutilized by the industry and consumers. To examine possible industry-based reasons for this situation an online survey of VR imaging professionals was undertaken in late 2005. The respondents were sourced from professional mailing lists and user groups available to the authors, and the data was collected using an open source survey tool. The respondents represent a small but fairly representative sample of the major players in this field; however care should be taken in generalizing from the results as no corresponding survey of either tourism marketers or of the use of VR technology by tourists themselves has been undertaken at this stage.

## Results of the Industry Survey

The aim of the survey was to determine how easy it is to produce VR images of tourist destination and heritage items, to determine if the technology, expertise, and knowledge required was a real barrier to its wider use and adoption in tourism marketing, or is the real reason for underutilization something else entirely? Our respondents (n = 80) were ICT professionals, with 57% having been in this industry for four or more years, and 86% for more than two years (Figure 2). Respondents self proclaimed status in the industry with respect to their expertise in VR simulations was expert (25%), advanced but not yet expert (45%), intermediate (19%) and novice (11%—Figure 3). Of the respondents, 86% produce VR images professionally, and 65% have produced VR images for tourism marketing purposes. Overwhelmingly however, 80% of respondents said that it was still difficult to produce such images and required specialist knowledge, equipment and expertise, but 92% believed that they were more effective than normal photographic images, and 80% believed that VR is more popular now than before in the industry. We also asked if they thought that consumers "enjoy" using VR imaging and if VR images more effectively promote tourism products than regular images. Again, over 90% of respondents thought this was true in both cases given their intimate contact with the tourism industry. The key issues for the respondents with respect to the further development of VR technologies for tourism came down to the following (Figure 4):

- Tourism operators are not aware of the technology.
- If they are aware, they believe it is very expensive at this time.
- Many Web designers also are not aware of the technology.
- If they are, they are reluctant to engage a specialist to translate their needs into suitable presentations.
- File size and download time remain a real concern (despite increasing broadband use).
- There is a prevailing fear that readily available browser software will not be capable of displaying the image.
- There is no "easy to use" software for potential consumers.

*Figure 2. ICT Industry experience of respondents*

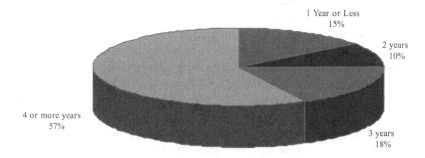

*Figure 3. Expertise status of respondents*

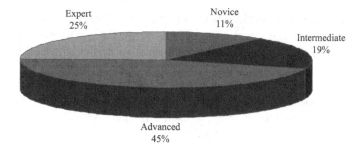

*Figure 4. Issues in the further development of VR technologies for tourism*

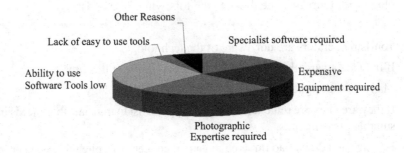

Until these concerns can be overcome, either through overwhelming user demand or through the advent of even newer technologies, the VR professionals surveyed concluded that there will be a continuing resistance to the use of 3D virtual reality techniques in tourism marketing. Instead, the current 2D enhanced methods will remain the standard at least for the short term future (to 5 years). The reason for this is the prevailing opinion amongst the professionals that while VR imaging and tourism appear to be a great fit, this is only really true in the context of skilled Web or multimedia advertising and promotion. Their view is that at the present stage of development a quality photograph is more usable, can be produced by far more people, can be used in both printed and Web-based media with little or no specialized training, and can be accurately judged for quality by tourism marketing professionals and the public in real time. Video and VR is presently restricted to knowledgeable producers and developers and used in Web, CD, or trade-show kiosk delivery. In these contexts VR is easier and cheaper to produce than a promotional video, but still more difficult than traditional photography.  It will only be when the cost and quality of VR imagery is close to that found in computer-based gaming that the tourism marketer and the tourist will consider the technique as having more than just novelty value, except perhaps for its uses in the heritage preservation field as outlined above.

In summary, the VR production industry appears to believe that tourism marketers are either not aware of the possibilities of this new technique for promotion, or that these are seen by the tourism industry as being just a different format of photography that costs more and doesn't dramatically improve public perception or use of the end product. Alternatively, it may be that the key problem is in fact that VR producers themselves do not know how to market their services to the tourism marketing and promotional people, and this problem itself ultimately reflects on the current low acceptance of VR for tourism promotion.

# Conclusion

This chapter undertook a brief overview of the available technologies and opportunities for the use of virtual reality in tourism marketing. It acknowledged that in almost all formulations of the tourism marketing model to date much has been made of the notion that tourism is unique because production and consumption occur not only at the same time but in the same place, and therefore that location or proximity is often *the* critical determinant of the take-up of tourism opportunities (e.g., Weaver & Lawson, 2002, pp. 222-223). But it then posited the question: what if the place variable could be removed from this equation through the further development of virtual reality techniques? The impacts of this possibility have been seen to include: less requirement for travel per se (perhaps); better and more real information about the physical actuality of a destination for the potential consumer (likely); price and service quality information very much simplified and improved (definitely), and changed tourism promotion strategies (undoubtedly). At the barest minimum, the uncertainties involved in relying on unverified 2D or text-based information for tourism travel decision-making could be considerably reduced using VR techniques.

Many educationalists and psychologists have noted that effective learning in human beings is closely associated with experiencing and therefore comprehending in a more structured way something that they have never seen before, or is dependent on being exposed to new and usable information that adds to and/or refines their existing knowledge base (summarized by Schwier, 1995, and many others). From these discussions certain general conclusions can be drawn about the likely responses of the tourist to virtual reality immersion environments. The most general one is that such users will notice and use the same way specific environmental features as clues to understanding and perhaps action on entering a new virtual space, just as they do in real space. For virtual reality tourism marketing to succeed then, authentic reproduction of a given environment (or as close as it is possible to get to it given available technology and funds) is required to convey the all-important sense of place. Secondly, the inclusion of accurate renditions of artifacts and action elements from the actual places being recreated (i.e., walk through and similar renditions) is essential to the creation of effective immersion environments. Despite the technical difficulties in doing this, and the expense of current versions of software and hardware, these criteria can now be fulfilled according to the VR professionals we surveyed for this discussion, so the use of virtual reality simulations of real places in order to provide either extra pre-travel information, or ultimately perhaps to replace travel entirely is now possible.

For the future, the VR industry is apparently much more excited about the possibilities inherent in these emerging technologies than the tourism and hospitality industry. Therefore it will require consumers (tourists) and their agents to reach the same level of understanding before their use will become ubiquitous throughout the tourism industry.  At the very least however these technologies now support the creation of a documentary and educational image bank of panographies (online virtual tours) for all sites registered as World Heritage by United Nations Educational, Scientific and Cultural Organization (UNESCO) and for hotel marketing, etc, thus enabling tourists and other users to visit and learn about such facilities and sites before actual travel or indeed to replace travel entirely. The availability in the future of more and more powerful and cheaper recording and display facilities for virtual tourism, ultimately in the form of personalized ubiquitous devices (Hoshino, 2005) that also provide GIS, travel information, and interpretation of language *and* artifacts (heritage archives and tourist attractions) in real time will allow the tourist the freedom to choose between a virtual reality experience and/or actual physical presence in that environment at will.

# References

Bednar, A. K., Cunningham, D., Duffy, T. M., & Perry, J. P. (1995). Theory into practice: How do we link? In G.J. Anglin, (Ed.), *Instructional technology: Past, present and future* (2nd ed., pp. 100-111). Englewood, CO: Libraries Unlimited, Inc.

Bierman, D. (2002) *Restoring tourism destinations in crisis.* Sydney: Allen & Unwin.

Bitgood, S. (1990). *The role of simulated immersion in exhibition* (Tech. Rep. No. 90-20). Jacksonville, AL: Centre for Social Design.

Buhalis, D. (1998). Strategic use of Internet technologies in the tourist industry. *Tourism Management, 19*(5), 409-421.

Buhalis, D. (2002). *eTourism: Information technology for strategic tourism management.* London: Pearson Education.

Buhalis, D., Jafari, J., & Werthner, H. (1997). Information technology and re-engineering of tourism. *Annals of Tourism Research, 24*(1), 245-248.

Cetron, M. (2001). The world of today and tomorrow: The global view. In A. Lockwood & S. Medlik, (Eds.), *Tourism and hospitality in the 21st century* (pp. 18-28). Oxford: Butterworth Heinemann.

Cooper, M. J. and Abubakar, B. (2004). The role of tourism bureaux in the development of tourist attractions in Australia: A case study of Hervey Bay, Queensland. *Journal of Hospitality & Tourism* 1(2), 1-10.

*Crownreef Web site.* (2005). Retrieved June 20, 2005 from http://www.crownreef. com/virtual_tour.cfm (java)

Gretzel, U., & Fesenmaier, D. R. (2002). Building narrative logic into tourism information systems. *IEEE Intelligent Systems, 17*(6), 53-64.

*Google Earth*. (2005). Retrieved July 17, 2005 from http://earth.google.com/tour/

Hall, C. M. (2000). *Tourism planning*, London: Prentice-Hall.

HarperCollins Dictionaries. (1996). *Collins compact Australian dictionary*. Sydney: HarperCollins.

Heung, V. S. (2003). Internet Usage by International Travelers: reasons and barriers, *International Journal of Contemporary Hospitality Management* 15(7), 370-378.

Hoshino, Y. (2005, July 16). *Relaxation research in a multicultural society*. Presented to the Science and Technology for Art III—Digital Archiving of Cultural Assets—International Symposium, Ritsumeikan Asia Pacific University.

Inkpen, G. (1998). *Information technology for travel and tourism* (2ⁿᵈ ed.). London: Pearson Education.

Ishida, T. (2002). Q: A scenario description language for interactive agents. *IEEE Computer* 35(11), 54-59.

*Kootenay Virtual Tours Web site*. (2005). Retrieved June 20, 2005 http://www.kootenayvirtualtours.com/topics/accomm/eagle/eagle_q.htm

Leiper, N. (1995). *Tourism management*. Melbourne: RMIT Press.

Morrison, A. (2002). *Hospitality and travel marketing* (3ʳᵈ ed.). New York: Delmar.

*Naturebase Web site*. (2005). Retrieved June 20, 2005 from http://www.naturebase.net/national_parks/shark_bay_qtvr.html (QuickTime)

*Optima Cruises Web site*. (2005). Retrieved June 20, 2005 from http://www.optimacruises.com/Am_virtual.asp;

Palmer, A. (1994). *Principles of services marketing*. London: McGraw-Hill.

Prideaux, B. (2000). Transport and tourism, past, present and future. In E. Laws & B. Faulkner (Eds.), *Tourism in the 21ˢᵗ century: Lessons from experience* (pp. 91-109). London: Continuum.

Prideaux, B. (2002). The cybertourist. In Dann, G. (Ed.), *The tourist as a metaphor of the social world* (pp. 317-339). Oxford: CAB International.

Psotka, J. (1995). Immersive training systems: Virtual reality and education and training, *Instructional Science* 23 (5-6), 405-431.

*Real World Imaging Web Site*. (2005). Retrieved June 20, 2005 from http://www.realworldimaging.com.au/

Ritchie, J. R. Brent. (1996). Beacons of light in an expanding universe: An assessment of the state-of-the-art in tourism marketing/market research, *Journal of Travel & Tourism Marketing* 5(4), 49-84.

Schwier, R. A. (1995). Issues in emerging interactive technologies. In G. J. Anglin (Ed.), *Instructional technology: Past, present and future* (2ⁿᵈ ed., pp. 119-127). Englewood, CO: Libraries Unlimited, Inc.

Sheldon, P. (1997). *Tourism information technology*. Oxford: CAB International.

*Sitepal Web site*. (2005). Retrieved January 2005, from http://www.sitepal.com

Sung, P., Lee, Y., Kim, Y., Kwon, Y. and Jang, B. (2000). Development of Virtual Cybertours in the virtual reality system, *Asia Pacific Journal of Tourism Research 3*(2), 45-50.

Vich-I-Martorell, G. A. (2002). The Internet as a marketing tool for tourism in the Balearic Islands. *Information Technology & Tourism* 5, 91-104.

Vogt, C. A., & Fesenmaier, D. M. (1998). Expanding the functional search model, *Annals of Tourism Research*, 25(3), 551-578.

Weaver, D., & Lawton, L. (2002). *Tourism management* (2nd ed.). London: Wiley.

Weber, K., & Roehl, W. S. (1999). Profiling people searching and purchasing travel products on the world wide Web. *Journal of Travel Research* 37(3), 291-298.

Weiermair, K., & Mathies, C. (2004). *The tourism and leisure industry: Shaping the future*. New York: Haworth Press.

Werthner, H., & Klein, S. (1999). *Information technology and tourism—a challenging relationship*. New York: Springer-Verlag.

Williams, P., & Hobson, P. S. (1995). Virtual reality and tourism: Fact or fantasy? *Tourism Management* 16, 423-427.

Witt, S. F., & Moutinho, L. (1995). *Tourism marketing and management handbook*. London: Prentice-Hall.

*World Heritage Tour Web site*. (2005). Retrieved March 2005, from http://www.world-heritage-tour.org

Chapter IX

# Towards Improved Business Planning Decision Support for Small-to-Medium Tourism Enterprise Operators

G. Michael McGrath, Victoria University, Australia

## Abstract

*In a recent study conducted for the Australian Sustainable Tourism Cooperative Research Centre, improved business planning was identified as one of the most pressing needs of small-to-medium tourism enterprise operators. Further significant problems confronting these businesses were coping with rapid change, complexity and uncertainty. System dynamics (SD) is especially well-suited to the modelling and analysis of problem domains with these characteristics and, in this chapter, we report on the development and implementation of a "tourism enterprise planning simulator" (TEPS) based largely upon SD constructs and technologies. Scenarios in which TEPS might be used to good effect are outlined and the potential benefits of this deployment are detailed.*

# Introduction

A number of tourism researchers have noted that there is a demand among prospective (and current) small-to-medium tourism enterprise (SMTE) operators for improved business planning tools (see e.g., Baker, 2000; Bergin-Seers, Jago, Breen, & Carlsen, 2005; Mistilis, Presbury, & Agnes, 2004). Moreover, there would seem to be a place for online, automated tools: whether as an adjunct to traditional sources of advice or as stand-alone products. Low-cost, generic business planning software products are inadequate because they fail to take into account contextual factors important to the tourism industry. There are, however, some impressive, recently-developed destination planning support tools and these are tourism-specific—examples being the "Tourism Futures Simulator" of Walker, Greiner, McDonald, and Lyne (1999) and the "Hotel Value Chain Profitability" model of Georgantzas (2003).

A feature of both these tourism planning and policy-making tools is that they are based upon system dynamics (SD) concepts, tools and techniques. SD has been around for over 40 years (see Forrester, 1961, for what is generally regarded as the seminal and most influential piece of work in the field), but has enjoyed something of a resurgence recently. To some extent, this is due to an increasing recognition (among researchers from many fields) that SD is especially suitable for capturing, modelling, and analysing: so-called "messy" problems; and key aspects of "change."

Messy problems have been defined by Vennix (1996, pp. 9-41) as being characterised by complexity, uncertainty, recursive dependencies, inter-related sub-problems, selective perception, self-interest, and, related to this, key stakeholders working from different views of the essential nature of the problem. A glance through any tourism/hospitality text should quickly convince the reader that these attributes all apply to the tourism domain: both at the destination level (see e.g., Ritchie & Crouch, 2003) and at the enterprise level (see Baker, 2000).

Change too is characteristic of the tourism industry. Indeed, in a recent study (McGrath, 2005), one of the most significant problems facing the Australian tourism industry was identified as rapid change: including technological change, major changes in the external business environment, and changes that are having substantial impacts at every point of the tourism supply chain (and at every level—from international to regional and local levels). The situation was summed up by one study participant as follows: "Not only are we shooting in the dark—we are shooting at a moving target" (McGrath & More, 2005, p. 4). Here, our interviewee was expressing a degree of dissatisfaction with: first, adequate data not being available to facilitate effective strategic planning; and, second, the fact that the tourism industry is moving so quickly that, even where accurate data is accessible in a timely manner, it is often outdated and relatively useless in much too short a timeframe. However, the quote would seem to apply equally to many other problems currently confronted by the industry.

In recognition of the above, the Australian *Sustainable Tourism Cooperative Research Centre* (STCRC) recently provided funding and support for a research project aimed at producing a *tourism enterprise planning simulator* (TEPS). Distinguishing features of TEPS are:

- Extensive use is made of SD modelling technologies and tools (for capturing and simulating key aspects of change).

- The enterprise simulator sits inside a destination-level simulator. In this way, TEPS addresses a major problem associated with the multitude of generic, low-cost business planning tools available—namely, they fail to take into account tourism-specific, contextual factors.

- TEPS operates at different levels of granularity. At the very fine-grained level, actual data is used to establish relationships and to instantiate model variables. At the more coarse-grained levels, a restricted set of destination archetypes is induced and users assign values to variables through an "impressionistic" (or fuzzy) process.

- Artificial intelligence tools (such as rule-based deductive inference, case-based reasoning and fuzzy logic) are used to complement the base SD technology employed.

In this chapter, we report on the development, validation and potential use of the tourism enterprise business planning tool. The focus of our initial research is on tourism accommodation enterprises and the chapter is organized as follows: background to the research is presented in the following section and this is followed by an overview of the design and implementation of TEPS. The following section deals with ways in which the simulator might be employed during tourism enterprise business planning and the benefits that flow from this. System validation, the current status of our project and future plans are then discussed and, finally, concluding remarks are presented.

# Background

## SMTEs and Business Planning

The Australian tourism industry employs approximately 5.9% of the total work-force, accounts for 5.9% of GDP, and contributes 11.2% of total exports (Tourism Australia, 2004, p. 22). There is some argument concerning the accuracy of these figures but the recent establishment of a "Tourism Satellite Account" (Smith, 2004) by the Australian Bureau of Statistics (ABS) means that tourism's contribution to the Australian economy is measured according to guidelines and methods established by the World Tourism Organization (WTO). This ensures that, at the vary least, local tourism statistics are derived consistently with the closest thing to a generally-accepted set of standards the international tourism industry has and that international comparisons may be made with a fair degree of confidence.

In excess of 90% of Australian tourism businesses are SMTEs (Sharma, Carson, & DeLacy, 2000, p. 3) and it has long been recognized that SMTE operators have to deal with myriad problems. For example, in a recent paper dealing with the local tourism industry's response to an Australian state government's "come online" initiative, Morrison and King (2002, p. 111) divided SMTE firms into Techno-whizzos, Early adopters, Wait-and-sees and Wilderness operators. Members of the Wilderness group were described as generally aged 45+, with no computer or interest in them, they felt they were too old to learn more and they viewed the Internet as a waste of time. They also had a dislike of officialdom/bureaucracy and were reluctant to participate in regional activities and networks. Somewhat depressingly, it was estimated that 60% of the SMTE sample were in the Wilderness category (with another 20% in the Wait-and-see group).

More generally, Gammack, Amaya Molinar, Chu, and Chanpayom (2004, pp. x –xi) analysed SMTEs in the Asia-Pacific region and nominated the following factors as significant inhibitors to enterprise development:

- A lack of a trained and professional workforce
- A lack of entrepreneurial skills among operators
- Low entry barriers—impacting on service quality, growth and business viability
- Lending arrangement and taxation regimes not conducive to SMTEs
- Conforming to (and supporting) sustainable regional infrastructure requirements
- Inconsistent and bureaucratic local authorities
- A lack of government recognition of the value of tourism
- A failure to recognize the potential benefits of industry clusters and collaboration
- Industry fragmentation and a proliferation of membership organizations
- A lack of technology (generally) and e-commerce (specifically) skills
- Relatively poor e-readiness and e-commerce uptake
- Scattered, poorly-integrated and difficult-to-locate business research information

A number of these factors might be classified under the broader heading of a "lack of strategic focus" and this has long been recognized as a problem among SMTE operators (see e.g., Sharma et al., 2000a; Mistilis et al., 2004; Morrison & King, 2002). This lack of attention to planning and strategy is evident in the Morrison and King (op. cit) analysis presented above and, more recently, Mistilis et al. (2004) identified the lack of a strategic focus as the main impediment to the uptake of online technologies among Sydney hotel operators. Nevertheless, there are indications that things might be changing for the better and, during another Australian study conducted by the author (McGrath, 2005, p. 72), one State Tourism Authority (STA) representative asserted that:

*Not a day goes by when we are not approached by at least a couple of prospective operators looking for help with their business planning. ... You can look at business planning as, maybe, a 14-16 step process. We talk to them [prospective operators] at Step 1, and the next time they hear from us is after they are established. Then, we are asking them for information! We need to do more for them.*

Thus, at least some SMTE operators are looking to improve their business planning and, given the high rate of enterprise attrition in this sector (Baker, 2000; English, 1995), some attempts have been made to provide the necessary support. For example, the Decipher tourism data warehouse (Carson & Richards, 2004) provides business planning support through its Web site, Tourism Victoria is planning to implement an online business planning product and the STCRC has recently released a business planning "toolkit" for property owners considering "Farm and Country Tourism" ventures (Fausnaugh, Waight, Higginbottom, & Northrope, 2004). TEPS is intended to complement these products (the current intention being to eventually implement it within Decipher).

A quick search using Google (and the keywords, "business planning software") returned just under 100 million matches. Even allowing for the fact that many of these are dead-ends, a brief perusal of a number of returned sites revealed a number of potentially useful business planning software aids. Thus, there is most definitely no shortage of generic business planning software. In addition, adding the word "tourism" to the search string led to a few sites that (on the surface) do seem to have something to offer the prospective SMTE operator (see e.g., the "Tourism Business Development Toolbox" at http://www.uwex.edu/ces/cced/tourism/).

Nevertheless (while admitting that our analysis was less than comprehensive), few of these online, tourism-related, business planning Web sites appear to be well-grounded in the holistic (or systemic) view of the "sustainable tourism system." This view is considered by some (e.g., Gammack et al., 2004, p. 1) to have its roots in the work of Brundtland (1987) and its many manifestations include the Mill and Morrison (2002) model (focusing on a "chicken-and-egg" like relationship between consumer travel decisions and destination marketing), the "triple bottom line" concept (Adams, Frost, & Webber, 2004; Elkington, 1999) (encompassing the natural, economic and cultural/social environments), and the "competitive destination" model of Ritchie and Crouch (2003). The WTO (1998) defines a sustainable tourism destination as a region where:

*... tourism development meets the needs of present tourists and host regions while protecting and enhancing opportunities for the future. It is envisaged as leading to management of all resources in such a way that economic, social and aesthetic needs can be fulfilled while maintaining cultural integrity, essential ecological processes, biological diversity and life support systems.*

## System Dynamics

The holistic view of a tourism destination seems to be now almost universally accepted among researchers and policy makers (if not industry practitioners) and, given this, it is perhaps a little surprising that greater advantage has not been taken of methods, tools and techniques commonly employed in SD (or "systems thinking") research and implementation to assist in the development of better business practices amongst SMTEs. SD has its origins in the work of Forrester (1961) and, more recently, has enjoyed something of a resurgence—largely due to Peter Senge's (1990) very influential work on "the learning organization," and to the development and release of easy-to-use, powerful, SD-based software modelling and simulation tools (such as *iThink*, *Vensim*, and *Powersim*). Recent examples of where SD has been used to good effect in tourism include the "Tourism Futures Simulator" of Walker et al. (1999), the hotel value chain modelling work of Georgantzas (2003), the tourism multipliers model of Loutif, Moscardini, and Lawler (2000), and the information architecture modelling work of McGrath and More (2005).

The SD component of TEPS has been developed and implemented using *Powersim* (Powersim, 2003). Within *Powersim*, models are developed in what is referred to as stock-flow format and a simple model is presented in Figure 1 below.

The basic building blocks of SD models are stocks (represented as rectangles), flows (represented as arrows with circular flow regulators attached) and converters (represented as circles). In our model, examples of stocks are Region Attractiveness, Enterprise Development and Region Development. There is a level associated with each stock, which can be an actual value or a value bounded by some artificial scale. Region Attractiveness (and, indeed, all stocks in our example) are measured on a 0-200 scale and we have set the system up so that, when the value of every stock level is at 100, the system is in equilibrium. Stock levels vary with flows, which may

*Figure 1. Example of a SD model—stock-flow form*

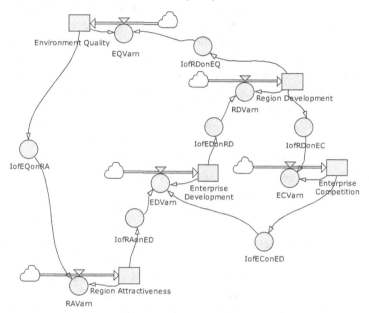

be inflows, outflows or bidirectional. For example, RDVarn (Region Development Variation) is a bidirectional flow such that:

$$Region\ Development_t = f(Region\ Development_{t-1},\ RDVarn_t).$$

That is, in our model, the region development level at time, *t*, is a function of the region development level at time, *t-1*, and the region development variation at time, *t*. These equations are the foundation of *Powersim's* formidable simulation capabilities. The third of our basic constructs, converters, serve a utilitarian role: they hold values for constants, calculate mathematical relationships and serve as repositories for graphical functions. In general, they convert inputs into outputs (hence, the name, "converter").

Earlier (see the introductory section), we noted that many issues and problems associated with tourism fall into a class of organizational problems defined by Vennix (1996, pp. 13-41) as "messy" and that problems of this type are characterised by complexity, uncertainty, interrelated sub-problems, recursive dependencies, and multiple interpretations of the problem's essence. He then makes the claim that among the key factors that impede our ability to resolve messy problems are: (1) limitations on our cognitive powers; (2) a tendency to grossly oversimplify or circumscribe complex problems; and (3) an inability to comprehend multiple, related feedback loops. Finally, he argues that a SD approach has the potential to overcome many of these problems and, furthermore, that (collaborative) development of a model may foster consensus, perhaps leading to increased acceptance of whatever decision is eventually taken. A considerable body of research has focused on understanding, and improving, benefits that can accrue during group model building using system dynamic modelling tools (see e.g., Anderson, Richardson, & Vennix, 1997; de Geus, 1994; Morecroft, 1994; Richmond, 1997; Vennix, 1996). If used judiciously, group modelling with SD tools can assist in mastering the learning problems listed above, as well as addressing the different viewpoints and beliefs which participants from various functional areas bring with them to any learning or decision making exercise.

Although the model presented in Figure 1 is a substantially simplified version of the version actually developed during our research, the complexity of the problem domain is clearly evident. This applies particularly to the feedback loops. For example: region attractiveness has an impact on enterprise development, enterprise development has an impact on region development, region development has an impact on the quality of the environment and the environment, in turn, has an impact on region attractiveness (thus leading us back to our starting point). Another feedback loop is: *Enterprise Development → Region Development → Enterprise Competition → Enterprise Development*. That is, an increase in enterprise development will (generally) result in an increase in region development which, in turn, might be expected to increase enterprise competition within the region. Finally, the increased enterprise competition may well lead to a decrease in enterprise development. This is an example of what the SD community refer to as a balancing loop: that is, enterprise competition acts as an inhibitor to unrestricted growth within the region. Another example of a growth inhibitor is environment quality.

Thus, our model contains a number of feedback loops. Vennix (op. cit), however, claims that many people are unable, at best, to understand the dynamics of a single feedback loop. Once multiple feedback loops are involved, even people who are experienced at interpreting feedback are unable to ascertain the behaviour of a system without resorting to a computer simulation (Anderson et al., 1997; Dangerfield & Roberts, 1995). During our research, we were able to adjust specific variables and observe the impact on other variables, over time, (through graphs automatically generated by *Powersim's* risk analysis software). This considerably assisted our end-users in improving their understanding of the complex, dynamic relationships present in the system. Vennix (op. cit) has argued that an advantage of involving decision makers from various areas in group modelling exercises is that they begin to understand that their actions not only affect their own areas and interests but may have major impacts on other stakeholders as well. This, in turn, may result in improved collaboration within the model development exercise itself.

Stock-flow models, however, are not all that suitable for collaborative model development, where end-users have significant input. In their most basic form though,

*Figure 2. CLD example—unintended consequences of well-meaning action*

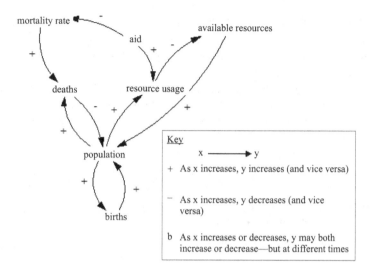

SD models are represented as causal loop diagrams (CLDs). A feature of CLDs is that they are both powerful and simple, relying as they do on just one fundamental construct: two variables, connected by an arrow, indicating a causal relationship. An example is presented in Figure 2, illustrating the "tragedy of the commons" archetype (Roberts, Andersen, Deal, Garet, & Shaffer, 1983), exemplified by the situation where, with cattle grazing on common land, incentives for individuals to increase herd size lead to overgrazing, eventual famine, and loss of livelihood (short-term benefits leading to long-term disaster).

The illustration presented in Figure 2 is taken from an actual case (WTO, 1998) concerning sub-Saharan African nomads who had survived sustainably in steady state for thousands of years. A well-meaning injection of aid in the 1950s resulted in a short-term lifespan and standard-of-living increase (mainly through new medicines and greater resource usage brought about by digging deeper wells). This, however, threw the system out of balance, leading to a longer-term agricultural and cattle grazing resource decrease, desertification, stock losses, eventual famine and an increase in deaths.

We now turn our attention to our tourism enterprise planning simulator (TEPS). For the reasons outlined above, we have chosen to specify and implement the bulk of TEPS using SD concepts.

## The *Tourism Enterprise Planning Simulator*: An Overview

The eventual plan is to implement TEPS within the STCRC's online, business assistance Web site, *Decipher* (Carson & Richards, 2004). A high-level view of the TEPS architecture is illustrated in Figure 3. The bulk of the model is specified and implemented within an SD framework. A knowledge base, implemented primarily as rules, sits within TEPS and is called to perform specific functions (such as the calculation of certainty factors based on a fuzzy logic approach). Values returned from the knowledge base component are used to dynamically instantiate variables within the SD model. One such function is the calculation of a region attractiveness value. However, in this case, users may opt to bypass the knowledge base and interact directly with the SD component (i.e., TEPS may be run as a stand-alone SD application). Moreover, to date, the bulk of our effort in developing our prototype has been directed towards the SD simulator. Consequently, in the remainder of this chapter, we shall focus on this component.

As noted above, during the previous ten years or so a number of excellent SD simulation software packages have been developed. As with almost any software tool, each of the leading tools have their "disciples" but, in our view, each of these tools have their strengths and weaknesses and tool selection often boils down to a matter of individual preference (and, oftentimes, familiarity with a previously used product). With this particular application, we opted to employ the *Powersim*

*Figure 3. TEPS: High-level architecture view*

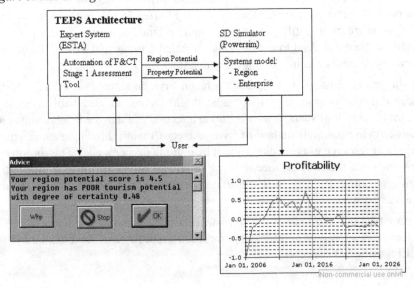

*Figure 4. Functional decomposition of SD component*

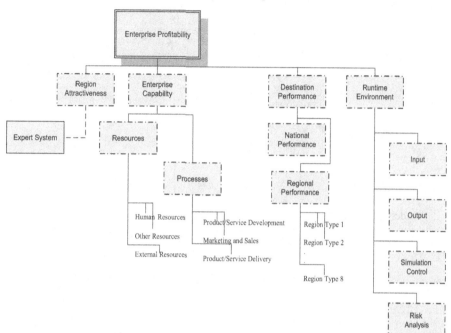

development studio (*Powersim*, 2003)—mainly because it has excellent functional decomposition facilities (and, as time goes by, we believe our model will need to be broken down to more precise levels of detail).

A functional decomposition of the SD component of our prototype is presented in Figure 4. The usual approach in developing an SD model is to: (1) specify the problem domain as a causal-loop diagram (CLD); and, then, (2) implement it in the slightly more complex stock-flow syntax employed by the software packages listed above (and illustrated in Figure 1). Here, because of space limitations, we restrict ourselves to CLD representations of our domain and a (slightly simplified) view of the Enterprise Capability component is illustrated in Figure 5.

Region attractiveness is at the core of the enterprise capability model. Attractive regions are natural targets for enterprise development and this leads to increased levels of enterprise development. More competition though, can have an adverse effect on enterprise profitability (e.g., through pressure to reduce tariffs) and this, in turn, may decrease motivation to invest further in enterprise development. Enterprise development also results in greater region development and, for the most part, this will lead to poorer environment quality. In turn, environmental despoilment (in the medium to long-term at least) will have negative consequences for both region attractiveness and enterprise profitability.

*Figure 5. Enterprise capability component: top-level CLD*

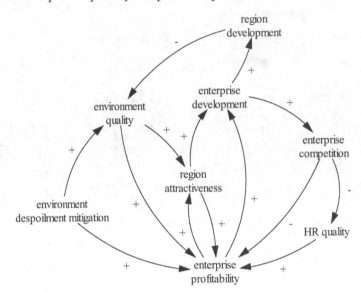

Thus, in these variables and causal links, we have a representation of (a variant of) the classic sustainable tourism model (discussed in the previous section). Essentially, if development is allowed to proceed unchecked, reinforcing loops will lead to increasingly greater levels of environment despoilment and lower enterprise profitability levels. Note, however, that environment despoilment mitigation has been included in the model as a mediating (or control) variable. That is, if a destination (collectively) is truly committed to protecting its natural resources this may keep the total system in balance and, also, work towards safeguarding enterprise profitability.

An additional variable included in our model is human resources (HR) quality. Effectively, increased enterprise competition will eventually lead to a reduction in overall HR quality (e.g., because of poaching and better staff taking advantage of opportunities elsewhere) and, as a consequence, remaining poorer-quality staff will have a negative impact on profits (i.e., customers can tolerate only so much!).

HR Quality is implemented in our SD prototype as a 2nd-level sub-module below Enterprise Capability (see Figure 4). The structure employed here was drawn from the STCRC 'Performance Measurement' toolkit, designed to allow small motel operators to benchmark and improve their operations (Bergin-Seers et al., 2005). At the time this chapter was being written, "human resources" was the only domain component (of those shown in Figure 4) that had actually been implemented. However, the intention is to progressively implement functionality corresponding

*Figure 6. Region attractiveness: Direct interaction through the SD control panel*

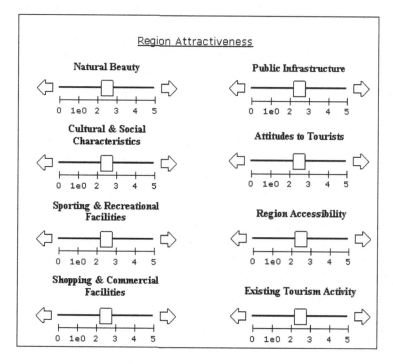

to the other resources and processes shown in Figure 4 (with the task scheduled to be completed by end-June 2006). Note though, that the prototype is still capable of producing useful outputs without lower-level modules being filled out with fine-grained detail (as shall be demonstrated in the following section).

Region attractiveness is calculated based on an approach presented in another STCRC toolkit; the "Farm and Country Assessment Tool (Stage 1)" (Fausnaugh et al., 2004). Using this toolkit, protective "Farm and Country" tourism operators are guided through a series of questions designed to assess the potential of their proposed tourism enterprise. One output from this process is a region attractiveness score and the functionality required to compute this value has been implemented within our expert system component. Alternatively, users may bypass the expert system and simply adjust a set of sliders within the SD component user interface (see Figure 6). Nevertheless, use of the expert system is recommended because: (1) users are alerted to many of the key factors that contribute to an attractive region; and (2) a "fuzzy logic" (Kosko, 1993) uncertainty handling routine assigns a "degree of confidence" level to the region attractiveness score calculated.

The Enterprise Capability module focuses on resources and processes specific to a particular (proposed) tourism accommodation enterprise. As noted earlier though, these are analysed within a destination context. More specifically, the National Performance component has been established so that simulation outputs accurately reflect the behaviour of key, national, accommodation sector indicators (e.g., total rooms, room nights occupied (RNO), seasonality, occupancy and revenue per RNO), on a quarterly basis over the period January 1998 to March 2005 (inclusive). Base data was taken from (ABS, 2005).

The SD simulator has been initialized to run for 29 quarters from the commencement of the current year. All variables are specified as indices. For example, RNO-national is an index of predicted RNO for total national visits (domestic and international), plotting percentage changes over time, on a quarterly basis against a base quarter. The March quarter of the current year is used as the base quarter and is assigned a value of 100. Where later values exceed 100, it indicates growth in comparison to the base quarter while values less than 100 indicate decline compared to the base quarter. The method is the same as that employed in (TRA, 2005) and the assumption is made that accommodation trends will be similar to actual figures observed in the seven years from January 1998 to March 2005 (ABS, 2005).

The National Performance model has been "tweaked" to emulate the accommodation sector behaviour of eight different region types. Users are required to select the region type closest to the destination in which they hope to establish their enterprise and enterprise performance will then be derived with reference to the selected region type's characteristics.

Tourism region types can be classified in a great many ways (e.g., by location, activities, climate, commerce/industry mix, population attributes, life-cycle stage, etc.) and Australian government tourism authorities (federal and state) have their own classification schemes. Following consultation with a number of government and tourism industry experts, however, we decided that the following region-type classification might suit our particular needs best: (1) Major Gateway; (2) Seaside (seasonal); (3) Seaside (year-round); (4) Coastal; (5) Provincial City (non-remote); (6) Rural; (7) Snowfields; and (8) Family Holiday. Whether this classification is effective will only be determined by actual experience with use of the simulator. We also should note that the system has been customized specifically for Australian conditions and would almost certainly require some modification before it could be used elsewhere (although it is unlikely this would involve changes to the model structure itself).

Finally, a detailed description of the runtime environment is beyond the scope of this chapter. We should note, however, that our user interface is similar to the "flight simulator" control panels commonly employed in SD applications (see e.g., Maani & Cavana, 2000, p. 116).

# Model Benefits and Usage

## Scenario 1: Basic Usage

Assume that we wish to examine the feasibility of setting up a motel in Anglesea—a small coastal town, about 70 minutes drive South-West of Melbourne. It has a superb surf beach and a fairly small population (chiefly retirees, commuters seeking a better lifestyle, and "weekenders"—mostly from Melbourne). The town has a large influx of tourists during the warmer months (particularly from December through to April) but experiences a significant drop-off in overnight visitors at other times—despite the town being right in the middle of the gateway to (the Australian state of) Victoria's major tourist attraction, the Great Ocean Road. In recent years, real estate prices have gone "through the roof": mainly because of a massive increase in demand from prospective "lifestylers" and holiday-home buyers, and limited capacity to increase housing supply and supporting infrastructure (without eating into surrounding coastal, national park and farming areas). The town has little in the way of industry and commerce outside of tourism-related enterprises but the wider region supports substantial farming activity.

Firstly, region attractiveness determinants have to be initialized. We elect to do this via the SD control panel (see Figure 6) and this yields a score of 130 (on a 0-200 scale). This relatively good score is largely the result of the assignment of maximum (or close to maximum) values for natural beauty, sports & recreational facilities, existing tourism activity and public infrastructure. These, however, are partly balanced by the assignment of comparatively-weak values to cultural & social characteristics, shopping & commercial facilities and attitudes to tourists.

*Figure 7.  TEPS : Sample output (enterprise profitability vs. year)*

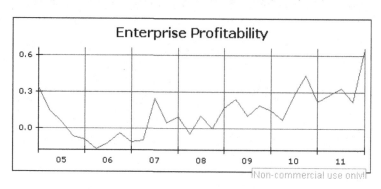

We might then set the remaining input parameters on the control panel as follows: Region Type to Seaside (seasonal); Environmental Damage Mitigation to Major; and, finally, we elect to leave the two HR-related parameters (HR Quality and HR Training Commitment) at their default values of average (HR issues are examined in some detail in the following two scenarios). Parameter initialization is now complete and running the simulation yields the enterprise profitability graph presented in Figure 7.

At first glance, these results appear to be quite encouraging—Figure 7 indicating that, after a couple of years of pain, a gradual improvement in profitability might occur. In reflecting on the simulation though, we might (for example) be concerned about the accuracy of the values we have assigned to some variables and, in particular, have considerable doubts about the component variables of the region attractiveness parameter.

Fortunately, *Powersim* has a powerful risk analysis package and, using this, we may investigate our model's sensitivity to changes in independent variables (or, more precisely, variables we decide to declare "independent" for some particular purpose). Basically, all that is required is to specify a mean and standard deviation for each of our independent (sub) variables, stipulate that Enterprise Profitability is the dependent (or effect) variable and, then, initiate a series of simulation runs (in our case, we use the recommended number of 40 runs) through the risk analysis software. The result is the "high-low" graph presented in Figure 8 and, here, it can be seen that around 80% of the variance (the area between the (90% and 10% lines) is within a 30% range (approximately). We conclude, therefore, that the model is not particularly sensitive to change in region attractiveness. We could then conduct further risk analysis experiments to determine precisely which variables (or combination of

*Figure 8.  TEPS: Example of a 'risk analysis' assessment*

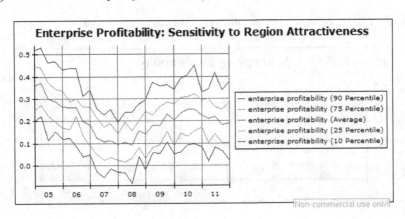

variables) do influence model behaviour most. The importance of conducting this type of "sensitivity analysis" has long been known in SD circles—early guidelines having been formulated by Coyle (1977, p. 193) almost 30 years ago.

## Scenario 2: HR Development

Assume we have some concerns related to the quality of local hospitality and tourism (H&T) staff we will be able to recruit for our start-up operation and, consequently, have decided that substantial staff training will be required. As such, through our TEPS control panel, we specify that our relative HR Quality is average and set the HR training commitment parameter to significant. The relevant simulation output resulting from these settings is presented in Figure 9.

*Figure 9. TEPS: Impact of HR development on quality*

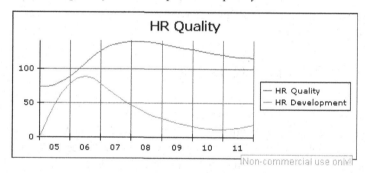

*Figure 10. TEPS: Unintended consequences of HR development activity*

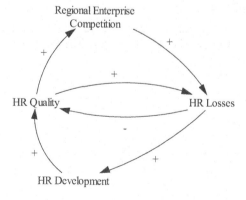

A brief perusal of the above diagram readily reveals two important features: (1) improvement in HR Quality lags some way behind investment in HR Development; and (2) after a considerable initial increase, HR Quality plateaus and then drops off somewhat. The lag between development and quality improvement would probably be expected but the second of these features is a little more complex and, while not an extreme case, it does represent an instance of the "fixes that fail" SD archetype (developed by the SD Group at MIT and detailed in Maani & Cavana, 2000, pp. 38-40). To understand what is happening here, we need to take a wider view of the system and, more specifically, the CLD representation presented in Figure 10.

With this "fixes that fail" example, we can see that investment in HR Development does, indeed, lead to a HR Quality improvement. However, this also results in two unintended consequences: (1) Regional Enterprise Competition intensifies (because we are now offering superior service to our competitors) and, consequently, some of our better staff may well be "poached" by our local opposition; and (2) we lose additional members of our newly-trained HR team to better-paying jobs outside our own region. Together, these contribute to substantial HR Losses and this, in turn, diminishes some of our recent, hard-won HR Quality gains. It also means that we have to invest even more in HR Development if our HR standards are to be maintained at the desired level.

## Scenario 3: Regional Marketing

In this example, we assume that regional commitment to environment despoilment mitigation is minimal and that, as a consequence, Region Attractiveness and (enterprise) profitability throughout the region will gradually decline over time. To arrest this deterioration, local authorities embark on a series of Regional Marketing campaigns. Simulation results are presented in Figure 11.

*Figure 11. TEPS: Failure to address fundamental problems in favour of quick fixes (smoothed to eliminate the impact of quarterly fluctuations)*

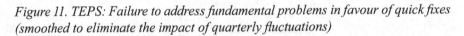
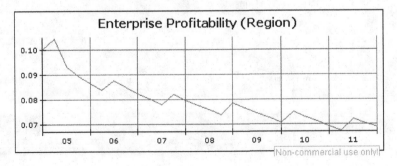

*Figure 12. TEPS: Over-reliance on quick fixes to fundamental problems*

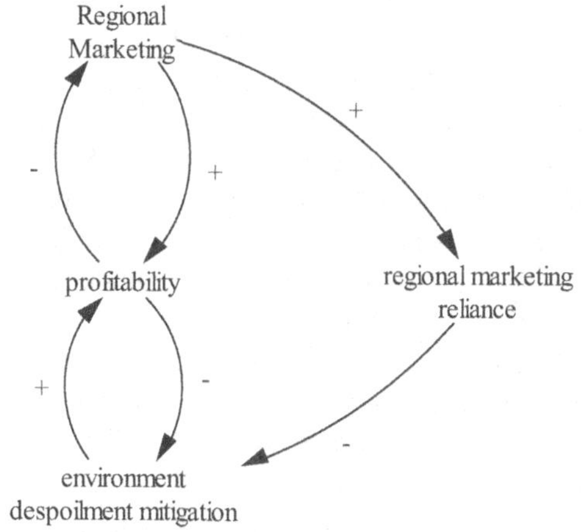

This is a classic instance of the "shifting the burden" SD archetype (Maani & Cavana, 2000, pp. 40-41), with our specific example being presented in CLD form in Figure 12. The essence of this archetype is that many (if not most) of us have a tendency to ignore long-term solutions to fundamental problems in favour of quick fixes. Thus, the Regional Marketing campaigns produce good results in the short-term but the overall enterprise profitability trend is still clearly downwards: the reason being that short-term benefits have produced an unfortunate reliance on marketing campaigns and, as a consequence, key regional stakeholders perceive less need to address the fundamental problem of environment despoilment mitigation.

# Model Validation, Implementation, and the Future

In the previous two sections, we have outlined the architecture of our TEPS system and demonstrated how it might be employed by our target users—primarily, prospective SMTE operators. The examples we have presented are specified at a fairly high level. Already though, a degree of complexity is apparent and this illustrates one of the benefits of SD modelling as claimed by its proponents: specifically, the approach can counter our tendency to over-simplify complex problems and issues into simple cause-effect relationships we can readily understand within the limits of our cognitive powers (Vennix, 1996). Of course, this is true of many conceptual modelling approaches and each of these have their own strengths and weaknesses. SD, however, is particularly well-suited to domains where feedback loops and time are significant (Richardson & Pugh, 1981) and both of these feature prominently in tourism models (see e.g., Ritchie & Crouch, 2003, pp. 60-78).

A fundamental motive behind the development of TEPS was to attempt to encourage SMTE operators to think more strategically and to take a wider and longer, systemic view of the destination in which they intend to establish, maintain and develop their enterprise. Consequently, in interacting with TEPS, they receive feedback on the realities of inherent system features and constraints: such as the delicate development-environmental balance, limits to growth, unintended consequences and side-effects, and the folly of concentrating on quick fixes at the expense of more fundamental solutions. Much of this was illustrated in the previous section and if we are, indeed, able to reach a critical mass of our intended users, then our software tool may contribute towards tourism destinations evolving towards the type of "learning organization" described by Senge (1990).

Thus, as noted above, this educational aspect has probably been the primary inspiration for our work. Nevertheless, the fact that our simulator is capable of producing graphs of projected Enterprise Profitability, HR Quality, Regional Enterprise Competition, Region Attractiveness, Environment Quality and more is intended to act as the trigger that might prompt our targeted users to interact with the model in the first place. Thus, it seems essential that our principal outputs should be "sensible"—to the extent that we must be able to convince the average user that our projections are reasonable. Consequently, the model and its implementation as TEPS must be validated and this is being accomplished via a two-stage approach: desk checking and field-testing.

SD models are notoriously difficult to validate (Richardson & Pugh, 1981). As noted by Forrester and Senge (1980, pp. 209-210), there is no single test which might be employed to validate a SD model but, rather, confidence in the model accumulates gradually as it passes more tests and as new points of correspondence between the model and empirical reality are identified. Maani and Cavana (2000, pp. 69-70), drawing on the work of Coyle (1983, p. 362), describe this process as consisting of:

- **Verification tests**, which focus on the equivalence between the structure and parameters of the real system and the model

- **Validation tests**, which are concerned with demonstrating the correspondence between the behaviour of the real system and the model

- **Legitimation tests**, which determine whether the model is in accord with any generally-accepted system rules

Essentially, the aim of validation is to "show that there is nothing in the model that is not in the real system and nothing significant in the real system that is not in the

Figure 13. *Model validation: Actual vs. TEPS results for AvRevPerRNO.*

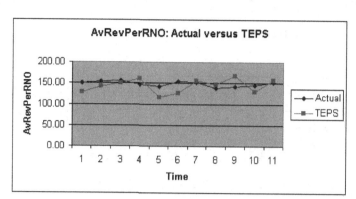

model" (Maani & Cavana, 2000, p. 69). An excellent example of how much of this can be accomplished through desk checking has been provided by Georgantzas (2003) where statistical measures, such as coefficient of determination and Theil's Inequality Statistics (TIS) (Theil, 1966), were employed to compare the predictive results of a SD model focused on various key measures of the performance of Cyprus hotels against actual data (over a 40 year period). Similarly, we have subjected our own model to similar tests, concentrating on measures such as occupancy, room nights occupied (RNO) and average revenue per room night occupied (AvRevPer-RNO). An example of one of our desk checking outputs is presented in Figure 13. This shows actual vs. predicted AvRevPerRNO for the region on which we based our Major Gateway generic region type.

The basis of Theil's approach is that the mean square error (MSE) is divided into three components: (1) bias ($U^m$); (2) unequal variation ($U^s$); and (3) unequal co-variation ($U^c$). The sum of all three components equals one and, briefly, a large $U^m$ indicates a potentially serious systemic error and, to a somewhat lesser extent, this applies to $U^s$ as well. If $U^c$ is large though, most of the error is unsystematic and, as noted by Sterman (2000, p. 877): "a model should not be faulted for failing to match the random component of the data." The TIS results for our example are presented in Figure 14 and, while they indicate that TEPS behaviour provides a reasonable approximation to reality (in this case anyway), there is significant room for improvement: specifically, the variance in our model is considerably greater than that of the actual data. In fact, this can be readily observed through a visual examination of the trend lines in Figure 13. The TIS results, however, are useful in that they quantify the extent of the various error types.

At the time this chapter was being prepared, much of the initial desk checking phase had been completed and, while some fine-tuning was still required, the model was

*Figure 14.   TIS breakdown of the Figure 13 AvRevPerRNO trend lines*

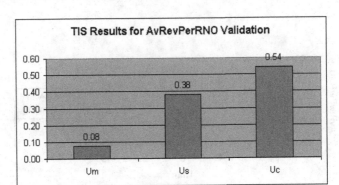

judged as being sufficiently mature that the next stage of validation could commence: that is, field-testing. To this end, negotiations were underway with a New South Wales (Australia)—based tourism authority concerning field-testing TEPS within their region. Testing protocols and other arrangements were in the process of being finalized and it likely that some preliminary results will be available by end June 2006.

Medium to long-term development will focus upon the following activities:

1.   Modifications and enhancements designed to address field-testing feedback and ongoing desk checking results

2.   Further development of the lower levels of the model; again, this will be largely driven by field-testing feedback

3.   TEPS is designed to operate at different levels of granularity. At the more "coarse-grained" levels users assign many of the system's parameters through an "impressionistic" process and this represents the current stage of development. At the very fine-grained level, actual data is used to establish key relationships and to instantiate model variables. Some of this currently takes place but one future development strand will focus on ensuring that, wherever convenient, variables will be assigned and relationships established automatically.

4.   As noted earlier, the simulator will be embedded within the STCRC's Decipher (Carson and Richards, 2004) tourism business planning toolkit. This will facilitate the automatic assignment of values to parameters discussed in (3) above. In addition, it also may provide some indication of whether there is any real interest in TEPS among its intended user base—SMTE operators.

5.   Further field-testing will be undertaken. At the very least, it is intended to test the simulator in an instance of each of the eight generic destination types for which the model has been customized.

Finally, as noted previously, although the current version of TEPS has been designed specifically for Australian conditions, we believe that the base model is sufficiently generic that it may well be suitable for any tourism destination and that the system has been designed such that it should be possible to conveniently customize it for different destination types (and instances of these types). Thus, while we have no specific plans at present, we aim to eventually test the model in an international setting and, thereby, go some way to establishing its external validity. Field-testing within the eight generic destination types we have identified as appropriate for the Australian context can be seen as a first step towards that objective.

# Conclusion

We have detailed the development, implementation and use of a tourism enterprise planning simulator (TEPS) based largely upon SD constructs and tools. The motivation for our work and particular approach was: (1) the need for improved access to useful business planning tools among SMTE operators; and (2) the fact that SD copes well with domains that are rapidly-changing and, in addition, can be classified as "messy" (Vennix, 1996, pp. 9-41).

Few would argue that the tourism landscape is evolving at an express (indeed, some might say terrifying) pace and issues that need to be considered when developing tourism enterprises are certainly messy (according to the criteria listed earlier). For example, Buhalis (2000) nominates the number of different stakeholders, stakeholder relationships and goals, contradictions between these goals, and difficulties in maintaining an acceptable and sustainable balance between the interests of stakeholders, natural resources and development activity as major problems that must be confronted in destination marketing and management—and tourism enterprises cannot be established in isolation from destination-level considerations.

Validation of SD models has long been a controversial issue. In particular, the inclusion of "intangible" variables (such as friendliness) in models has received substantial criticism (Legasto and Marciariello, 1980). However, as Campbell (2000) has noted, omitting such variables from models implies that they have a value of zero (or no impact) and, generally, of the infinite number of values that intangible variables might take, the only the only instantiation that is almost certainly wrong is zero! Moreover, considerable advances in SD model validation techniques have been made in recent years and, in the previous section, we demonstrated how one statistical approach might be used to good effect. In addition, the SD approach has been justified on its benefits and usefulness (Maani & Cavana, 2000, pp. 223-228).

For example, the model presented in Figure 5 contains four main feedback loops. As noted, Vennix (1996) claims that many people are unable to understand the dynamics of a single feedback loop. Once multiple feedback loops are involved, even people who are experienced at interpreting feedback are unable to ascertain the behaviour of a system without resorting to a computer simulation. Even though our example is substantially simplified (i.e., the total HR sub-domain is much more complex than the model illustrated in Figure 5), it clearly indicates the complexity of concept interrelationships and feedback loops within the tourism domain. Yet, it is already reasonably complex and, thus, our example illustrates another of the major benefits of the SD approach: namely that a graphical modelling approach can help to guard against over-simplification and promote shared understanding in both planning and research activity (Vennix, 1996).

Finally, ICT should work in a natural way to help grow the tourism industry. Yet, current research, including our own as discussed in this chapter, demonstrates that the reality is very different. SD offers a tangible solution to increasing our understanding of the field and leading us to more effective business planning and implementation. The use of such modelling approaches, however, must be grounded in improved ways of dealing with change as a norm—both for individual organizations and the industry as a whole. No longer can we afford the ostrich-like or reactive approach to change. Now we need change leadership that regards change as an opportunity and, as that classic management scholar Drucker (1999) suggests: focuses on policies for the future, encourages ways of looking for and anticipating change, finds appropriate ways to introduce change at micro and macro levels, and balances change and continuity appropriately. Only by so doing, by cleverly utilising technology and change management interdependently, will the industry and its individual organisations reap the benefits they offer individually and win the challenges the global industry confronts in the 21st century.

## Acknowledgment

This research was funded by the Sustainable Tourism Cooperative Research Centre (STCRC), an Australian Government initiative.

# References

ABS. (2005, March). *Tourist accommodation, Australia: Time series* (Rep. No. 8635.0). Canberra, ACT: Australian Bureau of Statistics.

Adams, C., Frost, G. & Webber, W. (2004). Triple bottom line: A review of the literature. In A. Henriques & J. Richardson (Eds.), *The triple bottom line: Does it all add up* (pp. 17-25). London: Earthscan.

Andersen, D. F., Richardson, G. P. & Vennix, J. A. C. (1997). Group model building: Adding more science to the craft. *System Dynamics Review, 13*(2), 187-201.

Baker, K. (2000). *Project evaluation and feasibility analysis for hospitality operations.* Melbourne, Australia: Hospitality Press.

Bergin-Seers, S., Jago, L., Breen, J. & Carlsen, J. (2005). *Performance measurement in small hotels* (Tech. Rep. Project No. 70061). Gold Coast, Australia: CRC for Sustainable Tourism Pty Ltd.

Buhalis, D. (2000). Marketing the competitive destination of the future. *Tourism Management, 21*(1), 97-116.

Brundtland, G. H. (1987). *Our common future.* Federal Office for Spatial Development, Berne. Retrieved December 1, 2005, from http://www.are.admin. ch/are/en/nachhaltig/international_uno/unterseite02330/

Campbell, B. R. (2000). *Business process modelling: A system dynamics perspective.* Unpublished MSc(Hons) dissertation, Macquarie University, Sydney.

Carson, D. & Richards, F., (2004). Delivering technological innovation in tourism: Considerations in the implementation of decipher. In A. J. Frew, & P. O'Connor, (Eds.), *Information and Communication Technologies in Tourism 2004* (pp. 1-11). Vienna: Springer-Verlag.

Coyle, R. G. (1977). *Management system dynamics.* Chichester, UK: Wiley.

Coyle, R. G. (1983). The technical elements of the system dynamics approach. *European Journal of Operational Research, 14,* 359-370.

Dangerfield, B. & Roberts, C. (1995). Projecting dynamic behavior in the absence of a model: An experiment. *System Dynamics Review, 11*(2), 157-172.

de Geus, A. P. (1994). Modeling to predict or to learn? *Modeling for learning organizations.* OR: Productivity Press.

Drucker, P. (1999). *Management challenges for the 21st century.* New York: HarperBusiness.

Elkington, J. (1999). *Cannibals with forks: the triple bottom line of 21st century business.* Oxford: Capstone.

English, J. (1995). *Small business financial management in Australia.* London: Allen and Unwin.

Fausnaugh, C., Waight, P., Higginbottom, K. & Northrope, C. (2004). *Farm & country tourism—on your property: Stage 1 assessment tool.* Retrieved from the Australian STCRC Web site, http://www.crctourism.com.au

Forrester, J. W. (1961). *Industrial dynamics.* Cambridge, MA: MIT Press.

Forrester, J. W. & Senge, P. M. (1980). Tests for building confidence in system dynamics models. *TIMS Studies in the Management Sciences, 14,* 209-228.

Gammack, J., Amaya Molinar, C., Chu, K. & Chanpayom, B. (2004). *Development needs of small to medium size tourism businesses.* Toowong, Qld, Australia: Asia Pacific Economic Cooperation Secretariat (APEC).

Georgantzas, N.C. (2003). Tourism dynamics: Cyprus' hotel value chain and profitability. *System Dynamics Review. 19*(3), 175-212.

Kosko, B. (1993). *Fuzzy thinking: The new science of fuzzy logic.* New York: Hyperion.

Legasto, A. A. & Maciariello, J. (1980). System dynamics: A critical review. In A. A. Legasto, J. W. Forrester, & J. M. Lyneis, (Eds.), *System Dynamics, TIMS Studies in Management Sciences, 14.* New York: North-Holland.

Loutif, M., Moscardini, A. O. & Lawler, K. (2000). Using system dynamics to analyse the economic impact of tourism multipliers. In P. I. Davidsen, D. N. Ford & A. N. Mashayeekhi (Eds.), *Proceedings of the 18th International Conference of the System Dynamics Society* (pp. 132-232). Albany, NY: System Dynamics Society.

McGrath, G. M. (2005, June 19-20). Information needs within the australian tourism industry: A scoping study. In P. O'Connor & A. J. Frew (Eds.), *Proceedings of the Hospitality Information Technology Association Conference (HITA 05),* Los Angeles (pp. 47-78).

McGrath, G. M. & More, E. (2005). An extended tourism information architecture: Capturing and modelling change. In A. J. Frew (Ed.), *Proceedings of the 12th International Conference on Information Technology in Travel and Tourism* (pp. 1-12). Vienna: Springer-Verlag.

Maani, K. E. & Cavana, R. Y. (2000). *Systems thinking and modelling: Understanding change and complexity.* Auckland, New Zealand: Prentice-Hall.

Mill, R. C. & Morrison, A. M. (2002). *The tourism system* (4th ed). Dubuque, Iowa: Kendall/Hunt Publishing.

Mistilis, N., Presbury, R. & Agnes, P. (2004). The strategic use of information technology in marketing and distribution—a preliminary investigation of Sydney hotels. *The Journal of Hospitality and Tourism Management, 11*(1), 42-55.

Morecroft, J. D. W. (1994). Executive knowledge, models and learning. In *Modeling for learning organizations* (pp. 3-28). Oregon: Productivity Press.

Morrison, A. J. & King, B. E. M. (2002). Small tourism businesses and e-commerce: Victorian tourism online. *Tourism and Hospitality Research, 4*(2), 104-115.

Powersim (2003). *Powersim Studio 2003: Reference manual.* Bergen, Norway: Powersim Software AS.

Richardson, G. P. & Pugh, A. L. (1981). *Introduction to system dynamics modeling.* OR: Productivity Press.

Ritchie, J. R. B. & Crouch, G. I. (2003). *The competitive destination.* Cambridge, MA: CABI Publishing

Richmond, B. (1997). The strategic forum: Aligning objectives, strategy and process. *System Dynamics Review, 13*(2), pp. 131-148.

Roberts, N. H., Andersen, D. F., Deal, R. M., Garet, M. S. & Shaffer, W. A. (1983). *Introduction to computer simulation.* Reading, MA: Addison-Wesley.

Senge, P.M. (1990). *The fifth discipline: The art and practice of the learning organization.* Milsons Point, NSW: Random House.

Sharma, P., Carson, D. & DeLacy, T. (2000). National online tourism policy initiatives for Australia. *Journal of Travel Research, 39*(2), 157-162.

Sharma, P., Carson, D. & DeLacy, T. (2000a). Developing a business information data warehouse for the australian tourism industry—a strategic response. *Information and communication technologies in tourism 2000* (pp. 147-156). Vienna: Springer-Verlag.

Smith, S. L. J. (2004). The measurement of global tourism: Old debates, new consensus, and continuing challenges. In A. A. Lew, C. M. Hall & A. M. Williams (Eds.), *A companion to tourism* (pp. 25-35). Malden, MA: Blackwell.

Sterman, J. D. (2000). *Business dynamics: Systems thinking and modeling for a complex world.* Boston: Irwin McGraw-Hill.

Theil, H. (1966). *Applied economic forecasting.* New York: North-Holland.

Tourism Australia. (2004). *Australia's tourism facts and figures: At a glance.* Canberra, ACT: Australian Government, Department of Industry, Tourism and Resources.

TRA. (2005). *Domestic overnight travel: Recent trends and challenges.* Canberra, ACT: Tourism Research Australia.

Vennix, J. A. M. (1996). *Group model building: Facilitating team learning using system dynamics.* Chichester, UK: Wiley.

Walker, P. A., Greiner, R., McDonald, D. & Lyne, V. (1999). The tourism futures simulator: A systems thinking approach. *Environmental Modelling and Software, 14,* 59-67.

WTO. (1998). *Guide for local authorities in developing sustainable tourism.* Madrid: World Tourism Organization.

## Chapter X

# Collaborative Commerce and the Hotel Industry

Michelle Rowe, Edith Cowan University, Australia

Alfred Ogle, Edith Cowan Univeristy, Australia

## Abstract

*This chapter proposes a framework to consider the application of collaborative commerce (c-commerce) in the hotel industry. C-commerce and some general characteristics of the hotel industry are examined, followed by a discussion on the likelihood of c-commerce adoption by hotels. A case study of two five-star hotels located in Perth, Western Australia is considered in light of the framework. Corporate structure, information technology (IT) and its importance to organisation strategy, the role and attitudes of the general manager of each hotel to IT as well as the social identity of the hotel to c-commerce emerge as issues critical to c-commerce. This area of study is in its infancy and further research is required to more fully consider the issues.*

# Introduction

Hoteliers are notoriously secretive and have been reluctant to share information and ideas with others, especially their rivals, due to a "fear of information leakage" (Chung, Oh, Kim, & Han, 2004, p. 429). This paranoia manifests itself in the dearth of literature on strategic alliances in the lodging sector (Dev & Klein, 1993). But what if hoteliers saw themselves in a different light—sharing information and ideas—from a perspective of co-opetition (competitive co-operation) or collaboration? This chapter poses this question and probes the likelihood of hotels seeing themselves in this light. This issue will be considered in the context of collaborative commerce which will firstly be defined and explained.

Collaborative commerce (c-commerce) is the use of Internet-based technology that promotes collaboration in business. The emergence of c-commerce reflects a shift of focus to relationships between firms, not just transactions (Sheth, 1996). Network behaviour, which underpins inter-organisational relationships, is of interest to tourism and hospitality operators. The premise behind the formation of networks is the realisation that a single organisation is incapable or unwilling to cope with environmental conditions (Cravens, Shipp, & Cravens, 1993) and does not possess the skills and expertise needed to compete in that environment.

This chapter overviews the concept of c-commerce and investigates the relevance of this concept to the hotel industry generally by way of a case study of two five-star rated hotels located in Perth, Australia. Although collaborative strategies of international hotel chains have been explored (Fyall & Spyriadis, 2003), the authors seek to investigate the phenomenon with respect to a framework that considers c-commerce and its antecedents. To understand factors necessary for and to explain adoption of c-commerce, the domains of MIS, management and an industry perspective are all relevant—hence a multidisciplinary approach is taken.

The influence of the manager and ownership structure of the hotel are thought to be important factors in the adoption of c-commerce. Using case studies of Perth hotels, the chapter also raises the questions of what motivates general managers (GMs) to enter into relationships with competitors, the nature and extent of these relationships and the role of information technology (IT) within the organisation and in such relationships. These issues have not been widely researched, however ,and are considered here.

# What is C-Commerce?

C-commerce is the use of technology, especially Internet-based technology, that promotes collaboration amongst businesses. It consists of all of an organisation's

IT bases, knowledge management and business interactions with its customers, suppliers and partners in the business communities in which it interacts (Gartner Group, 1999; McCarthy, 1999). C-commerce can occur horizontally involving co-opetition, being a sharing of resources and information amongst competitors, or vertically along a supply chain.

C-commerce is the coming together of firms, including competitors, to exploit opportunities that arise. As global competition intensifies many organisations are forming partnerships as an expeditious way to keep up or to access unique or "pioneering" resources (Ring & Van de Ven, 1992, 1994). As stated, collaboration around IT is a response to an increasingly complex and dynamic market (Cravens et al., 1993). Increasingly it is argued that firms, especially small and medium enterprises (SMEs) must enter into such partnerships to survive in globalised marketplaces. Most tourism enterprises worldwide fall into the SME category and are known as small and medium tourism enterprises (SMTEs) (Buhalis, 1996).

## What are the Benefits of C-Commerce?

C-commerce is concerned with obtaining sustainable competitive advantage from the maximisation of value adding benefits obtained by working collaboratively with others via IT. The adoption of IT has been identified as a possible source of strategic competitive advantage (Yetton, Johnston & Craig, 1994) as well as a potential generator of innovation resulting in further competitive advantage (Ryssel, Ritter & Germunden, 2004).

C-commerce enables firms to "grow" their assets and access markets (Bitici, Martinez, Albores, & Parung, 2004; Ring & Van de Ven, 1992). Internal efficiencies can be generated by the sharing of information via IT within inter-organisational relationships (IOR) (Ryssel et al., 2004). It can be argued that collaborative enterprises or networks "create new and unique value propositions by complementing, integrating and leveraging each other's capabilities and competencies" (Dyer & Singh, 1998, p. 676). IT/ICT are critical drivers of integration and cooperation since they enable businesses to integrate activities and functions otherwise not possible (Joo, 2002).

Collaboration generates "relational rents" or "supernormal profits jointly generated in an exchange relationship" (Dyer & Singh, 1998, p. 662) that cannot be achieved individually. These authors contend that the competitive advantage of these partnerships requires the presence of four factors: relation-specific assets, knowledge-sharing routines, complementary resource endowments, and effective governance. For these relational rents or benefits to arise these elements are required. Often the question is if they are in place. Firms need to adopt a different approach to strategic planning and management to allow the creation of networks and associated infrastructure based on shared resources with other organisations (Chi & Holsapple, 2005). This requires strategic thinking, trust and a realization of the importance of co-opting rather than competition which typically exists amongst individual firms. Again these issues need to be considered generally and specially in relation to the hotel industry.

## The Hotel Industry

When considering the adoption of c-commerce, the industry context needs to be borne in mind. The ownership and corporate structure as well as management of the hotel, including the expertise, perceptions and influence of the GM and the role of IT in the property or chain are important factors influencing c-commerce adoption.

Inter-organisational systems (IOS), of which c-commerce is one type (see Chi & Holsapple (2005) for a more complete discussion), have been facilitated by electronic commerce. The tourist industry was one of the first industries to adopt information and communication technologies (ICT) (Garzotto, Paolini, Speroni, Proll, Retsch-itzegger, & Schwinger, 2004).

In the past, electronic data interchange (EDI) and electronic funds transfer (EFT) have been the technologies to enter into IOS. The standards required for EDI and its high set up costs have tended to act as a barrier for SMTEs to enter into IOS. This potentially is overcome by the Internet. It is possible for hotels to take advantage of the Web via collaboration around the net as a way to deal with excess capacity and increase occupancy rates quickly. This is the case within many chains as the role of online intermediaries has expanded dramatically, especially since 9/11 (Starkov, 2002). Individual hotels are better able to compete in an increasingly dynamic marketplace via the exploitation of the advantages of the Web (Grover, Teng & Fiedler, 2002) as evident in the widespread participation in "distressed Web sites" such as needitnow.com, Travelocity.com; wotif.com and participation in innovative distribution services such as auctions and disintermediation (Connolly, 2000).

Chains of hotels generally have in place integration of the property management system (PMS) with the corporate central reservation system (CRS) and global distribution system (GDS) systems although in the past SMTEs appeared to have been under-represented in most mainstream CRS and GDS (Go, 1992). CRS integration allows for individual properties to benefit from the extensive reach of the chains marketing network and to allow for cross selling amongst properties within the chain. A view held in the late 90s was that via seamless distributions channels, untapped opportunities could be availed to firms (Stern & Weitz, 1997). That view is validated with Internet-enabled GDS integration that allows chain properties to extend their reach beyond that of their chain marketing network whilst simplifying and streamlining the booking process, thereby enhancing customer service (Con-nolly, 2000) and creating competitive advantage. In some instances independent or non-chain properties subscribe to a non-affiliate reservation network which enables independent operators to obtain many of the benefits enjoyed by chain-affiliated operators (Kasavana & Brooks, 2001). This interoperability of systems is an example of c-commerce, especially the CRS which has been the most commonly used wide area network (WAN) application in hotels (Brooks, 1999). However, GDS provide hotel bookings only for major hotel chains (Dogac, Kabak., Laleci, Sinir, Yildiz, Kirbas, & Gurcan, 2004)—excluding small independent operators. Web service technology would overcome the advantage afforded to top tier players, however this is beyond the scope of this chapter.

What about sharing of information between rivals in a location? Is this likely? Given that many hotels are part of a chain, interoperable systems are in place which facilitates the flow of information within the organisation. This may mean individual hotels do not need to collaborate with hotels in situ. Where strong information flows occur within the organisation (effectively c-commerce between hotels making up the chain) the need for and hence adoption of c-commerce between competitors in one location is negligible and may not be necessary.

*Figure 1. Holistic view of the factors necessary for c-commerce adoption*

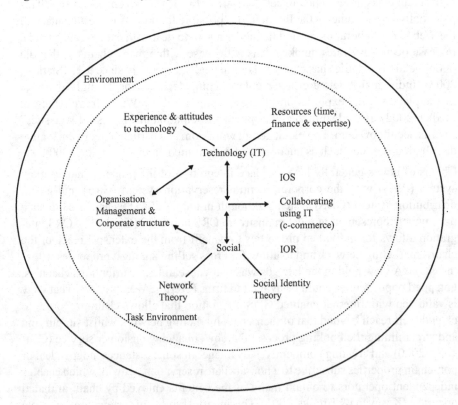

## Factors Considered Critical to C-Commerce Adoption

A review of the literature concerning c-commerce, IT, and inter-organisational theories as well as from the hotel industry perspective has been undertaken. In summary, c-commerce requires firms to develop a strategy, both short and long term; adopt appropriate business models; develop and sustain appropriate collaborative cultures engendering trust; invest in IT to facilitate information and knowledge sharing; and set in place appropriate organisational structures to enable collaboration (Kalakota & Robinson, 1999).

A framework depicting critical factors underlying c-commerce adoption is set out in Figure 1. The nature of management and management's attitudes to IT and risk taking as well as the corporate structure of the hotel are important factors shaping attitudes towards c-commerce. To understand networking or the c-commerce relationship, consideration needs to be given to two broad groups of theories: network or inter-organisational relationships theory and social identity theory.

# Discussion of Proposed Framework

## Organisation

Decisions to adopt IT are made by management. This can either reflect corporate policy, as is the case for chains, or, where management is autonomous such as is the case for independents, organisational decisions. Attitudes to and experiences of management tend to influence subsequent decisions and predispositions (particularly from the perspective of traditional decision making techniques—see Fulop, Linstead, Lilley, & Clarke, 2004) and this is the case with respect to IT.

Issues concerning ownership, management structure and degree of centralisation of decision making, including IT, come into play here and influence attitudes to IT and collaboration. These are important to the hotel industry as discussed.

## Technology (IT)

Firms make IT decisions either to generate cost savings or to enable a value added strategy to be pursued. Cost savings tend to be the strategy adopted where IT is peripheral to the business and where management's experience of IT is limited. The concern is for efficiency and systems to be in place to help achieve this. A value added strategy is appropriate (Levy, Powell, & Yetton, 2001) due to strategic necessity or where management is seeking growth and understands the connection between IS and added value.

C-commerce requires a strategic decision to invest in and collaborate around IT with others. Without a strategic view of IT c-commerce cannot arise and certainly would not be considered. Where a strategic view of IT is adopted the benefits flowing from investments in IT (including c-commerce) are likely to add value and generate potential competitive advantage as discussed earlier in this chapter. Responsiveness to the market and latest technologies available which customers may demand could be a driver for IT adoption. In such case IT is seen to provide a "strategic opportunity" to improve business performance and potentially generate competitive advantage rather than merely be an operational tool to increase efficiency.

## Resources

Resource based theory of the firm (Caldeira & Ward, 2003; Feeny & Willcocks, 1998) suggests that firms are characterised by a set of competencies or skills and capabilities that are important to enable it to achieve a sustainable competitive advantage. IT is part of that resources set. Important to c-commerce is the availability of resources dedicated to its implementation and also to adaptation of systems with "partners." These resources include time to plan and focus on future directions, rather than operational issues, financial resources to invest in software and hardware, and expertise of management, IT advisors or an IT "champion." SMEs have limited resources and generally do not possess the technical know how or resources to, for example, maintain effective Web sites (Gonzales, 2004). A coming together or collaboration is a means to overcome such limitations as access to scarce resources, including skills, information and knowledge is facilitated (Macpherson, Jones, Zhang, & Wilson, 2003).

## Social Network Theory

Network theory refers to cooperative IORs that include strategic alliances, partnerships, coalitions, joint ventures, franchises, network organizations and c-commerce. A variety of motivations underpins the formation of cooperative relationships such as access to new technology, markets, development of economies of scale and complementarity of skills as well as risk sharing (Powell, 1987; Ring & Van de Ven, 1992).

The literature indicates that IT is not the driver underlying c-commerce, rather relationships precede any collaboration around IT (O'Keefe, 2001). This indicates social bonds should be created first before c-commerce is possible. The development of informal connections via networking is critical to subsequent c-commerce. Some assert that once a relationship exists the use of IT within that relationship encourages a commitment to the relationship, thereby enhancing the relationship (Grover et al., 2002).

Without the cultivation of relationships, firms are not able to capture the full value of technology (O'Keefe, 2001). Such a coming together will only occur if the shared benefits are acknowledged and are deemed to be worthwhile. Perceptions of these benefits and a willingness to engage in c-commerce are influenced by attitudes to and experience of IT as well as the availability of resources able to be dedicated to c-commerce.

Whilst technology is central to c-commerce, it is the willingness to share information rather than the technology per se that potentially can constrain the relationship (Mason, Castleman & Parker, 2004; O'Keefe, 2001). Attitudes to knowledge and the willingness to share information with others are critical. Knowledge is seen as a source of competitive advantage. The sharing of this knowledge though potentially undermines this advantage since the knowledge gained by cooperation may be used for competition (Levy et al., 2001). This can only be overcome through the generation of trust, commitment to the relationship and an agreement to not act opportunistically, enforced by endogenous systems agreed and adhered to.

Participants in networks are likely to be entrepreneurial in nature—identifying opportunities, mobilising resources, and looking beyond resource limitations. This requires a boundary spanning approach—a willingness to interact with others "outside the organisation so as to obtain valuable information from the task and general environment" (Jones & George, 2003, p.173). Entrepreneurs are more likely to boundary span and network as they recognise the benefits in sharing ideas and information with participants either in similar or different industries. It is a contention of the authors that participants in networks and c-commerce are more likely to be entrepreneurial firms that are growing (Chell & Baines, 2000).

Table 1 summarises factors that are considered to be important to the adoption of c-commerce from a network theory/IOR perspective. Some factors pertain to the individual organisation whilst others relate to the dynamics and interaction between the potential partners and often develop over time as negotiations unfold.

Trust is identified as a critical factor to collaboration—without it there can be only limited mutual obligation between cooperating partners. Trust is a prerequisite for knowledge sharing and is fundamental to the question "to collaborate or not to collaborate." Whilst trust is difficult to achieve, it is possibly the most crucial aspect for success (O'Keefe, 2001) and is a precursor to commitment (Morgan & Hunt, 1994).

The concept of inter-firm adaptation has been considered in extensive research into IORs (Brennan, Turnbull, & Wilson, 2003). Adaptation (Hallen, Johnson, & Sayed-Mohammed, 1991) is a central feature of a working business relationship. It requires combined investment by both parties to the relationship, especially to shared IT systems in the case of c-commerce. This creates durable economic bonds between the partners. The willingness to adapt behaviour or to be flexible, for example, via adaptation to overcome difficulties experienced in an IOR, is important in generating trust.

*Table 1. Summary of main factors necessary for collaborative IORs/c-commerce*

| Factors pertaining to individual organisation | Factors pertaining to interaction of potential partners |
|---|---|
| • Commitment and trust<br>• Adaptation<br>• Level of investment in IT within the firm and level of Enterprise Application Integration<br>• Network competence<br>• Willingness to share information/enter into relationship (trust)<br>• Willingness to behave in fair/equitable manner (trust)<br>• Motivation behind co-opting<br>• Personality/values/beliefs of proprietor<br>• Organisation culture/collaborative culture<br>• Reliance on trust/endogenous systems<br>• Goals/vision, for example, growth<br>• Growth of the SME | • Commitment and trust<br>• Adaptation<br>• Congruency<br>• Track record with partner (trust)<br>• Motivation behind co-opting<br>• Reliance on trust/endogenous systems<br>• Goals/vision, for example, growth<br>• Interaction/dynamics and negotiations between parties |

Whilst trust and commitment and other characteristics depicting relationship quality are necessary for c-commerce, the lack of participation in collaborative ventures may reflect a weaker identification with social groups outside the organisation. This is what social identity theory argues.

## Social Identity Theory

Social identity theory (Tajfel & Turner, 1979) identified the importance of the social self which contrasts with the individual self. Cooperation (Kramer, 1993) with other decision makers, and so willingness and propensity to enter into c-commerce, is a function of the strength of one's personal identity viz that of a collective identity. When personal identities are salient, the focus is on personal goals and outcomes. For cooperation with others to occur then, the salience of one's collective identity needs to transcend one's personal identity. Motives of decision makers are more complex than ego (Axelrod, 1984; Kramer, 1993), with self-interest being one variable explaining co-operation. This has implications for c-commerce adoption in that the benefits of collaboration and the importance of a collective view preceding such cooperation need to be considered.

This is supported by other authors (Terry, 2003) who assert that individuals seek to improve their social identity and are motivated to belong to high status groups. This has implications for establishing c-commerce.

## Consideration Regarding the Hotel Industry

A number of these issues are now considered in relation to the hotel industry. The hotel industry is characterised by corporations or chains and independent operators. The benefits from c-commerce are considered to be greater for independents since they tend not to have the critical mass associated with top tier players (i.e., chains) and because they do not have in place strong collaborative arrangements, which exist internally within chains.

Interoperable systems already exist in chains, but do not exist amongst independents. Independents appear to resort to subscription to affiliate reservation networks that allow non-chain properties to participate as overflow facilities (Kasavana & Brooks, 2001) rather than network amongst themselves. This reliance on existing intermediaries potentially may be a barrier to c-commerce adoption. However it presents itself as a way for "independents to maintain their individuality and distinctive methodology, while still benefiting from the economies of scale that an affiliation with a larger group of like-minded properties can offer" (Travel Impact Newswire, 2004).

Where a hotel is owner managed and therefore has greater autonomy to determine policy, the GM is more likely think strategically and boundary span and so consider collaboration and initiate relationships fundamental to c-commerce. C-commerce though requires interoperable systems and the development of relationships, so may evolve over time, reflecting a typology of IOS developed elsewhere (Chi & Holsapple, 2005). Softwares that are available to facilitate such sharing of information as well as the Internet and the semantic Web are means by which this difficulty can be overcome. These issues fall outside of the scope of this chapter.

In relation to issues of size and resources, while medium sized hotels may *prima facie* employ more than 200 employees (the upper limit of medium enterprise in Australia) (Australian Bureau of Statistics, 2002) according to full time staff equivalent figures (FTSE) many fall into the category of a medium size employer. However, the context of the hotel in relation to an international corporation needs to be considered. Secondly, whilst many hotels use IT in a comprehensive and integrated manner in their operations and indeed within the chain (if this is relevant), much of its application is operational rather than strategic in nature.

# Case Study

Many of the issues discussed can be illustrated by the experience of two five star hotels located in Perth, the capital city of Western Australia.

Hotel A is a franchisee of a world renowned chain of hotels, the reputation of the chain and the brand generating its competitive advantage. There is a reliance on corporate policy and IT decision making. Built in 1973, this purpose built CBD hotel has 390 rooms and overlooks the scenic Swan River. Its target market is corporate clientele. Around 70% of its guests are domestic corporates and 10% are international corporates. The international name and its acclaimed loyalty program make this hotel more attractive to international corporates compared to regional chain or independents.

The GM is an industry veteran with 35 years industry experience, with 20 of those years employed in this hotel chain. Commencing as a bartender, he progressed into food and beverage management and then engaged in hotel general management.

Thirty-six percent of room bookings are made via chain-related reservation channels with corporate systems critical to the operation of this hotel. Decisions regarding IT are centralised and little autonomy is given to the GM in this regard. The GM saw IT as being ancillary to strategy and perceived it as being a tool to increase efficiency of the business. This reflects the centralised approach taken by the hotel towards IT and the longstanding position this GM has had within this chain. Whilst the future application of IT such as self check-in and check-out is recognised, since people and personalised service are at the heart of the business, such technologies are not likely to become reality. Certainly any decision in this area would be made at the Head Office level.

The nature of the corporate structure means that intra-chain networking is critical with a substantial reliance on integration with sister hotels in terms of room reservations. Interoperable systems exist in-house and thus between hotels, with systems determined by the corporation rather than by individual hotels.

This hotel relies on formal networks via Australian Hotels Association (AHA) rather than initiating relationships with external organisations. There is a willingness to participate in the industry practice of sharing information such as occupancy and roomrate figures. The hotel is a stable and mature business, placed third in the Perth market in terms of revenue per available room (REVPAR). Seventy percent of its policies are brand driven and therefore while the GM has the prerogative to cater to the distinct conditions of the individual property, autonomy is restricted.

Hotel B belongs to small regional chain. This particular chain was unique in that each property within the chain is owner managed and independently operated in terms of policies and procedures (P&P). Housed in what was originally the Australian Taxation Office built in 1968, the building was converted into a hotel in 1996 and has 306 rooms affording Swan River views. Located in the CBD, its target market is corporate guests with currently 60-70% of its clientele being domestic corporates. The GM has been in the hospitality industry for 20 years, first as a dishwasher in his family restaurant in Perth, then shifting to food production. Focusing on production, he worked up to Chef de Cuisine, then became interested in the service aspects of the industry taking on a position of Food and Beverage Manager, Executive Assistant Manager and then GM of this hotel in 2002.

The GM had a greater degree of autonomy with respect to IT investments and decision making and indeed strategic direction for the hotel. IT adoption was seen as potentially generating strategic opportunity for the business (Engsbo, Saarinen, Salmi, & Scupola, 2001) and a means to set the hotel apart from the competition. The hotel is the market leader in the Perth market in terms of REVPAR and is growing and innovative. In part this reflects the nature of the GM—younger, more entrepreneurial and who looks to IT as a means by which strategic advantage can be achieved. He is unrestricted by a chain corporate culture and so is less restricted in his decision making. Personal relationships between counterparts are important to this GM, indicating that the synergy between peers within the chain was strong.

The GM tended to take the initiative with regard to networking amongst competitors, was open to changes occurring with respect to IT and is more entrepreneurial and boundary spaning in its interactions with those outside of the organisation to obtain valuable information from the task and general environments (Jones & George, 2003). This was recognised as being a way to increase the quantity and richness of information available to the hotel to aid decision making in a dynamic and competitive environment. This openness to IT innovation adoption is typically not a trait of hoteliers hailing from food production due to the limited opportunities for such adoption in the kitchen area. This GM admits that he is somewhat of an anomaly in this regard.

Attitudes toward technology is a factor that differentiates the approaches of the two hotels and this reflects individual traits such as age, length of tenure, level of entrepreneurship, and background. In addition to these individual factors, corporate culture and decision making practices and degree of centralisation of decision making come into play.

## Discussion

Firms engaged in c-commerce do so because they recognize the strategic benefits, however c-commerce demands significant investment in IOS. A commitment to the relationship requiring investment in IT from a long term perspective then is critical. Efficiency no longer is the sole motivation for IT adoption (Levy et al., 2001).

This is an important point—one hotel saw IT purely as a tool to increase efficiency and so took a passive role, relying on corporate IT strategy. The other had a more strategic approach generally in their business and towards IT.

In part this reflects the nature of the ownership of the hotel, that is, owner managed as well as the attitudes of the GM to IT and change generally. Whilst the independent hotel recognized the value adding potential of IT, it is not likely that this will extend to c-commerce. This firm had a strong individual identity and whilst acknowledging the benefit in strategic alliances to win business and sharing information such as occupancy rates and possibly REVPAR with competitors, as is generally the case in this industry, evidence of further collaboration is not apparent.

This chapter proposes that organisations must possess certain characteristics for effective c-commerce adoption—these are embodied in the framework set out in Figure 1 and Table 1. The lack of these characteristics and low level of awareness of the benefits of c-commerce would act as an inhibitor to c-commerce adoption. For the hotel industry c-commerce of sorts exists amongst chains anyway and so since relationships are focused inwards within the chain generating a high corporate identity, the drive for relations outside that corporation is less.

From the case study it is evident there is a lack of a social identity amongst players in the industry in situ, other than membership of the AHA provides. Whilst hotels have a track record of adopting IT as discussed it tends not to be strategic. Certainly there is no real evidence of integration of IT within corporate strategy, reflecting a view of IT as a tool to increase efficiency of operations. The strategic benefits and competitive advantage IT could generate for the business need to be understood for c-commerce to be entered into.

Research is required to determine whether the factors embodied in the framework proposed here are critical antecedents to c-commerce adoption. The relationship between these and or other factors identified by subsequent research needs to be investigated more fully with respect to the hotel industry, both in Australia and overseas.

From the case study the influence of the GM, and management structure and decision making practices of the hotel are significant influencers to potential c-commerce adoption. Hotels that are part of a chain already have interoperable systems that facilitate information and knowledge sharing amongst the chain—this seems to be more important to individual hotels compared with potential collaboration with rivals in a location. This reflects the salience of individual identity viz social identity.

The autonomy of GM is a significant issue. GMs of hotels in a chain are more concerned with operational issues with strategy and policy determined at corporate level, including IT investment decisions such as PMS system and other softwares that are used. Since the GM in the owner managed hotel had a greater degree of autonomy, he is able to determine IT investment decisions which requires a more strategic view.

Investigation of the impact the external and task environments have upon c-commerce adoption in the hotel industry is important especially comparing contexts. Given that the majority of research regarding collaborative IORs and c-commerce has taken place in Europe the impact of the cultural and institutional settings needs to be acknowledged. The influence of parent companies upon individual hotel decision making also needs to be explored.

# Conclusion

In conclusion, c-commerce is an emerging phenomenon in many countries and industries. Little evidence exists as to its adoption generally, or amongst the hotel industry in particular. This chapter seeks to identify the factors critical to c-commerce adoption. The framework proposed in this chapter requires "testing" in hotels taking into account different national as well as other industry contexts so that validation or refinement can occur.

The notion that ownership structure and management significantly influence the business, its direction and so adoption of IT has significant relevance to the use of IT in the businesses studied here. Where the GM had little interest and involvement in IT the likelihood of innovative uses of IT was less.

Where a strategic view of the use of IT is taken by management collaboration around IT is deemed to be more likely. However this is complicated by issues of ownership structure and centralisation of IT and policy. The case study discussed here would indicate c-commerce is likely to be adopted by the independent sector of the industry where managers have greater autonomy to enter into such partnerships. Chains already collaborate around IT and so share information online and via CRS. Because of this and reliance on centralised IT decision making, individual hotels are less likely to enter into such relationships in situ.

Overall, there seems to be a strong relationship between the attitudes of GM to IT and their strategic vision and the role of IT and likelihood to adopt c-commerce. Where c-commerce exists in-house (that is in large chains) there is no need to consider entering into such collaborative arrangements with competitors. The rate of adoption, should it occur, will be slow until benefits are perceived. The influence of the corporate structure and the role of the GM are factors that significantly influence the likelihood of c-commerce adoption in the hotel industry. Such adoption is not likely at least at this point in time due to the factors outlined here.

# References

Australian Bureau of Statistics. (2002). *Small business in Australia* (cat. 1321). Canberra: Australian Bureau of Statistics.

Axelrod, R. (1984). *The evolution of cooperation.* New York: Basic Books.

Bititci, U., Martinez, V., Albores, P., & Parung, J. (2004) Creating and managing value in collaborative networks. *International Journal of Physical Distribution and Logistics Management, 34*(3), 251-268.

Brennan, D., Turnbull, P., & Wilson, D. (2003). Dyadic adaptation in business-to-business markets. *European Journal of Marketing, 37*(11/12), 1636-1665.

Brooks, R. M. (1999). *From the hotel property's perspective: The network computing alternative: Hotel online.*

Buhalis, D. (1996). Enhancing the competitiveness of small and medium-sized tourism enterprises. *International Journal of Electronic Commerce, Electronic Markets, 6*(1), 1-6.

Caldeira, M. M., & Ward, J. M. (2003). Using resource-based theory to interpret the successful adoption and use of information systems and technology in manufacturing small and medium-sized enterprises. *European Journal of Information Systems, 12*, 127-141.

Chell, E., & Baines, S. (2000). Networking, entrepreneurship and microbusiness behaviour. *Journal of Small Business Management, 12*(3), 195-215.

Chi, L., & Holsapple, C. W. (2005). Understanding computer-mediated interorganisational collaboration: A model and framework. *Journal of Knowledge Management, 9*(1), 53-75.

Chung, K. Y., Oh, S. Y., Kim, S. S., & Han, S. Y. (2004). Three representative market segmentation methodologies for hotel guest room customers. *Tourism Management, 25*(4), 429-441.

Connolly, D. J. (2000). Trends 2000: Shaping the Future. In *Proceedings of the 5th Outdoor Recreation & Tourism Trends Symposium,* Lansing, MI (pp. 73-83).

Cravens, D. W., Shipp, S. H., & Cravens, K. S. (1993, March). Analysis of co-operative inter-organisational relationships, strategic alliance formation and strategic alliance effectiveness. *Journal of Strategic Marketing,* 55-70.

Dev, C., & Klein, S. (1993, February). Strategic alliances in the hotel industry. *Cornell Hotel and Restaurant Administration Quarterly,* 42-51.

Dogac, A., Kabak., Y., Laleci, G., Sinir, S., Yildiz, A., Kirbas, S., & Gurcan, Y. (2004). Semantically enriched Web services for the travel industry. *SIGMOD Record, 33*(3).

Dyer, J. H., & Singh, H. (1998). The relational view: Cooperative strategy and sources of interorganisational competitive advantage. *The Academy of Management Review, 23*(4), 660-680.

Engsbo, M., Saarinen, T., Salmi, H., & Scupola, A. (2001). A framework of adoption of e-commerce in networks of SMEs. In *Proceedings of IRIS 2001*, Ulvik, Norway.

Feeny, D. & Willcocks, L. (1998). Core IS capabilities for exploiting information technology. *Sloan Management Review, 39*(3), 354-367.

Fulop, L., Linstead, S., Lilley, S., & Clarke, R.J. (2004). Decision making in organisations. In   S. Linstead, L. Fulop, & S. Lilley (Eds.) *Management and organization: A critical text* (pp. 462-494). New York: Palgrave.

Fyall, A., & Spyriadis, A. (2003). *Collaborating for growth: The international hotel industry.* Paper presented to Riding the Wave of Tourism and Hospitality Research, Council of Australian University Tourism and Hospitality Education Conference (CAUTHE), Coffs Harbour, Southern Cross University.

GartnerGroup. (1999) Gartner Group identifies c-commerce supply chain movement: An emerging trend in collaborative Web communities. *GartnerInteractive.* Retrieved from http://gartner5.gartnerWeb.com/public/static/aboutgg/presrel/

Garzotto, F., Paolini, P., Speroni, M., Proll, B., Retschitzegger, W & Schwinger, W. (2004, August 30-September 3). Ubiquitous access to cultural tourism portals. In Proceedings of *Database and Expert Systems Applications, the 15th International Workshop (DEXA'04)*, Zaragoza, Spain.

Go, F. (1992). The role of computerised reservations systems in the hospitality industry. *Tourism Management, 13*(1), 22-26.

Gonzales, M. V. (2004). Application of information technologies in the commercialisation and management of tourist products and destinations, in intermediate regions: Reticular integrated strategies. In *WISICT '04: Proceedings of the Winter International Symposium on Information and Communication Technologies*, Cancun, Mexico.

Grover, V., Teng, J. T. C., & Fiedler, K. D. (2002). Investigating the role of IT in building buyer-supplier relationships. *Journal of the Association of Information Systems, 3*, 217-245.

Hallen, L., Johanson, J., & Seyed-Mohamed, N. (1991). Interfirm adaptation in business relationships. *Journal of Marketing, 55*(2), 29-37.

Holsapple, C. W. & Singh, M. (2000). Toward a unified view of electronic commerce, electronic business, and collaborative commerce: A knowledge management approach. *Knowledge and Process Management, 7*(3), 151-164.

Jones, G. R. & George, J. M. (2003). *Contemporary management* (3rd ed.). Boston: McGraw Hill.

Joo, J. (2002, Summer). A business model and its development strategies for electronic tourism markets. *Information Systems Management*, 58-69.

Kalakota, R. & Robinson, M. (1999). *Frontiers of electronic commerce*. Reading, Massachusetts: Addison-Wesley.

Kasavana, M. L. & Brooks, R. M. (2001). *Managing front office operations*. MI: Educational Institute of the American Hotel & Lodging Association.

Kramer, R. M. (1993). Cooperation and organisational identification. In J. K. Murninghan (Ed.), *Social psychology in organisations: Advances in theory and research* (pp. 244-268). London: Prentice Hall.

Levy, M., Powell, P., & Yetton, P. (2001) SMEs: Aligning IS and the strategic context. *Journal of Information Technology*, 1i6(3), 133-44.

McCarthy, J. (1999) Gartner foretells of collaborative commerce. *Breaking News: IDG.net*. Retrieved from http//www.idg.net/idgns/1999/08/16/GartnerForetellsOfCollaborativeCommerce.shtml.

Macpherson, A., Jones, O., Zhang, M., & Wilson, A. (2003). Reconceptualising learning spaces: Developing capabilities in high-tech small firms. *Journal of Workplace Learning*, *15*(6), 259-270.

Mason, C., Castleman, T., & Parker, C. (2004, May). Knowledge management for SME-based regional clusters. In *Proceedings of CollECTeR*, University of South Australia, Adelaide.

Morgan, R., & Hunt, S. (1994). The commitment-trust theory of relationship marketing. *Journal of Marketing*, 5i8(3), 20-38.

O'Keefe, M. (2001) Building intellectual capital in the supply chain: The role of e-commerce. *Supply Chain Management: An International Journal*, *6*(4), 148-151.

Powell, W. (1987). Hybrid organisational arrangements. *California Management Review*, *30*, 67-87.

Ring, P. & Van de Ven, A. (1992). Structuring cooperative relationships between organisations. *Strategic Management Journal*, *13*, 483-498.

Ring, P. & Van de Ven A. (1994) Developmental processes of cooperative inter-organisational relationships. *Academy of Management Review*, *19*(1), 90-118.

Ryssel, R., Ritter, T., & Germunden, H. G. (2004). The impact of information technology deployment on trust, commitment, and value creation in business relationships. *Journal of Business & Industrial Marketing*, *19*(3), 197-207.

Sheth, J. (1996). Organisational buying behaviour; past performance and future expectations. *Journal of Business and Industrial Marketing*, *11*(3/4), 7-24.

Starkov, M. (2002). *The Internet: Hotelier's best ally or worst enemy? What went wrong with direct Web distribution in hospitality?* Retrieved March 23, 2005 from http://www.hotel-online.com/NEWS/PR2002_4th/Oct02_InternetAlly.html

Stern, L. W., & Weitz, B. A. (1997). The revolution of distribution: Challenges and opportunities. *Long Range Planning, 30*(6), 823-829.

Tajfel, H., & Turner, J. C. (1979). An integrative theory of intergroup conflict. In W. G. Austin & A. S. Worchel (Eds.), *The social psychology of intergroup relations* (pp. 33-47). Monterey, CA: Brooks/Cole.

Terry, D. J. (2003). Social identity and diversity in organisations. *Asia Pacific Journal of Human Resources, 41*(1), 25-35.

Tetteh, E. O. & Burn, J. M. (2001). Global strategies for SMe-business: Applying the SMALL framework. *LogisticsInformation Management, 14*(1/2), 171-80.

*Travel Impact Newswire.* (2004, December 1). Edition 81.

Yetton, P., Johnston, K., & Craig, J. (1994, Summer) Computer aided architects: A case study of IT and strategic change. *Sloan Management Review.*

## Chapter XI

# Sex Tourism
# and the Internet:
## Information, Amplification,
## and Moral Panics

Jerry Eades, Ritsumeikan Asian Pacific University, Japan

## Abstract

*This chapter examines the relationship between the Internet and sex tourism. It argues that interest in sex tourism in the media erupted in the early 1990s, about the same time that the Internet itself was becoming popular. The relationship between the two was both positive and negative. On the one hand, the Internet has allowed members of sexual subcultures to contact each other and for new forms of sex tourism to be marketed. On the other hand, the Internet also provided a platform for those opposed to sex tourism to raise the profile of the issue, in the process conflating images of sex tourism with those of Internet pornography, pedophilia, and child abuse, particularly in relation to tourism destinations in the Southeast Asian region. It has therefore aided the amplification of moral panics surrounding these issues. This sensational coverage has, however, tended to overshadow other forms of sex tourism, including those in which consenting adults meet together in resorts of clubs for recreational sex with each other. Thus, while the Internet has created moral panics and led to crackdowns in certain sections of the sex tourism market, it has allowed other alternative lifestyles to flourish on an unprecedented scale in an increasingly liberalized environment.*

# Introduction

Probably no sector of the tourist market has been more affected by the rise of the Internet than that of sex tourism. In fact, as will be shown below, until the advent of the Internet, "sex tourism" as a concept was rarely discussed in the media, even though sex as a motivation for travel has a very long history. But the relationship between sex tourism and the Internet also is extremely complex and contested, as befits such a controversial subject.

In this chapter, I first argue that the emerging literature on sex tourism has, in general, tended to concentrate on the commercial provision of sex to the exclusion of other types of sex tourism, with the greatest attention being given to the relations between prostitutes and tourists in Southeast Asia.

Second, I argue that in relation to this particular type of tourism, the Internet has proved a double-edged sword. Even though it has provided greatly enhanced opportunities for members of a wide variety of sexual interests, orientations and subcultures to contact and interact with each other, it also has provided an environment in which certain types of sex tourism have been increasing demonized by the media, civil society, and the politicians, resulting in the imposition of increasingly severe regulation and sanctions in a number of countries. The Internet has greatly assisted the stereotyping of the "sex tourist" as typically an overweight middle-aged Western male on the prowl for underage sex victims in the main Asian tourist resorts. This in turn has resulted new type of crime being brought onto the statute books in many countries, such as accessing and downloading child pornography. It also has made it possible for interest groups such as ECPAT (originally "End Child Prostitution in Asian Tourism")[1] to get their message across more effectively, increasing the pressure on governments to take action. In the mid-1990s, a number of countries introduced new legislation controlling the extraterritorial sexual activities of their nationals, and a number of well-publicized prosecutions have taken place since. Media reporting and its dissemination on the Internet have generally contributed to the sense of moral panic and indignation surrounding this issue, as well as conveying the comforting impression that something is being done about it, a questionable assumption given the small number of prosecutions and the large number of tourists.

My third argument, however, is that prostitution in Southeast Asia is only part of the story. Elsewhere, other forms of sex tourism involving consensual sex between tourists are flourishing, having been greatly facilitated and supported by the Internet. Far from experiencing increasing pressure from the law, these activities in some countries are enjoying an increasingly liberalized legal environment. The Internet acts both as an important source of information for the participants, as well as (to judge by the massive popularity of some of the sites where this information is disseminated) a significant source of entertainment for the casual *cybervoyeur*.

The chapter is therefore divided into five main parts. In the first, I discuss the definitions of sex tourism current in the literature, and the paradigms of its main variables offered by previous writers. The crucial variable, I will argue, is that of the power relations between participants in sexual activity. Where sex tourism involves the free participation of consenting adults with broadly equal power and rights in the relationship, there are clearly moral and legal problems than when some of the participants are coerced into sex because they are poor, vulnerable or under age.

Second, I look at the stages through which sex tourism typically develops in particular countries, in relation to other processes of economic growth and the development of a tourist market.

Third, I look at the growth of interest in sex tourism in the media, using online databases of press material that have developed into an important research tool in the last decade. Press databases are not only a good source of information on the topic, but also good indicators of the fluctuations of public interest in different countries concerning these issues over time. Here, I discuss how specific issues turn into moral panics speeded by the Internet, attracting both media attention and official action.

Fourth, I look at those types of sex tourism that have not generated as moral indignation as those involving prostitution or the exploitation of children, though clearly they are flourishing and even expending, both in cyberspace and in the flesh.

In the final section, I consider the policy implications of all this, for social theory and the future of sex tourism.

## Defining Sex Tourism

In general terms, sex tourism is not difficult to define: tourism in which the primary object is sexual activity, either sexual contact with others (local sex workers, other tourists) or sexual stimulation and arousal, usually leading to orgasm either alone or in company. However, the forms and sites of sex tourism have evolved considerably over the years, particularly as sex has become a less tabooed subject of discussion in the developed countries, and as would-be entrepreneurs (including organized crime) have devised new forms of sexual activity and exploitation for the purposes of profit.

In their pioneering monograph on sex tourism, Ryan and Hall offer the following thoughts on defining their subject:

*Sex tourism may be defined as tourism where the main purpose or motivation of at least part of the trip is to consummate sexual relations. It might be though that these relationships are usually of a commercial nature. However, the apparent solidity of such a definition soon starts to fade as the marginalities and states of sexuality start to be explored in more depth. ... Although sex tourism exists throughout the world, it has come to be primarily associated with the travel of tourists, usually male, in the developed world to less developed countries. One of the main attractions is the important cost differential that exists in the provision of both tourist and sexual services in the developing world compared to such provision in the industrialized world ... Therefore one of the key issues which thee present work addresses is the relationship between visitor and prostitute ...* (2001, p. x)

This initial definition points the way to much of their subsequent discussion. Although they state that the meaning of "sex tourism" is extremely wide, and need not necessarily involve a commercial transaction, they do nevertheless devote most of their time to male sex tourists buying sexual services in developing countries, particularly Thailand.

But despite this focus, they first offer three other sets of insights into the general nature of the field. The first concerns the range of activities and the variable degree of physical contact involved in sex tourism:

*The sex tourism industry also takes different forms ranging from the production of videos, through to nude dancing in which no physical contact occurs and the tourist acts as voyeur, and tourism-related prostitution, of which there are several major forms.* (Ryan & Hall, 2001, p. xi)

The key variable here is that of physical contact, though in practice dividing lines are fuzzy. For instance, exotic dancing is nowadays difficult to separate from lap dancing, and that can involve a considerable degree of physical contact, usually depending on how much the observer is prepared to pay (Lewis, 2002; Liepe-Levinson, 1998). It also can act as the curtain-raiser for other forms of sexual activity, to be negotiated separately.

Their second insight is a set of dichotomies through which different types of sex tourism can be differentiated from each other, according to whether the sexual activity is (a) voluntary or exploitative; (b) commercial or non-commercial and (c) enhancing or degrading for self-identity (Ryan & Hall, 2001, p. 49). The third of these is problematic, as is quite possible given the transient nature of sexual excitement that clients find their self-identity enhanced during the transaction itself, only to feel degradation later. The other two variables yield a four-fold table, one cell of which (non-commercial exploitative sex) seems of limited importance, while the three others more likely to arise in the real world. Recent literature suggests that many sex workers rate their work positively and reject their stereotyping as "victims" (e.g., Kempadoo, 1998, p. 2 and later chapters in the same volume), but it is usually commercial. Child prostitution would fall into the category of commercial and exploitative, while consensual sex between fellow tourists could be classified as voluntary and non-commercial—though whether it is ultimately identity enhancing or degrading for the participants is more difficult to ascertain objectively. But what we are left with here is the broad distinction between commercial sex (whether involving exploitation, by definition as some feminists would argue, or voluntary action) and consensual non-commercial sex.

Other models are of course possible, and I would suggest four continua which would extend those of Ryan and Hall to cover a wide range of sex-tourism activities. The first is the extent to which these activities are purely local or regional in nature (such as locally based swinging) to those which become the object of tourism, for example, commercially developed clothing optional and other "adult" resorts and the various casual and institutional activities a that go with them. A second continuum is the extent to which participation in sexual activity is the object of the exercise, rather than just viewing sex. This differentiates, for instance, the voyeur from the participant at dogging or swinging sites, and strip shows from prostitution, though lap dancing with bodily contact (Lewis, 2002) or audience participation in sex shows (Liepe-Levinson, 1998) are intermediate cases. A third dimension is how far the participants are professional sex workers, as opposed to casual amateurs, similar to the commercial-noncommercial dichotomy of Ryan and Hall. Clearly where professional sex workers are involved, there are economic and legal implications which do not arise when consenting adults are meeting for the free exchange of sex. It also may relate to a fourth dimension, the power relations between the participants, and the extent to which the sex workers themselves are willing participants in these activities, in other words Ryan and Hall's voluntary-exploitative dichotomy. Over the last two decades, as sex tourism has become an issue on the international radar, it has become clear that there are some extremely unpleasant forms of human trafficking involved, though in other cases participants may enter the sex industry on a more voluntary basis with a longer term goal in mind, as described for Dominica by Brennan (2004a, 2004b) or the Filipina hostesses and entertainers in Japan described by Garcia Dizon (2004, 2006). Finally, there is the question which most concerns this chapter, the extent to which the Internet has impinged on or amplified each of these types of activity.

## The Development of Sex Tourism

A third group of insights into sex tourism provided by Ryan and Hall (2001, chapter 7, based on Hall 1992) arise out of a developmental model they present of its origins. The stages are those of (a) indigenous prostitution, (b) economic colonialism and militarization, (c) substitution of international tourists for occupation forces and rapid economic development (Hall, 1992) and (d) the internationalization of legal and political responses.

Their argument can be summarized as follows. In many of the countries of East and Southeast Asia, the sex industry has a long history, going back to indigenous institutions in precolonial times. Even though they discuss mainly the origins of prostitution in Southeast Asia, it could be argued that this applies especially to Japan and China. Historically, many cities have had zones of license, in which sex industries and other forms of entertainment have flourished. These date back to the ancient world, where many of them were paradoxically associated with temples, perhaps not surprising given a large influx of religious pilgrims interested not only in religion (for typical instances in the literature, see Flemming, 1999; Lerner, 1986; Rosner, 1998; Toorn 1989). In the early modern state, many cities developed entertainment zones, perhaps the best example being that of the Yoshiwara in Edo (Tokyo), also located near one of the largest temple complexes in the city (Bornoff, 1991; Longstreet & Longstreet, 1970; Seidensticker, 1983; Seigle, 1993).

The Yoshiwara brought together the worlds of *kabuki* theater, *sumo* wrestling and the sex industry, with both female and male (Leupp, 1995) sex workers. This was the floating world of the great Edo print artists, and *shunga* or erotic pictures formed a large part of their output, despite official disapproval and censorship. Yoshiwara survived as a zone of prostitution into the 20th century, when it was closed down by a government concerned with public morals and the spread of sexually transmitted disease. Ironically the area is now the site of a large number of "soapland establishments" where sex workers provide sexual services within the context of giving the clients a bath (Bornoff, 1991; Seidensticker; 1990). China had a similar tradition of courtesans, which in the 20th century also developed into a large-scale prostitution industry in major cities such as Shanghai, with close links with both gangsters and politicians (Hershatter, 1997; Lintner, 2002).

In the 20th century, therefore, the rise and transformation of the sex industry took place under the influence of colonialism and the presence of the military. As Ryan and Hall (2001, p. 140) put it:

*In this stage the occupied culture's general acceptance of various forms of prostitution has been used as a justification for economic or military enforced prostitution or, as in the case of Japanese militarism in the 1930s and 1940s, was used as a means of exercising power on host populations. In addition, this stage commences the economic dependency of certain sections of host societies on the selling of sexual services as a means of economic growth and development. For example, in the case of Taiwan, hot spring resorts which provided for the spatial concentration of tourist-related prostitution activity were first developed under the Japanese colonial era between 1895 and 1945.*

As Japanese colonialism and emigration expanded in the early 20th century, networks of Japanese brothels were set up around the world, into which Japanese women from poorer families were recruited to service a largely Japanese clientele (e.g., Yamazaki, 1990). As is well known, during the Pacific War, the Japanese forced large numbers of non-Japanese women into prostitution as "comfort women" to service the imperial army throughout the region (Hicks, 1995; Watanabe, 1995). Less well known but increasingly well documented were the American arrangements to provide "rest and recreation" or "R&R" facilities for their troops, in Korea, the Philippines and elsewhere. It has been estimated that since the Second World War, up to a million Korean women have been involved in one way or another servicing the sexual needs of American servicemen (Lie 1995; Matsu & Sharnoff, 1977; Moon, 1997, 1999; Soh, 1996). Similarly, there were an estimated 12,000 registered and 8,000 unregistered hostesses in Olongapo City in the Philippines, serving the Subic Naval base and Clark Air Force Base (Law, 2000; Moselina, 1979; Philippine Women's Research Collective, 1985). Local city ordinances were changed to regulate the trade, and clear prostitutes off the streets and into clubs, a profitable source of income for local business (Claire & Cottingham, 1982). Similarly, the growth of the sex industry in Thailand stemmed partly from contracts to provide R&R services for the American troops fighting in Vietnam (Bishop & Robinson, 1998).

In the third of Ryan and Hall's stages, therefore, governments promoted sex work for the military, which later gave way to government-promoted sex work as a way of attracting foreign tourists. Prostitution and the commoditization of sex were presented as patriotic, promoting economic development, and creating jobs for the rest of the country. In Thailand, the process was helped by the image of the country promoted by popular culture, in the form of the *Emmanuelle* novels and films. Manderson (1997) suggests that Thailand was irrelevant to the plot of the original Sylvia Krystel film, which appeared in 1974: it was just a western soft-porn fantasy that could have been located anywhere. Nevertheless, it did help reinforce the image of Thailand as a sexual paradise in the Western tourist industry, and Patpong was soon firmly established in the guidebooks as a must-see site, the center of the burgeoning sex industry (Manderson, 1992). Thailand also established a reputation as a center for gay tourism, thanks to its comparative tolerance of homosexuality (Jackson, 1997, 2003; Sanders, 2002). Increasingly, sex tourism was becoming a literary theme, a shown by the success and notoriety of the work of Michel Houellbecq.

An important feature of the growth of sex tourism in post-war Asia was the emergence of Japan as the regions first economic superpower. After the Second World War, Japan had gone through its own occupation experience, and this continued for many years in Okinawa, which remained under American administration until 1972. Relations between the population of Okinawa and their American neighbors have remained difficult, and there have often been sexual undertones to the relationship, as when American servicemen were involved in the rape of a young Okinawan girl in 1995 (Eldredge, 1997). But as the Japanese economy revived, Japan began to play an increasingly important part in the regional sex industry as consumers. The group solidarity of the Japanese salarymen was often reinforced by works outings to popular *onsen* (hot springs) and other resorts in Japan, and some of these outings involved having a good time with local sex workers (for examples, see Constantine, 1993). As the Japanese economy expanded, this Japanese tradition of company sex tourism increasingly moved offshore, and trips to Thailand, the Philippines and even China as described below, became common (Bornoff, 1991; Brown, 2000). The Japanese also began to receive adverse comment in the press, and Japan started to come under increasing international pressure to clean up its act.

The Japanese response was in part to import the sex workers into Japan itself. With the increasing level of education in Japan, the falloff in the birthrate, and the increasing prosperity of the nation as a whole, the traditional sex industry itself started to collapse and run out of recruits. The solution was to simply import girls from countries which Japanese tourists had long since been patronizing to fill the gap. As the bubble economy expanded in the late 1980s, so did the population of foreign migrants. Some of the women coming in were brought in by organized crime under highly exploitative conditions: pay was poor, passports were seized, and much of the money the girls earned went straight back to the brokers who had brought them as payment for transport, accommodation and loans incurred on the way (Brown, 2000). Others came in more independently, one of the incentives being the chances of finding a husband in Japan. By the 1980s, there was a severe shortage of potential brides in some parts of the country, particularly in the rural areas, and in smaller towns and cities where the population was dropping rapidly. Foreign brides were an obvious solution to the problem. Even though there were problems with many of the marriages, they did at least legitimate the women's presence in Japan, and the birth of children with Japanese citizenship further strengthened their rights of residence (Garcia Dizon, 2004). Many Thai and Filipina women came in under special "entertainment" visas as a cover for their employment as hostesses or sex workers, and there were numerous complaints from women in the Philippines when the quota of visas was drastically reduced at the end of 2004 (Garcia Dizon, 2006).

The restructuring of the Asian sex tourism market from a military to civilian clientele leads into the fourth stage proposed by Ryan and Hall (2001), that of rapid economic development and international controls. Korea and Taiwan, like Japan, have gone through a period of high speed economic growth, and their birthrates also have fallen, the implication being that they too will probably follow the Japanese pattern of the collapse of the domestic sex industry, followed by the offshoring of sexual encounters and/or the importation of sex workers from elsewhere in the region. Meanwhile, sex tourism continues to flourish elsewhere in the region (Brown, 2000), including the Philippines (Law, 2000), Thailand (Bishop & Robinson, 1998; Seabrook, 2000; Truong, 1990), Vietnam (Marsh, 2006), Cambodia (Cater, 1995), and China (Jeffreys, 2004).

In the period from September to December, 2003, a particularly colorful scandal in China was widely reported by the international media. The affair, with its heady mixture of sex and nationalism, generated a considerable body of discussion and debate, much of which can be readily tracked down in the press databases.[2] It concerned a party of Japanese tourists from Osaka who reportedly had stayed at a hotel in the Chinese resort city of Zhuhai from 16-18 September. They had been joined there by a large contingent of Chinese women, and the result was widespread and prolonged sexual activity. The authorities were alerted and raided the hotel: after investigations, 14 people were prosecuted in December 2003 for their part in arranging the event, and sentenced to varying periods of imprisonment. The two most serious offenders were given life sentences. The Japanese tourists returned to Japan, and attempts to extradite three of them back to China were refused. The company concerned denied any wrongdoing in the affair, though they received a large number of indignant telephone calls and emails from the outraged public. The hotel in Zhuhai, together with another one where similar events were said to have taken place, was closed for a time, but eventually allowed to reopen under stricter controls than before. A number of local security officials were dismissed, presumably for allowing all this to happen on their watch.

Several features of the affair are noteworthy. The first is the vagueness about the numbers of people involved, and the extent of what actually happened. The number of Japanese men involved is variously given as 185, 285, or 400. The number of sex workers involved ranges from about the same as the men in some accounts to as many as 500 in others. Presumably over the three days of the party, people came and went so figures are understandably hazy. In any case, clearly a large number of people were involved and the event required a considerable amount of planning.

Second, because the Japanese were involved, discussions in the media drew heavily on Sino-Japanese history, increasing the sense of outrage at what had happened. In fact, it appears from other sites on the Internet that the hotels in Zhuhai had a reputation for being good places to find sexual companionship, at more reasonable prices than other cities in the region (Zhuhai is close to Canton, Macau, and Hong Kong). So what happened there was probably not unprecedented—apart perhaps from its sheer scale. Most of the participants were probably blissfully unaware that the date of their trip to China coincided with the anniversary of the "Manchurian Incident" of 1931, which marked the start of full-scale hostilities between the Chinese and Japanese. However, this fact was soon picked up by the Chinese and international media. Parallels were quickly drawn between the behavior of the Japanese invaders of the 1930s and the contemporary Japanese tourists, and the choice of date was presented as a deliberate attempt to humiliate the Chinese. It also happened that the date of the trial in December 2003 coincided with the anniversary of the Japanese entry to Nanjing in 1937. This also was quickly picked up by the media, allowing additional parallels to be drawn with the Japanese invasion.

Just to make matters even more complex, this was only one of a number of issues which affected Sino-Japanese relationships during the summer of 2003. Others included the location of an oil pipeline from Russia, the discovery of deposits of mustard gas left over from WWII, and disturbances between Japanese and Chinese students at Northwest University, Xian, China. Taken together, these various incidents provoked a sense of crisis in Sino-Japanese relations, reflecting not only Chinese hostility towards Japan, but also increasing nationalism in China. But what is clear is that the availability of the Internet exacerbated the crisis, through helping to popularize Zhuhai as a sex tourism destination, making the news of the scandal widely available, and allowing the Chinese public to coordinate their protests to the administration.

Generally since the early 1990s, however, several factors have produced an increasing outcry against sex tourism, and have led national governments to increase their efforts to try and exert greater control (Hall, 1998; Seabrook, 2000).

The first factor which lay behind these changes was the HIV/AIDS pandemic which spread quickly from the early 1980s, and increasingly came to affect countries with large sex tourism industries. As Ryan and Hall note, the Thai Public Health Ministry started to campaign against prostitution and sex tourism in 1989, because of their realization that AIDS could pose a problem for tourism as a whole, and for the wider economy. The Asia Development bank calculated that the costs to the economy could rise to $3.5 billion a year by the end of the century (Ryan & Hall, 2001; see also Beyrer & Stachowiak, 2003).

A second factor was an increasingly vocal campaign against human trafficking, and in particular the trafficking and sexual exploitation of women and children. This had long been an issue in Asia (Brown, 2000), but with the collapse of communism in Eastern Europe, the problem soon began to appear there as well. By 1993, it was reported that in Amsterdam, "Young women are being lured out of Eastern Europe by offers of jobs in the West. But there their passports are taken away and they find they have been sold as prostitutes" (Henley, 1993, Guardian Features section, p. 12). Trafficking in both the former Soviet Union and China soon became highly organized (for a comparison between the two countries, see Shelley 2005.) Indeed, increasing numbers of East European women began to appear in the bars and nightclubs of East Asia. These issues also were attracting increasing attention from the media, as discussed in the next section.

## Sex Tourism and the Media

By the mid-1990s, it became clear that the Internet had opened up not only immense possibilities for collecting information, but also for talking about sex online and accessing pornography. As with earlier new technologies, calls soon grew strident for the policing, censoring and regulation of the Internet, but the way it was designed (with decentralized structure and control), and the desire of the courts, particularly in the U.S., not to limit freedom of speech means that it remained largely unregulated, apart from some states such as Singapore, China, or the Islamic countries which have made heroic efforts to filter out information which they find unacceptable.

An important strand in the debate over regulation of the Web has been that concerning sex tourism and, by implication, pedophilia and child pornography. Indeed, so strong emphasis on pedophilia and pornography in discussions of sex tourism, that other forms of sex tourism noted above and involving consenting adults have often been largely ignored.

The development of these issues as a "moral panic," taken up by the media, pressure groups and politicians, can be documented in the major online press databases, many of which date back to the period before the rise of the Internet[3]. As a simple measure of the importance of these issues, the number of hits in each time period can easily be verified. Here I have used major publications included in the LexisNexis Total Research database, because of the ease with which large quantities of information can be downloaded from it. Using "sex tourism" as a search keyword, the database produced the following numbers of hits for each year from 1990 onwards.

As can be seen, in the early 1990s, sex tourism was hardly mentioned by the world's media as a concept at all, though clearly sex was already of major importance in the tourist industry, as Truong's pioneering study of Southeast Asia shows (Truong, 1990). Interest continued at a low level, until 1995-1996 when there was a massive jump. After a dip for a few years, media interest in the subject picked up again in 2003, and remains high until the present (the results for the first six months of 2006 are similar to those for 2005).

*Table 1. References to sex tourism in major world publications, 1990-2005 (Source: LexisNexis Total Research, Major World Publications)*

| Year | References | Year | References |
|------|-----------|------|-----------|
| 1990 | 8 | 1998 | 145 |
| 1991 | 17 | 1999 | 130 |
| 1992 | 22 | 2000 | 134 |
| 1993 | 29 | 2001 | 156 |
| 1994 | 38 | 2002 | 146 |
| 1995 | 156 | 2003 | 175 |
| 1996 | 255 | 2004 | 290 |
| 1997 | 141 | 2005 | 267 |

The sequences of events explaining this pattern seems to be as follows. By 1990, there was increasing concern about sex tourism in a number of quarters. First, national governments which were increasingly concerned with the international images of their country, particularly Thailand. During the 1980s, sex tourism slowly started to emerge as an issue, particularly in Thailand, as the number of tourists escalated, from less than 100,000 in the 1960s to five million a year by the late 1980s. In 1987, the Thai government launched a "Visit Thailand" campaign to promote the country as a tourist destination. Two thirds of the resulting visitors were men, and it was estimated that around 223,000 were there for the purposes of sex (Poole, 1991).

Second, medical authorities were increasingly concerned with the spread of AIDS which was starting to take an increasing toll in the country's sex industry. Reported cases from 100 in 1989 to 14,000 in May 1990, and there were estimates that 25 percent of the nation's sex workers were HIV positive. By 1993, Thailand was said to have one of the world's highest infection rates (Brangin 1993).

Third, there was pressure from NGOs and activists concerned with the welfare of women and children, many of them with links to the churches. The most important of these was ECPAT, whose Web site became one of the best sources of material on the issue, and which issued a series of influential country profiles and reports.[4]

Fourth, there was a growing concern about human trafficking and illegal immigration worldwide, exacerbated by the collapse of communism in Eastern Europe, as noted above. Countries like Hungary also were beginning to use the sex industry as a way to draw the tourists. "The sex ship sets sail early but the sex castle stays open late. If you miss both there are nightclubs with nude go-go dancers and erotic 'live' shows. This may look like Bangkok but it is Lake Balaton, once Hungary's most popular resort now touted as the new playground of European sex tourism" (Beck, 1990, Overseas News section). AIDS was starting to spread in Eastern Europe as well.

Finally the increasing visibility of pornography on the Internet became linked with these other issues in the media and the public imagination, and discourses of sex tourism took on the form which has predominated in the academic literature ever since. As a reaction to this, politicians were spurred to rapid action, given that this was an issue on which they found it easy to reach consensus across the political spectrum. Governments began to consider action (Seabrook, 2000): in 1990, Thailand, the Philippines, Taiwan and Sri Lanka were holding talks Britain, Germany, Switzerland, the United States, France and the Netherlands on joint action against pedophiles, and by the autumn of 1991, Germany was starting to take the lead in taking action against its nationals abusing children on holiday abroad (Ingham, 1991). Soon, calls for similar action were being heard in Australia and elsewhere (Skeggs, 1992). By late 1993, even French MPs were calling for curbs on sex tourism.[5]

The contribution of the Internet to the debate was therefore threefold: (a) to make available material which people found offensive on a massive scale and therefore force public discussion of the issue; (b) to give a voice to the various pressure groups campaigning for greater controls and (c) to disseminate media reports of these issues, the measures being taken, and their policy implications. The new legislation were touted as giving police a powerful tool in pursuing pedophiles, reinforcing the idea in the public imagination that the possession of images was synonymous with actual pedophilia. The British Home Office claimed that international collaboration had led to success: "Operation Starburst in 1995" led to 20 prosecutions in the UK and over 100 worldwide, and "Operation Cathedral" in 1998, which involved collaboration between 15 countries and seizures of 750,000 images.[6] In 2000, the British Home Office announced that it was setting up a new unit to deal with pedophiles within the National Criminal Intelligence Service, putting it in the same league as sabotage, terrorism, and international money-laundering. Despite all this publicity, however, it is doubtful how effective these measures have actually been in deterring these kinds of activities, given that the number of prosecutions has been modest compared with the supposed numbers of sex tourists. Also, the people prosecuted have included a number of high-profile individuals whose activities only came to light accident. This is most obvious in the case of Paul Gadd, well known in the 1970s as rock star Gary Glitter, which received enormous publicity in the United Kingdom (e.g., Aglionby & Barnett, 2005; Bainbridge & Aglionby, 2005; Drummond, 2002, 2003; Drummond & Fresco 2005; England & Barnes, 2006; Mackay 2006).

In 1999, Gadd took his computer to the local branch of PC World for repair. The technician noticed that there were a large number of pornographic images on the hard drive, many of them of children, and reported the matter to the police. Gadd was charged with downloading child pornography and jailed for four months, though he was cleared of charges of actual sex with children. The case received immense publicity. On his release, Gadd flew to Cuba, but soon attracted attention there and was expelled. Cuba was increasingly being identified by the Western media as a haven for sex tourism, and apparently also wanted to clean up its act.[7] Gadd then moved on to Phnom Penh in Cambodia in the late summer of 2001.

Unfortunately, he arrived at a time when both the British and Cambodian governments were attempting to take a hard line with alleged pedophiles and sex tourists. One Briton had already been jailed in Cambodia for sex offences, while another had been jailed in Britain for having sex with a 13-year old girl while in Cambodia. Early in 2002, the Cambodian Minister of Women's Affairs demanded Gadd's deportation from the country. Gadd spent the next two years moving between Cambodia, Thailand and Vietnam, with a series of court battles to resist attempts to remove him. By the summer of 2005, he had moved to Vietnam, but was arrested in November of that year on charges of having sex with a 12-year old girl in Vung Tau, a resort town popular with foreign oil workers, where prostitution was presumably not unknown. However, Gadd was difficult to ignore because of the media attention that followed him in his travels. Eventually, after charges of rape were dropped after payment of compensation, he was sentenced to three years in jail in March, 2005. In an interview with the BBC, he denied that he had slept knowingly with girls below the age of consent, and suggested that he might return to the UK after his release. As a reaction to this and similar cases, the British government put forward proposals to place overseas travel restrictions on registered sex offenders in future.[8]

Gadd's misfortunes were clearly made worse by his former fame and the tenacity with which the tabloid press followed the twists and turns of the story. He was not a sex tourist in the conventional sense, nor had he been convicted of actual pedophilia in his original trial. Before the new legislation of the mid-1990s, he might not have been convicted of any offence at all. However, the media coverage of his case persistently linked the issues of pedophilia, pornography and sex tourism, and articles in the popular press on sex tourism often referred to the Gadd case, just as accounts of the Japanese in Zhuhai tended to end with references to Nanjing.

## Couples and Sex Tourism:
## Swinging, Dogging, and Adult Resorts

As the history of the 19th and 20th century often shows, new communications technologies are often adapted to the sex industry with considerable speed. Earlier studies have shown that sex lay behind much of the popularity of the Minitel system in France during the 1980s (Castells, 1996), even though it was designed for more mundane uses such as looking up telephone numbers and paying bills.

Once the Internet itself was in place in the early 1990s, sex-related usage escalated. As with Minitel, sex became the most popular area of discussion in many of the bulletin boards and chat rooms that proliferated on the Internet, and dating and matchmaking sites took over from the agony columns of the magazines and newspapers (Merkle & Richardson, 2000). Dating sites had the added advantage that they could a much wider region, would be read by many more people, and provided facilities like e-mail and the instant exchange of photographs through ICT, the first of a new generation of instant messaging facilities. The matchmaking engines often had room for information on sex, age group, sexual preferences, appearance, location, and personal statements, as well as email addresses that could be used for more general purposes. Clearly many people using these sites are hiding behind adopted personae and Internet pseudonyms, but much of the information is probably genuine, as shown by the large number of unflattering self-descriptions and the number of participants in older age groups to be found on these sites. Some commentators have seen the emergence of a new culture of "encounter" arising as a result (Holden & Tsuruki 2003).

What these chat sites and matchmaking services also allowed was the proliferation of groups with similar unorthodox sexual preferences. Perhaps the largest of these were the swingers, couples and singles meeting together either to exchange partners or for group sex. "The lifestyle" as it is often known became popular in the 1970s as part of the counter culture in America, and among the sexually more adventurous in Europe. It continued to spread, despite the onset of AIDS, thanks to the almost universal use of condoms. It tends to be found most often among middle class highly educated couples, including many who are middle aged, many of them churchgoers (Bergstrand & Blevins, 2000). It has even spawned its own associations (such as the International Lifestyle Association, NASCA International for the U.S., or the Sexual Freedom Coalition for the UK) and its own genre of guidebooks (e.g., Bellemeade, 2002; Thomas, 1997). The Internet has provided swingers with three important forms of information: the location and personal details of other singles and couples and their various interests, the location of clubs and other meeting places, and chat rooms and notice boards where people can interact online or post their fantasies, experiences, photographs and videos.[9] The number of people using these sites appears to be enormous. At the time of writing, Swinging Heaven in the UK claimed to have over half a million members, with nearly a quarter of a million singles or couples including photos or videos in their advertisements. There is at least one case in which a couple turned a Web site documenting their sex lives into a multi-million dollar business.

Many Web sites cater to gay men and women as well, though they also have their own specialized sites. As the popularity of the Internet spread, a variety of sexual subcultures soon appeared online as participants were able to describe themselves and their preferences to each other.[10] The Web sites also began to provide information on travel to tourist centers with active sex service industries and sub cultures such as San Francisco, Berlin and Amsterdam (Brants, 1998; Wonders & Michalowski, 2001), and the kinds of attractions and activities available there.[11] This was part of a realization of the significance of the gay tourist market and the potential for businesses in catering to it (Clift, Luongo, & Callister, 2002). An online cruising culture is not confined to the West, but also has developed in Japan as well (McClelland, 2003). As with heterosexual couples, contacting partners online offers participants several advantages. It allows discretion, especially in countries where homosexuality is still either criminalized or discriminated against. Messages reach a much wider audience than they otherwise would, and potential partners are able to exchange photographs and discuss sexual preferences before actually meeting.

Making contact with potential partners does not necessarily overlap with tourism, but it often does. Many Web sites have information on a wide variety of "erotic vacations," adults-only resorts (many of them "clothing optional," and sex clubs located there which cater either the straight or the gay market.[12] There is probably a continuum between clubs which cater mainly for the local or regional crowd, as in the cities of northern England which are not major tourist centers, to those which cater almost entirely for tourists, such as those in the major tourist resorts aimed at a swinging clientele. The physical layout of the clubs, whether straight or gay, appears fairly uniform. There is usually an area for meeting and preliminary socializing, often centered around a bar. There also is a shower area, communal "play" areas featuring around large beds or mattresses, and sometimes private rooms to which couples and groups that require more intimate surroundings can move. Other common features include rooms with mirrors, rooms with bondage equipment and/or swings, glory holes, saunas, steam rooms, hot tubs, pools or Jacuzzi, and TV screens showing pornographic movies. One club in the UK has even imported a camper van and gravel into one of its playrooms, to recreate the outdoor dogging experience without the risks (for dogging see below). The Web sites often have space for visitor's comments, which can range from the enthusiastic to the highly critical.[13] One of the main issues in straight clubs is whether or not to allow entry to single men. It seems to be a universal problem for the swinger community that there are more men wishing to participate than women. Opinions are divided about letting in single men. Some argue that more men are needed to keep the party going, given that they tire and give up more quickly than women. Others argue that too many single men get in the way, and spoil the fun. The result is a paradoxical fee structure in which often single men pay more than couples and women are often admitted free. Some times of the week in many establishments are restricted to couples and single women only, with themed gay, bisexual, fetish-wear, S-M, or "greedy girl" evenings.

Demographic and locational imbalance creates a market demand for more informal venues for the voyeur community, and another developing niche in the market for amateur sexual services is provided by isolated spots where singles or couples meet informally for sex, often in the evening or at night. In the UK, this is now known as "dogging" though its antecedents, such as gay men frequenting public toilets for sex (Humphreys, 1975) or casual exhibition and open-air sex on nude beaches (Douglas, 1977), have been around for a long time. The new element in dogging is that exhibitionism and group sex tend to take place in car parks or other places which are accessible to vehicles, and that information on sites and activities is mainly spread by the Internet. This is an ideal medium for listing such locations, given that there are frequent changes of venue in response to police surveillance. The police can find out where the action is as easily as the doggers, simply by surfing the net.

However, generally these activities are taking place in an increasingly liberal atmosphere in most countries in the West. Most of the EU countries have now adopted the liberal and relaxed attitudes to sex which have long been the norm in France, Holland and Scandinavia. Pornography (other than child pornography) is readily available, sex clubs are increasingly popular, and expressions of open sexuality, including gay sexuality are increasingly recognized. Clothing optional and gay-friendly resorts and hotels are multiplying, and couples post their experiences, fantasies, photographs and action videos on the Internet, as sources of information for each other, and free entertainment for other surfers.

# Conclusion

As can be seen from the discussion above, the relationship between the Internet and sex, including sex tourism, has been extremely complex over the last decade. First, the relationship is not entirely one way: to judge from the preponderance of sex-related material in lists of the most popular Web sites, it was access to potential partners and the forbidden fruit of pornography that helped the Internet take off in the first place. In the late 1990s, the top sites on the Internet were nearly all concerned with sex or pornography. Now, the most popular sites are the search engines Google and Yahoo, technical sites such as Microsoft, or news sites such as the BBC. The sex sites only start much lower down the list. Now that the Internet has been with us for a number of years, it is becoming possible to assess the impact of this relationship on the wider society, and here the three terms which feature in the subtitle of this chapter, information, amplification and moral panics, may be useful headings under which to summarize my findings.

Sex has historically always been an important motivation for tourism, and the sex industry has grown up alongside the travel industry from ancient times. However, "sex tourism" as an issue in the media and the popular consciousness is comparatively recent. The data from the online press databases suggests that there were very few references to it at all before 1995-96, when it first became the subject of widespread media attention and debate. This happened to coincide with the takeoff of the Internet, and the merging images of pornography, child abuse, prostitution in the popular imagination meant that sex tourism began to appear more regularly as an issue.

It is undeniable that, for better or worse, sites dealing with sex-related materials are incredibly popular, and presumably many people are using them as portals to free entertainment rather than active participation. However, the dating sites show hundreds of thousands of people registering their profiles and participating in email, and presumably a significant number of these are doing so in order to meet real people. The popularity of these activities is shown by the proliferation of adult vacations, erotic tourism, clothing optional resorts, and guidebooks catering to the people who use them. This is a niche market, but the Internet is significant because it can make available information on so many of them in a single search. It has taken over the role of the small personal ad in the newschapters or the contact magazines which started up in the 1970s, but performs it infinitely more efficiently. Meanwhile, of course, the drop in the cost of transport over the years has meant that the possibility of actually meeting potential partners also has greatly increased.

It is difficult to know how many people are involved in alternative lifestyle options, but what evidence there is suggests that it is significant, particularly in the wealthier and more highly educated sectors of society. The AIDS epidemic precipitated a crisis in the 1980s, but the swinging fraternity has long since embraced the condom, and in any case there are plenty of other things to do which don't involve the exchange of bodily fluids. Meanwhile, governments in the West seem to have come to terms with the situation: the legal regime is increasingly liberal, policing is increasingly relaxed, and the impossibility of controlling and regulating what consenting adults choose to do with each other is recognized. When things get out of hand, there is discrete regulation. The amount of sex and exhibitionism behind the main beach in Cap d'Agde a few years back worried the authorities because many families used the beach. The solution was typically Gallic and pragmatic. During the holiday season, the area to the back of the beach was declared a "nature reserve," and the public was kept out by mounted police patrols. Daytime swingers moved elsewhere instead. Once the kids were back in school, controls were relaxed, the swingers returned to the beach, the police disappeared, and the *status quo ante* was restored.

If the Internet can inform, it also can amplify. It would be interesting to research the pattern of spread of information and associated activities, not only for sex, but for many other activities as well. As the popularity of a subject takes off, the increase in information on the Internet is exponential at first, reaching a plateau as virtually everyone who is interested is accessing information online. Interest might fall off later as new fads appear, though in the case of sex this has yet to happen. The power of the Internet may therefore mean that social trends are amplified and accelerated, reaching a plateau more rapidly than they otherwise might have done.

However, the Internet also can amplify indignation, dissent and protest, creating moral panics that led, in the case of sex tourism, to regulation with breathtaking speed. As images of child prostitution, pornography and sex tourism merged in the media and on the net, governments and politicians felt impelled to act, as being soft on sin was simply not an option for them. No matter that the legislation was badly framed, that it seemed to some to perpetuate images of colonial paternalism (Noh, 1997), or that it actually led to the arrest of very few individuals (Fraley, 2005), including some like Gadd whose activities were discovered more or less by accident.

As more dispassionate observers have noted, sex tourism involving prostitution is likely to continue for good economic reasons, the poverty of the families concerned, and the differential cost of sex between countries. The way forward, they argue, is improving the conditions of sex workers, given that policing and regulation are virtually impossible. The implication is not to try and stamp out sex tourism, or to keep it off the Internet, but to use the Internet to empower and educate the sex workers themselves (Law, 2000), on the assumption that an increasing number of them will gain access as costs continue to fall, for example through the merging of mobile phone and Internet technologies in the years to come.

# References

Aglionby, J. & Barnett, A. (2005, November 20). Gary Glitter could face a firing squad. *Observer*, New pages, p. 1.

Bainbridge, B. & Aglionby, J. (2005, November 26). Sex tourism Accusations against Gary Glitter throw spotlight on Vietnam: Tracking down child abusers: Police forces unite to fight world problem. *The Guardian*, London, final ed., p. 7.

Beck, E. (1990, August 14). Hungarian resort launches love boat. *The Times*.

Bellemeades, K. (2003). *Swinging for beginners: An introduction to the lifestyle.* New Tradition Books.

Bergstrand, C. & Blevins, J. (2000, Oct. 10). Today's alternative marriage styles: The case of swingers. *Electronic Journal of Human Sexuality, 3.* Retrieved from www.ejhs.org

Beyrer, C. & Stachowiak, J. (2003). Health consequences of trafficking of women and girls in Southeast Asia. *Brown Journal of World Affairs, 10*(1).

Birmingham Post. (2003, April 16). New ban to stop perverts going abroad for child sex. *Birmingham Post*, p. 9.

Bishop, R. & Robinson, L. S. (1998). *Night market: Sexual cultures and the Thai economic miracle.* New York: Routledge.

Bornoff, N. (1991). *Pink samurai: Love, marriage & sex in contemporary Japan.* New York: Pocket Books.

Branigin, W. (1993, December 2). Asia Faced With AIDS Catastrophe. *The Washington Post.*

Brants, C. 1998. The fine art of regulated tolerance: Prostitution in Amsterdam. *Journal of Law and Society, 25,* 621-35.

Brennan, D. (2004a). Women work, men sponge, and everyone gossips: Macho men and stigmatized/ing women in a sex tourist town. *Anthropological Quarterly, 77*(4), 705-33.

Brennan, E. (2004b). *What's love got to do with it? Transnational desires and sex tourism in the Dominican Republic.* Durham, NC: Duke University Press.

Brown, L. (2000). *Sex slaves: The trafficking of women in Asia.* London: Virago.

Castells, M. (1996). *The rise of the network society.* Oxford: Blackwell.

Cater, N. (1995, October 23). Crackdown on child sex. *Herald Sun.*

Claire, R. & Cottingham, J. (1982). Migration and tourism: An overview. In *Women in development: A resource guide for organisation and action* (pp. 122-138). Geneva: ISIS Women's International and Communication Service.

Clift, S., Luongo. M., & Callister, C. (Eds.). (2002). *Gay tourism: Culture, identity and sex.* London: Continuum.

Constantine, P. (1993). *Japan's sex trade*. Tokyo: Tuttle.

Douglas, J. (1977). *Nude beach*. Thousand Oaks CA: Sage.

Drummond, A & Fresco, A. (2005, November 22). Gary Glitter could face a firing squad. *The Times* (London), p. 17.

Drummond, A. (2002, April 28). Glitter faces deportation in crackdown on sex tourism. *Scotland on Sunday*, p. 13.

Drummond, A. (2003, January 8). Pervert thrown out of Far East hiding place; Glitter in Jail again. *The Express*, p. 10.

Eldredge, R. (1997). The 1996 Okinawa Referendum on U.S. base reductions: One question, several answers. *Asian Survey, 37*(10), 879-904.

England, V. & Barnes, A. (2006, March 5). Glitter to be deported to Britain after his release in November. *Independent on Sunday* (London), p. 47.

English Media Service. (2003, September 29). Sex scandal prompts anti-Japanese sentiments in China. ANSA English Media Service.

The Express. (2000, January 5). Police go online to net cybergangs. *The Express*.

Express on Sunday (2000, January 9). Police target Internet merchants of porn. *Express on Sunday*.

Flemming, R. (1999). Quae corpore quaestum facit: The sexual economy of female prostitution in the Roman Empire. *The Journal of Roman Studies, 89*, 38-61.

Fraley, A. (2005). Child sex tourism legislation under the Protect Act: Does it really protect? *St John's Law Review, 79*(2), 445-483.

Garcia Dizon, J. (2004). *Philippine migrants in Japan: Networks, strategies, narratives and the negotiation of identity.* Unpublished MA dissertation, Ritsumeikan Asia Pacific University, Beppu, Japan.

Garcia Dizon, J. (2006). Revisiting the OPA phenomenon: What's next for Filipino migrant workers to Japan?" *Ritsumeikan Journal of Asia Pacific Studies, 20*, 69-84.

Gould, T. (2000). *The lifestyle: A look at the erotic rites of swingers*. Firefly Publishers.

The Guardian (1993, December 11). French MPs back sex tourism curb. *The Guardian*.

The Guardian (2003, September 29). Japanese "orgy" claim sparks outrage in China. *The Guardian,* Final ed.

Hall, C. M. (1992). Tourism in South-Eat Asia. In D. Harrison (Ed.), *Tourism and the less developed nations* (pp. 64-74). London: Belhaven Press.

Hall, C. M. (1998). The legal and political dimensions of sex tourism: The case of Australia's child sex tourism legislation. In M. Oppermann (Ed.), *Sex tourism and prostitution: Aspects of leisure, recreation and work* (pp. 87-96). New York: Cognizant Communication.

Henley, J. (1993, September 10). Stolen bodies. *The Guardian* (London).

Hershatter, G. (1997). *Dangerous pleasures: Prostitution and modernity in twenti-eth-century Shanghai.* Berkeley, CA: University of California Press.

Hicks, G. (1997). *The comfort women.* New York: Norton.

Holden, T. & Tsuruki, T. (2003). *Deai-kei:* Japan's new culture of encounter. In N. Gottlieb & M. McLelland (Eds.), *Japanese cybercultures* (pp. 39-49). London: Routledge.

Humphreys, L. (1975). *Tearoom trade.* Chicago IL: Aldine.

Independent, The. (2003, December 13). Trial of 14 Chinese over huge orgy fuels anti-Japanese sentiment. *The Independent* (London, UK), Foreign ed, p. 15.

Ingham, R. (1991, September 7). Germany acts on sex tourism. *The Independent.*

Jackson, P. A. (1997). Kathoey><Gay><Man: The historical emergence of gay male identity in Thailand. In L. Manderson & M. Jolly (Eds.), *Sites of desire, economies of pleasure: Sexualities in Asia and the Pacific* (pp. 166-190). Chicago: University of Chicago Press.

Jackson, P. A. (2003). Gay capitals in global gay history: Cities, local markets, and the origins of Bangkok's same-sex cultures. In R. Bishop, J. Phillips & W. Yeo, (Eds.), *Post-colonial urbanism: Southeast Asian cities and global processes* (pp. 151-163). New York: Routledge.

Jeffreys, E. (2004). *China, sex and prostitution.* London: Routledge.

Kempadoo, K. (2002). Introduction: Globalizing sex workers' rights. In K. Kempadoo & J. Doezema (Eds.), *Global sex workers: Rights, resistance, and redefinition* (pp. 1-28). New York: Routledge.

Law, L. (1997). A matter of "choice": Discourses on prostitution in the Philippines. In L. Manderson & M. Jolly (Eds.), *Sites of desire, economies of pleasure: Sexualities in Asia and the Pacific* (pp. 232-261). Chicago IL: University of Chicago Press.

Law, L. (2000). *Sex work in Southeast Asia: The place of desire in a time of AIDS.* London: Routledge.

Lerner, G. (1986). The origin of prostitution in ancient Mesopotamia. *Signs, 11*(2), 236-254.

Leupp, G. (1995). *Male colors: The construction of homosexuality in Tokugawa Japan.* Berkeley CA: University of California Press.

Lewis, J. (2000). Controlling lap dancing: Law, morality, and sex work. In R. Weizer, (Ed.), *Sex for sale: Prostitution, pornography and the sex industry* (pp. 203-216). New York: Routledge.

Lie, J. (1995). The transformation of sexual work in 20th-century Korea. *Gender and Society, 9*, 310-327.

Liepe-Levinson, K. (1998). Striptease: Desire, mimetic jeopardy, and performing spectators. *The Drama Review, 42*(2), 9-37.

Lintner, B. (2002). *Blood brothers: Crime, business, and politics in Asia.* Chiang Mai, Thailand: Silkworm Books.

Longstreet, S. & Longstreet, E. (1970). *Yoshiwara: The pleasure quarters of old Tokyo.* Tokyo: Tuttle.

Mackay, N. (2006, March 5). Leader of the gang: Gary Glitter's not the first western paedophile to prowl Southeast Asia. It's just that he got caught. *The Sunday Herald*, p. 37.

Manderson, L. (1992). Public sex performances in Patpong and explorations of the edges of imagination. *Journal of Sex Research, 29*(4), 451-475.

Manderson, L. (1997). "Parables of imperialism and fantasies of the exotic: Western representations of Thailand—place and sex. In L. Manderson & M. Jolly (Eds.), *Sites of desire, economies of pleasure: Sexualities in Asia and the Pacific* (pp. 123-144). Chicago IL: University of Chicago Press.

Manderson, L. & Jolly, M. (Eds.) (1997). *Sites of desire, economies of pleasure: Sexualities in Asia and the Pacific.* Chicago IL: University of Chicago Press.

Marsh, D. (2006, May 5). Vietnam wakes up to child-sex trade. *South China Morning Post*, p. 8.

Matsui, Y. & Sharnoff, L. (1977). Sexual slavery in Korea. *Frontiers: A Journal of Women Studies, 2*(1), 22-30.

McClelland, M. (2003). Private acts/public spaces: Cruising for gay sex on the Japanese Internet. In N. Gottlieb & M. McLelland (Eds.), *Japanese cybercultures* (pp. 141-155). London: Routledge.

Merkle, E.R. & Richardson, R.A. (2000). Digital dating and virtual relating: Conceptualizing computer mediated romantic relationships. *Family Relations, 49*(2), 187-192.

Moon, K. H. S. (1997). *Sex among allies: Military prostitution in U.S.-Korea relations.* New York: Columbia University Press.

Moon, K.H.S. (1999). "South Korean movements against militarized sexual labor. *Asian Survey, 29*(2), 310-327.

Moselina, L. (1979). Rest & recreation: The U.S. naval base at Subic Bay. *Tourism and Prostitution* (pp. 17-20). Geneva: ISIS (International Bulletin 13).

Noh, E. (1997) "Amazing grace, come sit on my face," or Christian ecumenical representations of the Asian sex tour industry. *Positions, 5*(2).

Philippine Women's Research Collective. (1985). *Filipinas for sale: An alternative Philippine report on women and tourism*. Quezon City: Philippine Women's Research Collective.

Poole, T. (1991, October 15). Tourists who exploit women and children. *The Independent*, Living, p. 16.

Rosner, B. W. (1998). Temple prostitution in 1 Corinthians 6:12-20. *Novum Testamentum, 40*(4), 336-351.

Ryan, C. & Hall, C. M. (2001). *Sex tourism: Marginal people and liminalities*. London: Routledge.

Sanders, D. (2002). "Some say Thailand is a gay paradise. In S. Clift, M. Luongo, & C. Callister (Eds.), *Gay tourism: Culture, identity and sex* (pp. 42-62). London. Continuum.

Seabrook, J. (2000). *No hiding place: Child sex tourism and the role of extraterritorial legislation*. London: Zed Books.

Seidensticker, E. (1983). *Low city, high city: Tokyo from Edo to the earthquake*. New York: Knopf.

Seidensticker, E. (1990). *Tokyo rising: The city since the great earthquake*. New York: Knopf.

Seigle, C. S. (1993). *Yoshiwara: The glittering world of the Japanese courtesan*. Honlulu: University of Hawaii Press.

Shelley, L. (2005). "Russian and Chinese trafficking: A comparative perspective. In S. Stoecker & L. Shelley (Eds.), *Human traffic and transnational crime: Eurasian and American Perspectives*. Lanham, MD: Rowman & Littlefield.

Skeggs, P. (1992, November 11). Call for law on tourist sex. *Herald Sun*.

Soh, C. S. (1996). The Korean "comfort women" movement for redress. *Asian Survey, 36*(12), 1226-1240.

Sunday Times. (2002, November 24). Pedophiles may lose passport. *Sunday Times* (London), p. 30.

Thomas, P. (1997). *Recreational sex: An insider's look at the swinging lifestyle*. Peppermint Publishers.

The Times. (1999, November 15). Havana is haven for sex tourists and paedophiles. *The Times* (London).

Toorn, K. van der. (1989). Female prostitution in payment of vows in Ancient Israel. *Journal of Biblical Literature, 108*(2), 193-205.

Truong, T.-D. (1990). *Sex, money and morality: Prostitution and tourism in Southeast Asia*. London: Zed Books.

Watanabe, K. (1995). Trafficking in women's bodies then and now: The issue of military "comfort women." *Peace and Change, 20*(4), 501-514.

Wonders, N. A. & Michalowski, R. (2001). Bodies, borders, and sex tourism in a globalized world: A tale of two cities—Amsterdam and Havana. *Social Problems, 48*(4), 545-71.

Yamazaki, T. (1999). *Sandakan Brothel No.8: An episode in the history of lower-class Japanese women.* Armonk, NY: M.A. Sharpe.

# Endnotes

[1]   ECPAT describes itself as "a global network dedicated to ending the commercial sexual exploitation of children." In 1996, its original name, "End Child Prostitution in Asian Tourism," was changed to "End Child Prostitution, Child Pornography, and Trafficking in Children for Sexual Purposes" (http://www.ecpat.net/eng/ecpat_inter/projects/sex_tourism/sex_tourism.asp, accessed 7/706).

[2]   For a sample of press coverage at the time, see for example, "Sex scandal prompts anti-Japanese sentiments in China,"ANSA English Media Service , Monday , September 29, 2003; "Trial of 14 Chinese over huge orgy fuels anti-Japanese sentiment," Independent (London, UK) , foreign ed , p. 15, Saturday, December 13, 2003; "Japanese "orgy" claim sparks outrage in China," The Guardian - Final Edition, September 29, 2003.

[3]   Wikipedia defines "moral panic" as "a mass movement based on the false or exaggerated perception that some cultural behavior or group of people, frequently a minority group or a subculture, is dangerously deviant and poses a menace to society" (http://en.wikipedia.org/wiki/Moral_panic).

[4]   Many ECPAT publications can be accessed from the ECPAT site, http://www.ecpat.net/eng/index.asp.

[5]   "French MPs back sex tourism curb," *The Guardian*, December 11, 1993.

[6]   "Police go on-line to net cybergangs," *The Express*, January 5, 2000; "Police target Internet merchants of porn," *Express on Sunday*, January 9, 2000.

[7]   "Havana is haven for sex tourists and paedophiles," *The Times* (London), November 15, 1999.

[8]   "Paedophiles may lose passport," *Sunday Times* (London) November 24, 2002, p. 30; "New ban to stop perverts going abroad for child sex," *Birmingham Post*. April 16, 2003, p. 9.

[9]   For typical examples see http://www.intimateassociates.com/swingers/about_us.php (Intimate Associates), and http://www.theila.org/publicpages/links.shtml (International Lifestyle Association) for the U.S., or http://www.swing-

ingheaven.co.uk/ (Swinging Heaven) for the UK. Currently, the most popular adult sites in the U.S., ranking 31 (34 in the UK), is AdultFriendFinder.com.

10   These sites are too numerous to mention individually, but a selection can be accessed through portal sites such as Gay Crawler, http://www.gaycrawler.com/.

11   Gay tourism already has its own Wikipedia site (http://en.wikipedia.org/wiki/Gay_tourism) which includes information on major tourist destinations and a selection of links, including the International Gay and Lesbian Tourist Association, http://www.traveliglta.com/.

12   See for example http://www.4swinging.com/DEFAULT.htm.

13   For typical comments for UK clubs, see http://www.swingingheaven.co.uk/clubs/index.html.

# Section III

# Case Studies

Chapter XII

# Digital Imaging Trek:
## A Practical Model for Managing the Demand of the Digitally Enabled Traveller

Stephen C. Andrade, Johnson & Wales University, USA

Hilary Mason, Johnson & Wales University, USA

## Abstract

*This chapter introduces the concept and activities of the digitally enabled tourist and the impact such as tourist has on the travel and tourism industry. It summarizes the existing and emerging technical environments that encourage the use of hand held digital recording devices and personal Internet communications. Additionally, it looks at ways tourists publish and exhibit digital visual and written artifacts of their travel experience. The chapter introduces general types of digital communication infrastructure to be considered by the industry to create an experience to support this type of tourism. The authors hope that further understanding of the digitally enabled tourist will inform travel professionals to better facilitate commerce and practice in the industry.*

# Introduction

Technology has had a great influence on the tourism and travel industry. In recent years digital communication platforms and technologies have evolved and become accessible to a wide mainstream audience of tourists and travelers. Organizations engaging in travel and tourism commerce need to understand this wave of innovative behavior among their customers. From cell phones to high speed wireless Internet connection to the variety of creative ways customers have applied digital technologies—the travel and tourism industry is being widely affected by these emerging trends in information and communications technologies (ICT). Is the digitally enabled traveler the wave of the future? How will companies and services shift business models to optimize the experience of people with digital devices? Are there commercial opportunities embedded in these? What does a traveler need to know to keep current with changing technologies? It is critical that services providers and travelers alike stay informed, because one thing is certain, technological innovation and change will be a constant companion for the travel and tourism industry.

This chapter provides insight into technology trends that will be helpful to the practitioner, student, educator and the tourist-travelers themselves. Being prepared to meet the new demands of customers will provide rewarding experiences for parties on all sides of the tourism equation.

# Background

Since the wide spread use of the telephone in the 1920s, information and communications technologies (ICT) have had a great influence on the industry of tourism. In the 1990s, the wide spread use of powerful desktop computers, enterprise wide systems, and the World Wide Web (WWW) continued to transform the way business was conducted in all facets of the travel and tourism. While ICTs have had a dramatic impact on the mechanics of tourism business practices, the virtual explosion of new inexpensive digital communication technologies is transforming the experience of tourism from the traveler's point of view.

The new generation of hand held mobile technologies, the expansion of wireless (WiFi) networks and the surge in digitally hosted social interchange services present new opportunities for engaging all sectors of the tourism industry. This new generation of technologies also presents new challenges to the industry to structure services with the digital service users in mind.

New services that provide online collaborative and social interaction through the World Wide Web now shape and influence vast communities of millions of online customers. Traveler-centered mobile technologies are increasingly used for many activities embedded in the tourist and traveler experience. This chapter will explore the model of the digital imaging trek and the digitally enabled traveler as a way to structure experiences to satisfy the demand of the technically savvy traveler in a world of advancing mobile technologies and online services. It also will provide basic technical background about the devices and infrastructure that drives these technological innovations.

Understanding the use of advanced hand held devices from the traveler's point of view is becoming more critical to tourism industry providers. Both new and veteran professionals in the tourism industry need to think about how these technologies influence the customers' choices, activities and ultimately their economic decisions about tourism. Customers have eagerly adopted the cheap and easy to use digital technologies. Tourism professionals need to understand the role mobile digital technologies play in the expanding global tourism field. For customers, mobile digital technologies are helping to shape the experience of tourism from initial research of a destination, through the reservation process to the final visual record of the experience.

Mobile digital technologies include a wide array of products that are inexpensive and easy to use. When mobile digital technologies are used to shape a tourist's experience they become powerful digital communication tools reaching out to an infinite audience of like-minded users on the World Wide Web. New products in cellular telephony, visual still imaging, motion and sound recording, wireless digital connections to the World Wide Web and the services on the World Wide Web, all converge to offer a digital environment unlike any before it. The combinations of these technologies are dynamic, unique and ever expanding. These digital technologies are in a constant state of enhancement—services become faster, devices become more powerful and feature-rich, and prices come down. This evolution of technology is known as "Moore's Law" (see Figure 1). Just what is Moore's Law and why is it important?

*Moore's Law is the observation made in 1965 by Gordon Moore, co-founder of Intel. In it he states that the number of transistors per square inch on integrated circuits had doubled every year since the integrated circuit was invented. Moore predicted that this trend would continue for the foreseeable future. In subsequent years, the pace slowed down a bit, but data density has doubled approximately every 18 months, and this is the current definition of Moore's Law, which Moore himself has blessed. Most experts, including Moore himself, expect Moore's Law to hold for at least another two decades.* (http://www.webopedia.com)

Consider what it means to double the capacity of digital technologies every 12-18 months. Few if any physical systems or resources in the world of tourism have this capacity and potential. Moore's Law not only means faster and better technology,

*Figure 1. Moore's Law*

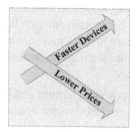

Moore's Law predicts: Computer chip devices get faster as prices come down over time.

it also enables dynamic changes in the way people use technology. In fact, it is difficult to predict exactly how consumers will respond to innovative devices and new digital gadgets. Tourism professionals need to understand this dynamic process and prepare for the digitally enabled traveler.

## Who is the Digitally Enabled Traveler?

The digitally enabled traveler is a new breed of traveler equipped with devices, connectivity, skill and motivation to create and access real-time, online, rich media knowledge bases of travel and tourism experience.

The digitally enabled traveler is motivated by the same principles as the conventional tourist. People involved in tourism are visiting locations for leisure, recreation, sight seeing, vacation and other activities. The global travel industry hosts not only tourists, but professional travelers on professional missions as well. People travel for business, cultural, scientific, educational, governmental and other kinds of activities in the world of global tourism. Most forecasts for travel of all types indicate a steady rise of 4% a year over the next decade. Even a causal observation in any busy transportation hub, such as an airport or train station will reveal how critical mobile technologies and wireless connections are to both the recreational and professional traveler alike.

People who travel with digital devices are highly motivated to stay connected to business and social networks. Minimally, most travelers today require basic voice and Internet connectivity service to maintain contact with families and tourism providers. Travelers want to stay in touch with the sources of lodging, travel bookings, reservations and other critical contacts during their trip. Some travelers thrive on constant digital connection to not only monitor progress in plans, but also stay in touch with their virtual communities.

Beyond the basic business function and family contact, travelers are using a wide array of digital devices to capture, record, edit, and exhibit the experience of tourism and travel. The days of a single film camera used in a casual manner to take pictures of highlights are over. As the tourism industry embraces near-endless global locations for travel destinations, travelers are highly motivated to capture and share their experience with digital recording and connection devices. Why? In spite of all the technical gadgetry, it is still human nature to want to discover and share a new experience. This mode of communication has been going on for generations, only now, it is played out on a global digital stage.

Digital still and video cameras along with powerful laptops and hand held devices have opened new territory for the digitally enabled traveler. These new digital technologies also offer new service-business opportunities for the tourism industry.

Today's digitally enabled traveler is highly motivated to stay in-touch with a virtual community of people through services on the Internet. With millions of people subscribing to World Wide Web sites that host virtual communities the trend of communicating in digital interactive space has been set. Social networking through digital services is widely accepted as common practice. This segment of the technology service industry is rapidly growing as the each successive generation matures into an economic demographic that can afford the expense of travel and tourism. Millions of people are now involved in what is called "social networking." As counter intuitive as it may seem, the way to establish human bonds is through digital technologies. Numerous Web sites have been established as sources for self-published digital image galleries, digital video galleries, audio files, user profiles, and blogs.

## Social Networking: The Latest Trend

Social networking systems are an emerging technology that is beginning to have a significant influence on how people communicate. Social networking systems are Web sites that offer a collaborative or shared virtual experience, generally around a particular theme or human interest. Visitors to the site can connect with each other through shared attributes, such as interests, activities, or geographic location.

Some social networking sites, such as Facebook (http://www.facebook.com), are designed simply to facilitate the process of making social connections. Other sites, such as Delicious (http://del.icio.us), offer a core application, such as allowing users to share Web site bookmarks. An essential quality of a social networking site is that it must allow users to share information via a network of nodes (users) and connections (users with similarities). Users also can easily identify other users with similar interests.

Most social network sites utilize the community to develop an ontology via tagging. Tagging is a simple method of allowing users to attach key words to a piece of data. Users searching for those keywords can then locate a wide variety of matching media. This works on the assumption that humans will generally choose similar terms to describe similar items. Most of the time, the assumptions works well, and people network with other people's experiences.

*Figure 2. Sample tag cloud*

Tags are often represented in a "tag cloud" (see Figure 2). Larger text indicates a more popular tag. Other visualizations include history, topics, and information origin. This visual model of popularity makes these sites friendly to even the most non-technical visitors.

Social networking sites are beginning to have a large impact in business. Consider the common professional activity of attending industry-specific conferences. Attendees meet for seminars, meals, and networking. Several attendees may take photos of this event. They can upload their photos to a photo networking site such as Flickr (http://www.flickr.com), and tag them with the name of the conference. Anyone searching for the conference would be able to find a complete photographic record of the event.

Social networking has even made an impact in tourism. "Where Are You Now?" (http://www.wayn.com) is a site that connects travelers, for logging trips and comparing destinations, finding travel buddies, and making friends with like-minded people. WAYN even helps with off-line networking by allowing users to send SMS (short text messages) to each other's cell phones.

Social networking presents an innovative solution to the problem of information overload. By organizing information collaboratively, useful content filters toward the people who would most like it, while useless content is dropped altogether. Finally, it is a core technology with implications that will touch all disciplines in the years to come.

A blog, or "Web log" for short, is a collection of posts around a theme or topic collected on a Web site. At the time of this writing, blog search firm Technorati (http://www. technorati.com/) was tracking 25.4 million blogs with 1.9 billion links.

A blog is a collection of time-stamped journal entries on any possible topic. Blogs cover every subject from politics to education to technology to one particular person's social life. Some blogs are only of interest to a few people while others have thousands of readers daily.

The Pew Internet Survey estimates that about 11%, or 50 million people, read blogs. (http://www.pewInternet.org/PPF/r/113/report_display.asp). Eighty percent of people contacted by the Business Blog Consulting Web site, a site focused on the growing use of blogs in business, believe that blogs are not a fad. Traditional media outlets (such as the BBC) have begun to add blogs to their media offerings.

The digitally enabled traveler is motivated to share experience in an immediate, visual and highly subjective manner. For a digitally enabled traveler, the personal reaction to a destination like a museum, a historic site, or a travel adventure is typically recorded as a highly personalized written blog. The digitally enabled traveler will supplement the blog with a gallery of digital images. The gallery will then be linked to a short video, compressed for Web hosting, of the activity at the site. With a reasonably fast wireless Internet connection or access to a local Internet café, this material can be posted within minutes of the experience, or in some cases, in near real time. Digitally enabled travelers with the proper digital gear and Internet connection can produce a personalized digital stream of video, images and words. Often defined as "rich" media, the mix of all these files—sound, still, motion, text—are a critical and creative connection to a virtual world for the digitally enabled traveler. For the digitally enabled traveler, contact with the social network on the Web is critical. This technical and artistic practice is easy to achieve and among the members of the digital generation, a routine and necessary activity.

Table 1 offers a way to understand the devices, practices, skills, and motivations of a digitally enabled traveler.

*Table 1. Understanding the devices, practices, skills, and motivations of the digitally enabled traveler*

| Device | Connectivity | Skill | Motivation |
|---|---|---|---|
| Cellular phone with low resolution camera function | Commercial wireless network, satellite connection in remote areas<br><br>Multifunction chips available for international functionality<br><br>Limited WWW access if available | Easy to use, entry level skill | • Basic voice communications; real time voice conversations with social and business network; voice mail.<br>• Basic e-mail if function available<br>• Basic organizational information: names, addresses, telephone, fax<br>• Basic low resolution images, very limited storage<br>• Limited to real time voice based research and basic business functions such as reservations, bookings, and so on<br>• Limited keyboarding if necessary |

*Table 1. continued*

| Hand held multifunction PDA- personal digital assistant | Commercial wireless network, satellite connection in remote areas<br><br>Multifunction chips available for international functionality<br><br>Limited WWW access if available | Entry to moderate level, requires some experience | • Voice function if feature available on device<br>• E-mail<br>• Moderate organization of rich information itinerary, dates, addresses, images, URLs, and so on<br>• Low resolution imaging if available, limited storage<br>• Wireless connectivity to basic navigating on WWW<br>• Basic keyboarding for research and booking business functions such as reservations, bookings, and so on |
| --- | --- | --- | --- |
| Battery power laptop with wireless connectivity | Commercial or free wireless, Internet café, locally provided high speed network connection<br><br>Satellite connection in remote areas<br><br>Wireless chip functional in international standards<br><br>Access to rich sources of information on WWW | Moderate to advanced, able to detect wireless signal; may require some basic problem-solving<br><br>Powerful image editing software applications | • Voice over IP if function available<br>• E-mail, online social networking, post digital images and video<br>• Advanced organization of rich information on device's data sources<br>• Edits and stores high resolution still images and digital video with sound<br>• Likely to use laptop for extensive research and business functions such as reservations, bookings, and so on<br>• Uses laptop as critical extension of travel experience; connectivity to online, social network a priority |
| Digital still camera | Direct connect to laptop or other device with Firewire.<br><br>Interconnect to Web through computer device | Easy to expert level skill | • Record images<br>• Record technical file type and related information<br>• Field edit<br>• Organize image files<br>• May be critical to business communications<br>• Critical to social network and social communications |
| Digital video camera | Direct connect to laptop or other devices with Firewire | Easy to expert level skill | • Record motion and sound<br>• Record technical file type and related information<br>• Field edit: shoot to edit<br>• May be critical to business communications<br>• Critical to social network and social communications |

*Table 1. continued*

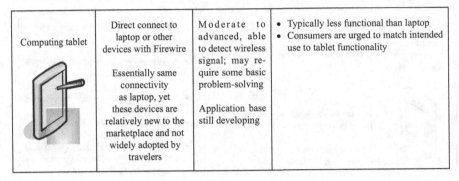

| Computing tablet | Direct connect to laptop or other devices with Firewire<br><br>Essentially same connectivity as laptop, yet these devices are relatively new to the marketplace and not widely adopted by travelers | Moderate to advanced, able to detect wireless signal; may re-quire some basic problem-solving<br><br>Application base still developing | • Typically less functional than laptop<br>• Consumers are urged to match intended use to tablet functionality |
|---|---|---|---|

Professionals in travel and tourism should understand that the focus of these technologies is the individual consumer, not necessarily the business enterprise.

## Digital Imaging Trek: A Model for the Tourism Industry

The digitally enabled traveler is equipped with an endless array of digital products designed to capture and record the tourism experience. Through these devices travelers are highly motivated to stay connected to virtual communities online. Patrons of tourism will use their technology skills to create visual and rich media collateral—high quality digital media artifacts. There are countless Web-based outlets to connect the traveler's experience and collateral to an eager virtual community and social interaction network. As digitally enabled tourism becomes an expectation among patrons and customers, tourism professionals need to understand and shape usage models.

The model of the digital imaging trek proposes information and technical architectures to capture travel experience, create a virtual record of tourism, and meet the demands of the digitally enabled traveler.

From early times of travel, the notion of a "trek" has long been regarded as a journey of self-exploration for the traveler. Many tourists and travelers today are seeking a heightened experience as part of their tourism through digital communication technologies. Putting practice in to models, especially the practice of the digital imaging trek, is a way to understand the processes and practices of the digitally enabled traveler (See Figure 3). Using all the digital tools available, a digital trekker will produce files from a wide range of sources and self-publish material in two methods; saved as CD-based files (or some other permanent memory such as DVD or portable USB Flash Memory) or published on the World Wide Web.

*Figure 3. The general digital imaging trek model embraces technology communication devices and self publishing*

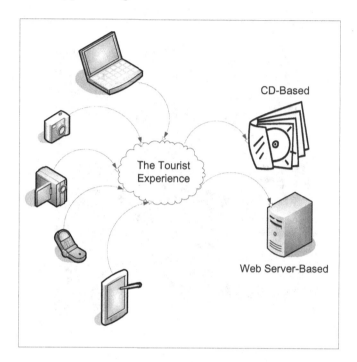

A typical day on digital imaging trek starts with a destination selection. Digitally enabled travelers will turn to the Internet to locate and decide upon a location. Whether it is a museum, a regional historic location or a cultural performance, the digitally enabled traveler will seek all types of information from Web site based services to make plans. When made available on a Web based system, transportation schedules, phone numbers, hours of operations, special information about exhibits, costs, and other related information about the region, are always instantly available to the traveler. Web based systems allow the digitally enabled traveler to acquire information regardless of time and in a preferred language.

in digital imaging trek model, the traveler is focused on acquisition of digital still and video images that record the daily experience of the trip. In any environment—built or natural—the visitor will always encounter new scenes that are novel, exciting, and educational and from the perspective of the traveler, representative of the tourism experience. With cheap recording memory in the form of Flash Memory, a digitally enabled traveler has near infinite storage space to capture images. Digitally enabled travelers also can edit on the fly. The advantage of digital imaging over

*Figure 4. Students and faculty from Johnson & Wales University on a digital imaging trek to Paris; wireless digital connection to the Internet is abundant in urban environments; checking e-mail and editing images in a street side café is now a common tourist experience*

traditional film imaging is in the use of storage and field editing. If an image is not worth keeping, it can be immediately erased. Images worth keeping are filed and stored until needed later.

As the day progresses on the digital imaging trek, travelers will want to spend time reviewing images, editing images, and corresponding to the social network with e-mail, uploads and blogs. Editing and organizing images are tasks that most travelers will conduct when time is available. Typically image editing is done on a portable laptop computer. Many people prefer to travel with laptop computers as they are light weight, highly functional, and a repository of software tools and information necessary to conduct digital imaging while traveling. (For the business traveler, a laptop is practically required gear for the trip.) Editing image files requires some time and concentration and will like occur during a break in activities. When editing still images with a popular image editing software such as Adobe Photoshop, travelers will crop, color-correct, merge and manipulate images.

Similarly, digital video footage also will be edited. Travelers on a digital imaging trek will likely download and edit video footage with commonly available video editing software such as Adobe Premiere or Apple's iMovie and Final Cut Pro. Still image editing software and video editing software is widely available. With basic skill and proficiency, digital travelers can achieve remarkably high quality results. For travelers on a digital imaging trek, it is the primary focus of experience and a rewarding achievement to acquire these images.

The ease of use of digital imaging equipment—still cameras, video cameras and laptops, promotes the phenomena of "hyper-imaging"—taking thousands of images to sort through later. Travelers who are serious about digital imaging are continuously shooting images throughout the day and night. The result of hyper-imaging is an overabundance of images and footage that must be sorted and organized. Powerful laptop computers with optimized internal and external storage are prefect for this task. Sorting and organizing images and footage is typically done to suit the desires of the traveler on a digital imaging trek. Images are categorized by group or class and notated with keywords for access at a later time. Various gallery and filing software makes the task of organizing relatively easy.

## A Short Primer on Digital Photography

Unlike film cameras, which store images on film, digital cameras capture images via electric sensors and store those images on reusable solid-state memory.

*Figure 5. Digital cameras are popular among travelers and tourists; they are portable, easy to use, and affordable*

The first digital cameras targeted toward consumers were released in the early 1990s. Since then the digital camera revolution has taken off, and there are hundreds of models available. Competition has remained fierce and manufacturers are producing digital cameras with limitless capacity. Just 15 years after the introduction of the first consumer digital cameras, current models are take pictures that are as high or higher quality than film cameras. Digital cameras take some getting used to, but tourists and travelers who taking digital imaging seriously will find numerous camera choices in the marketplace.

Digital cameras fall into three general categories: consumer, prosumer, and professional. Consumer cameras generally have a single, non-removable lens that mimics a standard 35mm film lens. However, manufacturers now produce consumer level models with nearly every feature of a traditional Single-Lens Reflex or SLR camera.

The term prosumer is a blend of "professional" and "consumer" and refers to consumers who demand more than the standard technology available while being unable to afford professional equipment. In the digital camera market, the prosumer devices are Single-Lens Reflex, or SLR, models, and are falling below the $1000 price point. Prosumers tend to be technologically savvy and more tolerant of quirks and bugs in new products.

Many professional photographers are moving entirely to digital photography, enticed by the low cost of shots, ease of printing, high resolutions, and ability to edit photos easily with software such as Adobe Photoshop. Professional cameras generally accept the same standard lenses as film cameras and store photos in RAW format, which allows for greater flexibility in editing. The RAW format can be thought of as a digital negative.

The editing and sorting activity is often a precursor activity to the act of e-mail, blogging and posting images on a Web site to interact with digitally connected social network. Travelers with a laptop and access to the Internet will use the online connection to communicate frequently and for sustained periods of time—sometimes hours at a time. If connectivity is available from a wireless service, the traveler with a laptop will connect, log in to services, and communicate on a frequent basis throughout the day. If the Internet connection is more concentrated, in an Internet café with computers for instance, the traveler will dedicate a portion of the day to connect and communicate online. It is not unusual to see Internet cafés through Europe and Asia, but the model is less attractive in the U.S. Internet connection services should allow the traveler to connect and spend as much time as necessary to conduct the typical activities as blogging, image posting, e-mail, checking itinerary, and so on. As the day winds down on the digital imaging trek, the digitally enabled traveler has acquired a new database of images, published and shared select image-files, and communicated stories of their experience with their social network online through e-mail and blogs.

*Figure 6. Digital imaging trek file types, platforms, and purpose*

| File Type | Hardware Platform | Software Platform | Purpose |
|---|---|---|---|
| Text file | Laptop, desktop, or handheld device with keyboard. Privately owned, or available through Internet cafe | Word processor-editor software | Written log of experience. Creating and sending attachments on e-mail. Creating and posting blog on Web services |
| Still image | Digital still camera Cell phone with still camera function Multifunction still and video camera | Embedded software in camera platform. Image editing with additional software on laptop or other device | Create a visual record of still images of travel experience. Sort and publish on Web server to share with social network. Send as attachments in e-mail. |
| Motion images | Digital video camera Cell phone with motion camera function Multifunction still and video camera | Embedded software in camera platform. Editing with additional software on laptop or other device | Create a visual record of motion images and sound. Edit and publishing on Web site to share with social network. Send attachments. |
| Hyperlink | Web based hosting services – social networks | Embedded feature on Web site | Allows author to 'link' from one type of information to another. Series of links create trails for others to follow. |

Taking pictures on a vacation is not new to the world of tourism, but digital equipment has changed the business and behavior equation. Given the proper technical infrastructure, images can be acquired and posted—essentially published—to a world-wide audience in a matter of minutes.

Digital photos are easy to share. Most photos are already stored on a computer or memory card, and it is a simple matter to upload them to the Internet, either through a private gallery (such as the digitaltrek.org site), or a social photography Web site such as Flickr (www.flickr.com).

Most thriving urban centers and developed destination resort complexes have a mature ICT infrastructure to support instant access to the Internet. Even smaller rural locations now boast access to the greater world of the Internet. The goal of a traveler on a digital imaging trek is to capture and publish images that reflect travel experience in new places and foreign cultures.

## Tourism and Information Architecture

It is critical that both traveler and tourism enterprise alike prepare for the use of digital technologies through "architecture." Travelers and organizations need to plan and think ahead of how to respond and conduct activities through the travel and tourism

*Figure 7. The architecture for wireless network and infrastructure model for digitally enabled traveler*

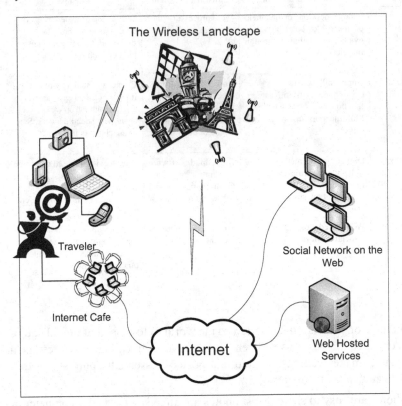

experience. While some things are left to chance or serendipity the deployment of digital infrastructure requires some thought. That plan is called "architecture."

Architecture for information services is similar to that of architecture for buildings—it is the deliberate planning, modeling, and delivery of ICT services. Architecture requires adopting a model of approach and solution, both in systems architecture and information architecture. How does a highly connected, fast speed digital environment that serves the digitally enabled traveler sprout up? It is not a singular act by any tourism organization, but a system wide policy approach of local and national partners in business and governmental bodies. In most cases, experts from companies that provide ICT services will consult on the array of services available in the technology marketplace.

Much of the communications infrastructure that has developed in the past decade is a confluence of commercial profit-driven interest, digital user culture, and regional policy and laws. The combined effect of the built ICT environment serves residents and visitors alike. Localities with new digital infrastructure enjoy digital connection to a broader world. Travelers to areas that are served with high speed digital services also reach out and use the infrastructure for all their related travel communication activities. This ever growing presence of widely accessible digital communication services represents different challenges to different cultures. While most Western cultural sensibilities accept the openness of access to the World Wide Web, other cultures are more circumspect and reserved, wishing to control the vast onslaught of information pouring out of the Web.

Cost has always been considered the primary barrier for entry in the world of ICT. The receding cost barrier—as Moore's Law predicts—has lowered the cost barrier, particularly with technology products and services. Tourist properties such as hotels and resorts now can achieve Internet access as easily as telephone access. In many instances, travel infrastructure such as airports, train stations, and the aircraft and trains themselves, provide Internet and advanced telephone access. Countries and regions are now adopting ICT's and installing a fiber-optic telecommunications system with wide spread wireless digital access points, which has distinct advantages over older, legacy "wire based" telecommunications infrastructures—particularly for the traveler. In some ways, the new fiber and wireless based connectivity infrastructure offers advantages for the digitally enabled traveler.

Of course, this entire ICT infrastructure model represents enormous business opportunity for the properties in which they exist. Hotels, resorts, travel destinations, travel hubs, restaurants, coffee houses, business outlets can differentiate themselves from competitors by providing ICT for a fee to the traveler. Travelers in turn, view access to ICT as a cost associated with travel and plan to spend money to acquire it. It is common for travelers to purchase short term access to ICT services at these sites on terms ranging from a few hours to several days.

When collaboration on planning and development of digital infrastructure occurs, the stage is set to promote services to the digitally enabled traveler. A highly developed infrastructure and usage model promotes rapid creation and publishing of rich media collateral by the digitally enabled traveler. All parts of the technology infrastructure work in unison to support the activities of the traveler.

Digital communication technologies of many platforms have become accessible to even the most inexperienced traveler. Mobile technologies of all types and sizes and wireless network signal have brought the Internet to the most distant of locations. This convergence of technical infrastructure and tourism presents opportunities and challenges to the tourism industry.

Yet even as the cyber-record of digital travel experience explodes, there are many issues the profession must consider. The more available common digital technologies become, the more travelers and tourism enterprises grapple with the complexity (and confusion) of choices including but not limited to privacy, intellectual property, systems integration, systems management, training, best practice, and so on.

# Digitally Enabled Travel: Knowledge Targets for the Novice

As the digitally enabled traveler becomes more of an influence in the world of travel and tourism, young professionals seeking degree based education and career opportunities in the field need to be familiar with basic technology. Whether looking at a college level curriculum or training opportunities for adults wishing to gain new skills, look for some of the topics covered here.

College level curriculum in hospitality, travel, and tourism programs should include an introductory level course in this area of digital technology. The topics taught in such a course do not necessarily have to be technical but young professionals entering the business should know the basics and be prepared to research and understand technology. A sample of college level curriculum might include topics such as the following.

## Foundations in Technology

Many professionals and educators mistakenly think that learners know all there is to know about basic computer operations, productivity software and Internet access, Web searching and surfing. While these topics are often part of many school systems, not everyone has mastered basic skill and techniques in all these areas. Interacting with computer interfaces and mastering the sophistication of some productivity tools such as word processing, spreadsheets, databases and browsers requires instruction, time and practice. Many colleges, universities, technical institutions and similar educational organizations offer courses in computer technology. The popular press is filled with instructional books complete with CD based video for those who are adept at self instruction. Many conferences, training seminars, and "Webinars" (seminars of text, sound, and motion hosted on the Web), offer similar instruction. Regardless of the model one uses to get trained, using digital technologies requires constant "tune ups" to one's skill set. Find the type of education that works for you and take advantage of it.

## Basic Information and Systems Architecture

Information and systems architecture introduces models to help solve problems in the field of technology. As with providing digital services for travels to use to communicate with social networks, technology applications start as a way to provide a solution to a problem.

While it is convenient to say technology will solve a problem or make some situation more efficient or less cumbersome, the idea has to be communicated in a visual model. Professionals in the world of information technology communicate regularly with visual models that reflect the structure or architecture of a system. Devices and the networks that connect them are shown so all can understand and agree on system solutions. Understanding basic architecture in work flow, information flow, and management, networking, service devices, client side devices, and so on will be very valuable for new professionals in the world of hospitality, travel, and tourism.

## Basic Web Design and Interface

Many professionals in the field of hospitality, travel, and tourism will likely be asked to participate in design teams to design and build Web sites that will host information for customers or be used internally as sources of information for the business enterprise. Conceptualizing and building a Web site is a skill that requires practice and experience although of software tools such as Microsoft FrontPage and Adobe (formerly Macromedia) Dreamweaver make it easy to try this activity. With a little training in software features of such applications, college level courses can quickly teach students the essentials in basic Web site design. This is both a technical and creative challenge, but most people quickly see the results of a little effort. For people just wishing to start with a simple Web site to host information about a trip or a destination, these tools are cheap, accessible, and relatively easy to learn.

## Basic Digital Imaging and Image Manipulation

There are an abundance of off-the-shelf software tools in the marketplace that will introduce college student (or anyone with the motivation to learn) skills in digital imaging and image manipulation. While many people have digital cameras a course on digital photography will introduce a wide range of topics from composition to technical specifications. Understanding the wide range of options in today's digital cameras can be helpful for young professionals who need to deal with a customer base that is armed with the latest camera gadgetry. Learning the process involved in capturing an image and uploading an image to a devices that can store the image in important. More knowledge in these areas will help improve customer empathy and ultimately customer satisfaction.

Editing images in software like Adobe Photoshop has a double benefit to a college curriculum. Students with added technical skills such as digital photo editing are in more demand. Many businesses need such skills to help with developing creative collateral to promote the commercial activity of the business. Understanding the creative process from image acquisition to image editing also will help the professional in dealing with agencies that provide that service.  For instance, image editing is a time consuming activity, and in negotiating advertising contracts, such knowledge will be helpful.

## Desktop Publishing

Desktop publishing is a content area that will provide a young professional with the knowledge of how to put assets such as text and images together in print collateral to serve the business. Even in the digital age, many businesses still have a great need for printed products to advertise, inform and attract potential customers. Tourism properties still have a great need for pamphlets, brochures and signage to keep customers informed about policies, regulations, events, calendars, and so on. A course in desktop publishing will give practitioners an opportunity to learn a skill that will help promote and organize business. In desktop publishing, students can learn how to conceive and construct various types of print pieces using software such as Microsoft Publishing or Adobe Indesign.

## Editorial, Content Creation and Content Management

While learning technical tools is vital, helping young professionals identify and manage the message is critical to the success of travel and tourism businesses. Courses that emphasize the basics of how to construct the message in both text and visual design are important for a basic college curriculum.

## Systems and Technology Primer for the Digitally Enabled Traveler

As digital communications platforms and technologies have become adopted by a wide mainstream audience two factors have been critical to widespread use—practicality and ubiquity. Along with the explosion of digital gadgets, contemporary travelers now have high expectations of availability of connectivity and complimentary technologies.

If the tourism industry is to appropriately harness and cater to this new and demanding audience, the industry must build a model of digitally enabled travel that supports both traditional goals of tourism and the new goals of digital media acquisition. Understanding the pieces of the technology puzzle can serve as a starting point.

Several recent world events have highlighted the role mobile technology plays on the world stage. The first images of the London tube bombing in 2005 came from the cell phone cameras of survivors. These images were published by the BBC and forwarded around the world within minutes of the attack. Similarly dramatic images, particularly digital video, were quickly spread after the 2005 tsunami disaster in the Indian Ocean. Whether it is a global or local scale, digital imaging devices are ever present and serve as eyes to the world. Building a world class digital environment brings with it many more challenges, not just in the technical realm, but in the human realm as well.

## A Word on Privacy and Security in the Digital Age

Privacy, security of information, copyright, information ownership, censored, and uncensored material are all issues that become concerns of the industry when technology is introduced. It is a grey area because decorum and respect relies as much on personal behavior as it does on personal technology. Travelers with powerful digital recording tools must understand the local cultural norms, as well as the global broadcast power of the World Wide Web.

Privacy is an important and sensitive issue. Visitors to a Web site may be reluctant to share information—such as their e-mail address—because they fear that their personal information will be sold and they will be subjected to unsolicited advertisements. Spam, the endless barrage of meaningless e-mail advertising, has become an onerous burden to all citizens using online tools. It is best avoided by constricting the use of e-mail addresses.

Information that may be personal or sensitive, such as vacation photos or a travel journal, should be posted with care. In many cultures people do not wish to have their images posted for the world to see. Privacy for individuals is a sensitive matter. Even in public tourism venues, digital photographers are challenged when taking images and asked to refrain. Religious and private properties often post requests to refrain from photography and video recordings.

Institutional Web sites should consider developing a privacy policy, or a legal statement that reflects what the institution may and may not do with information provided by users. The World Wide Web Consortium (the standards body for the Web) has developed the Platform for Privacy Preferences (P3P) (http://www.w3.org/P3P/), a standardized language which provides Web site administrators with a simple and automated way to quickly generate a customized policy for their site. Individual digital travelers, eager to capture a unique image, must apply their own standards. The golden rule though is "do unto others" as you would have done to yourself. Consider the impact of each image that is posted.

Travelers must be aware of their physical safety and security at all times. Broadcasting information on the Web can add to this worry. For example, travelers, especially solo-travelers, are advised against posting a personal and complete itinerary until their trip is complete. No only does it tell the world where you will be, but it also tells the world where you are not. Home safety as well as trip safety is the paramount concern.

*Table 2. Core components of an information technology system*

| Technology | Location | Skill-level | Description |
|---|---|---|---|
| Computer Client | Computing cluster such as an Internet café, business service office, hotel lobby, etc. One or more for use by customers | Basic to advanced software such as e-mail, word processing, file management; basic computer knowledge | The computer client serves as the starting point for the customer. Recreational and business travelers alike will budget time and funds to access basic computing services such as e-mail, word processing, file uploading. |
| Laptop Computers | Anywhere, travelers port and manage | Basic to advanced software such as e-mail, word processing, file management; basic computer knowledge | A laptop computer is a computer client and the traveler's link to the Internet and workstation for writing blogs or editing digital photos. |
| Card Readers | Anywhere | Basic computer knowledge required. | Digital cameras accept different memory cards depending on brand. A generic card reader will allow any computer to read any card from any camera, with no additional software. |
| Portable Storage | Anywhere | Basic computer knowledge required. | Backups are a major issue for travelers concerned about potential data loss (from theft or equipment failure). A portable hard drive (or a device that can burn CD's) provides a cheap and easy backup solution on the road. Small and easily packed. |
| Network-wired | Anywhere | Intermediate to advanced computer knowledge required to build and support. Entry level user knowledge to access and use. | Wired Internet connections are generally located in institutions (such as hotels, business services, universities), and may incur a cost for access. |

*Table 2. continued*

| | | | |
|---|---|---|---|
| Network-wireless | Anywhere | Intermediate to advanced computer knowledge required to build and support. Entry level user knowledge to access and use. | Wireless Internet connections can be found in built environments, particularly popular in urban settings with restaurants, parks, museums, hotels, and cafes. |
| Mass Storage | Any secure building location, typically attached to host devices such as advanced workstations or mainframes. | Intermediate computer knowledge required to configure, install and support. | A mass storage device, is a very large, commercial grade hard drive. It supports data and functions core to large businesses. While computer users may see the results of such devices in a routine Web search, these devices work in the background of daily user activities. |
| Servers | At a hosting company; typically a technology company which provides a secure physical location, as well as technical knowledge to support services. Locations are typically built specifically to house the servers. | Advanced technical skills in Web hosting and server based data services. | The server will host all of the content for a Web site and code for Web applications such as a gallery or blog. Often a class of computers known as workstations; function solely as servers. A hosting service provider will maintain and support all server hardware and software. Computer users access these devices through client computers to update Web sites, post images in galleries and blog. |

With reasonable precautions, a Web site can *increase* safety. It allows a large number of people to check in on the well-being of travelers. While theft and other dangers cannot be eliminated, careful use of a Web site, instant messaging, and e-mail can reassure those back home. The personal technology of a digital enabled traveler is an attractive target for thieves. Common sense should guide the novice and experienced traveler in protecting personal possessions.

# Web Hosting:
## What Travel and Tourism Professionals Need to Know

All Internet applications such as a Web site or a search engine run on a server. The server is a computer workstation in a class of computing machines that is specially constructed to manage the constant demand of service to clients on the network. Servers require special software and in most cases, comparably advanced knowledge and skill to configure and maintain. While it is possible to run a server in-house, it involves purchasing a machine, installing and supporting an operating system and applications, and maintaining an "always-on" Internet connection. Managing a server requires routine management as well as prompt response emergencies, 24 hours a day, 7 days a week. For most travel and tourism providers, becoming a technology company is a distraction from the core business. It is generally advisable that any business requiring a host on a server be outsourced to a Web host business provider.

A Web host is a company that provides space on their Web servers, use of their programs, and a certain amount of bandwidth use for a monthly cost. Often referred to as a "solutions provider" or a "Web hosting service" the hosting company will handle all computer hardware and software issues such as installations, configurations, backups, updates, and any unforeseen maintenance. Of course, solution providers contract these services for a fee, but competition works in this marketplace as it does in any other, and a shopper is wise to research and compare costs and services among a range of businesses.

There are many Web hosting companies and there are many attributes to consider when researching them. Choosing a hosting company is a long-term commitment.

*Table 3. Qualities for evaluating a hosting company*

| Factor | Description |
|---|---|
| Reputation | Every company must market itself on its reputation for service to customers. Ask for reference of other businesses that have used the services. Search for comments on the Web about the company and its performance. Are there any instances of how the company performed in a crisis, such as a virus attack or power failure? Have you toured the facilities or conducted due diligence on the company? |
| Reliability | Does the company publish statistics on technical performance? What level of support and customer service contact is there? Will you be able to contact people in off hours? What kind of technology do they support? Is there a specific platform or hardware and software and do you recognize the vendor? Ask about back-up, power supply, physical security, data security, and so forth. Do they publish their reliability data? Conduct an Internet search through popular search engines to find information about them. |
| Technology | Is the hardware and software platform up to date and current? Can you speak to vendors who supply the company with technology. Do they publish any related information about platforms? |
| People | Making a business agreement is as much about people as it is price structure. Have you met the principals of the company? Are you generally familiar with their organization and business structure? Do you have confidence in the people you have met? Is there generally superior business communication to your proposals? |

Transferring a site from one hosting service to another generally involves several days of unreliability and possible downtime. Carefully consider all of the factors onlined in Table 3 before making a decision.

All of these considerations are important indicators of a successful Web hosting experience. Remember, anyone can run a server, including a college student living in an apartment with a space for a computer on a network. Make sure that you are dealing with a professional company that has a reputation for handling routine business as well as crises. Like the travel and tourism industry, professional protocol in handling technical matters as well as high grades on customer service are key to sound business practice in the technology marketplace.

As with every business, hosting is about people as much as technology. Find a company with knowledgeable employees who are happy to deal with their clients. You should find support personnel who are professional, courteous and eager to answer questions at your knowledge level, no matter how basic or advanced.

Every good host publishes their uptime (the amount of time the service has run without interruptions) and customer testimonials. Don't necessarily trust the quotes on the company's Web site; do an Internet search with any popular search engine (Yahoo, Google, etc.), and find out for yourself.

Once you have identified a few companies that you feel comfortable dealing with, consider the technical requirements of your project. The first decision is about the type of hosting that the project requires. The options are:

- **Dedicated hosting** means that you are leasing an entire computer, which gives you access to the entire hard drive and allows you to make certain configuration requests that are not possible on a shared machine. By leasing a server (rather than purchasing it and placing it in your office), you outsource the need for physical setup, administration and backup services. You also avoid the upfront cost of a powerful machine, and take advantage of your hosting company's ability to quickly purchase and maintain the machine with professional qualified vendors.

- **Shared hosting**, sometimes called managed hosting, means that you are leasing part of a server, which you will share with other customers. This kind of plan generally involves very low monthly fees (as low as $10/month) and provides complete technical support. Unless you are hosting multiple blogs or Web sites, a shared hosting plan is probably sufficient.

Travel and tourism organizations could have a range of needs to contract an outside hosting provider. Setting up a Web page to inform customers of features and offerings of a property or package, or architecting more advanced online services for customers may be among the ideas you will have. The next step in this process of selecting a hosting provider is to explore what you want to do with your hosting provider. The type of service you offer will determine the software applications that the hosting provider will need to run on the server. Additionally, your requirements will guide the features that you'll select for the server. Each software package will list the special requirements on their Web site, but some general guidelines are:

- **Static Web page:** Simple Web pages that hyperlink information that is relatively static. Information does not change too often. Static Web pages require little to no special software or technical support.
- **Downloadable images:** No special requirements, similar to static Web page
- **Image gallery with uploading:** Image galleries containing collections of image (often hundreds and thousands) require server-side programs. Server side programs mean that special software has been loaded and manipulated to provide an easy user interface and experience. A database will be required to track and maintain a medium to large size collection of gallery images.

*Table 4. Criteria for evaluating Web hosting services*

| Feature | What to Look For |
| --- | --- |
| Technical Support | At the very least, 24-hour e-mail technical support. Also consider telephone support (generally, the company promises to address your problem and call you back within 24 hours). |
| Domain | Most hosting plans include one domain registration (for example, www.yournamehere.com) for free. Make sure that the price for a second is reasonable (not more than $20/year). |
| Disk space allocation | Disk space, the space on the hard drive that is allocated to you, should be adequate for your application. Storing Web pages or blogs requires a small amount of space, while storing photographs requires multiple gigabytes. Look for at least 10GB of space. Also, research in advance what it will cost to expand your allocated space. Understand the incremental hikes in cost for more disk space. |
| Server-side program access | The applications that you wish to run will guide your need for server-side program access. In general, look for PHP, which is a coding language that manages how customers see and interact with your services. |
| E-mail addresses | Your plan should offer the ability to create your own me@mydomain.com e-mail addresses. Web-based e-mail access is a nice feature for frequent travelers, and is offered at no additional cost by many hosts. |
| Bandwidth | Bandwidth refers to the total amount of data transfer between your server and visitors to your Web site. More bandwidth is good. Understand that bandwidth to the end user is limited by their personal connection and rate of speed. |
| Statistics | It's always helpful to know exactly how many visitors your site has. Hosting companies typically provide this information with some graphics and analysis. |
| Databases | If you wish to run a dynamic application such as a blog, you'll need access to a database. |
| Operating System | Your operating system choice should be guided by your application requirements. Most hosting plans are based on either Linux (which tends to be cheaper), or Windows. |

- **Blogs:** Blogs, or written text entries also require special server-side software to accepted entries, organize them and display them, blog software, like image galleries is generally database-driven.

Several hosts offer blog-friendly plans that require minimal configuration and no technical skills. Lists of these can be found at http://wordpress.org/hosting/ and http://www.sixapart.com/movabletype/hosting.

Identify your minimum technical requirements. In general, look for the criteria listed in Table 4.

## More Technical Tools of the Digitally Enabled Traveler

Digitally enabled travelers will quickly embrace new and experimental technologies. For them, it is a challenge to figure out ways to adopt a technology and make it work in the daily flow of travel.

For instance, instant messaging, or "IM," is a technology for rapid-fire asynchronous messaging across a network. Instant messages can be thought of "instant e-mail," and are generally used to communicate to a select social network, but often composed on the computer screen while doing something else. Digitally enabled travelers multitask on the computer—that is, they conduct more than one activity at the same time—with ease.

IM was first popularized in the mid-1990s by ICQ, a product introduced by Mirabilis Ltd in 1996. Mirabilis Ltd was later acquired by America Online, which ran a competing product called "AOL Instant Messenger," or AIM. By acquiring ICQ, AOL became the largest operator of instant messaging networks in the world.

Other competitors include Microsoft, which offers an instant messaging feature as part of the Microsoft Network (MSN), and Yahoo!, which offers the feature as part of their community-building options. All of these services are free to use, though some may display advertisements.

Unfortunately, all of these services are based on proprietary protocols and do not interoperate. Therefore, a digital traveler must choose the service that most of the people that they wish to communicate with use. If this is not practical, digital travelers can invest in a product such as Trillian, from Cerulean Studios (http://www.ceruleanstudios.com/), which is an IM program that supports all major networks.

Instant messaging is favored by digital travelers, because it allows instant communication with anyone on the network, no matter where their physically located. If a device (such as a computer or cellular telephone) has Internet access, it can connect to an IM network. This is an extremely low-cost method for travelers to communicate with their social network of friends, family, and colleagues around the world.

More recently, voice over Internet protocol (VoIP) has become an important buzz-word in the latest digital tools becoming available to digital travelers. VoIP is a technology for transmitting traditional "telephone calls" over the Internet. Imagine using a laptop as a phone and conducting routine two-way audible conversations. Such calls are indistinguishable from normal Internet data and promise to make international conversational calls extremely cheap. Imagine no more phone calling cards and the end to frustrated travelers trying to decipher local and international calling codes.

While still in the early stages, VoIP is available to any digital traveler with a laptop, speakers, and a microphone. Services such as Google Talk or Skype (http://www.skype.com/) are up and running and can be used to converse with telephone quality audio for free. Skype also offers "Skype Out," which permits computers to connect with telephone numbers anywhere in the world for extremely reasonable rates.

Needless to say, it is important for travel and tourism organizations to be familiar with trends such as VoIP for two reasons. The early adopters of such technology—the digitally enabled traveler—are the bell weather for change in the industry. It won't take long for entrepreneurial technology providers to create a competitive business model for VoIP and shift the commerce to a new marketplace.

## Convergence and Future Trends

Given the rapid evolution of digital communication tools, both hardware and software based, it is not hard to imagine that many of these products will continue to transform.

The technology industry is creating faster, lighter, devices that better integrate with each other. This trend of "convergence" is one to watch for. It wasn't long ago that a cell phone was simply a way to have voice conversations with other parties. To-day, other features have converged on the platform of a cell phone. Is a cell phone a camera, a video recorder, a video viewer, organizer and personal digital library? The answer is "yes"—it is all those things and more.

A digital camera is no longer a camera; it is an image processing workstation. Images can be acquired, edited, filed, and stored. Images are dynamic files that merge and morph into other applications and devices through infrared proximity connections.

The ubiquitous iPod from Apple computer started off not too long ago as a just another platform for listening to music. Today an entire lucrative industry revolves around providing rich media content for viewing on a tiny screen. Need an exercise multimedia instruction package for keeping fit during travel, it can be purchased and downloaded to your iPod.

# Conclusion

Digital gear to enhance the travel and tourism industry is a constantly evolving marketplace. The future is part evolution and part revolution, from wildly popular devices to culturally challenging information flow. Regardless of the intricacy, allure or popularity of digital devices, the seasoned digitally enabled traveler will always find ways of incorporating new devices and new services to enhance experience and communicate to a social network in digital space. Travel and tourism providers must influence the role of the digital imaging trek by understanding the role they themselves play in this ever changing landscape. Who is the provider, the host, the arbitrator of this new world of digital travel? By seeing and understanding the big digital picture, tourism and travel providers will retain perspective and offer quality services to patrons worldwide.

# Note

- All images are provided with permission to reproduce by the authors.
- Illustrations are public domain license free illustrations from Microsoft Visio.
- Figures representing models are provide with permission to reproduce by the authors.
- Illustrations in models are public domain license free illustrations from Microsoft Visio.

## Chapter XIII

# Feeling Welcome:
## Internet Tourism Marketing Across Cultures

Wolfgang Georg Arlt, University of Applied Sciences, Germany

## Abstract

*If used in a proper way, the Internet can be a powerful cross-cultural incoming tourism communication tool. This chapter examines to what extent the opportunities are utilized which are offered in the virtual sphere to extend across physical and cultural distances a welcoming hand to potential visitors from far-away source markets. The discussion is based on the results of a study about the non-german language Web sites of Central European DMOs, conducted in 2002 and updated in 2006, and the results of a study of German-language Web sites of non-European NTOs and DMOs, conducted in 2005. It can be shown that an increase in multilingual Web sites within the period under review can be recognized, but that an increase in cross-cultural awareness of the providers of such Web sites is still lacking.*

# Introduction

"Tourism destinations are probably one of the most difficult "products" to market, involving large numbers of stakeholders and a brand image over which a destination marketing manager typically has very little control." (Palmer, 2004, p. 128) In the 21st century, both the expectations as well as the actual experiences are informed by all kind of communication received via media beforehand and by interpretation through different kinds of "cultural mediators" (Ooi, 2002), which influence and shape the "tourists gaze" (Urry, 2002), especially in international tourism.

These complex processes are only accessible for the tourism industry in a very limited way, as images are not simply the result of promotions put forward by companies or destinations (Goodall & Ashworth, 1988). The brand image for example of Arab countries for European tourists can be traced back to the Orientalism (Said, 1978) fortified by Flaubert and French painters like Delacroix, Decamps, and Fromentin (Lemaire, 2000). The way these countries are portrayed in the news in a situation of increased fears of terrorism also will influence the image. Peer-group information and the travellers own experiences play an often even more important role here, forming the image according to the descriptions by friends and colleagues who have actually been there and on the background of own former visits to foreign countries.

Nevertheless, some degree of influence of the brand building based on "image" by the responsible destination marketing organization is possible and in fact an important part of the marketing strategy for a given destination (Chon, 1991). This influence is growing with the "otherness" of the destination (Bieger, 2002). The degree of otherness is perceived in the same way as distances are perceived in tourism—not in kilometres, but in accessibility, including accessibility in a cultural and lingual sense. The less well-known, the more exotic a destination is, the greater the chance to influence the image through tourism marketing activities. One important tool for such long-range marketing activities in the 21st century is undoubtedly the Internet.

If used in a proper way, the Internet can be a powerful cross-cultural incoming tourism communication tool. This chapter examines to what extent the opportunities are utilized which are offered in the virtual sphere to extend across physical and cultural distances a welcoming hand to potential visitors from far-away source markets. The discussion is based on the results of a study about the non-german language Web sites of Central European destination marketing organizations (DMOs), conducted in 2002 and updated in 2006, and the results of a study of German-language Web sites of non-European national tourism organizations (NTOs) and DMOs, conducted in 2005. It will be found that an increase in multilingual Web sites within the period under review can be recognized, but that an increase in cross-cultural awareness of the providers of such Web sites is still lacking.

# Tourism and Internet Marketing

Within a single decade, the Internet has developed from an obscure network for scientists into an indispensable daily tool for about 16% of the world population. The number of Internet users, doubling from approximately 500 million in 2001 (Globalreach, 2005), to more than a billion in 2005 (Internet World Statistics, 2006), has surpassed the number of international travels, which grew from 684 million to 808 million border-crossings in the same period (WTO, 2006).

Not counting the 2% of Internet users both in Africa and in Oceania, roughly one third each of the global Internet users are located in the USA, in Asia and in the Europe respectively. In 2000, English was still the mother tongue of 50% of all Internet users. By 2006, the user community can be divided by languages into three almost equal parts, having English, another European or an Asian language as their respective mother tongues. Comparing the situation in 2001 and in 2006, English lost ground dramatically especially to Chinese and to "smaller" languages, documenting the fact that the Internet has outgrown its mainly North American beginnings.

Travel and tourism is one of the major fields of Internet usage. In terms of sales, tourism products like air tickets, hotel rooms and last-minute packages for domestic and short-haul tourism are the most common products sold via the Internet except books. Here the Internet's main function is to act as a booking machine. In 2002 online travel sales reached US$27 billion in the North American and 8 billion €

*Table 1. World Internet users by mother tongue 2001-2006 in % (Sources: September 2001 data: GlobalReach, 2001; November 2004 and March 2006 data: Internet World Statistics, 2006)*

| Language | 2001 | 2004 | 2006 |
|----------|------|------|------|
| English | 43 | 35 | 31 |
| Spanish | 7 | 7 | 8 |
| German | 7 | 7 | 6 |
| Italian | 4 | 4 | 3 |
| French | 3 | 5 | 4 |
| Portuguese | 3 | 3 | 3 |
| Dutch | 2 | 2 | 2 |
| Chinese | 9 | 13 | 13 |
| Japanese | 9 | 8 | 9 |
| Korean | 4 | 4 | 3 |
| Others | 9 | 12 | 18 |
| Total users | 505 million | 801 million | 1022 million |

*Figure 1. World Internet users by mother tongue 2001-2006 in % (Sources: September 2001 data: GlobalReach, 2001; November 2004 and March 2006 data: Internet World Statistics, 2006)*

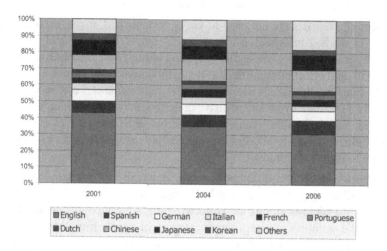

in the European market, capturing 14% and 5% of the total market respectively (Marcussen, 2003). For 2005, the European market expanded to 25 billion € (10%) (Marcussen, 2006). The total value of online travel sales worldwide reached US$49 billion in 2005 and climbed further to US$65 billion in 2005 (eMarketer, 2005), not the least fuelled by no-frill airline ticket sales.

Internet marketing has, as has been recognized by the industry, a number of advantages against other media:

- Reduced costs compared to advertisement and promotional activities
- Easier to update than brochures and pamphlets
- Easier and cheaper to handle compared to telephone hotlines
- 24-hour availability of information (Douglas & Mills, 2004; Mills & Morrison, 2002)

For Incoming tourism, especially for long-haul leisure travel, the dominant usage and the main advantage of Internet Web sites is quite different. Decision-making for travel requires qualified information and confidence, making the Internet first of all an image-building tool, important to help deciding whether to go to a specific new destination, to stay for a shorter or longer period, or to use specific services of a company at the destination. Incoming tourists, especially when not travelling to neighbouring countries, are by necessity less spontaneous. Perceived images will therefore play a more important role in their decision for or against travelling to certain destinations or using certain services, whereas online booking will be less relevant in a situation of unfamiliarity with the destination.

New incoming tourists are not easy to target. Established, major markets can be reached via sending information to known customers, by traditional public relations work, fair attendance, advertisements, and so on. These measures are however costly, time- and effort consuming and typically do not reach minor—or underestimated—markets. Potential visitors from new source markets can be more easily targeted by a dedicated Web site, which can be found by the customer wherever he or she lives. No other medium can beat the Internet as the cheapest, most convenient and most efficient way to address these potential customers in distant countries, belonging to different cultures.

What culture and cultural differences mean, especially for tourism, is a topic of hot debate (Reisinger & Turner, 2003; Trompenaars & Hampden-Turner, 1998). Hofstede (2001) defines culture as "collective programming of the mind which distinguishes the members of one group or category of people from those of another" (p. 9). and, according to Paul A. Herbig, "over 450 definitions of the word culture exist" (Herbig, 1998, p. 11). However, this is not the place to enter the "relevance of culture" debate, as at least the existence of cultural differences is not disputed in the tourism literature.

A differentiation of the classical "guest-host" interrelation scheme (Smith, 1989) should be introduced here. Marion Thiem (1994) developed the thinking tool of four different tourism cultures. Extending the well-known distinction of Goffman (1959) of the front stage and the backstage of a destination, she points out the difference between the daily-life cultures of the travellers home region and the specific culture of travellers away from home, which differs considerably from the daily-life culture in factual behaviour as in self-perception. Similarly the inhabitant of the destination also has a daily-life culture as well as another culture which is the one shown to the tourists purposely, being it as a "genuine fake" (Brown, 1996) or a "mediated authenticity" (Ooi, 2002). The form of this presented culture might also be different for different target markets.

For cross-culture tourism marketing—online as well as offline—this communicated culture has to be adapted to each source market culture accordingly, stressing common points or explaining local culture in terms which relate to the source culture and are therefore easier to understand and probably more sympathetic to the receiver. In international business the seller is expected to adapt to the buyer, this is the "Iron Rule #1" for cross-culture marketing, according to Gesteland (2002, p. 15).

For the cross-culture Internet marketing of destinations and attractions this author proposed in an earlier study an expansion of this "Iron Rule" to three "Golden Rules," namely that the the potential customer/visitor has to be able to:

- **Find the online information**
- **Understand the online information**
- **Feel comfortable about the way it is presented** (Arlt, 2005)

The technical problem of finding has become smaller with the availability of better global search engines. Still a domain address which is neither a .com-address nor a top-level domain of the targeted market (for instance .de, .at., .ch in the case of German-speaking customers) and/or a non-intuitive address like "www.aspureasits-gets.com" or "www.fac.de" will make it harder for the user to locate the Web site. Keywords in the language of the target markets and links from other, local Web sites will enhance the visibility of the Web site.

Understanding starts with language. As stated above, only a third of all Internet users share a common mother tongue, English, even though many Internet users are able to understand English to different degrees. However, information given on a Web site conveys not just the facts, it also shows respect and attention paid to the speakers of other languages—or the lack of it. To make visitors feel welcome, to make them feel that "they thought about me," providing information in the mother tongue of the visitors will make a huge difference in supporting a positive bonding beyond the mere availability of useful facts. According to Forrester Research, Web site visitors stay twice as long on a local language Web site compared to an English Web site (De Palma, 1998). "Even customers who speak English prefer sites that offer their local language as well as local product selections, relevant payment options, and localized versions of customer service" (Torris, 1999). Toru (1998) and Auh (1998) underline the importance of multilingual sites for Japan and Korea. Kralisch and Mandl (2006) point out that even for bilingual speakers of a 'smaller' language "the use of their native tongue can represent an additional service that discriminates a product from others by enhancing its value/perception" (p. 2). This statement is supported by their research which shows clear preferences by users for native language Web sites if given a choice.

Besides the question of the usage of different languages, would-be visitors from afar will in many cases request information that is much too obvious for local users to be mentioned. Few Chinese will need to be informed about the fact that the shops are open seven days a week in China; for a German this might be a useful reminder helping to shape their travel plans. Illustrations and webcams can provide additional useful non-verbal information, providing information like the dressing style of the locals, architectural features, daily life behaviour etc. which will elude the attention of members of the local culture but provide useful insights for viewers with different cultural backgrounds.

To make potential visitors feel comfortable is the most complicated but also most rewarding part of cross-culture internet marketing. To provide the address of a German-speaking dentist for potential German visitors may need a bit of extra research, but to provide this information will put to rest one of the many worries of potential German visitors to an overseas destination and will help to turn anxiety into pleasant anticipation. Colours and symbols have different meanings in different cultures. Web sites overflowing with colours and moving graphic objects may look interesting and cute to some visitors but confusing, kitschy or even offending (Becker, 2002) to others. An Asian Web site which uses colours perceived as "typical Caribbean" will mystify the European Web site visitor. The expected carriers of trustworthy information will vary—they will have to be "authorities" for visitors from more hierarchical orientated societies and peer group members for individualistically moulded visitors.

"You cannot not communicate, especially across cultures," Paul Watzlawick stated 40 years ago (Watzlawick, Beavin, & Jackson, 1967). While such a comment probably overstates the communication problem, destination Web sites that obviously do not care about foreign, especially non-English speaking tourists by not providing useful information, or providing static or outdated pages for them are in danger of sending a signal to such potential visitors that suggests: "You are not welcome here."

## Measuring the Cross-Cultural Service Quality of Tourism Web Sites

Many tourism sites, especially of NTOs and DMOs, cannot use online sales as a measurement, as they typically do generate little or no revenue of their own (Tierney, 2000). Nevertheless, the evaluation of the effectiveness of their Web sites is needed to learn about the relation between cost and effect, to facilitate continuous improvements and to compare the performance of the site with its competitors and industry peers (Morrison, Taylor, & Douglas, 2004).

Studies on Web site evaluation have been conducted for a decade with the emergence of agreed methods for Web site evaluation. Murphy, Forrest, Wotring, and Bryner (1996); Murphy, Forrest, and Wotring (1996); and Kasavana, Knutson, and Polonowski (1997) can be counted among the pioneers of Web site evaluation, concentrating on hotels and restaurants. Among the first evaluations for tourism Web sites are the studies of Hanna and Millar (1997) and of Cano and Prentice (1998). A list of major Web site evaluation studies is provided in Morrison et al. (2004, p. 241). All these studies rely on different forms of content analysis with different features and characteristics evaluated, mostly executed by just one expert.

With a few exceptions (e.g., Donthu, & Yoo, 1998; Furrer, Liu, & Sudharshan, 2000; Okazaki, 2004; Tsikriktsis, 2002), most surveys have given little attention to the special requirements of Web sites crossing linguistical and—more importantly—cultural borders. However, Sigala and Sakellaridis (2004) have tried to use Hofstede's cultural dimensions to developed global rules for culturally aware Web site design. Schegg, Steiner, Frey, and Murphy (2002) include language use as part of a "value-added service" within their five dimensions, the other four being service processes, customer relationships, creating trust and cybermarketing. Douglas and Mills (2004) mention "glocalisation" and the need "… to communicate in the language of the visitor thus opening the international gateway to the local products and services." (p. 277). The appeal that "the results of studies focusing on the cross-cultural differences in online search behavior … should be incorporated into Web site designing process to capture every cultural market segment since the Internet targets are worldwide" (Jang, 2004, p. 45) is seldom translated into criteria for Web site evaluation. Even so, implicit cultural values are part of any evaluation when for instance "uncluttered" Web pages are seen as an asset of any Web site regardless of the targeted audience (Morrison et al., 2004, p. 250).

## The Present Research: Results of Two Studies

The two studies presented here are based on earlier research of the author in cross-culture Internet marketing, starting originally outside the field of tourism. Through a series of studies on cross-culture Internet marketing in tourism, for instance about the multilingual and multicultural content of the regional British Tourist Board Visitor Web sites, eight groups of criteria were developed and refined, taking into account different research approaches found in the literature (Arlt, 2001, 2002a, 2000b, 2003, 2005).

Points were given for 65 weighted criteria under the headings of "accessibility," "languages," "technical quality," "design quality," "international content," "target group specific content," "topicality," and "interactivity."

Visibility, technical quality, design quality and target group specific content made up the first cluster, each evaluated with a maximum of 100 achievable points awarded. The other four criteria, that is, language, specific content, topicality and interactivity were awarded a 50% higher weighting, as these aspects have been found in earlier studies to be especially responsible for the evaluation of the usage of the opportunities of virtual cross-cultural communication. Each criterion was evaluated with a maximum of 150 achievable points. Altogether a maximum of 1,000 points could be achieved.

Even though the main topic of the research was cross-cultural marketing, visibility, technical, and design quality were included as "[i]t seems imperative that any holistic Web site evaluation approach must have at its foundation an assessment of the technical details of the site design. Insufficient attention to site design and search

engine positioning greatly reduce the value of good content and sound marketing."
(Morrison et al., 2004, p. 246)

For each criterion 80% of all possible points (80 and 120 points respectively) were
awarded according to five to eight sub-criteria each (see Appendix A). The other 20%
of each criterion were awarded for special outstanding offers, making it possible to
award single achievements not included in the sub-criteria. For each sub-criterion
the full points or a fraction could be awarded.

The first study using the methods described above was conducted in March 2002,
with an update done in April 2006. It analysed the internationality of the official
tourism Web sites of 60 DMOs in Germany, Austria and the German-speaking part
of Switzerland. The selection was done in the following way: For Germany, the 30
cities and communities with the highest numbers of foreign overnight stays according to the German national statistics (Statistisches Bundesamt, 2001) were selected,
provided that they offered any foreign language content on their tourism Web sites.
Accordingly, twelve destinations could not be evaluated, including three out of the
dozen of most foreign-visited destinations (Düsseldorf, Medebach, and Gunderath),
and destinations down to the No. 43 on the list, Boppard, entered the evaluation
process. Similarly, for Austria the 15 communities with the highest number of foreign
overnight stays were selected according to the national statistics (Statistik Austria,
2002). In Austria only one destination (Mittelberg) had to be dropped because it did
not offer any foreign language content. For Switzerland, only destinations in the
German-speaking part of the Swiss Confederation were used, excluding ski resorts
like St. Moritz and Klosters and cities like Berne and Geneve. As no ranking for
foreign overnight stays is provided, all destinations being named on www.myswit-
zerland.com as important international destinations were chosen, provided that they
had more than 20,000 inhabitants, were located in the German speaking Cantons
of Switzerland and offered foreign language content. Many of these destinations
failed on the last criterion, offering content only in German even though they are
visited by many Swiss and foreign guests speaking other languages. In the end, 15
destinations could be evaluated for German-speaking Switzerland.

The Austrian capital Vienna emerged as overall winner and the only destination
that reached very good marks (890/1000) in this study. Five other destinations
could claim a good result with more than two thirds of the points available, namely
Zurich, Saalbach-Hinterglemm, Berlin, Innsbruck, and Sölden. Four out of the six
best Web sites were provided by Austrian communities, whereas in Germany and
Switzerland only the respective biggest city could achieve a satisfactory score. Three
Swiss, five Austrian, and 11 German destinations were awarded more than half of
the maximum number of points, nine other destinations achieving more than 400
points and a "passed" mark.

No less than 26 mainly German and Swiss destinations, almost half of all Web sites
evaluated, failed to reach even 40% of the possible points and must be regarded as

providing a rather negative brand image to non-German speaking potential visitors (for the list of all 60 cities see Appendix B).

The main problems could be summarized as follows:

- Many important destinations did not provide any non-German content at all, ignoring the information needs of the 98% of mankind not speaking German.

- Foreign language content was offered in most cases in English only. Online content in other languages was rare, even when printed information was available in other languages.

- Almost all Web sites showed a lack of consistency. Positive or original solutions in one part contrasted with erroneous or lacking offers in other parts. Coincidence or arbitrariness played a big role: for example, links often led to German language content without warning or explanation.

- The major advantages of Internet communication, topicality and interactivity were seldom used. Especially information about upcoming events, which is less easy to find for potential visitors in other countries, was not translated. Foreign language content was often outdated, even when the German content was up-to-date.

- Very rarely non-German pages of the Web sites evaluated used interactive elements like newsletters, guestbooks, or instantly downloadable information. The opportunities to get information about the visitors to the Web site were almost totally ignored, as were the chances to get in contact with foreign media or travel company representatives in international source markets. Offering pictorial current information by using webcams to show daily life in a destination in real-time was seldom used.

- A check of the quality of the foreign language content at regular intervals is obviously almost never done. Broken links and very outdated information were found much more often on the non-German than on the German content pages.

- An adaptation to special source markets and their interest and culture was seldom found. Special navigation, different colours, additional content, and so on were lacking. Information was not offered with a customer orientation. For example maps showing the location of the destination within Europe, information about foreign language church services, addresses of mosques, and so on were almost never provided. Target-group specific content proved to be the least developed part, with just eleven out of the 60 evaluated Web sites reaching more than half of the total points awarded.

- The fact that tourism and holidays should be connected to fun and happiness was communicated only by some of the Austrian Web sites. On the German and Swiss-German pages old buildings instead of smiling visitors, art historians lectures instead of specific ambience and complicated feedback forms instead of photographs of the contact person clearly dominated.

- Especially negative impressions were given by English-language parts of Web sites which seemed to have been abandoned long ago. In addition, some DMOs openly refused to send out information material to addresses outside the home country. Visitors were further angered on many Web sites by sentences like "For more information please consult the German pages" or very bad translations obviously done by a non-native speaker.

After four years, the Web sites were revisited. Out of the top 10 Web sites of 2002, Vienna still remained clearly the best international DMO Web site in German-speaking Europe, with now 14 languages and adapted content for most of them. The second-placed Zurich still offers a technically excellent Web site, however with only English content and little interactivity. Saalbach-Hinterglemm, Sölden, and Lech kept their lively style, by creating the infrastructure for a foreign language community, by taking care to provide foreign language texts also for webcam explanations, and so on. Berlin and Bremen now offer 10 languages each, with special content added especially for the FIFA World Cup 2006, whereas Innsbruck and Baden-Baden in April 2006 still included content on their Web sites about the possibility to visit the Christmas markets of 2005. Trier offered an up-to-date international Web site with different content versions for different target groups, putting for example information about the Karl Marx museum on the Chinese language homepage only. Leipzig, the number 11 of the 2002 study as best East German city also added content for the FIFA World Cup 2006 and even provides as a rare treat links to the homepages of its sister cities.

Out of the four German and Austrian cities among the top 12 international destinations, which did not provide any foreign language content on their Web sites in 2002, only Düsseldorf had improved its offer by 2006. However, even though Düsseldorf is still the no. 6 of the international destinations in Germany, only a partial English Web site is offered. Current events are still only provided in German and some links, leading for instance to the important Caravaggio exhibition to be held later in 2006, are not working.

The bottom 10 destinations of 2002 continued to show many shortcomings. Bonn still expected visitors to understand *"Zur englischen Startseite"* (to the english homepage) as the description of the button to click to get to some English—non-current—content. St. Gallen, Schaffhausen, Rüdesheim, Solothurn, and Brunnen showed no improvement with information up to two years old and no information on events in foreign languages. "If you understand a little German you might find some useful information on our site" the Schaffhausen site states rather frankly.

Neustift provides information in seven languages but on a Web site done in an rather amateurish way. Real improvements were shown only by the two big German city Web sites of Frankfurt and Köln. Both include more languages now, Köln even offers a Chinese-German language guide and multi-language news provided by Deutsche Welle (German International Radio). However, both Web sites showed still a limited interactivity, a confusing embedding of international into German content (Köln) and a German sense of humour (Frankfurt): "Please note that we only offer this service (events calendar) in German due to the large amount of topical information available."

To summarise, after four years more languages are used, but almost no improvement in intercultural skills are displayed. The big German cities are getting a push from the FIFA World Cup 2006. Some small destinations keep their advantage in international customer orientation, many others still do not give much thought to their international visitors and provide English language content only out of a sense of duty but without any enthusiasm or professionalism or even insight into the gains that can result from it.

For the second study presented here, which was conducted in August/September 2005, the opposite approach was used. This time German-speaking tourists were chosen as the target group to answer the question: how are non-European destinations using targeted Web sites to lure German-speaking tourists to their shores? The choice of German was based—besides the background of the researcher—on the fact that German-speaking people are both prolific Internet users and ardent international travellers.

In the three mainly German-speaking countries Germany, Austria and Switzerland, Internet usage is above 55%, resulting in 62 million Internet users, representing almost 7% of the world Internet population against the fact that only 2% of the world population speaks German (Globalreach, 2005). At the same time, German-speaking tourists are responsible for no less than 15% of all international tourism expenditure. Germany, as the number one tourism spending nation in 2004 was the source of US$71 billion tourism spending outside Germany. Austrian and Swiss travellers added another 11 and US$9 billion respectively in their international spending (UNWTO, 2006). If segmented by languages, German-speaking tourists with US$91 billion expenditures represent by far the biggest purchasing power in international tourism after tourists from English-speaking countries. Even if taking into consideration that about 80% of the German-speaking outbound travellers stay within Europe, US$18 billion for the remaining 20% inter-continental travellers still represent an out-of-continent tourism purchasing power equalled only by US citizens.

The culture of German-speaking people can briefly be described in Hofstede terms as showing very high uncertainty avoidance levels, very low power distance levels, medium high individuality and masculinity levels, and rather short-term orientation.

This results, speaking very generally, in a pronounced interest in planning on the basis of clear and extensive information, the wish to find out by themselves rather following advice, to see "behind the curtain," and a rather high wish for security as well as education. These characteristics are more pronounced in long-haul leisure tourists who tend to be better educated and/or older than the average German-speaking traveller (Hofstede, 2001).

For the 2005 study, 500 Web sites of NTOs and DMOs of national and regional destinations as well as important cities and well-known attractions, relevant for German outbound tourism, were visited. The destinations and attractions were selected by using statistics from the German National Tourism Board and through analysis of major German tour operators' catalogues. To mirror the search behaviour of German tourists, only Web sites recognisable as the "official" Web sites of the destinations and attractions were considered, not Web sites of third parties or private partner companies in Central Europe. Geographically all areas outside Europe were considered, including the Americas, Asia, Africa and Oceania. As the whole world minus Europe was taken as the chosen research area, obviously no comprehensive study was possible. The 500 Web sites chosen do, however, reflect an important part of the information interests of German-speaking intercontinental tourists.

The content analysis of the Web sites was conducted in two steps. In a first step, all Web sites were checked for possible German-language content. A minimum of two pages German-language content was set as a minimum level, to eliminate Web sites that offer no more than a few welcoming sentences. Out of the total sample, 50 Web sites could be identified which offer more than one page of German-language content. In a second step, the remaining 50 Web sites were analysed twice by a group of students of the University of Applied Sciences in Stralsund and by the author in August/September 2005, using a standardized evaluation form. Results were compared and discussed in a panel meeting.

The study revealed again a widespread disregard of cross-culture Internet marketing. Many major non-European tourist destination and almost all major non-European tourist attractions do not have any German-language content at all. Within the 50 analysed Web sites with German-language content, practically all major mistakes possible in cross-cultural Internet marketing could be found. Accordingly even the Web site with the most favourable evaluation for its German-language content, www.australia.com, could secure only 67% of the maximal points possible. Only seven Web sites returned results above 60% of the possible points, with another 13 above 50%. 30 out of 50 Web sites (60%) did not reach half of the achievable points, risking to rather annoy visitors to the Web site than to inspire them to visit their destination or attraction (all results can be found in Appendix C).

The strengths of the Web site could be found mainly in those criteria that are relatively independent from cultural differences: visibility, technical quality and overall design quality. The weaknesses were found in the core cross-culture criteria, showing a lack of knowledge of and/or a disregard in cross-cultural Internet marketing.

Some common mistakes and omissions, ordered according to the criteria evaluated are as follows:

- **Visibility:** Without an intuitive and/or local URL, German language metatags and extensive linkage, many Web sites failed to show up in Google.de or Google.com searches. Offers to bookmark the Web site or to list the page as the user's homepage were almost never made.

- **Language:** Many Web sites were done by professional agencies, using native German speakers as translators. Some however obviously used their own personnel to create rather funny, if unassuring texts. Only the top performers offered all information in translation, most giving only a partial translation, often with German-labelled links, which lead without warning to pages in English or other languages. Opportunities to create bonding and empathy by comparing proverbs in German and in the local language, relating descriptions of sights to German fairy tales, poems, and so on were not used at all.

- **Technical quality:** Technically most Web sites were of a quite good standard. Even so, sitemaps were often missing and search functions frequently not working. Generally speaking, functionality is the area with the least problems, here the Web agencies producing the Web sites have their core competence.

- **Design quality:** Most Web sites had a professional-looking design. However, a customization towards preferences of different user groups was nowhere to be found. For German preferences many Web sites appear to be too overloaded with information, not well enough ordered in the presentation of the information and simply too kitschy. The top performers offered not only automatic language recognition but also a function to change to other languages, important for German speaking users entering the Internet from a computer whilst already in the destination or in a third country.

- **Specific content:** Specific content is the area where most omissions were found. Information was generally simply translated without taking into account the target group's specific interests. Frequently information, which is self-evident for locals, was not provided for visitors who may not have known about it. Specifically, access information and maps showing the location within the greater region were often missing, as were webcams. More specifically, information about German language services in the country, from guided tours to bakeries to doctors to libraries with German newspapers was almost never provided. Such information is not only of factual value—indeed many such facts are only needed after arrival—but also serve to reassure visitors that such services are available when they are needed. The German obsession with planning and predictability is not catered for.

- **Target group specific content:** One of the strengths of Internet information provision is the possibility to include many extra areas for special interest. A certain amount of information was provided by most Web sites on outdoor activities and local food. However, information for business travellers or students looking for internships, press releases, and so on was seldom to be found. Many countries or cities have twinning or other spartnership arrangements with German localities. Sometimes also associations of destination-born persons now living in Germany exist. These existing connections could be used to support the arising bonding possibilities; however, this opportunity is missed in most cases.

- **Topicality:** The second-most important difference between a guidebook and a Web site is the possibility to include up-to-date information on the Web site. Potential visitors can be guided towards specific events, festivals, and so on which might strengthen their decision to travel to the destination or to stay longer than otherwise planned. As many long-haul travellers have fixed return-date flights, such information needs to be communicated well before departure to the destination. Web sites which do not show the date of the last update, sometimes giving an event for "November" without mentioning the year, can annoy visitors. Some Web sites had German-language versions that seemed to be never updated, showing event calendars several years old.

- **Interactivity:** The most important difference between a guidebook and a Web site is the possibility to interact with the visitors and potential customers. Brochures can be offered as .pdf-files for instant download, newsletters give the opportunity to communicate on a regular base, ePostcards help to spread the URL of the Web site, games give reasons for repeat-visits to the Web site. Providing the opportunity for users who have already been to the destination to put peer information on the Web site themselves, to report about their best experiences, or to upload their favoured snapshots, are readily used when offered. Likewise a "matching tool" to find potential fellow travellers, peer-group ratings for specific services and attractions or links to customers' blogs make all the difference between "advertisement" and real information, especially for users from Hofstedian low power-distance societies like Germany, Austria or Switzerland. Unfortunately, in the field of interactivity only very few of the analyzed Web sites showed any creativity.

# Conclusion

The results of the two studies discussed here show the prevailing problems of adequate use of the Internet as a communcation and marketing tool for inbound tourism. Most German, Austrian and Swiss-German DMOs are offering no more than a slimmed English version of their Web sites without the crucial elements of topicality and interactivity. Likewise, designers of non-European Web sites for German-language speaking potential customers fail to understand the importance of communicating to the customer and potential visitor in his or her own language, in his own way and style, taking into account specific interests and characteristics. The importance of facilitating communication with and among customers from a specific culture in their own terms is still clearly underestimated, even though this could be used as a crucial brand image building tool. As a result even most of the Web sites that are providing German language content are technically working well but fail to transfer a positive specific image to such a large and affluent source market as the German-speaking countries.

Effective Internet communication across cultures is about much more than having a static Web site with some pages translated word by word into another language or simply betting on the language abilities and cultural adaptability of potential visitors. To improve the communication quality is not mainly a financial question but rather a question of customer orientation. By allowing customers to voice their wishes and ideas about the style and content of the Web site both online and while they are staying in the destination can provide the customers' point of view needed to customize the Web site successfully.

Cross-cultural Internet tourism marketing is a powerful instrument to support inbound tourism. In 2006, NTOs and DMOs spend more time and money on providing multi-language static information on their Web sites than they did a few years earlier, but the missing topicality, interactivity and content customization that often occurs is however endangering the positive brand image building effect for potential visitors with different cultural backgrounds. More efforts are needed to convey the message that visitors from all source market can feel truly welcome.

# References

Arlt, W. (2001). *Internationalizing your companies' Web site.* Paper presented at MediaMit Congress, Munich, Germany.

Arlt, W. (2002a). *Internet as cross culture marketing-tool for inbound tourism. A comparison of non-German language Web sites of German, Austrian, and*

*Swiss-German tourism promotion institutions*. Paper presented at Leisure Futures Conference, Innsbruck, Austria.

Arlt, W. (2002b). *Internet as a cross culture incoming tourism communication tool*. Paper presented at Wales Tourism Alliance Conference, Cardiff, Wales.

Arlt, W. (2003). Connecting with cultures. *Locum Destination Review, 11*, 43-46.

Arlt, W. (2005). A virtual Huanying, Selamat Datang and Herzlich Willkommen!—The Internet as a cross cultural promotional tool for tourism. In C. Haven-Tang, & E. Jones (Eds.), *Tourism SMEs, service quality and destination competitiveness: International perspectives* (pp. 325-336). Wallingford: CAB International.

Auh, T.-S. (1998). *Promoting multilingualism on the Internet: Korean experience*. Paper presented at UNESCO INFOethics '98, Monaco.

Becker, S. A. (2002). An exploratory study on Web usability and the internationalization of US e-businesses. *Journal of Electronic Commerce Research, 3*(4), 265-278.

Bieger, T. (2002). *Management von destinationen*. München: Oldenbourg.

Brown, D. (1996). Genuine fakes. In T. Selwyn (Ed.), *The tourism image: Myths and myth making in tourism* (pp. 33-48). Chichester: John Wiley & Sons.

Cano, V. & Prentice, R. (1998). Opportunities for endearment to place through electronic "visiting": WWW homepages and the tourism promotion of scotland. *Tourism Management, 19*(1), 67-73.

Chon, K. (1991). Tourism destination image modification process: Marketing implications. *Tourism Management, 12* 68-72.

de Mooij, M. (2005). *Global marketing and advertising. Understanding cultural paradoxes* (2nd ed.). Thousand Oaks: Sage.

DePalma, D. A. (1998). *Strategies for global sites*. Cambridge, MA: Forrester.

Donthu, N., & Yoo, B. (1998). Cultural influences on service quality expectations. *Journal of Service Research, 1*(2), 178-186.

Douglas, A., & Mills, J. E. (2004). Staying afloat in the tropics: Applying a structural equation model approach to evaluating national tourism organization Web sites in the Caribbean. In J. Mills, & R. Law (Eds.), *Handbook of consumer behavior, tourism and the Internet* (pp. 269-294). Binghamton: Haworth Hospitality Press.

eMarketer. (2005). *Online travel worldwide report 2005*. Retrieved April 2006, from http://www.emarketer.com

Furrer, O., Liu, B. S., & Sudharshan, D. (2000). Culture and SQ perceptions: Basis for cross-cultural market segmentation and resource allocation. *Journal of Service Research, 2*(4), 335-371.

Gesteland, R. R. (2002). *Cross-cultural business behavior* (3rd ed.). Copenhagen:

Copenhagen Business School Press.

Globalreach. (2002). *Online language populations*. Retrieved November 2002, from http://www.glreach.com

Globalreach. (2005). *Online language populations*. Retrieved September 2005, from http://www.glreach.com

Goffman, E. (1959). *The presentation of self in everyday life*. New York: Doubleday.

Goodall, B., & Ashworth, G. (Eds.) (1988). *Marketing in the tourism industry: The promotion of destination regions*. London: Croom Helm.

Hanna, J. R. P., & Millar, R. J. (1997). Promoting tourism on the internet. *Tourism Management, 18*(7), 469-470.

Haven-Tang, C., & Jones, E. (2005). *Tourism SMEs, service quality and destination competitiveness: International perspectives*. Wallingford: CAB International.

Herbig, P. A. (1998). *Handbook of cross-cultural marketing*. Binghamton: Haworth Press.

Hofstede, G. (2001). *Culture's consequences: Comparing values, behaviors, institutions and organizations* (2nd ed.). Newbury Park: Sage.

Internet World Statistics (Ed.). (2006). *World Internet usage and population statistics*. Retrieved April 2006, from http://www.internetworldstats.com/stats

Jang, S. (2004). The past, present, and future research of online information search. In J. E. Mills & R. Law (Eds.), *Handbook of consumer behavior, tourism and the Internet* (pp. 41-50). Binghamton: Haworth Hospitality Press.

Kasavana, M. L., Knutson, B. J., & Polonowski, S. J. (1997). Netlurking: The future of hospitality Internet marketing. *Journal of Hospitality & Leisure Marketing, i*(1), 31-44.

Kralisch, A. & Mandl, T. (2006). Barriers to information access across languages on the Internet: Network and language effects. In *Proceedings of the Hawaii International Conference on System Sciences (HICSS-39)*, Track 3.

Lemaire, G.-G. (2000). *L'univers des Orientalistes*. Paris: Edition Menges.

Marcussen, C. H. (2003). *Trends in European Internet distribution / Trends in the US online travel market 2000-2002*. Denmark: Centre for Regional and Tourism Research. Retrieved August, 2003 from http://www.crt.dk/uk/staff/chm/trends.htm

Marcussen, C. H. (2006) *Trends in European Internet distribution of travel and tourism services*. Denmark: Centre for Regional and Tourism Research. Retrieved April, 2006 from http://www.crt.dk/uk/staff/chm/trends.htm

Mills, J. E., & Law, R. (Eds.). (2004). *Handbook of consumer behavior, tourism and the Internet*. Binghamton: Haworth Hospitality Press.

Morgan, N., Pritchard, A., & Pride, R. (Eds.). (2004). *Destination branding. creating the unique destination proposition* (2nd ed.). Oxford: Elsevier.

Morrison, A. M., Taylor, J. S., & Douglas, A. (2004). Web site evaluation in tourism and hospitality: The art is not yet stated. In J. E. Mills & R. Law (Eds.), *Handbook of consumer behavior, tourism and the Internet* (pp. 233-252). Binghamton: Haworth Hospitality Press.

Murphy, J., Forrest, E. J., & Wotring, C. E. (1996). Restaurant marketing on the Worldwide Web. *Cornell Hotel and Restaurant Administration Quarterly, 37*(1), 61-71.

Murphy, J., Forrest, E. J., Wotring, C. E., & Brymer, R. (1996). Hotel management and marketing on the Internet: An analysis of sites and features. *Cornell Hotel and Restaurant Administration Quarterly, 37*(3), 70-82.

Okazaki, S. (2004). Do multinationals standardise or localize? The cross-cultural dimensionality of product-based Web sites. *Internet research: Electronic Networking Applications and Policy, 14*(1), 81-94.

Ooi, C.-S. (2002). *Cultural tourism & tourism cultures*. Copenhagen: Copenhagen Business School Press.

Palmer, A. (2004). The Internet challenge for destination marketing organizations. In N. Morgan, A. Pritchard, & R. Pride (Eds.), *Destination branding. Creating the unique destination proposition* (2nd ed.). Oxford: Elsevier.

Reisinger, Y., & Turner, L. W. (2003). *Cross-cultural behaviour in tourism. Concepts and analysis*. Oxford: Butterworth-Heinemann.

Said, E. (1978). *Orientalism*. New York; London: Pantheon Books.

Schegg, R., Steiner, T., Frey, S., & Murphy, J. (2002). Benchmarks of Web Site design and marketing by Swiss hotels. *Information Technology & Tourism, 5*(2), 73-90.

Selwyn, T. (Ed.). (1996). *The tourism image: Myths and myth making in tourism*. Chichester: John Wiley & Sons.

Sigala, M. (2004). Reviewing the profile and behaviour of Internet users: Research directions and opportunities in tourism and hospitality. In J. E. Mills, & R. Law (Eds.), *Handbook of consumer behaviour, tourism and the Internet* (pp. 93-104). Binghamton: Haworth Hospitality Press.

Sigala, M., & Sakellaridis, O. (2004). Web users' cultural profiles and e-service quality: Internationalization implications for tourism Web sites. *Information Technology and Tourism, 7*(1), 13-22.

Smith, V. L. (Ed.). (1989). *Hosts and guests: The anthropology of tourism* (2nd ed.). Philadelphia: University of Pennsylvania Press.

Statistik Austria. (Ed.). (2002). *Statistisches Jahrbuch 2002*. Wien: Statistik Austria.

Statistischen Bundesamtes. (Ed.). (2000/2001). Tourismus in Zahlen 2000/2001. Bonn: Statistisches Bundesamt.

Thiem, M. (2001). Tourismus und kulturelle Identität. *Aus Politik und Zeitgeschichte, 47*, 27-46.

Tierney, P. (2000). Internet-based evaluation of a tourism Web Site effectiveness: Methodological issues and survey results. *Journal of Travel Research, 39*(2), 212-219.

Torris, T. (1999). *The best of Europe's e-commerce*. Cambridge, MA: Forrester.

Toru, N. (1998): *Multilingualism on the net*. Paper presented at UNESCO INFOethics '98, Monaco.

Trompenaars, F., & Hampden-Turner, C. (1998). *Riding the waves of culture* (2nd ed.). New York: McGraw-Hill.

Tsikritsis, N. (2002). *Does culture influence Web site quality expectations? An empirical study*. Paper presented at the Decision Sciences Institute 2002 Annual Meeting.

Urry, J. (2002). *The tourist gaze* (2nd ed.). London: Sage.

Watzlawick, P., Beavin, J. H., & Jackson, D. D. (1967). *Pragmatics of human communication*. New York: Norton.

UNWTO United Nations World Tourism Organisation. (2006). *Facts and figures*. Retrieved April 2006, from http://www.world-tourism.org/facts/menu.html

# Appendix A:
# Criteria and Sub-Criteria with
# Maximum Achievable Points

| 1. Visibility | 100 |
|---|---|
| URL intuitive | 10 |
| Links to other Web sites | 10 |
| Recognizable as official page | 10 |
| Google.de Rank 1-20 („x Tourismus") | 10 |
| In Google.de under URL-Name | 10 |
| .de/at/ch address | 10 |
| Metatags in source code | 10 |
| Metatags in German | 10 |
| Special Visibility (e.g., bookmarking) | 20 |

| 2. Language | 150 |
|---|---|
| Level of German translation quality | 30 |
| Additional other language 1 | 10 |
| Additional other language 2 | 10 |
| Additional other language 3+ | 10 |
| German version easy to find | 10 |
| German version full translation | 10 |
| First page German | 10 |
| Quality of German language used | 30 |
| Special Language (e.g., proverbs) | 30 |

| 3. Technical quality | 100 |
|---|---|
| Loading time short | 20 |
| Screen size optimized | 10 |
| Functioning Sitemap | 10 |
| No special browser needed | 10 |
| Functioning Search function | 10 |
| Functioning Quickfind/Shortcut | 10 |
| Functioning Flash w/ Skip function | 10 |
| Special technical quality (e.g., downloads for software) | 20 |

| 4. Design quality | 100 |
|---|---|
| Design quality according to German taste and expectations | 30 |
| Navigation simple | 15 |
| Design adapted for diff. versions | 15 |
| Design meeting regional style image | 10 |
| Links easy recognizable | 10 |
| Special design quality (e.g., automatic language recognition changeable) | 20 |

| 5. Specific content | 150 |
|---|---|
| Extent of information in German | 15 |
| German language further information | 15 |
| German language guiding offered | 15 |
| Map with location in the country/region | 15 |
| Map with location in the continent | 15 |
| Access information from Germany | 15 |
| Working Webcam | 15 |
| Working weather report | 15 |
| Special specific content (e.g., German associations in the destination) | 30 |

| 6. Target Group specific content | 100 |
|---|---|
| For German tour operators | 10 |
| Information Nature/Hiking | 10 |
| Information local/special food | 10 |
| Information for Journalists | 10 |
| Information for Internships | 10 |
| Information for business travellers | 10 |
| Information public Internet access | 10 |
| Information German church services | 10 |
| Special target group specific content (other than above) | 20 |

| 7. Topicality | 150 |
|---|---|
| General information up-to-date | 20 |
| Current events | 30 |
| Information about last site actualization | 10 |
| German and other language versions same level of topicality | 20 |
| Prices quoted in Euro | 10 |
| Special bargain offers | 15 |
| Specific current information (snow, wind, festivals) | 15 |
| Special topicality (e.g., real-time information feeds) | 30 |

*continued on following page*

| 8. Interactivity | 150 |
|---|---|
| Functioning contact e-mail | 15 |
| Functioning e-mail Form | 15 |
| Functioning E-Shop | 15 |
| Mailing of Information material to Germany possible | 10 |
| Brochures for download (pdf) | 15 |
| Subscription offer for Newsletter | 20 |
| Functioning Guestbook/Chat in Germany | 15 |
| Functioning E-Postcards | 15 |
| Special interactivity | 30 |

# Appendix B:
# Ranking of 2002 Study

| Rank | Destination | Points |
|---|---|---|
| 1 | Wien | 890 |
| 2 | Zürich | 745 |
| 3 | Saalbach-Hinterglemm | 710 |
| 4 | Berlin | 695 |
| 5 | Innsbruck | 675 |
| 6 | Sölden | 670 |
| 7 | Baden-Baden | 645 |
| 8 | Bremen | 640 |
| 9 | Lech | 640 |
| 10 | Trier | 615 |
| 11 | Leipzig | 610 |
| 12 | Gstaad | 600 |
| 13 | Regensburg | 585 |
| 14 | Rothenburg | 580 |
| 15 | Salzburg | 565 |
| 16 | Zell am See | 560 |
| 17 | Scuol | 555 |
| 18 | Hamburg | 550 |
| 19 | Heidelberg | 545 |
| 20 | Nürnberg | 545 |

| Rank | Destination | Points |
|---|---|---|
| 21 | Essen | 540 |
| 22 | Engelberg | 535 |
| 23 | Ischgl | 525 |
| 24 | Stuttgart | 500 |
| 25 | Tux | 500 |
| 26 | Luzern | 465 |
| 27 | Wiesbaden | 460 |
| 28 | Garmisch-Partnkirchen | 445 |
| 29 | Aachen | 435 |
| 30 | Mayrhofen | 430 |
| 31 | Mainz | 425 |
| 32 | St. Anton | 420 |
| 33 | Würzburg | 420 |
| 34 | Bad Ragaz | 415 |
| 35 | Karlsruhe | 395 |
| 36 | Eben/Maurach | 390 |
| 37 | Seefeld | 385 |
| 38 | Lübeck | 375 |
| 39 | Gersau | 370 |
| 40 | Kirchberg | 360 |

*continued on following page*

| Rank | Destination | Points |
|------|-------------|--------|
| 41 | Zug | 355 |
| 42 | Boppard | 350 |
| 43 | Basel | 340 |
| 44 | Braunwald | 330 |
| 45 | Mannheim | 325 |
| 46 | Augsburg | 315 |
| 47 | München | 315 |
| 48 | Hannover | 305 |
| 49 | Winterberg | 295 |
| 50 | Dresden | 280 |

| Rank | Destination | Points |
|------|-------------|--------|
| 51 | Brunnen | 265 |
| 52 | Köln | 260 |
| 53 | St. Gallen | 255 |
| 54 | Schaffhausen | 250 |
| 55 | Solothurn | 240 |
| 56 | Frankfurt | 235 |
| 57 | Andermatt | 220 |
| 58 | Neustift | 220 |
| 59 | Rüdesheim | 215 |
| 60 | Bonn | 200 |

# Appendix C:
# Destinations, Web Sites, and
# Achieved Points of 2005 Study

| Destinations | Web sites | Points achieved |
|--------------|-----------|-----------------|
| Australia | http://www.australia.com | 670 |
| Trinidad & Tobago | http://www.visittnt.de | 660 |
| Canada | http://www.travelcanada.ca | 650 |
| Korea | http://german.tour2korea.com | 635 |
| Costa Rica | http://www.visitcostarica.com | 630 |
| Peru | http://www.peru.info | 620 |
| Morocco | http://www.tourism-in-morocco.com | 615 |
| Japan | http://www.jnto.go.jp | 590 |
| New York City (USA) | http://www.nycvisit.com | 590 |
| St. Lucia | http://www.stlucia.org | 585 |
| Hong Kong | http://www.discoverhongkong.com | 580 |
| Israel | http://www.goisrael.de | 575 |
| Taiwan | http://www.taiwan.net.tw | 575 |
| Bahamas | http://bahamas.de | 565 |
| Hawaii (USA) | http://www.gohawaii.com | 560 |
| Québec (Canada) | http://www.bonjourquebec.de | 555 |
| New Zealand | http://www.newzealand.com | 540 |

*continued on following page*

| Malaysia | http://www.tourism.gov.my | 530 |
|---|---|---|
| Tasmania (Australia) | http://www.discovertasmania.com.au | 530 |
| Seychellen | http://www.aspureasitgets.com | 515 |
| Thailand | http://www.tourismthailand.org | 495 |
| Mexico | http://www.visitmexico.com | 490 |
| Nova Scotia (Canada) | http://novascotia.com | 485 |
| Singapore | http://de.visitsingapore.com | 485 |
| Serengeti Park (Tanzania) | http://www.serengeti.org | 480 |
| Turkey | http://www.reiseland-türkei.info | 465 |
| India | http://www.india-tourism.com | 465 |
| Fiji | http://www.bulafiji.de | 450 |
| Pennsylvania (USA) | http://www.pcvb.org | 445 |
| South Africa | http://www.southafrica.net | 440 |
| Jamaica | http://www.visitjamaica.com | 435 |
| Florida (USA) | http://www.visitflorida.com | 430 |
| Namibia | http://www.namibiatourism.com.na | 430 |
| Tunisia | http://www.tunisietourisme.com.tn | 405 |
| Costa Rica | http://www.costarica.tourism.co.cr | 400 |
| Yucatan (Mexico) | http://www.mayayucatan.com | 400 |
| Kerala (India) | http://german.keralatourism.org | 395 |
| Western Australia | http://www.westernaustralia.com | 380 |
| China | http://www.fac.de | 365 |
| La Reunion | http://www.la-reunion-tourisme.com | 365 |
| Merida (Mexico) | http://www.merida.gob.mx | 365 |
| Myanmar | http://www.myanmar-tourism.com | 365 |
| Belize | http://www.travelbelize.org | 360 |
| Brazil | http://www.turismo.gov.br | 360 |
| Florida Keys (USA) | http://www.fla-keys.com | 350 |
| Puerto Rico | http://www.gotopuertorico.com | 325 |
| Maldives | http://www.visitmaldives.com | 275 |
| Vancouver (Canada) | http://www.tourismvancouver.com | 265 |
| Iguacú Waterfalls | http://www.fozdoiguacu.pr.gov.br | 250 |
| Edmonton (Canada) | http://www.edmonton.com | 240 |

## Chapter XIV

# Changing Technological Trends in the Travel Behaviour of Older Tourists

Ian Patterson, University of Queensland, Australia

## Abstract

*This chapter examines the growth in usage of information technology and the Internet by older adults. We are becoming an ageing society with seniors and baby boomers now responsible for a larger share of all holiday spending. The Internet provides a perfect vehicle for the travel industry however, many seniors are still fearful about using the Internet, and perceived problems still exist with credit card security, quality control and privacy issues. In the future, Internet travel bookings are likely to increase with the growth in baby boomers who generally prefer to use the Internet. This will further encourage the use of discount fares however it will place increased pressure on the future role of the travel agent. Furthermore the authors hope that through an understanding of the technological needs of older adults, it will inform tourism providers about the best ways to attract older people to use Internet sites for all aspects of their travel needs.*

# Introduction

We are becoming an ageing society. The United Nations has recognised the fact that the older generation are growing rapidly, and has estimated that over two billion people will be aged 60 years and over by the year 2050, and this will account for 22% (or one out of five) of the world's population compared to 10% in 2000. These demographic shifts will be seen across all continents (United Nations, 2000). For example, McNeil (1991) stated that, "… as amazing as it seems, over one-third of all Americans were born between 1946 and 1964" (p. 22). Australia's ageing population also is increasing, from around 12% in 1999 to between 24% and 26% by 2051, or one in four people (Australian Bureau of Statistics, 1999).

On a global scale, the world is becoming increasingly aware of the significant impact that older adults (and in particular, baby boomers) will have on the tourism industry in the decades ahead (Goeldner, 1992). The direct consequence of this ageing pattern is that in the future, seniors will be responsible for a larger share of all holiday spending. For example, in 1999 over 593 million international travellers were aged 60 years and over. This accounted for around a third of all holiday spending by this segment.  By 2050 this figure is projected to be greater than 2 billion trips (World Tourism Organisation, 2001).

As a result of this change in the demographic profile, the tourism and leisure industry is increasingly targeting the 65 years and over market because older adults generally are regarded as having greater amounts of free time and discretionary income to spend on travel, and as a result have become a significant growth market (Javalgi, Thomas, & Rao, 1992). This is because many baby boomers perceive themselves to be younger in age and in outlook, more in control of their lives, and increasingly more self-reliant. Baby boomers typically feel a decade younger (average of 10.2 years) than what their actual age is, and as a result often prefer to spend their holiday activities with younger people (Cleaver & Muller, 2002).They often seek out new and different leisure experiences that are often challenging and soft adventure activities, as well as being skillful and knowledgeable consumers that are generally satisfied with their lives (Patterson, 2002).

Today, the Internet has provided a perfect vehicle for the travel industry, as online travel Web sites have allowed consumers to have increased power over their travel planning, as well as providing them with a quick, easy and cheaper way of booking holiday travel. Traditionally, older consumers have been slower to embrace new technologies such as computers and the Internet in comparison to younger people. Many seniors are still fearful of using the Internet, and a widespread belief exists that information and communication technologies (ICT) are only for the young. This attitude is slowly changing as more baby boomers are approaching the retirement age.

# Aims of the Chapter

This chapter will discuss the use of information technology and the Internet by older adults, to assist them in making more informed decisions about future tourist destinations, and provide cheaper travel bookings. Some of the important research questions that will be asked in this chapter are:

1. Are older adults still reliant on travel agents to help make travel decisions for them?

2. Do older adults feel confident that they can use computers and the Internet to gather travel information?

3. In the future, will older adults use the Internet to plan and make their own travel bookings?

# The Traditional Role of Travel Agents

In the past, travel agents have served as both information providers and planning/booking providers for a large number of travellers, particularly when planning international overseas travel (Oppermann, 1997). In the 1990s travel agencies emerged as one of the top three information sources used by tourists for overseas travel, as well as the means to arrange travel to destinations that people had not previously visited (Duke & Persia, 1993; Mihalik, Uysal, & Pan, 1995).

The first serious attempts at research focussing on the role of the travel agent began in the 1980s. These studies set out to discover how consumers perceived the role of the travel agent, and the reasons why people chose a specific agency to make travel bookings. Bitner and Booms (1982) were quick to predict that the role of the travel agent needed to change in the future—from the traditional role of a clerk, to a salesperson, and ultimately to a travel councillor. They suggested that if travel agents were to survive in the future, they needed to adopt the following radical changes to the way they do business:

• To use more aggressive marketing techniques to segment the market and to better communicate with their clients

• To have a better command of product line and profitability analysis

• To expand their use of highly sophisticated information systems and equipment

• To gain a thorough knowledge of travel destinations and requirements for each of the market segments

- To develop an understanding of how to interact and to successfully negotiate with suppliers

Sheldon (1986) examined the role of the travel agent from an economic perspective. The author affirmed that the main function of a travel agent was to reduce the time and money spent on information and transaction costs for consumers, as well as providing promotional expenditure for suppliers. Sheldon found that basic package tours provided a bigger discount to the consumer (15%) than all-inclusive tours (-3%) in his study.

Kendall and Booms (1989) investigated the way that consumers chose, used, and reacted to communications from retail travel agencies. They administered a questionnaire to 660 respondents in the Seattle region using a random digit dialling technique, as well as conducting several focus group workshops to discuss issues that were associated with people's views about travel agencies. The authors found that word of mouth communication was heavily relied upon, and as a result many travel agencies developed many loyal clients. The researchers found that consumers will sometimes call a travel agency that is listed in an advertisement to compare basic information and prices, but will always go back to their regular agency for the actual bookings and payments.

Kendall and Booms (1989) concluded that if travel agents were to survive, they needed to develop greater knowledge about the specific needs and expectations of their clients. This included information about the types of restaurants they preferred; local attractions or side trips they wanted to go on; leisure activities that they liked to participate in; and the destinations and types of hotels, resorts, and transportation they preferred. Consumers rated the importance of gaining knowledge from all types of information sources higher than their own physical comfort when visiting an agency. In regard to their physical needs, some clients were particularly attracted by the specific location of the retail travel agency operation and the pleasantness of the office décor, while others preferred to use the telephone when dealing with the agency. Kendall and Booms (1989) concluded that travel agents needed to develop more sophisticated marketing techniques and to have a thorough understanding of consumer needs so as they could effectively compete in the travel marketplace.

Richards (1995) was interested in discovering whether travel agents were able to provide customers with travel information by helping them to bridge the information gap. This was because many consumers were becoming more skilled in accessing specialised product knowledge through their own sources, and as a result were increasingly becoming more advanced in their means of information retrieval than travel agents themselves. With this in mind, Oppermann (1997) focused his research on resident's perceptions of travel agency service attributes and compared them to travel agents beliefs about what customers found to be important. He collected responses from 266 travel agencies and 400 New Zealand residents, and found that there was a wide gap between resident's perceptions and the travel agent's actual beliefs. He argued that travel agents needed to be more aware of their client needs in order to remain competitive, and thereby to ensure long-term viability. Oppermann (1997) concluded that travel agents needed to lift their current performance because they were being placed under increasing pressure from other competitors in the travel industry. For example, the increased availability of tourist information on the Internet combined with direct booking and payment facilities were now seen as detrimental to travel agencies.

Oppermann cited several authors who also had forecast the demise of travel agencies because of the increasing competition from the Internet. Lewis, Semeijn, and Tala- layevsky (1998) for example, expressed concern about the future of travel agents, given the increased trend toward information technology. The researchers noted that there had been a significant reduction in agency commissions paid by airlines to travel agencies, due to the increasing use of the Internet by consumers that had enabled them to obtain current travel information and to make direct airline reservations more easily. Because of these changing customer demands and travel patterns of senior customers, this has resulted in increased expectations in relation to value and convenience, as well as the emergence of increasingly knowledgeable consumers who were quickly becoming more proficient users of information technology.

As noted previously, the traditional travel industry structure consisted of a huge network of travel agencies that had a complete monopoly on information, prices and bookings. However, this is now changing and increasingly being challenged by travel providers who have direct access to customers through Web sites provided through the Internet. This has particularly become evident in the airline industry where carriers such as Virgin Airlines in Australia and Southwest Airlines in the U.S. sell most of their cheaper tickets on the Internet without the use of travel agents. Even the established airlines such as American and United are now using direct channels such as line services, the Internet, and toll-free telephone numbers to reach their customers. Eliminating the human aspect has minimised costs for the airlines and as a result they can now offer discount fares that are exclusively available to online users as well as promoting the use of electronic ticketing (Lewis et al., 1998).

However, although they are increasingly becoming under threat from new techno- logical advances, travel agents are still performing many important services for their travel consumers. Some still act as information brokers by passing on information from suppliers of travel products to consumers. They process transactions of print- ing tickets or forwarding money and often act as advisers to travellers. Aspects such as trust and social contact are still important to some consumers particularly when planning leisure travel, as well as face-to-face communication with an agent at a physical retail location is still seen as important for many older travellers. In the future, the highly competitive nature of the travel industry and the declining commissions paid by airlines may lead to the widespread consolidation of some smaller travel agencies. The success of travel agents will depend entirely on their ability to, "… capture the market's loyalty, ensure access to travel information while providing value-added services, and develop winning product strategies supported by information technology" (Lewis et al., 1998, p. 25).

In Scotland, one travel agency, Stewart Travel Centre, has responded to Internet travel companies cutting into their business by refocusing their strategic direction (Edry & Sennott, 2004). Stewart had noticed that there was a large number of cruise ships launched in the 1990s and decided to concentrate on advertising cruise packages. By 1999, he had created Scotland's Cruise Centre which became the largest in the country with nearly half of his 5,000 annual customers booking cruises. Stewart also has moved into other profitable niche areas such as gay and senior travel, adventure vacations, and even pet travel. In the future he felt that travel agents needed to embrace the Internet more, and help customers to sort through the information over load on the Web. Although the Internet may be cheaper and easier for simple trips, travel agents are still needed to sort out difficult itineraries and complex long-haul travel. Their skills and experience will still be needed to sort out such problems as arranging connecting flights, and to inform travellers about the plethora of rules and regulations that apply to travel within different overseas countries. Many older clients in particular like to spend time talking over their travel plans in person, therefore they prefer to book through a travel agent rather than through the Internet (Edry & Sennott, 2004).

## The Use of Computers and the Internet by Older People

In the later part of the 20th century, a technological revolution began to occur with the development and mass production of the personal computer (PC), video games, cable TV, and mobile telephones. In addition, the Internet soon became available and started to form a link between the multiple forms of information and communication technologies (ICT).

In the 21st century, increasingly larger numbers of older people are learning to use a computer and the Internet. For example, only about 30% of Americans aged 55 and over owned a computer in 1996. By 2001 these figures had increased to 37.1% (Adler, 2002). However, the majority of older people aged 65 years and older still do not have any Internet access. In the United Kingdom, although there has been a huge increase in the use of the Internet to 62% of the British population, the usage rate dropped to 33% for the 55 to 64 year age group, and to just 6% for those over 75 years of age (National Statistics Survey, 2003). This has been attributed to the lack of adequate training, unfamiliarity with computer technology, or uncertainty about how the Internet can be used as a useful resource for them. Others are

*Figure 1. Computer usage across different age groups between 1998-2002 (Source: Household Use of Information Technology, Australia [8146.0])*

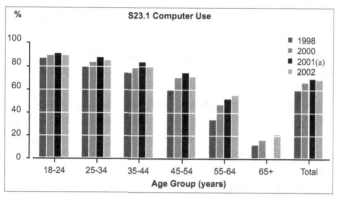

*Note: (a) Data for 2001 not available for persons aged 65 years and over*

disadvantaged because of their low income, poorer education and/or lower social class status (Castells, 1998). As a result, Internet usage is mainly concentrated in the younger end of the over 50 age group. However, baby boomers who are presently aged between 42 and 60 years of age will rapidly increase the percentage of computer users as they become older. This is because many baby boomers are well educated and wealthy and because of this, have favourable attitudes toward the use of computers (Kawamoto, 2003).

In Australia, the Australian Bureau of Statistics (2002) found that around one in five older people used a computer in 2002 which is slightly lower than the American figures (ABS, 2002). That is, only 21% of older people aged 65 years and older used a computer compared to 89% of persons aged 18 to 24 years (see Figure 1).

Older people who use computers were more likely to use them at home for personal and private purposes (92%). Other uses were for educational purposes (19%), work or business (16%) and voluntary or community work (13%). Only 13% of older people aged 65 years and older used the Internet, with 4% using it to pay their bills such as their car registration or local government rate payments. Over a third of older people (36%) stated that they had no need to order goods and services via the Internet, or had not bothered to try.

A recent study in the United States by the Kaiser Family Foundation (2004) specifically looked at the use of the Internet for informing decisions about health and health care options. The foundation found that less than a third (31%) of Americans aged 65 years and older had used the Internet. However, they noted that 70% of the next generation of seniors who are presently aged 50 to 64 year age group were regular users of the Internet. These differences in usage figures were quite striking with only 21% of older adults going online to access health resources compared to 53% of the 50 to 64 year olds. The foundation concluded that there was a "digital divide" between the two age groups and this placed older people who were most in need with limited access to information on which to base important health care decisions.

A report titled "Older Americans and the Internet" reinforced the findings of the Kaiser Foundation. They stated that despite the significant gains among seniors, "... most Americans aged 65 and older live lives far removed from the Internet, know few people who use e-mail or surf the Web, and cannot imagine why they would spend money and time learning how to use the computer" (AScribe Health News Services, 2004, p. 2). However this is quickly changing as a growing group of younger baby boomers in the 50 to 60 year age group have become significantly more attached to the Internet. Lee Rainie, the author of this report, concluded, "Internet users are gaining momentum. Internet users in their 50's who work, shop, and keep in touch with friends and family online will age into, and transform the wired senior population" (AScribe Health News Services, 2004, p. 2).

Several studies have investigated the benefits of computer usage for older adults. A study by White, McConnell, Clipp, and Bynum (1999) at Duke University concluded that teaching older adults to use computers to access the Internet and e-mail has resulted in a trend toward reduced loneliness. White et al. (1999) found that computers had a beneficial effect on older people's psychosocial wellbeing as well as expanding their social support network. White and his colleagues also noted that involvement in a network of online support and chat groups, helped older people to feel connected to society, and was a strong predictor of lower levels of perceived life stress. The Kaiser Foundation (2004) reinforced this, with their study findings that 34% of seniors considered e-mail and the Internet as an important part of their lives that they did not want to do without. Furthermore, over half (56%) of seniors who used e-mail stated that it made it a lot easier for them to stay in touch with family and friends.

The importance of social support networks has been emphasised in other studies of older adults. Wright (2000) found that older adults were able to meet a diverse group of individuals not only from the same cohort group but also to make intergenerational contacts. Wright concluded that these online support groups helped older adults to feel more connected to society, as sharing one's life with others helps to validate their experiences as human beings. This is especially true for individuals who spend a great deal of time on the Internet, and generally results in relatively strong relationships beginning to form. For a number of people, their relationships with Internet friends were regarded as similar to a surrogate family, even though they had met online and were complete strangers beforehand. Furthermore, Antonucci (1990) and Wright (2000) noted that greater involvement with Internet support networks was a better predictive of lower perceived life stress than age or the number of hours per week communicating on the Internet.

Morrell, Mayhorn, and Bennett (2000) conducted a study to document the use of the World Wide Web among a sample of 381 (151 men and 230 women) in different age groups in South Eastern Michigan. The breakdown in age groups were 108 middle-aged (aged 40-59), 181 were young-old adults (aged 60-74), and 92 were old-older adults (aged 75-92). Two versions of a World Wide Web questionnaire were mailed to respondents, one directed at current users of the Web while the other directed at nonusers. The researchers found that only nine of the 92 old-older adults indicated that they were current Web users. Users were found to be younger, better educated, more likely to own a computer, have a higher household income, and lived with someone who was a nonuser. The authors concluded that age was a good predictor of Web use, and the reason that the old-older age group did not use the Web was because of a lack of computer access and knowledge.

Sourbati (2002) conducted focus group and individual interviews with 18 older tenants and six care staff in sheltered accommodation schemes in North London. This accommodation service employed care staff on a 24-hour basis and provided a communal Internet facility and free Internet sessions. Sourbati (2002) wanted to ascertain what benefits were provided by Internet access for older people living in sheltered accommodation. Firstly, she found that encouragement that was provided by family, social networks, and care staff generated a lot of interest about using the Internet among older people. Several saw it as a way of providing opportunities to engage in constructive leisure activities and hobbies, find companionship, communicate with others, and keep in contact with modern society.

One retired tenant stated "… I would love to be able to use the Internet. Because that's tomorrow, I mean if I had a few bob and I wanted to buy something I'd buy the Internet … I'd use it for entertainment, I could tap into information, companionship" (Sourbati, 2002, p. 2).

Secondly, she found that there were barriers and obstacles to their use of the Internet. These included physical disabilities such as arthritis, dexterity problems, or declining vision had caused problems. Lack of technical support and assistance by community support officers who also lacked basic Internet skills were issues that also needed to be dealt with. Such computer devices as the mouse could cause difficulties for older adults when performing such skills such as dragging, clicking, or fine positioning. "The only thing I find hard now which I have only ever used once is what do you call it … the mouse, you know, it kept going here, there and everywhere" (Sourbati, 2002, p. 2). Older adults also may become confused and frustrated by the unfriendliness of interface designs such as small font sizes, using pull-up or drop-down menus, or having a poor colour contrast background (Lee, Godbey, & Sawyer, 2003). Although these barriers exist, several organisations such as the University of the Third Age, ElderHostel, and SeniorNet are helping older adults to gain computer knowledge through a wide range of educational programs and training.

## Elderhostel (www.elderhostel.org)

In 1999, Elderhostel was one of the Internet winners at the annual CIO Web Business Magazine awards. Elderhostel began with a very basic site in 1995 however in 1997, the president of Elderhostel, Bill Berkeley, decided to expand of this site as one of his major objectives. Among the changes that occurred, the customer mailing list was expanded by 25% and online registrations were encouraged. This saved the organisation $87,000 as Elderhostel promoted an appeal to save the environment resulted in a growing number of clients who no longer received paper catalogues. Instead, regular customers received e-mail notification when a new catalogue went online. The online catalogue was improved by including details about accommodations and information of special interest to those with physical limitations. The site allows customers to register, check their status, cancel or transfer courses, go on a mailing list, change their information, send e-mails, and make donations. In fact, online donations have outpaced mail contributions, and the average gift has been 30% higher than donations that are made through the mail. The site also supported meaningful surveys and experimental programs. Future plans include peer program reviews and a discussion forum. Elderhostel has attributed their success to design that is tailored to suit over 55-year olds, such as readable print, minimal graphics and allowance for small screens (www.cio.com/archive/Webbusiness/070199_interwinners.html).

## SeniorNet as an Educational Provider (www.seniornet.org)

SeniorNet was established to provide education for older adults so as to enable them to gain greater access to computer technology (Grodsky & Gilbert, 1998). SeniorNet began in 1986 as a research study that was aimed at encouraging seniors to use a computer. The study found that under the right conditions, older adults adapted well to using digital technology. Over time, SeniorNet soon established an infrastructure of learning centres specifically designed to cater for older adults which has now grown into a national network of 128 learning centres covering 35 states in the United States. Adults who are 50 years and older can enrol in an inexpensive eight week class ranging from an introduction to computers, to creating your own Web page. These classes are peer taught by more than 1800 older adult volunteers who have previously taught more than 120,000 older adults to use computers and the Internet.

The mission of SeniorNet is centred on inclusion and independence, and classes are places where comfort and community are stressed, and older students are encouraged to ask questions and work at their own pace. By going online, older adults can also locate new friends and gain support in difficult times. For example, SeniorNet has established a grief support discussion group where people can find comfort and support when necessary. Other intergenerational projects such as "Living Archives" were launched in 1993 and this has enabled school students to electronically connect and interact with seniors, and at the same time to encourage participation by older adults in this form of electronic classroom. The project focuses on such specific topics as World War II, the 1950s, the civil rights movement, space travel, and women's liberation. This has enabled a high school student in Alabama for example, to communicate with a Holocaust survivor in Arizona, or a senior citizen who marched with Dr Martin Luther King Jr. to share that experience with students across the country (Grodsky & Gilbert, 1998).

Adler (2002) stated that in the future, the widespread availability of broadband networks will play a major role in supporting and enhancing the lives of older adults. High-speed broadband networks offer several important advantages over slower narrowband networks: first, they make it possible to add high-quality two-way video to today's voice and text communications. Second, they provide instant access to rich multimedia content. Third, broadband's "always on" feature makes communications more convenient and supports a broad range of continuous, unobtrusive monitoring services. Finally, once broadband networks, both wired and wireless, become ubiquitous, users will be able to access any content from anywhere at any time.

While broadband applications will be of value to many segments of society, some applications will be of special importance to seniors. Among the key benefits that ubiquitous broadband networks offer to older adults are:

- **Enhancing communications with family and friends:** High-speed, always-on networks will dramatically enhance the ways in which people communicate and share their lives on an on-going basis. High quality video will be added to today's voice and text communications providing opportunities for richer interactions.

- **Expanding opportunities for lifelong learning:** Current experiments with "e-learning" have demonstrated the potential of online education for older adults, particularly for those with limited mobility. Online "classrooms without walls" will bring engaging educational experiences to seniors at home, and will help prolong the careers of older workers by providing instant access to continued training in the workplace.

- **Improving the delivery of health care services:** Broadband technology may have the greatest impact on the lives of seniors in the area of health. As people get older, the cost of the medical services they use also increases. One promising approach to improving health care delivery is a greater use of "tele-medicine" services. Broadband networks will make it possible to deliver high quality medical services to older adults, including remote diagnoses and continuous health monitoring in ways that are convenient for both patients and providers.

- **Supporting independent living:** One of the most innovative uses of broadband networks will be to help people remain independent as they age and become more frail. Research is currently underway to develop an "aware home" that will unobtrusively track the behaviour of residents, automatically provide needed services, and call for help when needed.

- **Creating new options for entertainment:** As broadband access grows, so will the range of entertainment options available to everyone, including older adults. Greater bandwidth will expand the opportunities to provide content designed for specific audiences and give individuals the ability to customise the programming available to them.

For these benefits to be realised, a number of barriers will have to be overcome. These include ensuring that new services are easy for older adults to learn and use, guaranteeing that online applications are private and secure, and creating a legal and regulatory environment favourable to the rapid deployment of broadband networks (Adler, 2002).

Adler (2002) presents the following future scenario of Madge Gunderson, 88 years old, and the year is 2012:

*Madge is able to keep to keep in close contact with her family thanks to a constant stream of communication back and forth. As she sits down to breakfast she picks up a wireless tablet about the size of a pad of paper and scans a list of half a dozen messages that have arrived overnight. She sees that a video e-mail message has arrived from her 21-year old grandson who is teaching English in Japan. She could play the message on her handheld tablet, but she decides to watch it on a larger flat screen that hangs on the wall of in her kitchen. The screen is in fact a normal digital television set containing some additional circuitry that allows it to connect to and interact with other systems through a wireless home network. Using her tablet as a remote control, Madge turns on the wall screen and calls up the message. Madge is amused to see that the grandson wants to introduce one of his students named Toshio who wants to practice his English skills. His English is less than perfect, but she is able to follow his description of a kite-flying festival he had participated in. The message then cuts to a few seconds of video of brilliantly coloured kites flying in a clear blue sky. Madge likes the image of the kites so much that she replays this segment. She freezes the video of the kites and sends the image to an electronic picture frame that sits on the kitchen counter, replacing another picture that had been in the frame for the last few months. At the end of the message, Toshio asks Madge if she would be kind enough to send him a message back. She considers* *using a digital video camera in the room to create a video response, but decides that she doesn't look good enough at this hour of the day to be seen, even in an online message. So she records a short audio message politely thanking Toshio for his message and telling him how she enjoyed seeing the kites. When she is finished, she sends the message to her grandson for delivery to his student. As she scans the rest of her message list on her tablet, she sees one from her physical therapist who explains that he has some new exercises that he'd like Madge to try and asks her to schedule an appointment. She links to a calendar showing the therapist's schedule and sees that he has an open slot at the end of the morning. She taps on that time on the tablet's touch sensitive screen, and her name is automatically entered (the system recognises that it is Madge who is calling and knows that she is one on the therapist's patients). After going through her messages, Madge shifts to a display of the front page of the Washington Post which remains a daily habit, even though she rarely reads the printed version of the paper. She scans the headlines and reads a few stories, then calls up a calendar of her activities for the day. She sees that she is scheduled to meet a friend for afternoon tea then tutor a group of second graders in a local after-school program which she does every week ... Since Madge no longer drives a car, her calendar automatically reserves a ride to her appointments through a local para-taxi ... As Madge drives to town she gets a call from her granddaughter in Boston who is eager to show her a drawing that she made that morning at school. As Madge only has her handheld phone with a small video display, she tells her granddaughter that she will look at the picture when she gets home where she will be able to see it on the big screen. As Madge arrives at the school she decides to turn off her pocket phone. All of this technology is helpful, she thinks, but sometimes it's a good idea <u>not</u> to be too connected!* (pp. 8-9)

# The Use of Internet Technology for Travel by Older Adults

The Internet is a technological innovation which is having a profound influence on all aspects of people's lives. The Internet is gaining rapidly on other forms of media such as television and newspapers in terms of time spent on these types of media (Heichler, 1997). The travel industry in particular has consistently been identified as one of the main industries that is most likely to be affected by the growth of the Internet. Machlis (1997) stated that travel was the single largest revenue generator among consumers on the Internet, totalling US$800 million in 1997.

In 2005 the Travel and Tourism Industry (TIA) estimated that 56% of the 216.1 million adults in the U.S. currently use the Internet. This translates to over 120 million adults of which 84% state that they are travellers, meaning that they have taken at least one trip of 50 miles or more away from their home in the past year. This translates to a market of 101.3 million online travellers. More frequent travellers who state that they have undertaken five or more trips annually, have an even greater likelihood of using the Internet with 75% indicating that they use it (Green & Cook, 2005).

Several studies have looked at the increased growth in Internet purchases for travel by older people. Age has been found to be an important demographic variable in terms of the likelihood of older adults using the Internet for a browsing search for travel information, purchasing, and perceptions about security. A study by GTRC (1998) found that mature individuals were less likely to use search engines to reach an Internet site than by traditional means such as through reading magazines and newspapers. This study also found a significant relationship between a traveller's age and the likelihood of making purchases over the Internet. This is because as people age, they appear to be more suspicious about the quality of products that are available, with almost 50% of potential travellers over 50 years of age citing the quality of the goods as a problem when making purchases over the Internet. Mature individuals also were less likely to admit that they would use their credit card over the Internet (GTRC, 1998).

Weber and Roehl (1999) provided a profile of consumers who purchased travel via the Internet. These researchers at Georgia Tech conducted a WWW survey in 1997 to track the growth and changes of the Web user base. The survey was conducted online with participants completing questionnaires that were posted on the Web. Their study found that age and education were significant variables, and that people who were younger (25 years or younger), or older (over 55 years of age) were less likely to purchase travel arrangements online than people in other age groups. Furthermore, respondents with four-year college degrees or postgraduate qualifications were more likely to purchase travel online than people with lower educational levels. Travel purchasers also were more likely to have previously been online for a period of four or more years. The most frequently cited reasons for *not* purchasing products online were credit card fraud, no assessment of product quality, privacy issues, and the preference to purchase locally. The researchers concluded that the major challenges facing online travel retailers were to address the issues of credit card security and data access. They concluded that consumers must feel confident that the information being provided was safe and could be used ethically and appropriately (Weber & Roehl, 1999).

In a further study by Bonn, Furr and Hausman (2000), they interviewed a sample of almost 14,000 travellers during a recent trip to Tampa, Florida. The researchers divided the sample population into three representative age groups: Generation X'ers, Baby Boomers, and Mature Travellers. A small number of travellers from England,

Canada, Germany, and Brazil (11.2%) completed the questionnaire, while 88.8 % of the total sample was residents of the United States. The authors found that the U.S. respondents, particularly Generation X'ers and Baby Boomers consistently stated that they were the most likely users of Internet services for travel purposes. Mature travellers were less likely to make use of the Internet to book a trip as the trend line in their study indicated nearly flat growth until 1999. However, future growth in Internet usage among mature travellers is likely to increase as a result of the continuing maturation of the baby boomer population, rather than any change in behaviour patterns of present-day mature travellers.

These latest figures are encouraging, with seniors who now use the Internet increasing by 47% between 2000 and 2004. In February 2004, a survey found that 22% of Americans aged 65 years or older had access to the Internet and this has increased from 15% in 2000. This translates to about 8 million Americans who are aged 65 years or older that presently use the Internet. By contrast, 58% of Americans aged 50 to 64 years, 75% of 30 to 49-year-olds, and 77% 18 to 29-year-olds currently go online. In particular, 41% of the older age group 65 years and older have made travel reservations online at the end of 2003. This is a 16% increase since 2000 and showed a growth rate of 64% (AScribe Health News and Services, 2004).

## Why is the Internet Becoming More Popular for Travel Bookings by Older Adults?

Several reasons have been suggested:

- Allows customers to shop around for the lowest fares for trips and accommodations
- Provides a more personalised service with large amounts of useful information available
- Helps consumers to better understand the products by using multimedia, such as fantasy vacations and 360 degree virtual tours
- Saving money in a paperless environment
- Increases the convenience of obtaining information at home, and supporting a customer focussed strategy
- The Web dramatically decreases the time it takes to make travel reservations and plans. (Turban, 2004)

# Examples of Successful Travel Web Sites for Use by Older People

## *Travelocity (http://www.travelocity.com)*

Regarded as the leader in the category of mega-travel sites, this is the third largest Web site on the Internet. This site provides consumers with a myriad of services, ranging from car rentals, train bookings, hotel reservations, and information on every conceivable destination and complete vacation packages. It maintains a user friendly interface over which transactions are processed. The site is simple to use, and a consumer can literally book an airline ticket with 3 clicks. It also continues to add value to the site by introducing new personalised services to customers.

## *Wal-Mart (http://www.walmart.com)*

Wal-Mart has moved into the booming and profitable world of Internet travel sites. In 2000 it launched its new site which offers airline tickets, car rentals, and hotel reservations to customers. The site is extremely simplistic and provides nothing other than the basics and is easy to use for older travellers.

## *United Airlines (http://www.shopzilla.com)*

In July 1999, United Airlines and Buy.com announced a strategic alliance between the two which capitalised on the booming online travel industry. Specifically, it was a strategic business move to get into the mega-travel site sector which had become very profitable. This site offers the typical array of hotel, car, and planning services. This idea was later modified to target college students CollegeTravelNetwork.com. In January 2000, United announced a partnership with Delta Airlines, Northwest Airlines, and Continental Airlines to develop a site devoted to airline travel that will offer fares that can be only found on the Internet.

## *REI Adventure Travel (http://www.rei.com)*

REI.com is one of the growing sites that specialises in adventure travel. REI has experienced a 22% increase in sales since 1998, and now offers around 4,000 trips each year. Adventure Travel has bought out Adventure Travel and this has allowed them to provide a dynamic Web wizard search engine that enables customers to plan an adventure trip by searching its database based on parameters of destination and activity, and then narrows it down by price, and so on. REI also is the sole provider of adventure gear and other paraphernalia.

Suggestions for successful travel sites for older travellers:

- Focus on customer service.

- Keep the site as simple as possible and use larger print to make it easier to read for older people.

- Provide as many services as possible to create a one-stop shopping site for travel without sacrificing simplicity.

- Utilise java script and intelligent agents to further personalise the site for older visitors.

- Attempt to form strategic alliances with other companies with complimentary core competencies.

- Look to move into regions that are untapped and have a huge market potential such as Asia.

# Conclusion

In 1998, people who were over 50 years of age and who were intent on travelling were more likely to use the traditional advertising media such as through travel agents, magazines, and/or newspapers. Travel agents in particular have, and still are providing an important service for older travellers especially if they are travelling overseas. Many older adults still prefer word of mouth communications with their travel agent, many of which have built up a loyal clientele of older people over the years that still rely on them for travel information, advice and personalised booking services. Several academics have challenged the traditional role of the travel agent stating that they need to change their mode of operations from a salesperson and clerical worker, to become a travel councillor if they want to remain competitive with online booking and Internet services, especially in the airline and hospitality industries. That is, a good travel agent needs to develop more sophisticated marketing techniques and detailed information about travel destinations, as well as an understanding the specific travel needs of different segments of the older adult market if they wish to stay in business.

Many older people still lack knowledge about, and access to computers while others do not feel confident about using the Internet. However, there are many benefits of using the Internet such as developing an increased social support network, and improved contacts with friends, relatives, and family members through e-mail services. Furthermore, surfing the Web can increase a person's knowledge and skills and help to re-establish and maintain an older adult's sense of empowerment and confidence.

Finally, cognitive improvements through the learning of new technologies also have been noted, and studies have shown that older adults have substantially increased their ability to feel mentally alert, challenged, and useful (Lee et al, 2003).

Recently, through such organisations as Senior Net and the University of the Third Age, older people are learning how to use computers in relaxed and comfortable settings close to their homes. This has encouraged the use of intergenerational projects with schoolchildren, who can now instantaneously interact with seniors through the use of electronic classrooms. Adler (2002) also stated that the widespread availability of broadband networks will play a major role in supporting and enhancing the lives of older adults. These benefits include enhancing communications with family and friends, expanding opportunities for lifelong learning, improving the delivery of health care services, supporting independent living, and creating new options for entertainment. For these benefits to be realised, a number of barriers will have to be overcome. These include ensuring that new services are easy for older adults to learn and use, guaranteeing that online applications are private and secure, and creating a legal and regulatory environment favourable to the rapid deployment of broadband networks.

Although younger consumers are more likely to make online bookings for travel purposes, older people are becoming increasingly more confident in the use of this form of information technology. Perceived problems still exist with such aspects as credit card security, quality control and privacy issues. However, the numbers of people aged 65 years and older in the United States who are using the Internet has increased from 15% in 2000, to 22% in 2004, an increase of eight million Americans. This will further increase with the growth in the number of baby boomers who are generally proficient in their use of the Internet, and prefer to take advantage of its services in relation to online purchases. This has encouraged the use of discount fares for international travel however it places greater pressure on the future role of the travel agent, as it may eventually eliminate them as a broker for travel transactions.

# References

ABS (Australian Bureau of Statistics). (1999). *Older people: Australia, A social report* (Cat. No. 4109.0). Canberra, ACT: AGPS.

ABS (Australian Bureau of Statistics). (2002). *Household use of information technology, Australia* (Cat. No. 8146.0). Canberra, ACT: AGPS.

Adler, R. P. (2002). *The age wave meets the technology wave: Broadband and older Americans.* Retrieved 30 June, 2006 from http://www.seniornet.org/downloads/broadband.pdf

Antonucci, T. C. (1990). Social supports and social relationships. In R. H. Binstock & L. K. George (Eds.), *Handbook of aging and the social sciences* (pp. 206-226). San Diego, CA: Academic Press.

AScribe Health News Services. (2004, March 25). *22 percent of Americans age 65 and older go online: Many more are shopping, doing health research, making travel reservations* (pp. 1-2).

Bitner, M. J., & Booms, B. H. (1982). Trends in travel and tourism marketing: The changing structure of distribution channels. *Journal of Travel Research, 21*, 39-44.

Bonn, M. A., Furr, H. L., & Hausman, A. (2000). Employing Internet technology to investigate and purchase travel services: A comparison of X'ers, boomers and mature market segments. *Tourism Analysis, 5,* 137-143.

Castells, M. (1998). *The information age. Volume 3: End of the millennium.* Oxford, UK: Blackwell.

Cleaver, M., & Muller, T. E. (2002). The socially aware baby boomer: Gaining a lifestyle based understanding of the new wave of ecotourists. *Journal of Sustainable Tourism, 10,* 173-190.

Duke, C. R., & Persia, M. A. (1993). Effects of distribution channel level on tour purchasing attributes and information sources. *Journal of Travel and Tourism Marketing, 2,* 37-56.

Edry, S. L., & Sennott, S. (2004, April 19). Cruising for customers: Contrary to popular belief, the Internet hasn't killed off travel agents. It's turned them into savvy specialists. *Newsweek International,* p. 58.

Green, C. E., & Cook, S. D. (2005). *Travelers' use of the Internet* (2005 ed.). Washington DC: Travel Industry Association of America.

Goeldner, C. R. (1992). Trends in North American tourism. *American Behaviouralist Scientist, 36,* 144-154.

Grodsky, T., & Gilbert, G. C. (1998). Seniors travel the information superhighway. *Parks and Recreation, 33,* 70-74.

GTRC. (1998). *GVU's 10th WWW user survey.* Atlanta, GA: Georgia State University Press.

Heichler, E. (1997). Internet lacks content for women. *Computerworld, 31,* 64.

Javalgi, R. G., Thomas, E. G., & Rao, S. R. (1992). Consumer behavior in the US travel marketplace: An analysis of senior and non-senior travellers. *Journal of Travel Research, 31,* 14-19.

Kaiser Family Foundation. (2004). *E-health and the elderly: How seniors use the Internet for health.* Retrieved June 30, 2006 from http://www.kff.org

Kawamoto, K. (2003, November-December). Older adults and the Internet. *Interface: The Journal for Education, Community and Values.*

Kendall, K., & Booms, B. (1989). Consumer perceptions of travel agents: Communications, images, needs, and expectations. *Journal of Travel Research, 33,* 29-37.

Lee, B., Godbey, G., & Sawyer, S. (2003). The changing roles of computers and Internet in the leisure lives of older adults. *Parks and Recreation, 38,* 22-25.

Lewis, I., Semeijn, J., & Talalayevsky, A. (1998). The impact of information technology on travel agents. *Transportation Journal, 37,* 20-25.

McNeil, R. D. (1991, September/October). The recreation profession and the age revolution: Times they are a 'changin'. *Illinois Parks and Recreation, 22,* 22-24.

Machlis, S. (1997). Profits eludes travel sites. *Computerworld, 32,* 53-54.

Mihalik, B. J., Uysal, M., & Pan, M.-C. (1995). A comparison of information sources used by vacationing Germans and Japanese. *Hospitality Research Journal 18/19,* 39- 46.

Morrell, R. W., Mayhorn, C. B., & Bennett, J. (2000). A survey of World Wide Web use in middle-aged and older adults. *Human Factors, 42,* 175-184.

National Statistics Survey. (2003). Retrieved June 5, 2006 at http://www.statistics.gov.uk

Oppermann, M. (1997). Service attributes of travel agencies: A comparative perspective of users and providers. *Journal of Vacation Marketing, 4,* 265-281.

Patterson, I. R. (2002). Baby boomers and adventure tourism: The importance of marketing the leisure experience. *World Leisure Journal, 44*(2), 4-10.

Richards, G. (1995). Retailing travel products: Bridging the information gap. *Progress in Tourism and Hospitality Research, 1,* 17-19.

Sheldon, P. J. (1986). The tour operator industry: An analysis. *Annals of Tourism Research, 13,* 349-365.

Sourbati, M. (2002). *Internet use in sheltered housing: Older people's access to the new media and online service delivery.* Joseph Roundtree Foundation: Digital Age series.

Turban, E. (2004). *Electronic commerce: A managerial perspective.* New Jersey: Pearson/ Prentice Hall.

United Nations, Division for Social Policy and Development, Department of Economic and Social Affairs (2000). *The sex and age distribution of the world populations: 1998 revision.* Retrieved June 30, 2006: http://www.un.org/esa/population/publications/ageing/Graph.pdf

Weber, K., & Roehl, W.S. (1999). Profiling people searching for and purchasing travel products on the World Wide Web. *Journal of Travel Research, 37,* 291-298.

White, H., McConnell, E., Clipp, E., & Bynum, L. (1999). Surfing the net in later life: A review of the literature and pilot study of computer use and quality of life. *Journal of Applied Gerontology, 8*, 358-378.

Wright, K. (2000). Computer-mediated social support, older adults, and coping. *Journal of Communication, 50*(3), 100-118.

World Tourism Organisation. (2001). *Tourism 2020 vision: Global forecasts and profiles of market segments, 7*. Madrid, Spain: World Tourism Organization.

# About the Authors

**Wayne Pease** is the associate dean (Fraser Coast) for the Faculty of Business, University of Southern Queensland and lectures in information systems at the Fraser Coast Campus of the University of Southern Queensland. He has published over 30 books, refereed articles, and book chapters. His employment background is in senior management with Queensland Health and has worked in higher education since 1998 when he accepted a lecturing position in information systems at the then new USQ Fraser Coast Campus. His research interests include electronic commerce and its impact on rural and regional communities; payment and security systems in electronic commerce; collaborative commerce; Web design and Web data delivery systems including DBMS integration and query optimisation; and windows application development.

**Michelle Rowe** has vast experience working in management and marketing roles in service organisations and as a lecturer in management and marketing (since 1990). Currently Michelle is undertaking PhD studies looking at collaborative commerce adoption by SMEs. Michelle is interested in the ways SMEs perceive and use ICT from the perspective of e-commerce and collaboratively, taking a multidisciplinary approach. This research has also focused on the digital divide, with the aim of assisting SMEs in rural and regional Australia. She has written generally from this perspective. Michelle also is interested in the application of electronic and collaborative commerce in various industries.

**Malcolm Cooper** is vice president international cooperation and research, and holds the position of professor of tourism management in the Graduate School of Asia Pacific Studies, at the Ritsumeikan Asia Pacific University (Beppu, Japan). He is a specialist in tourism management and development, environmental management, water resource management, and environmental law, and has published over 80 books, refereed articles, and book chapters. Dr. Cooper is the Asia Pacific regional editor for *Tourism Research International* and sits on the editorial boards of other international academic tourism journals. He has held previous appointments at the Universities of New England, Adelaide, and Southern Queensland (Australia), and Waiariki Institute of Technology (New Zealand) and has worked in the environmental planning and tourism policy areas for federal, state, and local governments in Australia, and as a private tourism consultant to the governments of China and Vietnam.

\*\*\*

**Stephen C. Andrade** is chair of the Computer Graphics Department and associate professor at Johnson & Wales University (Providence, Rhode Island, USA). He has been involved in technology development and education for 25 years, working in computer research, advanced telecommunications, and higher education. He works within the field to apply new technologies to human pursuits, especially in travel and tourism. As a faculty member, he regularly leads undergraduates through extreme mobile computing experiences in international capitols. Mr. Andrade makes his home in Rhode Island and is an active writer, presenter, and contributor to the professional community.

**Wolfgang Georg Arlt** was born in 1957. He has an MA in sinology and a PhD in political sciences from FU Berlin in Germany. He has served as professor for leisure and tourism economics at the University of Applied Sciences (Stralsund, Germany), as a visiting professor at several Chinese universities, and as a research fellow of Japanese Society for the Promotion of Science. He is the leader of China Outbound Tourism Research Project.

**Jerry Eades** is a professor of Asia Pacific Studies, Ritsumeikan Asia Pacific University (Beppu, Japan), and Senior Honorary Research Fellow at the University of Kent (Canterbury, UK). He graduated with a PhD in social anthropology from Cambridge and has taught in West Africa, the UK, and Japan, including the University of Tokyo and the University of Kent. His research interests over the years have included West Africa, the Asia Pacific, migration, urbanization, tourism, the environment, and higher education reform. His most recent books are *The Making of Anthropology in East and Southest Asia* (ed. with Shinji Yamashita and Joseph Bosco, Berghahn 2003), and *The 'Big Bang' in Japanese Higher Education* (ed. with Roger Goodman and Yukmiko Hada, Trans Pacific, 2005).

**Vladimir Garkavenko** holds a master's degree from the Kiev State University (Ukraine) in French and Arabic Languages and Literature. He also holds a MBS in Management from the Department of Management and International Business from Massey University in Auckland. He is in his last year of PhD studies at the Auckland University of Technology. His doctoral thesis deals with the impact of ICT on New Zealand travel industry in general and on the travel agents sector in particular. Currently, Mr. Garkavenko is a lecturer of tourism at the School of Tourism and Hospitality at the Waiariki Institute of Technology (Rotorua, New Zealand).

**Călin Gurău** is professor of marketing at Montpellier Business School (France). He is a junior fellow of the World Academy of Art and Science (Minneapolis, USA). He worked as marketing manager in two Romanian companies and he has received degrees and distinctions for studies and research from University of Triest, Italy; University of Vienna (Austria); Duke University (USA); University of Angers (France); Oxford University; and Southampton Business School and Heriot-Watt University (UK). His present research interests are focused on marketing strategies for high-technology firms and internet marketing. He has published more than 25 papers in internationally refereed journals, including *International Marketing Review*, *Journal of Consumer Marketing*, and *Journal of Marketing Communications*.

**John W. Houghton** is currently a professorial fellow at Victoria University's (Australia) Centre for Strategic Economic Studies (CSES) and director of the Centre's Information Technologies and the Information Economy Program. He has had a number of years experience in information technology policy, more general industry policy and related economic research. He has published and spoken widely on information technology, industry, and science and technology policy issues. He has co-authored several chapters of the OECD publications *Information Technology Out-*

*look* and *Communications Outlook*, and written a number of reports for the OECD and International Telecommunications Union. He also produces regular updates on the Australian ICT industry, sponsored by the Australian Computer Society, and has authored and co-authored numerous industry and science policy reports for a range of industry associations, state and federal government. Houghton was awarded a National Australia Day Council, Australia Day Medal for his contribution to IT industry policy development (1998).

**Roopa Jakkilinki** is a PhD research scholar at Victoria University (Melbourne, Australia). She gained a Master of Science in Computer Science (2004) at Victoria University. Jakkilinki gained a graduate diploma in Computer Science at Victoria University (2002), and she gained a postgraduate diploma in information technology (2001) from MAHE (India). She completed her Bachelor of Arts in Computer Applications (1999) from Andhra University (India). Jakkilinki has been employed as a sessional tutor at Victoria University. She also has worked as a research assistant for a project funded by STCRC.

**George Kakaletris** is a graduate of the Department of Physics of the University of Athens (Greece) and has obtained his MSc degree from the Department of Informatics and Telecommunications of the same organisation. In the past, he worked for several years for Greek IT companies, initially as an S/W engineer and later as an S/W architect, IT project manager and an R&D department director. He has experience in designing, developing, and deploying integrated IT systems for both the public and the private sectors, and he has participated and technically managed several EU and nationally funded research projects. Among the systems he has designed and implemented are real time data delivery services, major financial applications, data management systems, and various tools. He is certified by Microsoft Corporation as an MCP (1999) and currently he is a PhD candidate, employed as a research associate of the Department of Informatics and Telecommunications of the University of Athens.

**Dimitris Katsianis** received an Informatics degree, an MSc in signal processing and computational systems from the University of Athens (Greece), Department of Informatics and Telecommunications. He is a research fellow with the Optical Communications Group, participating in several European R&D projects. He has worked as an expert scientific advisor with several firms in the field of techno-economic & network design studies. His research interests include broadband communications and methodology of network design with techno-economic aspects. He has more than 45 publications in journals and conferences in the field of techno-economics and telecommunication network design and he serves as a reviewer in journals and conferences.

**Neil MacNeil** was born in the UK, but moved to New Zealand in the mid- 1990s, and has since made it his home. He recently has returned to New Zealand following almost five years in Japan. As an associate professor with Ritsumeikan Asia Pacific University, Neil developed e-learning initiatives and delivered a range of IT based courses, as well as playing a fundamental role in the development of Web-based services within the university. He currently is involved with online education initiatives in New Zealand as well as providing independent IT consultancy services to a range of clients in the UK and Japan.

**Hilary Mason** is an instructor in computer graphics and new media at Johnson & Wales University (Providence, Rhode Island, USA). She has studied computer science at Grinnell College and Brown University and is interested in using innovative technologies to solve problems in hospitality, business, and education.

**G. Michael McGrath** earned his PhD from Macquarie University (1993). He is currently a professor of information systems at Victoria University (Melbourne, Australia). He has over 20 years experience in the IT industry—mostly at Telstra, Australia, where he worked in a variety of positions. These included an executive-level position, as manager of information architecture within the organisation's Corporate Strategy Directorate. His current research is focused mainly on the development of a high-level information architecture for the Australian tourism industry and on issues associated with the takeup and diffusion of online technologies among small-to-medium tourism enterprises (SMTEs). In recent years he has conducted research and consultancy work for Telstra, IBM, Centrelink, Department of Industry Science and Tourism (DIST), and National Office for the Information Economy (NOIE). He has authored over 100 refereed journal and conference papers.

**Patrick S. Merten** is a research assistant at the International Institute of Management in Technology (IIMT) at the University of Fribourg (Switzerland). With a master's degree in information management, he conducts research in information and communication technology (ICT) management. For his PhD studies he especially focuses on the effects of mobile technologies and mobile business on the airline industry.

**Simon Milne** is a professor of tourism at the Auckland University of Technology (New Zealand), where he directs the New Zealand Tourism Research Institute (www.nztri.org). Simon completed his PhD at Cambridge in 1989 and then taught at McGill University, Montreal (until 1998). Dr. Milne has considerable international experience in economic impact assessment, labour market analysis, small and medium enterprise performance, and the formulation of tourism development strategies. Much of his recent research has focused on the links between information technology, tourism, and economic development.

**Alfred Ogle** is a PhD candidate at Edith Cowan University (Australia), School of Marketing, Tourism and Leisure. Currently a sessional lecturer at ECU, he was previously an assistant professor in hotel management at the Institute for Tourism Studies in Macau SAR. Alfred received a Swiss diploma in hotel management from Hotelconsult, a BS degree in hotel and restaurant management from the University of Houston, and a MSc degree in training and human resource management from the University of Leicester. A Certified Hospitality Educator (CHE), his areas of research interest is hotel accommodation design and hotel guest-management interface. Prior to his entry into academia, Alfred was in hotel front office operations in North America and Asia with his last position as front office manager of a Holiday Inn property in Malaysia.

**Ian Patterson** is an associate professor in the UQ School of Tourism at the University of Queensland (Australia), Ipswich campus. He is head of leisure and recreation and was research director for the school (between 2001 and 2004), teaching courses in tourism and leisure behaviour and sport management. He completed his PhD at the University of Oregon (1991). He has published over 60 scholarly publications including refereed journal articles, an edited book, book chapters, conference papers, and consultancy reports. He is mainly interested in researching healthy older people who are undertaking tourism and travel and all types of physical activity programs.

**Mohan Ponnada** is a research assistant for the Travel Recommender System project funded by the Sustainable Tourism CRC at Victoria University (Melbourne, Australia).

**Nalin Sharda** gained BTech and PhD degrees from the Indian Institute of Technology—Delhi (1974 and 1984, respectively). Presently, he teaches and leads research in multimedia and Internet communications at the School of Computer Science and Mathematics, Victoria University. He has worked in the IT industry, taught at Curtin and Murdoch Universities (Australia), and held visiting/adjunct positions at Florida Atlantic University (USA); Jaypee University of Information Technology

(India); and Karlstad University (Sweden). Sharda's current research interests and related publications include application of the Internet and multimedia systems to enhance communications and the development of tourism ICT systems. Sharda has developed a number of conceptual models for integrating the art, science and technology of multimedia systems, including: multimedia design and planning pyramid (MUDPY), a meta-design framework for multimedia systems design; and movement-oriented design (MOD), a new paradigm for designing the temporal aspect of multimedia systems.

**Thomas Sphicopoulos** received a physics degree from Athens University (Greece, 1976), a DEA degree and doctorate in electronics both from the University of Paris VI (1977 and 1980, respectively), and the doctorate in science from the Ecole Polytechnique Federale de Lausanne (1986). He worked in Thomson CSF Central Research Laboratories on Microwave Oscillators (1976-1977). Sphicopoulos was an associate researcher in Thomson CSF Aeronautics Infrastructure Division (1977-1980). He joined the Electromagnetism Laboratory of the Ecole Polytechnique Federal de Lausanne (1980) where he carried out research on applied electromagnetism. He has been with the Athens University engaged in research on broadband communications systems (since 1987). Sphicopoulos was elected as an assistant professor of communications in the Department of Informatics (1990), as associate professor (1993) and has remained a professor in the same department (1998-present). His main scientific interests are microwave and optical communication systems and networks and techno-economics. He is leading about 30 national and European R&D projects (RACE I and II, ACTS, RISI, HCM, COST, Eurescom, and so on) including Synthesis and TITAN. He has more than 120 publications in scientific journals and conference proceedings. He is also a reviewer in journals of IEEE and IEE and auditor and evaluator of RACE and ACTS projects. He is the chairman of the IEEE LEOS Chapter (Bulgaria, Greece, Romania, and Yugoslavia). Sphicopoulos has been an advisor to several organisations (since 1999) including EETT (Greek NRA for telecommunications) in the fields of market liberalisation, spectrum management techniques, and technology convergence.

**Dimitris Varoutas** holds a physics degree and MSc and PhD diplomas in communications and techno-economics from the University of Athens (Greece). He is a lecturer on telecommunications techno-economics in the Department of Informatics and Telecommunications in the same university (since 2005). Varoutas has been participating in European R&D projects (since early 1990s) in the areas of telecommunications and techno-economics. He also participates in or manages related national and European activities for techno-economic evaluation of broadband strategies, telecommunications demand forecasting, price modelling, and so on. His research interests include telecommunications and techno-economic evaluation of network architectures and services. He has published more than 45 publications in refereed journals and conferences, including leading IEEE publications. He is an IEEE member and serves as reviewer in several, including IEEE publications and conferences.

# Index

## G

Gadd, Paul (a.k.a. Gary Glitter) 272, 273
Galileo 7, 85
  system 124
GARMIN 123
gateway
  /SAP session 146
  mobile location center (GMLC) 130
gay
  tourist market 274
  travel 344
general packet radio services (GPRS)
        119, 122, 160
  /UMTS Phones 132
Generation X'ers 352
geographic information system (GIS)
        127, 130, 160
global
  distribution system (GDS) 7, 51,
        54, 55, 56, 58, 81, 85, 87, 89,
        90, 97, 99, 100, 102, 103, 105,
        110, 245
    new entrants (GNE) 100, 105
    supplier 88, 98, 100
  positioning system (GPS) 123, 124,
        127, 128, 141, 160
    device 124, 131
    receiver 122
  system for mobile telecommunications
        (GMT) 119
  travel industry 289
GM 252, 253, 254, 255
GMLC 160
Google Talk 312
graphical user interface (GUI) 33, 105
  layer (GUIL) 33
GSM 122, 125, 128, 160
  mobile terminals 132
  positioning 125, 127
guest-host interrelation scheme 318
gyroscope 127

## H

harmonize ontology 31
head-mounted display 190

high-speed
  circuit switched data (HSCSD) 119, 160
  downlink packet access (HSDPA)
        120, 160
HIV/AIDS 269, 271
HLR 142
hosting 309
hotel value chain profitability 216
HTML 132, 160
HTTP 140, 146, 147, 160
human
  resources (HR) quality 226, 231
  trafficking 271
hybrid recommender system 166

## I

IDR cycle 57
ID tag 127
illegal immigration 271
image-based geographical interface 199
imaging technology 201
IMAX 206
in-flight entertainment and communication
        system (IECS) 108
incoming tourism 317, 318
inference engine (IE) 33
infomediaries 51
information
  -based economy 77
  and communications technologies (ICT)
        2, 3, 4, 5, 6, 15, 51, 55, 60,
        61, 62, 66, 68, 77, 92, 94, 96,
        105, 107, 110, 160, 203, 238,
        245, 273, 287, 300, 301, 340,
        344
    adoption 53, 59
    infrastructure 18, 299, 301
    introduction 59
    services 300
  revolution 77
  systems (IS) 160
  technology (IT) 27, 78, 116, 160, 243,
        247, 251, 253, 255, 341, 343
    providers 103
instant messaging 311

round trip time (RTT)  125, 161

**S**

secure sockets layer servers  21
Semantic Web  27, 135
  application  27
semi-automated business environ-
      ment research (SABER)
      7, 79, 81, 84, 85
semi-immersive systems  182
SeniorNet  348
senior travel  344
server  307
service
  -oriented
    approach  117
    architecture (SOA)
      117, 136, 137, 142, 161
    access point (SAP)  142, 147, 161
sex
  industry  265, 266, 267, 271, 273, 276
  tourism  261, 262, 263, 264, 266, 267,
      269, 270, 271, 272, 273, 276
    industries  269
    tourists  272
  worker  264, 267
sexual subculture  274
SGML  132
sharable content object (SCO)
      170, 171, 174
  reference model (SCORM)
      170, 173, 174, 175, 178
shared hosting  309
short text messages (SMS)
      119, 126, 130, 161, 291
  /MMS  131, 146
simple object access protocol (SOAP)
      102, 161
SITAR  87
Skype  312
small and medium enterprise (SME)
      12, 17, 20, 66, 244, 248
small and medium tourism enterprise
      (SMTE) 2, 12, 20, 22, 216, 218,
      219, 220, 244

operator  219, 233
smart phone  32
social
  identity theory  250
  network theory  248
spam  305
standardised package tour  5
START  85
State Tourism Authority (STA)  219
static information sources  27
super-passenger name record (super-PNR)
      101
sustainable tourism cooperative research
      centre (STCRC)  217, 224, 238
swingers  264, 273, 274
Synchronized Multimedia Integration Lan-
      guage (SMIL)  172, 173
system
  architecture  303
  dynamics (SD)  216, 220, 231, 238
    applications  228
    archetype  232, 233
    component user interface  227
    constructs  237
    control panel  229
    framework  224
    model  220, 234
    simulator  228
    tools  222
  task model  39

**T**

tag  291
  cloud  291
Talea  32
target group specific content  321
technical quality  321
techno-whizzos  218
telecommunication networks  78
Theil's inequality statistics (TIS)  235
THISCO  89
threatened intermediaries hypothesis  55
time division multiple access (TDMA)
      161
time of arrival (TOA)  126, 161